The Performer
in Mass Media

The Performer in Mass Media

... IN MEDIA PROFESSIONS AND IN THE COMMUNITY

by William Hawes

University of Houston

COMMUNICATION ARTS BOOKS

HASTINGS HOUSE, PUBLISHERS
New York 10016

To Ella,
Kent and Robbie

Library of Congress Cataloging in Publication Data

Hawes, William, 1931–   The performer in mass media.

  (Communication arts books)
  Bibliography: p.   Includes index.
  1. Performing arts—Technique. 2. Mass media.
I. Title.
PN1590.T43H3   791'.028   77-14343
ISBN 0-8038-5824-8
ISBN 0-8038-5825-6 pbk.

Published simultaneously in Canada by
Copp Clark, Ltd., Toronto

Printed in the United States of America
Designed by Al Lichtenberg

CONTENTS

PREFACE

The focal point of every media production is the performer—sometimes animated, occasionally electronic, often animal, but principally human. Fine producing and directing, lavish studios, and shrewd management are valueless without the performer. The performer is greater than whatever exists in light, shadow and sound, for human performers link all of us through common understandings, sympathies, appreciations, entertainments and artistic delights. The gods of fortune single out a few performers to dwell with them on Olympus, where first names reign in awe and respect throughout the world. A far larger group of professional performers work in local and regional markets where their substantial skills in communication provide the threads that bind the hometowns of the earth. But the largest number of performers are the volunteers, the neighbors down the street.

This book is about human beings as performers—who they are, what they do, how they do it. Every performer I have ever seen or heard has helped to write some of it, especially my students in performance classes, radio and television programs, and films. Some of these contributors deserve personal recognition as well as my deep gratitude for their advice in the preparation of this manuscript. I am indebted to my colleagues at the University of Houston, especially my dear friend, Professor Emeritus Dr. Tom C. Battin, with whom I produced some 300 television programs . . . and to my manuscript readers Tom Jarriel, ABC Washington correspondent; Terry Jastrow, former staff producer-director for ABC Sports, now an actor in Los Angeles; Yvette Romero, an actress in New York; Rick Schieffer, newscaster, now on the Board of Directors, Green Valley Communications, Inc., Tucson . . . and to contributors David D. Connell, vice president for production, and Ed Gilbert, of the Children's Television Workshop, New York; Robert L. Hilliard, chief, Educational Broadcasting Branch, FCC, Washington, D.C.; Ron W. Irion, director of Broadcast Management, National Association of Broadcasters, Washington, D.C.; Russell F. Neale, publisher, and his staff at Hastings House, New York; James Rawitsch, creative director, Olesen, Hollywood; Jim Sanders, executive vice president/creative director, and John Heck, vice president, Week-ley & Penny, Inc., Houston; John Tracy, director, CBS and PBS, New York; Bob Wright, news director, and Brian Hill, KLOL, Houston; and Bill Worrell, sports director, KPRC-TV, Houston . . . and to the man-agement of Houston media, particularly Alvin Guggenheim, of Alvin Guggenheim & Associates, who has arranged so many meetings with cinema performers and directors, and the Gaylord Broadcasting Company's Crawford Rice, Gene Jacobsen and Clyde Formby, of KHTV, Houston, and James Terrill, of KTVT, Dallas-Fort Worth, for allowing me to present new talent since 1960 in a weekly TV series and/or numerous specials.

Part One:

THE PERFORMER

1: Cue-You're On!

"Who me?"

The Performer as a Communicator
>The Live Performance—The Prerecorded Performance—The Communicated Performance—The Remembered Performance

Circular Response
Image Control
Professional Performers
Community Experts as Presenters

THE INSTANT A person appears before cameras or speaks into a microphone, he or she forms impressions in the minds of those in the audience. That person is, in fact, a "performer." Performing is becoming commonplace with the increased availability of media ranging from home-movie making to network TV production. Every performer, amateur or professional, instantly creates an impression, favorable or unfavorable, in the minds of thousands—perhaps millions—of listeners and viewers. Hitherto relatively unknown individuals, caught in newsmaking circumstances such as a suspect on trial or a doctor who wishes to obtain funds for critical medical research, suddenly find that in order to gain favorable attention media must work for them. The rapid dissemination of information and entertainment by mass media—television, radio, cinema, recording—makes everyone, whether in media professionally or non-professionally, experience the role of a performer. For who is a performer? A performer is the newscaster, the actor, the minister, the teacher, the social activist who uses media to impart information and entertainment so that people respond through deeds and purchases, intellectual endeavors and the gamut of emotional experiences.

Professional performers traditionally are those who make their living from appearing in media. They use media consciously to influence an audience. They are newscasters, sportscasters, weather reporters, farm directors, home specialists and other journalists; disc jockeys, masters of ceremony, quiz masters, hosts, sales people and other announcers; singers, actors and actresses, dancers, musicians, variety artists and other entertainers.

The list has lengthened substantially in recent years, because many individuals (and groups) who are non-professional performers in a theatrical or journalistic sense are utilizing media to obtain their objectives. Included are politicians, attorneys, physicians, research scientists, diplomats, business executives, government officials, clergy, professional athletes, those concerned with public broadcasting, educators in instructional television and social activists. Today's performer in mass media comes from many walks of life.

THE PERFORMER AS A COMMUNICATOR

A performer's work can be observed at various levels. The first is the *live* performance which consists of what the performer actually says in total context. The second is the *prerecorded* performance which may or may not be an edited version of what the performer says. A third level is the *communicated* performance—that is, what the listener/viewer actually sees and hears within the environment of reception. A fourth level is the *remembered* performance. This is the latent, fragmented recall a listener/viewer has of a performer's work.

The Live Performance

Whatever a performer appearing "live" (in person) says or does on camera and microphone may be transmitted, altered or eliminated through noise substitution (bleeps), blackouts (audio/video deletion) or cutaways (alternate video) as his or her message is processed through media.* A performer is relatively certain that most of what has been said and done will be viewed and heard if the program is live, for producers have little recourse except blatant censorship. Responses from listener participants for call-in radio programs are delayed a few seconds so that radio producers can exercise the option of excising potentially injurious words. Some unedited interview programs noted for their candor have guests who are aware of legal limitations and who use discretion.

The Prerecorded Performance

Most programs are audiotaped, videotaped or on film. Exceptions are live portions of newscasts, sportscasts, some "instant" reports at the scene, and disc jockey continuity. Major portions of daily news and DJ programs are on videotape, film, disc or audiotape. They are referred to as *canned* segments. The opportunity for alteration of material in prerecorded programs is great. A discussion may consist of carefully selected questions and answers recorded over many hours. In its final form this discussion may be edited to a half-hour for a radio program, thus, a great deal of information is eliminated and the remainder may be somewhat out of context. Thousands of feet of film taken throughout the lifetime of a performer may be condensed into a one-hour documentary. Errors the public might see in live performance may be eliminated. In short, a performer appears at one's best, because the work has been carefully edited; consequently, edited tape may create the illusion that participants are always witty, brilliant people. Elec-

* For further description or definition of unfamiliar technical media terms, see the Glossary, page 313.

tronic alterations enable singers and dramatic readers to reach nearer perfection than they could when appearing live. As a result the listener/viewer sees and hears a careful selection and condensation of what really took place.

The Communicated Performance

The listener/viewer views the live or prerecorded performance in a unique environment, an odd physical and mental mixture of his or her thoughts and miscellaneous uncontrollable digressions. It is a wonder the perfomer communicates with a listener/viewer at all, because the vast amount of what such listener/viewer sees and hears is immediately filed subliminally in the brain never to be retrieved again. The listener/viewer tends to retain those bits of information or emotional experiences that activate and reenforce preconceived notions, thoughts or emotions. If the performer's message is in tune with the listener/viewer's thoughts and feelings, the listener/viewer will be motivated to action: to buy a product, to spontaneous reaction (laughing, crying) or reacting in a multitude of other ways. Only then has the performer communicated with someone.

The Remembered Performance

A performer has yet another level of his or her work to contemplate: Will the performance be remembered? If so, how much of it will be remembered? The recollection of a performance is based on the listener/viewer's mental and emotional state when the performance was seen and is likely to deteriorate with time, resulting in a confused recollection of the performance. If listener/viewers like the work of the performer a great deal, they may remember the performance in some idealized or romanticized way resulting in a vast audience and favorable publicity that may place the performer among the famous. The role of a media critic is often to articulate the assets and liabilities of a performer's work for posterity; so that a performer's work can be evaluated. A performer's work can be greatly enhanced by constructive critical judgment.

CIRCULAR RESPONSE

"Round and round she goes and where she stops nobody knows," Major Edward Bowes used to say as he hosted radio's *Original Amateur Hour*. Although Bowes was not reciting communications theory, he may well have. As a performer communicates with the audience and receives stimuli from it, the performer in turn is prompted to further action.

The communication process in mass media may be summarized in seven steps. First, the performer (communicator) conveys stimuli in appearance and voice. Second, the stimuli (message) are designed or formalized (encoded) in language, sounds and pictures by the performer. Third, the formalized message is transmitted through radio, television, film and disc (media) to the listener/viewer (communicant). Fourth, the listener/viewer picks out of the message the impressions that are stimulating. Fifth, the listener/viewer (now in the role of the communicator) responds emotionally, such as with applause or laughter, and intellectually, such as with a question to provide further stimuli (feedback) for the performer. Feedback, the sixth step, is so necessary for some performers that live studio audiences are required stimuli for top performances. Performers on *The Tonight Show* show depend heavily on a live audience in addition to viewer feedback which performers receive much later by mail, telephone and from ratings. Seventh, the performer gratified that he or she has made contact with the audience responds proportionately, the message being noticeably heightened or eventually terminated. A performer *must* evoke response from the audience.

This principle of communication theory is referred to as empathic or *circular response*. The concept when applied to performance says that upon appearance or utterance a performer instantly conveys information through media to the audience, the audience reacts and sooner or later the performer reacts to the audience reaction. In a live performance all of this takes place more or less instantly and continuously, but when a performer works through media, feedback from an unseen audience may be delayed.

IMAGE CONTROL

Of prime concern to a performer is what the audience thinks of him or her, professionally and personally. Close associates such as an agent or producer know what the performer thinks or does or how temperamental he or she is behind the scenes, off-camera and off-mike, but the audience knows only what it sees and hears while the performer is on broadcast media or film or what it reads in print media.

Appearances, interviews, and news items in all media tend to be selected by the performer's associates, so that the performer will always seem to be at one's best. These relatively few things the performer and associates wish to convey about the performer constitute the public image. Mastery over what the public sees and hears is called *image control*. The performer and associates select what they want an audience to see and hear so that the audience has a high regard for the performer professionally and personally. The task is complex and difficult, because an audience forms its opinion the moment it sees and/or hears the performer, continually changing its opinion as the performer provides new stimuli. "The image and the man are one and the same," Barbara Delatiner wrote in *Newsday*. "David Brinkley on the small screen is a twin for David Brinkley off-screen. The clipped, precise way of talking. The words carefully measured to say the most as succinctly as possible. The cigarets casually lighted but intensely puffed. The epitome of the cool personality. Brinkley also is cool away from the camera and the microphone. Not cold and aloof but rather low-key, generating warmth with his thoughts, not necessarily with his delivery. Only in one way are the public and private Brinkley apparently two different men. The fabled Brinkley wit was subdued."[1]*

The term image refers to the public's acquaintance of a person through media, not to the person as a human being. If, for instance, media reveal a performer in a socially acceptable context pursuing virtuous activities exclusively, it is likely the public will think of that performer as acceptable and virtuous. Glen Campbell, Doris Day, Sydney Poitier and Mickey Mouse are rarely shown any other way. An outstanding example of image control is the transformation of a young, divorced housewife and mother into the international sex attraction, Raquel Welch. Publicist Patrick Curtis is credited with skillfully and relentlessly changing her image. Her nose was straightened, breasts expanded with silicone, and body molded by diet and exercise. Every facial expression was choreographed by Curtis. Five years after Ms. Welch made her movie debut she received star billing in *100 Rifles.*[2] Less elaborate perhaps but equally persuasive was the transformation of Richard Chamberlain. For five years he was well known as TV's young Dr. Kildare, complete with golden hair and crisp white uniforms. In the late 1960s Chamberlain gave up the series to study Shakespearean theater in England. Emerging several months later with a British accent, shaggy brown hair, flarred bluejeans and a suede jacket, Chamberlain reaped praise from American and English critics for his TV role as Hamlet.

While image control is expected of a motion picture star and other media professionals, what about the community expert who becomes a media performer? How important is image control to that person? If his or her appearance is fleeting and the attitude casual, then image control is of no importance. If, however, the person sincerely wants to influence an audience, to enact legislation, to propagate an idea, to make money or disseminate information, the community expert must make a convincing presentation; in effect he or she must compete with

* Reference notes for each chapter are found in the section beginning on page 323.

professional performers. Anyone who plans to use media should know how to use them to advantage. Nowhere is this clearer than at the conclusion of TV/radio station editorials when qualified representatives of opposing views are invited to state those views in debate fashion. Frequently the response from the community expert is inept, because that person is debating not only an issue but also a media professional who uses media every day to make a convincing public presentation. Thus, it becomes increasingly evident that it behooves a community expert who appears as a presenter, if not as a professional performer, to use media as skillfully as possible.

Let there be no doubt image control is the same kind of media control some dictators or politicians use to create the impression of a just government working to benefit the people. Image control whether it is by government officials, a film star or a soap manufacturer is thought control. Professional performers want to control their images on media.

But there is another facet to the matter of image control: the public view. The public, weary from a quarter century of television viewing, a half century of radio, about 80 years of the movies and centuries of printed promotion does a great deal of selecting on its own. An audience tends to pick out what it wants to believe. It is acquainted with the illusions of filmdom. Recent publications concerning the "making" of the president of the United States have alerted the public to those techniques designed by media experts to create favorable public opinion. Needless to say, an on-going selective search for reality requires the public to be more discriminating in believing performers on media. The ramifications of this fascinating study can only be hinted at here; it is enough to remind performers that today's audience, raised on mass media, is paradoxically astute and naive. The performer must respond to this ambivalence in the public.

PROFESSIONAL PERFORMERS

Although a few people attempt performing later in life, perhaps along with or after a successful career in an unrelated field, most become interested in performing while in their early years at school. A young performer expresses ability through available organizations and activities such as speech contests, bands, plays, choirs, "ham" radio operation and student publications. Many high schools and elementary schools are fortunate enough to have radio, television and/or film facilities. The performer diligently takes lessons in music, dancing or voice, devoting a great deal of time to performance, because of personal and parental motivation. Usually a prodigy does not have to be told to practice for long hours. He or she uses every opportunity to appear before the public in church, school and the community.

This background is handily applied in college to academic work in departments of communication, drama, journalism, music, speech and liberal arts. The performer may pursue related activities like cheerleading or athletics. Depending largely on courses available, one enrolls in areas where specific performing interests can be developed. As the performer gains experience and as his or her work becomes better known, more opportunities arise. Cities and towns of all sizes frequently need entertainers and journalists—a part-time disc jockey on a radio station, an extra in a film being shot on location, a master-of-ceremonies job for a baton twirling contest, a "color person" for a local high school basketball game, a comic for a ladies' club, a singer in a pizza parlor, a musician in a dance band. The performer never knows when or where that first paying job will come, and never knows how long it will last. These uncertainities a person lives with as long as he or she is a professional performer.

Admittedly it is more difficult to be a performer on television. Frequently, the novice begins either by working in another medium first or accepts whatever job comes along in television with the hope that once he or she is in the station, performing ability will be recognized. The young professional performer soon learns to take advantage of every opportunity, especially if it is in performing. The performer accepts out-of-town assignments, one-night stands and benefits, and is aggressive in asking for work and showing what he or she can do. The aspirant is willing to work free if it will achieve his or her goals. For example, one young man who wanted to get into a local TV news department demonstrated his journalistic fortitude by waiting out a hurricane in a particularly vulnerable location as it hit the Gulf coast. Another wrote to a network offering to pay his own way if the network would allow him to join the sports staff when on location for a key sports tournament. Both young men were hired. A girl joined a civic organization so that she could make its public service spot announcements. She too was successful. Every performer has a different story to tell.

Blending a strong academic curriculum, perferably at a major college or university, and the job potential of a major market gives the beginning performer the best chance of accumulating both a degree and commercial *credits*—that is, a record of commercial experience—at the time of graduation. By doing so, the performer has a strong foundation. He or she may be fortunate enough to be absorbed on a full-time basis by the local station after working part time while attending classes. Some students, awarded internships in various communities, may be hired after the internship is complete. A performer must go wherever the work is, realizing that professional life is transient. The first job may last six months to two years; the second a bit longer. A performer is constantly looking for the *next* job, and therefore may seek the assistance of an agent. Even performers who are lucky enough to be hired in the hometowns or cities of their alma mater rarely stay for an extended period. Personal ambition and the necessity for station revitalization force the turnover even of excellent employees. Broadcast journalists are often told to get experience in smaller communities before trying the larger or the networks. Entertainers usually begin by working live in such places as nightclubs, amusement parks, community theaters, summer stock, restaurants and elsewhere prior to getting an opportunity in mass media. Many musicians try to cut a record hoping it will elevate them to the big time.

The road to media success can be discouraging, but it must be traveled if a performer is to be recognized. While most professional performers did not become well-known until they had worked in media for many years, many do make it rather quickly. There is no one formula for reaching the top.

COMMUNITY EXPERTS AS PRESENTERS

More community experts are using media to communicate with the public. These people are often highly skillful in their occupations but seldom in the utilization of media. For instance, why are many Sunday morning sermons on radio so long? Why are many TV teachers so boring? Why do many politicians appear incompetent? Why can't teenagers articulate their frustrations? Why do so many bank presidents look stodgy? Why do public relations representatives for petroleum and chemical companies seem to be against the community and for pollution? Why are the most needy members of society—the aged, the poor, the handicapped, the destitute, the uneducated, the incarcerated, the unsuitable—the least effective in pleading their causes on mass media? They use media *ineffectually*.

The president of the United States, members of Congress and local politicians are aware that their reelection may depend upon how successfully they use media. World tensions rise and subside with statements made by deplaning diplomats. Water bonds are voted, a city attorney's staff is increased, streets are improved, the public's attitude toward its police force changes when the power of mass media is mobilized properly. Business and industry, recognizing that media must be used purposefully, hire communication experts to make statements to media in event of off-shore oil well fires, plant explosions, train derailments, airplane crashes and other instances of public news interest.

Physicians are interviewed to endorse the requirements of a local hospital. Managers of automobile companies present a direct personal sales appeal to gain public confidence in their business. Athletes depend on media to perpetuate their reputations through play-by-play action, locker room comments and interviews. When the playing field is no longer a career possibility, a few of them join the sports staff of a radio or television station.

An increasing number of school administrators and teachers realize that they may be using media as presenters. In one elementary school morning announcements, once made on a public address system, are now on television. Children and teachers are presenters. A high school science teacher might have an entire series of programs on radio or television for which he or she is the principal presenter. In large school systems superintendents and supervisors, who once oriented teachers in the auditorium, now do so over closed circuit television. An awareness of media is growing among the students themselves as children in some schools produce short films of other children, thus giving them an early opportunity to work with media.

The utilization of media by community experts is increasing rapidly as concerned citizens realize how they can accomplish their objectives through media's proper use. Social activists including minority groups, clergy, civil rights lawyers, or indeed almost anyone with a cause, may plan to take advantage of media. Many low-income groups simply do not know how to use radio and television, but they are learning through evening classes held in churches, schools and common gathering places. As one Hispanic-American leader explained, "No one in the barrios knows how to use media to speak for Chicanos, so we are teaching them."

Even the housewife who wants some participation in her community is being called upon to provide everything from testimonials for a laundry detergent to running for the school board. Never let it be said that members of the family do not compete (when they appear on television or radio) with the most glamorous celebrities in the world. The family and friends of that relative or neighbor are even more concerned about such person's appearance than that of the famous. They want to be proud of the spokesperson for their cause. Children do expect to be proud of their parents on radio or television and vice versa.

Initially entertainers, journalists and commercial advertisers used mass media for communication, then came the educators, and now the social reformers. Public use of media is increasing. More and more individuals use mass media everyday to communicate purposefully with thousands of other people. The flow of information and entertainment is so profuse that the public has come to expect some sophistication in everyone who appears on media. After all, in mass media professional performers, community experts and amateur presenters compete for public attention.

2: Appearance

"An Olympian."

APPEARANCE IN MEDIA is part reality and part illusion. The reality is that which the camera cannot avoid revealing even though the performer might wish to—a pitted complexion, scars, a misshapen body. Inasmuch as nearly every aspect of a performer's physical appearance can be altered through make-up, lighting, costuming or surgery, most performers deal in illusion. Hair, eyes, nose, mouth, height and weight can be changed or controlled by the performer. So, the question arises, "How much should a performer change for his or her professional benefit?" There is no one answer. A performer's appearance, however, is linked to his or her psychological composition or personality. An individual is what he or she is, and the physical self reflects the inner being. A performer, therefore, should alter only that aspect of physical appearance that enhances, reflects and compliments the inner self. The performer who keeps in mind that each person is unique emphasizes whatever physical characteristics he or she chooses. Performance in media is primarily a matter of being outstanding. Physical differences contribute immeasurably to making a performer memorable to the public.

CLASSIC BEAUTY

Characteristics of male handsomeness and female pulchritude have changed very little over the centuries. True, there are times when a woman must lose weight here and there, use quite a bit of make-up or reduce it, have long hair or short, but for the most part her characteristics remain about the same. These characteristics were defined, refined and preserved in the magnificent Greek statues depicting Aphrodite, Apollo and the other gods and goddesses of Olympus. Centuries later Michelangelo's David and DaVinci's Mona Lisa repeated the classic proportions. Media celebrities and athletes of all races update the desire for similar proportions. Many health spas and exercise salons are adorned with Roman statues depicting the classic human form. Televised contests for Mr. and Miss America, Miss Universe and heroes of *Adam-12, The Rookies* and *Emergency!* perpetuate the Greek ideal.[1]

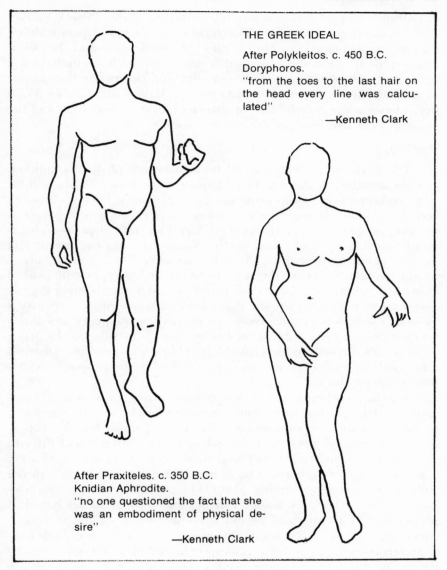

THE GREEK IDEAL

After Polykleitos. c. 450 B.C.
Doryphoros.
"from the toes to the last hair on the head every line was calculated"
—Kenneth Clark

After Praxiteles. c. 350 B.C.
Knidian Aphrodite.
"no one questioned the fact that she was an embodiment of physical desire"
—Kenneth Clark

Admittedly, for some Africans—the stately Watusi or the primitive pygmy, for example—and for some Orientals of slight build and fine bones, the classic Western figure is at variation. Since the fusion of Western and Oriental cultures during and after World War II, however, there has been a tendency for Orientals (Japanese, for example) to be taller, more muscular and generally conform to the classic Western ideal. Most performers yearn to be attractive in the classic tradition, while preserving the unique characteristics of their own personalities. Classic proportions—the Greek idea of wholeness—may be summarized along these lines: physical beauty is one with strength, grace, gentleness and benevolence.[2] Recent television deities are the "Bionic Man" and "Bionic Woman," played by Lee Majors and Lindsey Wagner. They are the combination of nature's fairest endowments and the imaginings of a technologically oriented society.

The Body

The performer's body should be in excellent physical condition, just like an athlete's. Ancient Greeks spent many hours on physical fitness. Top condition requires continuous maintenance, for a performer's body is constantly changing whether one wants it to or not. A person is growing or getting older throughout life. The shift in proportions is mostly notable in height and weight. Society dictates the norm: tall, slender people are considered more attractive. The average man's height has increased over the years to where he has reportedly peaked at five feet, seven inches, but most people would agree standing slightly over six feet is more desirable. Part of the mystique of the expression "Tall in the Saddle" comes from the notion that pioneers and Westerners were tall men. A romantic leading man is usually tall. He has a straight back, broad and level shoulders, a big chest, a narrow waist and hips and long legs. He is currently personified in the proportions of a football quarterback.

A romantic leading lady is shorter than most men who are considered tall. Her bustline and hipline measure nearly equally. She has a narrow waist and slim proportions over all. Historically female proportions have changed more than the male's, at times being rather full and at other times being rather stick-like. Ideal proportions are based upon a girl's figure during her late teens and therefore vary some with the culture. A teenager weighing about 115 pounds with the measurements of bust 34 inches, waist 24 inches and hips 34 inches has ideal proportions. This youthful period is consistently idealized in fiction. American culture gives scant allowance for maturation, and consequently does not allow for variations from the idealized norm, resulting in a youth-oriented appearance for everyone. Blacks and Latins are often excellent physical specimens while young, but for environmental reasons may physically deteriorate at an early age. Recent advertising has been toward encouraging Blacks and Latins to preserve a youthful appearance, especially when working in media.

The Face

Facial features should be relatively delicate for women and strong or angular for men, according to classic design. The Pietá of Mi-

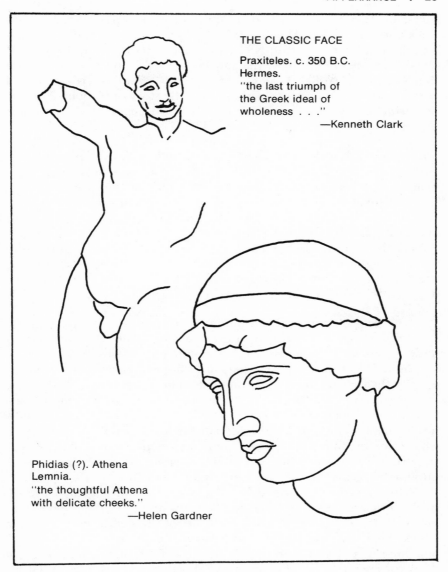

THE CLASSIC FACE

Praxiteles. c. 350 B.C.
Hermes.
"the last triumph of
the Greek ideal of
wholeness . . ."
—Kenneth Clark

Phidias (?). Athena
Lemnia.
"the thoughtful Athena
with delicate cheeks."
—Helen Gardner

chelangelo, Oriental water colors and porcelain figurines of recent centuries show a preference for fine features. To makeup artist Alan Demko, "I can't think of one person [as an ideal beauty]. I think of a composite Kim Novak's pretty nose, Mia Farrow's well-shaped mouth that isn't too large or too small, Diana Ross' huge eyes, Dominique Sanda's high cheekbones, Bianca Jagger's strong chin line and Audrey Hepburn's long neck."[3] Many women in media do not have delicate faces, yet they are considered beautiful—for example, Barbara Stanwyck and Lucille Ball. Male handsomeness in the classic sense is recognizable in the faces of Paul Newman, Robert Redford and Clint Eastwood. But one's face is more than an attractive design. ". . . even more than the voice," Clive Barnes wrote recently, "the face is the actor's prime instrument, the mirror of his soul, the story of his journey."[4]

Structure. Many beauticians classify the face in four categories: oval, square, round or heart-shaped. The classic face is the oval; it has the most pleasing and versatile proportions. This shape is somewhat longer than it is wide. The square face usually means the person has a strong jaw and chin line, often balanced by a more prominent forehead. The round face indicates that the width of the face equals the height. The heart-shaped or triangular face refers to a less pronounced chin line, perhaps a weak one with a normal forehead. Men have similar facial structure, but less attention is given to them, in part because the hair is the principal means of balancing the face and until recently men's hair styles have been too short to be of benefit in reproportioning the face. Although the oval is favored for both sexes, men are also depicted in contemporary art as having square faces with strong chin and jaw lines.

The classic face handily divides into thirds, preferably equal thirds: from the top of the forehead to the eyebrows, from the eyebrows to under the nose, from under the nose to the bottom of the chin.

Eyes. Eyes communicate a person's state of mind and level of energy by their color, shape, environment and expressiveness. Eyes come in many colors—shades of blue, brown and black are the most common. Green, violet and amber are less frequent. Most eyes are a mixture of many colors, making it difficult for many people to say exactly what color they are; hence, the vague terms "hazel" or "blue-green." Important too is the whiteness of the area surrounding the iris and pupil, redness and veins being undesirable.

The eyes may be round or somewhat almond-shaped, large or small, but large eyes are preferred. The appearance of the eye is determined by the surrounding features: shape of the socket, eyebrows and lashes. Typically, recessed eyes with heavy, long lashes and brows, depending upon fashion trends, provide attractive shadowing for eyes. A third consideration is expressiveness. This depends upon their clarity, uniformity, depth of color and sparkle which is associated with a healthy, intelligent person.

Nose. The nose is perhaps the most difficult feature to work with if it is oversized or too irregular. The classic nose is straight, about one-third the length of the face, and has even, balanced, rather small nostrils, and a smooth unblemished skin, devoid of pores or discoloration. The tip of the nose is slightly rounded, not pointed. Frequently people

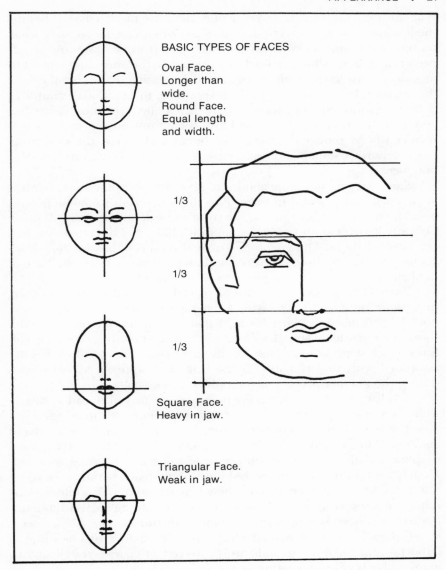

BASIC TYPES OF FACES

Oval Face.
Longer than
wide.
Round Face.
Equal length
and width.

1/3

1/3

1/3

Square Face.
Heavy in jaw.

Triangular Face.
Weak in jaw.

are not blessed with a classic nose. Common Oriental noses are small and tend to be scooped or flat. Black races often have large nostrils. Some eastern Mediterranean people have irregular cartilage resulting in a hump at the bridge of the nose. Sometimes hair grows inside nostrils and must be removed.

Mouth. The classic mouth has slightly pink, full lips. The upper lip is about the same size as the lower one. Both are nicely curved. Behind the lips are even, white teeth devoid of any fillings or dental work whatsoever. Some cultures consider gold fillings attractive, but most people prefer matching white enamel replacements for missing teeth. The mouth is considered by many the most expressive feature of the face, the surrounding muscles quickly responding to emotional stimuli by tightening, quivering or smiling. A pleasant smile is the most rewarding and graceful asset a person can have, for almost any error by a performer will be reduced or forgotten by an audience if the performer has a generous smile. A classic figure in a serious work rarely smiles, however.

Ears. An ear should be about the same length as the nose, tending to be small and graceful in form. Ears are a problem for some people, because they may stick out too far from the side of the head. Women can usually cover up unattractive ears with hair, and of course, surgery can make changes. The opening to the ear is on roughly the same horizontal plane as the tip of the nose and about midway from the back of the head.

Hair. Hair frames the face and provides a helpful variable in reproportioning it and intensifying facial colors. Hair color may or may not be uniform, particularly for light shades. The hue should be of uniform color to the scalp. Brown shades are common to Western cultures, black shades to the East and in warm climates. Blond shades are associated with cold climates. White hair, with appropriate variations during the graying process, is the only universal color.

A full head of hair is traditionally related to youth and strength, while baldness is related to aging and sometimes wisdom. Samson's power was said to be generated from his hair. Amount alone is not enough. Manageability is necessary and so is a natural tendency toward shaping or falling into place on the head to form a pleasing covering. Usually a slight natural curl is desirable. Many black people with tight, fine curly strands prefer to have their hair straightened, while various other races spend millions of dollars each year adding curl. A tendency toward curliness is common to some individuals and black races; straightness is common among Orientals. The texture of one's hair is important. Silky, shiny strands are preferred to coarse, rough or unmanageable bodiless fine strands.

INDIVIDUAL DIFFERENCES

Most human beings vary substantially from the classic ideal. These variations make them less than perfect, yet usually even more interesting to other human beings. The world indeed would be dull if everyone looked like everyone else. Overweight has made Kate Smith, Cass Elliott, Jackie Gleason, Oliver Hardy, and Lou Costello identifiable. Sophie Tucker used to lament in one of her songs, "Nobody loves a fat girl," but her admirers were legion. Twiggy, Cher and Ray Bolger are known for being very thin. Wilt Chamberlain is exceptionally tall. Raquel Welch, Jane Russell and *Playboy* pinups have large bustlines; Betty Grable and Marlene Dietrich were known for beautiful legs. Marilyn Monroe's figure, having many attractive proportions, helped make her a sex symbol of the 1950s. These exceptions in physical appearance helped to make these performers memorable. An identifying characteristic is often found in the face: Mick Jagger—lips; Lauren Bacall of the 1940s—"the Downunder Look"; George Gobel—brush cut hair; Joan Crawford—chin and jaw; Clark Gable and Bing Crosby—protruding ears; Gene Tierney—protruding teeth; Jimmy Durante and Bob Hope—odd shaped noses. Admirers of Greta Garbo believed she had a classic face.

Sometimes a physical exception to the classic proportions can be an asset. The performer must decide how to emphasize the distinguishing feature. If the feature coincides with the individual's presentation, if the individual likes the feature or does not want to have it surgically removed or altered or remolded through exercise, then it must be blended into the person's total appearance as a positive asset. To wit, the person chooses to live with it. Most people in media, whether appearing professionally or infrequently, prefer to present themselves for what they are without exceptional changes. This desire to develop one's self provides that unique quality to an individual and makes the person easily recognizable to the public. "People who look like people" are in demand occasionally for commercials. One woman over 65 enjoys playing "nice little old grandmother parts." Another at 55, without experience, is cast from time to time in training films and commercials. A third woman and her husband made a commercial showing three couples dancing. The women got their jobs through agents. A research scientist who uses videotape to playback the in-class performance of his aspiring science teachers asks them, "How do you want to look?" Rock singer Janis Joplin would have said, "The way I am, man."

SELF-EVALUATION

When performers take a good look at themselves, what do they see? What do others see? Chances are a performer sees everything unattractive, everything one would like to change, everything the performer thinks is more perfect in someone else.

A performer may see his or her own good points, but cannot evaluate them. The performer depends primarily upon the comments of others for that. A random sampling of comments from one's audience, one's family, friends and strangers will in time present a good idea of one's attractive qualities. A performance class in a professional school or college filled with students and an instructor who have the best interests of the performer in mind can provide valuable perspective. This special audience is a kind of talking mirror for the performer.

Self-evaluation consists of personal research based on opinions, viewing videotapes and films and intimate scrutiny in front of a mirror before a performer can truly determine his or her physical assets and liabilities. An educated professional performer will make this assessment early in life and revise the impression as he or she matures. Those performers who are already mature must undergo evaluation as quickly as possible if they are to have a place in a circle of younger competition. The community expert has been evaluating his or her appearance before a mirror also. It is human nature to do so, but it is the community expert's first appearance on media that typically alerts him or her to careful self-evaluation. If the community expert or company representative is to appear often on media, he or she may wish to enroll in continuing education classes in media performance.

		SELF EVALUATION CHART *Physical Data:* Height: Weight: Complexion: Body structure: Age: Sex:
Unretouched photographs of entire body. Front, profiles and back. Unretouched photographs of face. Front, profiles and back.		*Facial Data:* Structure: Eyes: Nose: Mouth: Ears: Hair:

A valuable method of self-evaluation is to have eight unretouched photographs taken: four of the entire body (front, profiles, and back) and four of the face front, profiles—a person's side views are dissimilar—and back. These photographs should then be carefully traced so that the performer has an outline of his or her entire body and face. The performer can use these tracings to alter features on paper before actually trying them.

3: Improving Appearance

"Magic Mirror on the wall who is fairest?"

Improving the Body
Height Control—Weight Control—Complexion Control—Maturation—Body Make-up—Clothing (Essential Clothing; Aesthetic Clothing; Accessories)

Improving the Face
Structure—Reproportioning the Face—Improving the Eyes—Improving the Nose—Improving the Mouth—Improving the Ears—Improving the Hair

FOUNDATIONS: This chart shows basic foundation colors listed by their suggested uses and manufacturers' numbers.

	Max Factor grease/cake/ stick	Bob Kelly creme stick	Ben Nye creme cake		Max Factor grease/cake/ stick	Bob Kelly creme stick	Ben Nye creme cake
JUVENILE GIRL - LEADING LADY	2A	S-3	L-1	**OLD AGE FEMALE**	4A	S-8	OLD AGE
JUVENILE BOY - LEADING MAN	7A	S-6	M-1	**OLD AGE MALE**	6	S-8	OLD AGE
MIDDLE-AGE FEMALE	4½	S-4	L-3	**BLACK SKIN (LIGHT)**	665-K	SC-50	25
MIDDLE AGE - MALE	5½	S-5	M-3	**BLACK SKIN (MEDIUM)**	665-M	SC-52	27
ORIENTAL, MALE/FEMALE	5 Female / 12 Male	S-9	24 Female / 23 Male	**BLACK SKIN (DARK)**	665-P	SC-54	30

ONCE HAVING EVALUATED his or her appearance, the performer decides what should be done to modify and presumably improve it. Appearance can be improved through exercise, make-up and/or medical treatment. Preliminary to these discussions is an understanding of how a performer creates illusion, through the manipulation of light and shadow. Such manipulation is common to the visual arts of painting, sculpture, theater and cinema. All colors have values that can be converted into shades of black and white, very dark colors being near black and very light colors near white. All other hues are somewhere in between. The range of variations in hues from black to white is called the *gray scale*. It might be said a performer molds his or her appearance in terms of light and dark values—that is, the gray scale. To an audience, pure white is the most "advancing" and pure black is the most "retiring" light value. Simply speaking, if one were to look at two performers—one white, one black—equally far away, the white performer would be easier to see than the black one. If the bodies of the two performers were identical, the white performer would still look closer and larger than the black performer. In other words the lighter the value the easier it is to see, the larger and closer it appears. This principle applied to performance is the basis for achieving three-dimensional effects in make-up and clothing. Specifically, a performer applies white make-up around the eyes to bring the sockets forward and dark make-up to recess them. A performer wears light clothing to show off a suntan, but wears a dark costume to accentuate a pale complexion.

Generally TV avoids the high contrast combinations of black and white, because the contrast tends to leave a semipermanent "image burn" on the face of the TV camera tube. Before the days of color TV, men would commonly wear charcoal-blue, -black, -brown or -gray suits with white shirts, thus creating undesirable high contrast. Nowadays men and women wear more colorful clothing, avoiding extremes and utilizing the central range of hues in the gray-scale. The performer must consider what clothing will look like in both black-and-white and color television. Color television is in wide use in many countries, but its use is far from universal and so compatibility is essential. Middle gray-scale colors such as pastel blue or green and certain flesh tones may appear as a single hue when viewed on black-and-white TV. An amusing example of this point occurs when a figure-fitting colored body suit suggests on a black-and-white TV receiver that the dancer is nude.

IMPROVING THE BODY

Physical improvement of the body is accomplished handily through exercise, which is largely a matter of forming good habits at a young age. The need for a good physical education program, including proper diet, exists at the pre-school level and continues throughout life. A person reaches his or her physical peak during the late teens—Olympic stars, models, showgirls and beauty contestants. Once a person leaves high school, works and assumes responsibilities of adult life, exercise programs in sports and other recreations are often abandoned, and he or she slips quickly into physical decline. Unfortunately, many young men and women are fat and/or bald, with missing teeth, weak muscles and/or poor skin. Much of this deterioration is caused by neglect.

Ron Fletcher, who has an exercise studio in Beverly Hills—Candice Bergen, Ali McGraw, Katharine Ross, Shirley Jones are clients—has a theory called "Body Contrology," a discipline designed to realign and recondition the body. Fletcher claims any body at any age can be improved. "All it takes is work." Discipline is the key to contrology. Fletcher's program demands total coordination of body, mind, spirit—and breath. "Only by bringing the four together through total concentration can control of the body be achieved," he explains. "The initial step is to find one's center, that place where one's balance is located. Once that is achieved, freedom to move the body at will comes. That allows the body to fill its life space with presence and authority."[1] Some celebrities keep themselves in shape by registering at $100-a-day spas such as La Costa, near San Diego, but most of the work can be done by exercising at home.[2] The discussion that follows will aid those performers who wish to slow the aging process and improve their present physical condition. Principal considerations are height, weight, complexion and maturation control.

Height Control

Proper exercise is essential for maintaining one's full height. If a performer is posture conscious, he or she will stand tall and erect by balancing one's weight on the balls of the feet and especially the joint of the big toes, pulling shoulder blades back and down, and putting chin forward but level. For sitting, one should slide the buttocks back, trying to sit tall, holding the torso straight, pulling the abdominal muscles in, shoulder blades back and down, and putting the chin slightly forward. Many people sit on the mid-part of the backbone, walk with slightly drooped shoulders or a humped back. Physical neglect often begins in formative years when adolescents perform tasks or develop poor habits which result in malformation of the bones. Physical exercise can develop one's frame properly during growing years and maintain it thereafter.

A steady, consistent approach to physical development is the better approach to keeping physically fit, according to experts. Many performers turn to dance. Dance combines physical discipline, grace and exercise. A performer may work out in a gym on the bars and mats or in some other sport such as swimming or tennis, but dance includes all of the exercises and aesthetic complements a performer requires. Dancer Paul Taylor has 90-minute classes which have three parts: a workout on the floor or barre, a free standing exercise and traveling through space. "There is no democracy," Taylor says. "The students do what the tyrant says or try someone else's class. Most dance classes are very strict in requirements and form."[3]

The illusion of height can be achieved in various ways. As much as two inches can be added to one's height by inserting lifts inside specially designed shoes, called *elevator* shoes. High-heeled shoes, when fashionable, accomplish the same purpose (Tony Orlando). If the performer keeps a weight level less than normal for his or her height, this too will help to create the illusion of tallness. At the 1972 Republican Convention an elevator, regulated from a nearby desk, kept all speakers at the same height and none taller than the President. Here are some suggestions for those who wish to seem taller:

1. Make maximum use of the height you have by perfecting your posture. Stretch and strengthen the spine through exercise, pull up the rib cage and hold the head high. Practice with a book on your head. This old reliable technique still works.

2. Comb and style your hair in front of a full length mirror, adding proportion and balance to the entire figure.

3. Keep your make-up simple, neat and delicate, using delicate colors, accents and fine false eyelashes if you wear them.

4. Wear the same color clothing to lengthen the line from head to toe. Women will probably benefit from showing a little more leg than fashion dictates at the time.

5. Keep all accessories simple and diminutive in proportion to your entire appearance.

Unusually tall persons should stand their full height and make the most of it. However, dropping the waistline, wearing low heels, patterns and coats a little long may help to reduce the illusion of height. The director can help a great deal by means of clever camera angles.

Weight Control

There is a direct relationship between weight, height and good health. Dr. Robert C. Atkins has suggested a simple formula for determining the relationship of one's height and weight. "To calculate the approximate degree of their overweight, if any, multiply the number of inches over five feet by five inches for a woman, seven for a man, then add one hundred."[4] Or, consult the weight chart at the end of this section. Note that performers keep within the ranges on the chart: TV's "Wonder Woman," Lynda Carter, for example, is 5 feet 8¼ inches tall and weighs 126 pounds; Cicely Tyson is 5 feet 3 inches and 100 pounds; Randolph Mantooth (John Gage of *Emergency!*) is 6-foot-1, 179 pounds.

Proper weight aids good health. So long as a performer consumes the proper daily nutritional requirements for one's body, the performer need not eat additional food. The fact is most people enjoy eating, and therefore they are prone to eat more calories than their systems consume each day. A performer who eats an excessive number of calories gains weight, one who does not eat enough loses it. Aside from certain glandular malfunctions or imbalances which are relatively rare, weight is the result of eating too much.

A performer can expect to look heavier on TV and film than in person. Some estimate as much as 10 pounds heavier, due in part to the aspect ratio of the picture—four horizontal units to three vertical units. If a performer wishes to control weight, he or she must regulate the amount and kind of food eaten. A simple calorie counter and the honest recording of each item eaten will show precisely where the intake exceeds the amounts of caloric energy used. (A calorie is a unit of measure which indicates the relative value of food consumed to energy used by an individual.) Many performers go on crash diets with or without the assistance of physicians. These diets frequently yield temporary results, but they may be dangerous because the body may not get sufficient nutrition to sustain health and energy. Dieting under a physician's direction is the better way. A person may lose several pounds within a brief period. The loss should allow the skin to contract gradually. Once a performer has attained a desired weight, he or she should maintain it by getting weighed every day, and by keeping within a five-pound margin *under* the desired weight.

The most effective diet program the author has observed is a combination of daily injections of human chorionic gonadotrophin (HCG), plus a rigorously supervised 500-caloric diet. This program was developed by Dr. A. T. W. Simeons.[5] For many this diet suppresses hunger. While some physicians discuss the suppression as psychological, other physicians have worked out the program in great detail.

The intense pressures of performing have forced Elizabeth Taylor, Connie Stevens and Dyan Cannon into fasting periods before media appearances; Lorne Green, Bill Conrad and Buddy Hackett have lost weight on The Rice Diet; Weight Watchers helped Carol Burnett and Ruth Buzzi; Tony Orlando used Dr. Stillman's high protein diet.[6]

While weight does not prohibit some performers from working in media (William Conrad in the *Cannon* series, James Coco in *The Dumplings*), it tends to prevent those who deviate greatly from normal weight in appearing in visual media in capacities other than entertainment. For instance, some singers are heavy, but rarely are journalists. (A few exceptions are those with reputations from another medium such as newspapers or radio.) Overweight performers are rather common in radio, however. Broadcast journalists, entertainers, politicians, clergy and others working in visual media as a rule are trim. Furthermore, young media participants recognize the personal values of weight control.

Aside from diet, there are several items on the market for reproportioning one's body. Undergarments such as Pantyhose have given birth to Lycra bodysuits which are lightweight and comfortable.[7] Girdles and corsets made of stiffer materials reshape various parts of the body especially the waist, hips and bustline. To the contrary, padding in shoulders, bustlines, hips, buttocks and limbs adds to the illusion of weight gain. Of course these items are concealed by clothing. Medical treatment such as breast expansion, discussed elsewhere, may add weight and/or reproportion the body. Although very thin females have been accepted for a long time, the underdeveloped male physique, once an advertising cliché—the "97-pound weakling,"—is presently appearing on media, and occasionally as a film hero. By contrast the fat man or woman is usually ridiculed, especially if they appear without clothing.

Clothing can be very helpful in adding or reducing weight by means of illusion. To shed pounds a performer wears clothes that hug the larger parts of the body, but not too tightly, such as A-line skirts and dresses and blouses that do not have excess material on the sides. Softly woven fabrics, a simple uncluttered look from shoulder to hem, dark hose, V-necklines, upswept hairstyles, hemlines that fall just below the knee or almost to the floor during the evening, pants covering most of the shoe, vertical designs and patterns, dark to medium colors, long narrow lapels on blouses, jackets and coats all contribute to a slimming effect. A heavy performer should avoid flat shoes and flat hair styles, horizontal stripes and patterns, gathers, pleats and large patch pockets, white or light solid colors, accessories like sashes and belts, hems above the knee, rough-textured fabrics such as tweeds, bulky wools, shiny fabrics, double breasted coats with wide lapels, turtlenecks, slim, tight, straight skirts. An opposite approach to most of these suggestions will add weight for the slender person.

DESIRABLE WEIGHTS FOR MEN AND WOMEN AGED 25 AND OVER[8]
In pounds according to height and frame, in indoor clothing, and shoes

HEIGHT		SMALL FRAME	MEDIUM FRAME	LARGE FRAME
		MEN		
Feet	*Inches*			
5	2	112–120	118–129	126–141
5	3	115–123	121–133	129–144
5	4	118–126	124–136	132–148
5	5	121–129	127–139	135–152
5	6	124–133	130–143	138–156
5	7	128–137	134–147	142–161
5	8	132–141	138–152	147–166
5	9	136–145	142–156	151–170
5	10	140–150	146–160	155–174
5	11	144–154	150–165	159–179
6	0	148–158	154–170	164–184
6	1	152–162	158–175	168–189
6	2	156–167	162–180	173–194
6	3	160–171	167–185	178–199
6	4	164–175	172–190	182–204
		WOMEN		
4	10	92– 98	96–107	104–119
4	11	94–101	98–110	106–122
5	0	96–104	101–113	109–125
5	1	99–107	104–116	112–128
5	2	102–110	107–119	115–131
5	3	105–113	110–122	118–134
5	4	108–116	113–126	121–138
5	5	111–119	116–130	125–142
5	6	114–123	120–135	129–146
5	7	118–127	124–139	133–150
5	8	122–131	128–143	137–154
5	9	126–135	132–147	141–158
5	10	130–140	136–151	145–163
5	11	134–144	140–155	149–168
6	0	138–148	144–159	153–173

Complexion Control

Light-skinned (Caucasian, Oriental, tan) and dark-skinned (dark brown or black, red) people provide a wide range of values on a gray scale which equates each skin hue to a color value ranging from black to white. (See Gray Scale.) The essential difference is that the darker the skin the less effective make-up may be for the purpose of creating illusion or changing one's appearance. Dark-skinned performers depend on the lighting expert in the studio to bring out their features. The skin color easiest to work with, and much preferred by many people, is a medium suntan shade in the middle of the gray scale.

Aside from color, the next greatest concern is clarity. The skin must be free of blemishes (scars, pimples, large pores, moles, veins, discoloration). Few faces are completely free from all of them. Cleanliness practiced from an early age is a great help in protecting one's skin. Dr. W. C. Duncan, president of the Houston Dermatological Society, recommends this routine:

1. Cleanse and rinse the face with cold tap water. This removes surface dirt.
2. Cleanse with soap and the hottest water you can stand, rinsing with hot water. This opens pores, removes make-up and dirt.
3. Cleanse with a wash cloth, using soap and hot water. Rinse with hot water.
4. Splash-rinse with cold water to close pores.[9]

Some performers, particularly teenagers, may need to alternate the use of an abrasive cleaner or pumice every other day. Otherwise, any standard bar soap is suitable for washing. Performers should also keep hands and nails away from the face, because they may bring dirt and infections to it. Medicated creams found in the drugstore are satisfactory in getting rid of blemishes. Blemishes should not be squeezed; dark skins are particularly slow to heal and tend to scar. One suggested lotion is Liquemat, an inexpensive formula combining color, water and alcohol; it may be worn by either sex. The sun is a danger to fair-skinned people who should stay out of the sun or use sun-screen lotions. The sun may also cause premature aging, wrinkles and blotches. Acne is common in both sexes during later adolescent years. Acne is caused by the stimulus of the male hormone, according to a popular theory, and so boys tend to have the more severe cases. Diet has little to do with acne; a person may be allergic, perhaps temporarily, to certain foods, however. (See Abnormalities.)

As a performer gets older, many factors influence the skin. Sun, loss of natural oils, facial movements and methods of applying make-up may damage the skin. Cosmetics can provide lubrication. Actress Joan Crawford, noted for her beauty, once said that she made a habit of using a moisturizer regularly, treating her face and neck in the same way. After showering she applied rose water and glycerin to her hands, elbows and joints because they dry out faster than the fleshy parts of the body.[10]

Maturation

Cosmetics, surgery and illusion will only go so far; a person's skin does age. On close observation a person's skin looks its age especially if the person is fair skinned. People having dark skins age much more slowly, perhaps by more than 20 years. Careful lighting, theatrical trickery, make-up, exercise, fashionable clothing and a normal time lag between production and release dates of films and videotapes preserve the illusion that some men and women are slow to age.

Facial movement is a major cause of wrinkles. Wrinkling brows and laughing permanently crease the face. For instance, the performer who frowns habitually soon sees lines between eyebrows and at the corners of the mouth. Some people unconsciously arch their eyebrows causing forehead wrinkles. Such habits once formed are difficult to change. A performer can try to reduce these wrinkles by massaging in a moisturizer and wearing a pad, purchased at a drug or department store, that is pasted across the wrinkled area during non-business hours at home. The pad serves as a reminder that these wrinkles are related to tension and habit and that the performer should relax the face.

So long as the skin remains relatively tight to the skeleton, a performer will appear youthful. Various skin tightening methods are applied, from daily face washing with water and a patting technique so as not to break down any tissues, to surgical procedures. (See Abnormalities). Women are not alone in a desire to look one's best. Since 1960, the men's grooming-aids business has tripled to become a billion-dollar industry.[11] Various techniques and products are on the market. One do-it-yourself facelift consists of small transparent, plastic discs that are glued in front of and behind the ears. An almost invisible cord is hooked into rings on the discs and drawn up over the crown of the head. Hair is combed to conceal the apparatus.[12]

Body Make-up

Those whose natural skin color is sufficiently intense for TV and film are fortunate. Occasionally make-up is applied to one's body, particularly the hands so that they do not look pale when next to the face. Legs, indeed the entire torso, may be covered with body make-up. Body make-up is difficult to work with because it sometimes comes off on clothing and deteriorates during shooting, so when possible, many performers prefer a natural suntan. Actor George Hamilton is said to head for a sunny climate whenever his natural tan starts to fade. Rarely, an exotic body make-up is applied, such as in the film *Goldfinger,* when a girl's entire body except for a small patch was sprayed gold; extreme care is used in the application and removal of this make-up.

Clothing

The purposes of clothing in media are (1) to provide essential covering, (2) to lend aesthetic attractiveness, uniqueness and/or vanity to the performer, (3) to mask unattractive features, and (4) to establish unusual costumes for entertainment programs (monsters, *Planet of the Apes*). The first three functions are of interest here.

Essential Clothing. Most performers want flexible clothing that is easy to wear, easy to maintain and looks presentable under many different conditions. A person who appears frequently in media realizes instantly that he or she either wears the same costume every week— newscasters wearing identical yellow sportscoats with the station's logo on the pocket, all singers wearing choir robes—or has the monumental task of wearing something different in every appearance. Hence, the program credits to certain stores for wardrobe—"Wardrobe by Botany 500," or a local store credit. The essential task is to get something besides one's favorite pinstripe suit or plain A-line dress to wear on every newscast. There is no inexpensive answer to this dilemma without borrowing the clothes. The performer rotates the wardrobe as well as anyone can and hopes that the public will not be too critical. Men have a better chance of getting away with this conservative approach than women do. Often women receive as much comment, especially from female viewers, on their appearance as they do on their program content, and so women must be more conscious of their wardrobe.

Furthermore, the temperature in a TV studio frequently varies a great deal: under lights on the set it is warm to hot, elsewhere in the studio it is cold from air conditioning. Bringing along a sweater or coat to a TV studio is a good idea.

Aesthetic Clothing. In general, clothing should reveal the graceful lines of the body, yield to the face and add color and warmth to the person. There are some exceptions, of course, wherein the costumes themselves, as in a musical revue, are the principal attraction. The most universally accepted costume for a man is a suit, shirt and tie and for a woman an unadorned dress of contemporary design and length. The clothes should fit smoothly without wrinkles. Many of the popular synthetic fabrics of polyester, acrylan and nylon are suitable if they are not too hot under TV lights. Plain fabrics have a conservative look, but accessories can easily be added. Patterned fabrics are sufficiently atten-

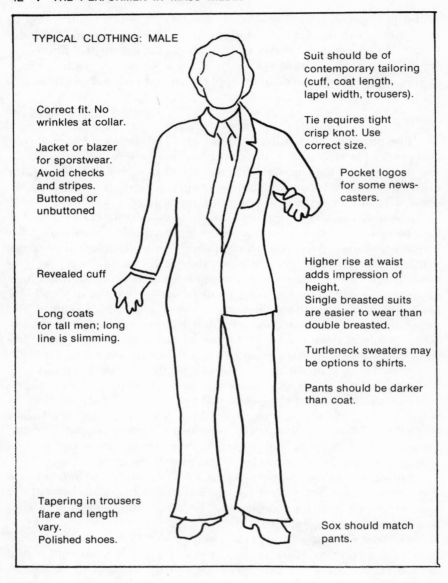

TYPICAL CLOTHING: MALE

Correct fit. No
wrinkles at collar.

Jacket or blazer
for sporstwear.
Avoid checks
and stripes.
Buttoned or
unbuttoned

Revealed cuff

Long coats
for tall men; long
line is slimming.

Tapering in trousers
flare and length
vary.
Polished shoes.

Suit should be of
contemporary tailoring
(cuff, coat length,
lapel width, trousers).

Tie requires tight
crisp knot. Use
correct size.

Pocket logos
for some news-
casters.

Higher rise at waist
adds impression of
height.
Single breasted suits
are easier to wear than
double breasted.

Turtleneck sweaters may
be options to shirts.

Pants should be darker
than coat.

Sox should match
pants.

tion-getting in themselves. Occasionally a check or plaid will have its
design reinforced by the electronic scanning in such a way that the pattern itself will appear to move or jump and draw unnecessary attention
to itself. These patterns should be avoided.

A performer tends to work toward a vertical look by wearing ver-

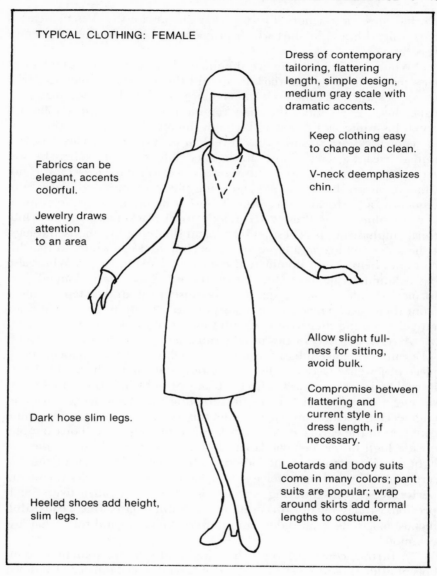

TYPICAL CLOTHING: FEMALE

Dress of contemporary tailoring, flattering length, simple design, medium gray scale with dramatic accents.

Keep clothing easy to change and clean.

V-neck deemphasizes chin.

Fabrics can be elegant, accents colorful.

Jewelry draws attention to an area

Allow slight full-ness for sitting, avoid bulk.

Compromise between flattering and current style in dress length, if necessary.

Dark hose slim legs.

Leotards and body suits come in many colors; pant suits are popular; wrap around skirts add formal lengths to costume.

Heeled shoes add height, slim legs.

tical stripes, height-increasing shoes or solid colors. If a performer wishes to lengthen the body line, he or she should wear a costume that emphasizes the vertical line. If a perfomer wishes to slenderize the body's appearance, he or she should concentrate on the center vertical panel in the attire, using dark retiring colors to the sides. In effect, this is what most performers do somewhat unconsciously. A man wears a dark suit with a light shirt which provides the attention-getting center vertical panel.

White and light colors are dominant. If a man wears white socks on a program along with dark pants and shoes (some athletes do this), the viewer will notice his ankles much more than if he had worn matching dark socks. Every time the man repositions his legs, the public will watch his white socks moving through the air. The same is true if his pants or socks are so short they reveal an inch or two of bare leg. If a woman wears a dark blouse and a very light or white skirt, she will seem to enlarge her hips. The viewer's eye will tend to seek the hot white areas on the TV screen, ignoring the gray hues and black; consequently, a performer uses white for what he or she wants to emphasize. In films, Elvis Presley frequently wore black pants and a white shirt, emphasizing his chest and face, and slimming his thighs and legs. If he appeared live in a large arena or club, he wore white, so that his costumes helped him dominate the stage by looking larger. White also has a luminous quality under powerful arc lights. Dark-skinned performers should use white sparingly because it will draw attention away from their face. They are safer keeping to a medium gray-scale color range, accenting their costume with touches of black and white.

Accessories. Accessories usually call attention to themselves. Accessories may enhance a basic costume—a well-designed or colorful tie, a piece of jewelry. Occasionally a piece of metal will catch the TV lights in such a way that it will reflect a beam of light into the camera lens causing a dark halo or "bloom" to surround the metal. In recent times engineering techniques have made this occurance, which was quite common in the earlier days of black-and-white TV, rare. For example, once a high luster, metallic lapel pin on a lady's dress caught the TV lights to the extent that the bloom covered more than half of the TV screen. Non-reflecting jewelry is now being made especially for media performers. Non-glittering jewelry is often very attractive. Semi-precious stones (agate), decorations of leather, lace, fine beads, dull metals, macramé, embroidery and flowers are warm and somewhat less common.

A further consideration is that rings and pins are sometimes symbols of affiliation with religious (Star of David), social (Order of Eastern Star) or professional groups (The Bell System, a pilot's wings), of economic status (large diamond) or of marital status (wedding band). They should be worn only if the performer considers the affiliation desirable to his or her public image.

IMPROVING THE FACE

"I don't believe there is such a thing as perfect beauty," Alan Demko, a well known make-up artist, has said. "That's why I think make-up is so interesting. We use it to create illusion. I think of myself as an image maker. It's a fascinating business to accentuate the positive and eliminate the negative in a face."[13] The principal means of alteration is make-up. The main function of make-up for mass media is to preserve a normal, healthy, vital appearance, to intensify or dramatize outstanding features, to change or minimize less attractive features, and to add oils to the skin which are lost through maturation. The objectives are accomplished with a great deal of experimentation and, with the exception of certain character parts in dramas, the use of minimum make-up. In general, women appearing on TV apply make-up heavier than street wear; and men apply little more than make-up essentials such as a base color. The objective, whether the performer is a media professional or a community expert using media, is to enhance the person's natural appearance with the use of make-up. The thin, translucent quality of Mia Farrow's skin is preserved with the use of minimum make-up consisting of a whipped cream base, pink blush and lip gloss. Raquel Welch prefers a sophisticated, shiny, intentionally made-up look requiring dark eyeliner around the entire eye, light eyeshadow on the lids of her large, deep set eyes, and a pearl finish heavy gloss lipstick. Luciana Avedon wears an over-all foundation for photography, and a moisturizer and blusher with a spot of pearlized powder on her nose. Her eyeshadow is a creamy peach which she blends into the cheek as a blusher. A plum color is sometimes added to the upper eyelid and a gray shadow to the lower to emphasize the eye. The brow is elongated with a brown pencil. She also wears "tons" of feathery, black mascara.[14]

Structure

A make-up foundation or base coat covers blemishes and eliminates shadows in the face caused by wrinkles extending outward from the corners of the eyes ("crow's feet") and sagging skin beneath the eyes ("bags") and intensifies the basic color of the skin. Most performers agree that a foundation is desirable. Some individuals such as sportscasters are reluctant to use make-up, but they soon realize that several thousand watts of TV light can bleach out the natural, energetic color so vital to a healthy, athletic-looking complexion. In modeling the face, a prime coat of white make-up, the most advancing color, is initially applied to especially dark areas and wrinkles. Then, most Caucasians cover the entire face with a base coat that is a shade or two deeper than the natural face tone. Black or brown people may not need a color base except to cover uneven pigmentation; they may prefer a moisturizer or an appropriate blend of powder if the face is prone to perspire. Shininess is characteristic of some races and youth, and so some blacks, especially blue-black people, prefer a shiny look which enhances their three-dimensional appearance. Many cosmetic firms have satisfactory make-up supplies which can be purchased directly or from many local department and drug stores. A foundation should be chosen for color and for providing or eliminating moisture. A grease or oil base make-up usually provides moisture; a pancake or water base make-up tends to eliminate it.

Reproportioning the Face

A good head of hair, a fine wig or toupee will do excellent things for balancing the face. For example, hair is swept up and combed high to balance a square chinline. Hair is left long, down and encouraged to move on to the face to soften the shape of a round face. A triangular face may be enhanced by long soft strands, sometimes parted in the middle of the forehead and inclined to flow inward to mask a weak chinline. Basic proportions can be changed when hair is moved onto one's face through bangs and side curls. For example, bangs will reduce a high forehead. A complex hairstyle can also call favorable attention to itself.

Generally, men with oval and square faces look better with moderately short hairstyles; men with round and triangular faces look better with longer styles, often parting in the center of the forehead and falling shoulder length. Hairstyles for both men and women depend in part on prevailing fashions. The amount and complexity of hairstyles for both sexes range from huge curly wigs of the eighteenth century to the bald pates often projected as being fashionable in some future century. Yul Brynner, Isaac Hayes, Redd Foxx and Telly Savalas enhance their identity by maintaining a bald head. A bald pate must be shaved about once a week with shaving cream, and then the skin is oiled to produce a shiny look. To many: "Bald is beautiful, Bald is sexy. Bald is distinctive."[15] Some men dare to wear an earring to reinforce the impression of power like a genie from the *Arabian Nights;* others prefer a mustache or beard or both. Beards do a remarkable job of concealing and/or balancing faces. A mustache has been an outstanding addition at times. A classic example is that of silent film star John Gilbert who was relatively unknown until he grew a mustache and became a matinee idol. Beards and mustaches are reserved primarily for character actors, however; few men appearing regularly on TV news programs or game shows wear them. Current magazines provide a good source for possible hairstyles that can then be recreated for either sex by a local hairstylist.

Improving the Eyes

For women, basic make-up for the eyes (in addition to the base coat on the skin) is eyeshadow which enhances the effect of the color of the iris. Usually the eyeshadow is applied to the top lid only, heavier near the iris and blended off as it moves toward the eyebrow. Sometimes it is applied to the entire socket and beyond. George Masters suggests muted eyeshadow. In one instance Masters used a brush to apply powdered eyeshadow which he paints all around the eye, including a quarter of an inch under the eye. "By using water to apply the eyeshadow, you can intensify it on the lid, then dilute it a bit for outward strokes, dilute it more for the area under the eye."[16] It dries nicely and stays in place without collecting in the creases or dusting off. Black mascara is usually applied to lashes; older women may prefer the softer effect of lighter mascara such as brown, light brown, charcoal or grey depending on one's coloring. A second use of eyeshadow is to recess the eye socket and thus create a more seductive look. A dot of pink is sometimes added near one or both tearducts to further enlarge and color the eyes. Eyeliner is usually run along the lower edge of the eyelid, and sometimes on the upper lid as well. Mascara is then applied to darken and lengthen the real lashes. Artificial lashes may be added to the upper lid either by applying them one by one or by applying a finely constructed set of lashes. Artificial eyelashes are purchased in various lengths, degree of curl, thickness and colors. Many performers who must be seen from long distances such as in concert or theater wear very long lashes. They may continue to wear them in television and film as a kind of identification. Liza Minnelli is a case in point. Her extremely long lashes give her an abnormally wide-eyed juvenile look. The eyebrow is emphasized by an eyebrow pencil which draws, in light feathery strokes, fine hairlike lines that enlarge, fill in and darken pale eyebrows.

Most men use little or no eye make-up, just enough to recover a natural look to their eyes that the base coat has covered up. Simply washing off the base coat around the eyelids is sometimes sufficient, especially if the man has naturally dark lashes and brows. Blond men frequently use a light brown pencil to darken their eyebrows and hairline on the forehead. Men use make-up but in less quantity. They apply eyeshadow above and sometimes below the eyes to recess sockets. They add eyeliner and mascara, for the same reasons a woman does. The effect of course makes the man pretty, which to a point is desirable in some male sex attractions. Some young rock stars use exotic make-up including glitter as part of their image (Mick Jagger). Such make-up usually is associated with "far out" artistic innovations, bisexual or homosexual appearance, or feminine characteristics in men. In any event men should not be hesitant in using make-up that will improve their appearance or public image. Make-up, is after all, a tool of the trade.

Improving the Nose

The nose can be emphasized by covering it with a base coat somewhat lighter than the rest of the face, a somewhat darker color will de-emphasize it. Either way, nose make-up is blended with the rest of the face. A nose can appear shorter if a line lighter than the base coat is applied on the top of the nose from the brow to a point two-thirds the way down the nose. The farther the line is extended, the longer the nose appears; and the wider the line, the wider the nose; the narrower the line, the narrower the nose. While useful in the theater, it may be difficult to make the line subtle enough for closeup TV or film; and so, many performers experiment before finding a completely satisfactory application.

Improving the Mouth

For centuries women have been painting their mouths. The intensity of the colors depends on the dictates of current fashion and a variety of cultural views. Women who are young, pretty or have good normal coloring to their lips can avoid make-up, but this is sometimes undesirable under media lights, if they wish to look natural. During the early 1940s lips were brilliant colors; a few years later they were fashionably pale. Lip rouge can enhance or tend to lessen the size of the mouth. Women with narrow lips often draw the desired shape of the lips slightly beyond the normal shape and brush in the desired color. The lips can appear fuller if highlighted with a lighter lip rouge or by mixing white with the principal color and applying it to the bottom lip. Some lip gloss is applied purposefully to add a luster or "wet look" to the surface, because moist lips are supposed to be more sexually attractive.

Men usually ignore their mouths. After applying the base complexion coat, they wipe off any coverage of the lips so that the natural pink color can be seen. Occasionally a man will apply a pale pink lipstick, making certain that it appears natural, and in no way effeminate, on the closeup camera. Male entertainers experiment with lip make-up primarily for exotic effect.

Men and women must be careful that their teeth are clean and white. Attractive teeth were definite assets for Jimmy Carter, Gerald R. Ford and Ronald Reagan during the 1976 political campaigns, according to orthodontist Dr. Benjamin Ichinose.[17] Smokers must pay special

PERSONAL MAKE-UP CHART

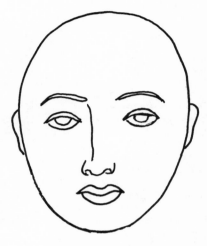

Name:
Age:
Complexion:
Straight/Character:

Make-up:
Base:
Blusher:
Eyes:
  Lashes:
  Shadow:
  Brows:
Powder:
Lipstick:
Body Make-up:
Hair:

(Outline your one-sheet photograph here.)

Special Requirements:

See color chart at the beginning of this chapter

attention to their teeth so that they do not yellow or darken. Now and then in a comedy routine or dramatic sketch a tooth must be blackened. Black enamel is temporarily painted over the surface of the tooth. A temporary white enamel can be applied to an unusually dark tooth. Capping teeth is discussed in a later chapter. Creating an unusual effect, Dr. Henry Dwork, a New York dentist specializing in the-

MAKE-UP SUGGESTIONS

Keep make-up off hair.
The lighter the hair color, the softer the lines in the face.
Use wigs to experiment with hair styles and color.

A white undercoat erases some
  wrinkles.
A short white line, shortens
  the nose; a long one
  lengthens it.
A broad one broadens it; a
  narrow one narrows it.
White applied to the lower
  lip make it fuller.

Apply base just under jaw
  and back to ears. All
  skin colors are attractive
  on media if properly lighted.
  A smooth foundation adds a
  blemish free healthy color
  under intense lights.

Brows should follow natural arch.
Eyeshadow recesses socket;
mascara and lashes make eye
  appear larger.

Brush on lipstick and highlight with lip gloss.

Rouge or blusher goes in hollow to define cheeks.

atrical work, constructed an elaborate denture that gave Marlon Brando the full-mouth look in *The Godfather*.[18]

Improving the Ears

Ears are usually ignored or covered by hair. Ears can be taped to the head to enhance their chances of growing close to the skull, but this almost certainly must be done at an early age. If the ears show, they should be covered with an even base coat as is the face. Very often the base color can blend off at the ears leaving them a paler hue than the more important face. Paler ears may appear slightly larger than normal; likewise a slightly darker base would tend to make the ears look somewhat smaller. In no case should a base coat be allowed to end abruptly before covering the ears or neck. Instead, it should blend off gradually.

BASIC COSMETICS

Item	Form	Application
Cleansing	Creme and lotion	For deep cleaning pores in skin.
Astringent	Liquid	For closing pores after cleansing.
Moisturizer or toning lotion	Lotion	For retaining or adding oil to skin.
Foundation or base	Solid, creme, liquid	For a matte finish to the skin. Should not streak. Cover stick gives added highlights to age lines and recessed areas.
Lipstick	Creme, solid	For coloring and reshaping lips.
Blusher	Solid, powder	For modeling and tinting areas of the face, especially cheeks. Rouge may be added.
Eyeshadow	Solid, creme	For modeling and tinting eyesocket.
Mascara	Liquid	For lengthening and darkening lashes. Artificial lashes may be a substitute.
Eyebrow pencil	Solid	For highlighting and adding to brows.
Polish	Liquid	For nails. Artificial nails may substitute for missing or misshapen nails.

Improving the Hair

Hair is very important to both sexes. The styles vary greatly. Styles for women are almost limitless, so key factors must be to wear (1) a style that is right for the performer; (2) a style that is consistent with the media and personal image; (3) a style that is fashionable, and hopefully, flattering; (4) a memorable style (Phyllis Diller, Veronica Lake); (5) a style that is easy to maintain under difficult conditions. Mainte-

HAIR LENGTHS AND STYLES

Very short, curly

Straight cap

Ear or shoulder length, forward flip

Shoulder length, curls

Upsweep with curled bangs, shoulder length curls in back

Hair length:

Ears

Shoulder

Mid-back

Low-back

STYLED STRAIGHT

NATURAL CURL

Brush cut

Short, parted, sideburns

Curly bangs, sweptback sides

Ear length, full look

Shoulder length, with flip

nance of hair takes a great deal of time. Most performers must spend time continuously keeping their hair clean, and cut—slightly long and loose, certainly not plastered down and, if necessary, colored. A simply designed, well defined hairstyle serves most women in media; but initially an attractive style may be difficult to achieve.

The principal styles for men are (1) traditional, (2) ethnic and (3) natural. The natural hairstyle is one the performer has little chance of changing. For example, the short, tight curly hair of some blacks. This slow growing hair covers the head in a minimum way. It cannot be altered. The longer-haired black can have the naturally curly strands straightened, if necessary, and then teased in various designs, some of which are extremely bouffant (the Afro). The Caucasian male and most Orientals who have long black hair that is straight and difficult to manage usually prefer moderate length sideburns and back. In recent times shoulder length hair has become popular with the younger men, having shortened it from the long locks associated with hippie and beatnik lifestyles.

The way a performer's hair is cut makes a difference. Blunt cut hair is cut straight across. Layered hair is blunt cut, but it is not all the same length. Tapered hair has an uneven cut and produces a soft effect. Graduated hair provides fullness for short hair as the underneath hair is cut so that it fluffs out the top hair. These hair cuts apply to both men and women.

Wigs are widely used by performers. Women can change hairstyles and colors almost instantly without damaging their own hair with constant bleaches; and men, especially older ones, find that hairpieces or toupees give them a more vital look, which is a personal psychological lift as well as enhancing them physically. Performers are encouraged to buy high quality hairpieces and to be fitted by qualified professionals who guarantee satisfaction. A good hair piece may cost a few hundred dollars. A poor, ill-fitting hairpiece can be damaging to a performer. A performer should plan ahead to a time when he or she may be partially or totally bald. Blonds are rather prone to lose their hair. Many men lose their hair before they are 30. In such cases a gradual transition should be discussed with hair experts at the early signs of hair loss.

4: Voice

"Her mistress's voice."

An audience must hear well. It wants to hear every word or sound without undue strain and frustration. Sometimes a performer mumbles, slurs sounds, speaks inaudibly; sometimes extraneous noise (static or electronic interference, overriding background music) prohibits the audience from hearing what is said. Some news reports from overseas (short wave) do this, some orchestras do this. Sometimes the volume is insufficient on the microphone. Whatever the cause, it must be corrected so that an audience can hear well. The audio portion of a TV program or film is equally important to the video; and, of course, in radio and music recording, audio quality is everything. To ascertain audio characteristics of a performer, he or she should examine their vocal capabilities and limitations.

A PROFESSIONAL ATTITUDE

After the shock wave of a performer's initial appearance has passed, an audience is polarized essentially as listeners. What will the performer say? How will he or she say it? The performer has then to inform, alarm, caress, tease, shock, amuse, embarrass, excite and/or frighten the listeners with, among other things, the voice. A performer's voice communicates by overtly and consciously moving the audience to respond, to understand, and to enjoy what the performer is saying. The performer knows he or she is influencing the audience, and the performer enjoys the challenge. After an initial impression of soft focus, a vision of fur and glitter, Marlene Dietrich uttered, "Hello . . ." as a throaty, worldly, eternal mating call instantly and consciously keynoting the television entertainment to follow. Walter Cronkite, in the typical attire of a conservative businessman, begins the *CBS Evening News* with, "Good evening," using the term as a throwaway for the news presentation to follow.

A performer should practice prodigiously. Good vocal communication requires rehearsal, and the amount of practice depends upon the degree of perfection the performer wishes to attain. A performer must read the copy a few times to be certain it is thoroughly understood. Then a performer reads it aloud several times to be certain that each syllable flows easily and clearly so that the listener will understand the message instantly. Rehearsal for radio may be adequate at this point, but rehearsal for TV must continue until the copy is adequately memorized or until the performer can look up from the copy or away from cue cards for sufficiently long periods to allow proper eye contact with the viewer or other performers. Some performers require much rehearsal, others are "quick studies." It makes no difference so long as the final performance is flawless. "Nothing else matters to anyone when all is said and done but how you sound on the air. To have that good air sound, one has to feel his job is important, and if he feels that way—the job is important to him and to others," according to Peter Jay, news director, KNBI, Norton, Kansas.[1]

Such perfection is something performers strive for far more than they attain. A performer with a good professional attitude wants to strive for voice improvement and is willing to invest a great deal of time in this accomplishment. Performers find after much hard work that once the obvious vocal irregularities are corrected, the less obvious ones are much more difficult to define and isolate. A speech coach, therefore, or someone with a keen ear and training in voice improvement listens for subtle irregularities and helps the performer correct them. Some suggestions for improving one's voice will be included in this chapter, but ultimately an individual's personal voice problems must be brought to the attention of a voice specialist.

Coinciding with the improvements suggested above is the necessary conditioning of the voice so that it can communicate effortlessly and tirelessly through media. This means that the performer must be in top physical condition because one's voice is often a reflection of one's general health; a person's voice may be the first indication of fatigue. The range of the voice, when tired, shortens; the timbre or quality of each low tone decreases. Eventually, a few shrill middle to high range tones carry whatever communication is necessary. Even these tones fray until a hoarse quality develops, and this yields to a half-vocalized whisper. Finally, no voice at all. Deterioration of the voice also comes from incorrect voice placement—too high or too low, extensive shouting such as at football games, and disease (tumors, colds) causing organic or functional disorders. Then too some people have much more vocal stamina and vocal timbre than others. Some fortunate beings—some disc jockeys for instance—seem to be able to talk indefinitely without noticeable voice fatigue.

PSYCHOLOGICAL ASPECTS

A number of scientists from various fields have concluded that the voice is the most efficient way of communicating. It carries information about the personality, mood and present state of functioning. No two voices are alike, so positive identification can be made by voice alone. Occasionally police investigators have made identifications of people by means of a "voiceprint," which is presently being perfected by Bell Laboratory researchers. Voices are very sensitive to the performer's entire physical condition. In the main, a voice depends on vigorous, internal energy, generated from good health, a desire to perform, a certain amount of personal daring or abandon while performing, self-confidence and a joy derived from performing for others. For example, this is a reporter's description of Liza Minnelli: "She was supercharged with power to spare. She tore through her numbers with her arms flung wildly as she raced across the stage, utilizing her every charm to perfection. The little girl with the big red lips and wild eyelashes hypnotized the audience with her every gesture and it seemed like every time she looked ready to collapse she would come charging back, spurred on by the wild ovations of the crowd."[2]

Relaxation, Tension and Fatigue

Relaxation is the key to a full rich voice. Often relaxation is not possible because of tension and/or fatigue. Relaxation is largely a state of mind. If a performer believes that the audience is friendly, that it wants to see the program, and/or if the performer has some experience, knows what to expect and likes what he or she is doing, the performer's voice will be relaxed and reflect it. Some performers are much better at being relaxed than others; they can set aside possible consequences of a bad performance by dissolving the notion of potential harm with the attitude, "I can do it. I know I'm good." Many other performers cannot be so positive about their work; they worry about whether they will be a success. Worry causes tension in the muscles of the entire body, particularly the throat. Tight muscles reduce the vibrations in the cartilage and bones limiting the richness of tone a performer could get from the voice. A tense voice is often harsh, strident, may salivate more, has less breath supply and control, may quaver, squeak or shift pitch unexpectedly. Fatigue is the other extreme. The muscles simply do not function precisely so the words are poorly articulated. Some voices tend to shift to higher pitch and are thin, when tired.

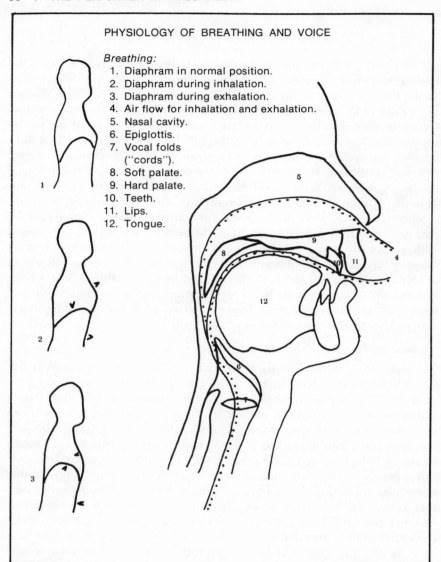

PHYSIOLOGY OF BREATHING AND VOICE

Breathing:
1. Diaphram in normal position.
2. Diaphram during inhalation.
3. Diaphram during exhalation.
4. Air flow for inhalation and exhalation.
5. Nasal cavity.
6. Epiglottis.
7. Vocal folds ("cords").
8. Soft palate.
9. Hard palate.
10. Teeth.
11. Lips.
12. Tongue.

PHYSIOLOGICAL ASPECTS

A human being produces sound by actually controlling a stream of air as it rushes from the lungs, up a tube called the trachea, past vibrators called vocal folds, into a large cave (mouth) of cartilage, muscle and bone. The stream of air is changed or modulated principally by the tongue, teeth, lips and hard palate into precisely the shape and amount the speaker desires before it is thrust from the mouth as an identifiable utterance.

Voice Quality

The resonant quality generated from the entire vocal mechanism in an individual is called *timbre*. Timbre includes all of the nuances and subtle reenforcement an air stream receives from vibrating bones and cartilage and from the size, shape and strength of associated muscles. No two voices are quite alike, because the throat, chest and mouth are not alike in any two individuals. A voice depends on organic construction as well as function. "Mellow," "harsh," "shrill" are efforts to classify vocal timbre. They are inexact, yet they recognize that we hear a distinct difference in voices. The reproduction of a single utterance is rather complex, for each vibration produces other vibrations, some in sympathy with the first vibration, some not in phase with it. Those in phase with it are said to be *in harmony,* those that are not are *dissonant.* These complications suggest why a human voice is unique. Unless a voice is altered surgically, timbre cannot be changed. It is comparable to a fingerprint.

Types of Vocal Quality

Most voices are a pleasant combination of various qualities. The dominant, clearly definable and noticeable kinds of voice quality are nasal, breathy, thin, harsh or strident, and hoarse. At times nearly everyone's voice depends upon these characteristics for expression. Those voices having these qualities in the extreme (i.e., to where they are uncontrollable) are probably the result of organic or functional disorder.

Nasal quality occurs either by allowing air to escape through the nose, produced for example by a cleft palate, or by preventing air from doing so, such as caused by a common head cold. The former is referred to as *nasality,* the latter *de*nasality. One of the best known performers to capitalize on the nasal quality of his voice was Rudy Vallee. Vallee became very popular on radio as a crooner of the late 1920s and '30s. In a comedy sketch with Edgar Bergen and his dummy, Charlie McCarthy, Vallee asked: "What is a ventriloquist?" Bergen replied: "I talk through my stomach." To which Vallee boasted: "I sing through my nose."

A breathy quality is popular with some female performers. Breathiness can produce an effective seductive utterance stronger than a whisper. Marilyn Monroe was extremely skillful at adding a breathy quality to her voice, projecting intimacy, mellifluous tones and a certain manipulation of the mouth and lips for sexual enticement. Breathiness is obtained by letting an abnormal amount of breath escape through the mouth with each utterance.

A thin voice has insufficient nuances; thereby reducing the full, rich qualities associated with a pleasant voice. Such a voice is used by comediennes like Lily Tomlin when playing the role of a harassed housewife or switchboard operator. The quality is rather common in some women and men who for years have pitched their voices too high, and in effect have only developed the high range during maturation. Comedian Don Knotts playing a nervous "milktoast" has made a career out of a high thin register.

A harsh voice is caused by the lack of nuances from primary and secondary vibrations in an entire pitch range, resulting in a rough, irritating and genuinely unpleasant quality. A similar sounding strident voice is produced largely by strain and tension. A hard-driving individual, such as often played by George C. Scott or David Janssen, may have a strident voice. The resonators in the throat and neck are tense.

A hoarse quality is unusual and can be quite useful, especially for a woman or a small child. This sort of frog-in-the-throat to foghorn utterance can be comic or in a mature woman, seductive. A deep hoarse voice helped to make Tallulah Bankhead's vocal signature, "Hello, dahlings." Carol Channing's similar vocal register is a combination of many qualities, some of which tend toward hoarseness. The truly hoarse voice may be caused by excessive shouting, laryngitis, polyps on the vocal cords and certain diseases. If a hoarse voice is sufficiently audible and if its range is not impossibly limited, its unique quality can be fascinating to listen to and thus memorable for the public. Marlon Brando's gravel-voiced characterization as "The Godfather" is one illustration.

Controlling the Air Supply

The greater the amount of air a performer can draw into the body, the longer one can speak without taking a breath, if the release of the air is properly controlled. The body may be thought of as a large balloon—if any portion of the balloon is restricted, the less air it will hold—and so it is with the body. The performer standing erect elongates the torso so that air can fill the body fully and easily. If one places the hands at the waist with fingers almost touching in front and thumbs to the rear and breathes deeply, he or she can feel the fingers being pulled apart as the body is inflated. A perfomer must learn to control inhalation, retention and exhalation of breath. The principal muscle controlling these activities is the *diaphragm,* located between the chest and the abdomen. An erect torso can take in the same amount of air whether standing, sitting or lying, but the air supply is more difficult to control in the latter positions.

Breathing. The amount of air inhaled depends largely on its use. A performer thinks of breathing from the clavicle, the thoracic cavity or the diaphragm. When a person inhales, the uppermost part of the body is filled first; that is, to roughly the upper trunk, the *clavicle* or collarbone. Panting is an example of air drawn to this level. More commonly air is taken into the upper lungs for normal breathing and speaking; this is the *thoracic* or chest cavity. Lungs are quite expandable and the lower region is used if an effort is made to relax the diaphragm sufficiently to fill the lower lungs. The diaphragm acting like a bellows helps to create the partial vacuum which draws air into the body and pushes the air out again on command with assistance from the intercostal muscles and the rib cage. Inhaling should be as quick, quiet and complete as possible; it should be reserved for ends of paragraphs, lines or phrases. Only amateurs gulp air within words or phrases or exhaust themselves in their delivery.

Breathing is not merely a matter of getting air into the body. It is more importantly getting air out. On expulsion, the air supply, shaped as a stream, is released in miserly fashion so that the performer inhales less frequently and uses the air more efficiently. One breathing exercise is to practice enunciating vowels within a few inches of a lighted candle without having the flame flicker. Another is reading long monologues aloud, allowing a minimum of inhalations. A third is to time oneself while sustaining a note or sound. Breath control takes daily practice.

Read each paragraph on one breath. . . .

1. This is the house that Jack built. (BREATHE)

2. This is the malt
   That lay in the house that Jack built. (BREATHE)

3. This is the rat,
   That ate the malt
   That lay in the house that Jack built. (BREATHE)

4. This is the cat,
   That killed the rat,
   That ate the malt
   That lay in the house that Jack built. (BREATHE)

5. This is the dog,
   That worried the cat,
   That killed the rat,
   That ate the malt
   That lay in the house that Jack built. (BREATHE)

6. This is the cow with the crumpled horn,
   That tossed the dog,
   That worried the cat,
   That killed the rat,
   That ate the malt
   That lay in the house that Jack built. (BREATHE)

7. This is the maiden all forlorn,
   That milked the cow with the crumpled horn,
   That tossed the dog,
   That worried the cat,
   That killed the rat,
   That ate the malt
   That lay in the house that Jack built. (BREATHE)

8. This is the man all tattered and torn,
   That kissed the maiden all forlorn,
   That milked the cow with the crumpled horn,
   That tossed the dog,
   That worried the cat,
   That killed the rat,
   That ate the malt
   That lay in the house that Jack built. (BREATHE)

9. This is the priest all shaven and shorn,
   That married the man all tattered and torn,
   That kissed the maiden all forlorn,
   That milked the cow with the crumpled horn,
   That tossed the dog,
   That worried the cat,
   That killed the rat,
   That ate the malt
   That lay in the house that Jack built. (BREATHE)

10. This is the cock that crowed in the morn,
    That waked the priest all shaven and shorn,
    That married the man all tattered and torn,
    That kissed the maiden all forlorn,
    That milked the cow with the crumpled horn,
    That tossed the dog,
    That worried the cat,
    That killed the rat,
    That ate the malt
    That lay in the house that Jack built. (BREATHE)

11. This is the farmer sowing his corn,
    That kept the cock that crowed in the morn,
    That waked the priest all shaven and shorn,

That married the man all tattered and torn,
That kissed the maiden all forlorn,
That milked the cow with the crumpled horn,
That tossed the dog,
That worried the cat,
That killed the rat,
That ate the malt
That lay in the house that Jack built. (BREATHE)

Resonance

"My body is like a tube," said singer John Davidson. "My whole body resonates." Resonance is the vibration of the vocal folds or "cords" and their surrounding environment of bones and cartilage. *Fixed* resonators cannot be changed in shape or size without surgery. They are the skull bones, the nose, the nasal sinuses, the windpipe, the chest bone and the ribs. *Adjustable* resonators can change in size, shape and tenseness. They are the mouth, the pharynx or soft palate at the back of the mouth, and the larynx. Vocal folds are left relaxed and open for breathing, producing no vibration, but they are tightened and vibrate during speech-producing voiced sounds such as "da," "ga" or "va." By contrast so-called unvoiced sounds—"f," "t" or "p"—restrict the air stream at the teeth (fricative) and/or lips (plosive), but no vibration of the vocal mechanism is required to form the sound.

Practice these exercises for improving your resonance, but do not strain or force your voice:

1. Strive for the complete relaxation of your throat by yawning several times.
2. Hum with your lips closed until you can feel your entire head vibrating.
3. Vocalize by sustaining each vowel sound for several seconds, maintaining the same pitch.[3]

Phonation

Phonation is the precise production of a phoneme or sound. Phonation may be thought of in three ways: articulation, pronunciation and communication. Articulation is a performer's ability to produce a sound clearly. Each language has its own collection of sounds which one must learn if he or she is to speak the language correctly and without a dialect. A common exercise in performance classes is to have each student pronounce words containing the common sounds—vowels, consonents, diphthongs—in the language. Common sounds in the English language are:

Vowels: beet, bit, bait, bet, bat, bath, bomb, wash, bought, boat, book, boot, bird, bitter, sun, sofa

Diphthongs: bite, how, toy, using, fuse, say

Consonants: poor, boor, time, dime, kite, guide, few, view, thigh, thy, sing, zing, shock, Jacques, chest, jest, how, when, mom, noun, sing, love, watch, yellow, run [4]

A voice coach knows immediately which sounds are articulated incorrectly. Once these sounds are brought to the student's attention, so that the student can hear the difference between what he or she is saying and what should be said, the student will probably be able to make the change and almost instantly improve most of those words containing the newly corrected sound. For example, the diphthong "i" is articulated in the Southeast as "ah" by holding the sound for a slow graceful release. This regional inflection may be all right when speaking with the folks back home, but if he or she aspires to national recognition or wishes to rally the nation to what is believed to be a national cause, the performer will need to use broadcast standards of articulation.

If articulation refers to the sounds producing parts of words, pronunciation is the enunciation of the entire word. In a country as large as the United States, there are going to be variations in pronunciation: "tomato—tomahto," "Cuba—Cuber," "junta—hunta." [5] Both pronunciations may be correct; one may be used nationally and the other regionally or locally. So long as communication is complete, no problems may arise. "Yp silanti" (Michigan) is pronounced "Iṕ silanti" and "Bur nett" (Texas) is "Burń it" to residents. Foreign names cause greater pronunciation difficulties. Even network pronunciation varies: "Kru chev" or "Kru chov," "Veet Nahm" or "Ve et Nam."

Professional commercial announcers, news people, politicians in national office and others—those people who presume to represent great segments of the population and who wish to communicate with all of their constituents by means of television, radio and film—use a general language with a popularly accepted standard of pronunciation. This standard, many authorities agree, is commonly found in the Middle West and California, and is referred to as "General American speech." The test for one who speaks General American is that the public cannot identify the person's native background, residence or race. Network newsman Hal Walker is an excellent example. A person must see him to know he is black and ask him to know where he is from. Pronunciation guides published by the networks and the wire services help to acquaint the performer with national standards of pronunciation. Voice lessons and a tape recorder should do a great deal, if the performer can hear the differences in inflection.

Regional dialects, racial dialects and international languages influ-

ence a performer's speech. Some performers of international renown—
black entertainers, English rock stars, French sex sirens and Southern
belles—have become very successful without changing their dialects.
Lady Bird Johnson's Texas twang is identified with her sincerity and
honesty. Lawrence Welk's dialect has added a unique and positive dimension to his TV image. Tom Jones's Welsh dialect adds a quality of
rugged strength. For comedians working in dialects, clear articulation
is essential because an audience must understand the meaning of all
words if it is to laugh at the punchline. Myron Cohen and Flip Wilson
must deliver both dialect and meaning if they are to be entertaining.
Many comedians suggest a dialect but modify it, as the audience
requires, for communication. Current trends in media suggest that
dialects enrich programs and so there is less effort to prohibit those
with dialects from newscasts, for example. Of course, a dialect can be a
definite advantage if a station overtly appeals to a minority or ethnic
population. Within the last decade, the idea that an individual's natural
dialect is 'correct' for that person, especially for interpersonal communication, has been taken seriously by teachers of speech and language across the country, in opposition to the tradition of a single standard of "correctness."[6] Mass communication is still wrestling with the
correctness concept.[7] Dr. Harold Weiss, who teaches phonetics at
Southern Methodist University, said there are 15 major dialects in the
United States, but basically the speech patterns are Southern, New England and Midwestern.[8]

Several books are available to the performer who wishes to improve his or her speech. Here are some examples of common errors:

Sound substitutions: git for get, sinator for senator, min for
men, jist for just, becuz for because, pressperation for perspiration, Illinoise for Illinois, pitcher for picture, whur for where,
witch for which, wear for where, what for watt, madder for matter,
baddle for battle, pilla for pillow, vury for very, coworse for coerse,
liberry for library, groshers for grocers, intertainmint for entertainment, mintal for mental.

Sound omissions: han for hang, son for song, han for hand, slep
for slept, goin for going, trus for trust, whi for white, chile for
child, spect for expect, fiel for field, an for and, playin for playing,
memry for memory, hunred for hundred, lil for little, s'pose for
suppose, mir for mirror, tempeture for temperature, genlmen for
gentlemen, hep for help, zackly for exactly, las for last.

Sound additions: acrost for across, cain't for can't, pome for
poem, athaletics for athletics, meilk for milk, mis chee vi ous for
mis chie vous, palm for palm (no "l"), placeda for placed.

Slurred sounds: desks, wasps, clasps, discs, doncha for don't you, valyabul for valuable, wanna for want to, harya for how are you, howjado for how do you do.

Misplaced accents: dé bate for de baté, com pár a ble for com par a ble, the até er for thé a ter, in creasé (verb) but in crease (noun), re fill' (verb) but ré fill (noun), a li' as for á li as, dis close for dis closé, in fá mous for in fa mous.

If you wish to improve your articulation, repeat these well known exercises as rapidly as you can.

1. How much wood would a woodchuck chuck in the woods if a woodchuck would chuck wood? If you were a woodchuck and would chuck wood, would you chuck wood like a woodchuck or would you chuck wood differently? No doubt, some woodchucks chuck more wood than other woodchucks. What would other woodchucks chuck, if some woodchucks chucked all the wood?

2. Peter Piper picked a peck of pickled peppers. How many peppers did Peter Piper pick, if Peter Piper picked a peck of pickled peppers.

3. A big black bug bit a big black bear.

Slovenly articulation is frequently caused from inactive muscles around the lips, tongue, jaw and soft palate. Exaggerated movements of these articulators while you are reciting nonsense syllables or vowels will help to make them limber. Self consciousness is a principal detriment to flexible articulators. You should practice exaggerated smiles stretching the lips, whistling, blowing, extending the tongue, moving the jaw up and down and side to side, humming and pronouncing words containing "m" and "n" sounds.

INTERPRETATION

Modulation of the voice can occur through mental demands placed on it, called *interpretation.* Interpretation is based on the logical and emotional response generated in the mind of a performer when a passage is recited or read. Every utterance is interpreted in some way, whether colorfully or flatly. For example, the sound "ah" can be interpreted in various ways producing different meanings: "ah" means understanding, "ah" means surprise, "ah" means dejection, "ah" means emotional satisfaction; "ah" means the last gasp of a fatal blow, "ah" means "I'm thinking," "ah" is the sound a patient makes when the doctor depresses the tongue, "ah" is a vowel. Interpretation varies in accordance with inflection or the willful or subliminal raising or lowering of pitch and volume in response to the text. Interpretation depends upon the rate, timing and tempo at which a selection is delivered. Interpretation is a subtle and complex art that requires variety and style. The more knowledgeable a person is of life, the better educated, the more experienced, the better chance he or she has of reflecting those changes in the voice, those nuances that stimulate response, that induce pleasure and action in listeners. Why will an audience listen to some performers like Henry Fonda as Clarence Darrow or James Whitmore as Will Rogers for an hour or two and will deny others five minutes? These actors, having years of experience, are able to bring to audiences new insight into the lives of the characters they portray, and they do it through interpretation.

Pitch

Every voice is capable of covering a range of frequencies from low to high. Some voices can produce a far greater pitch range than others. The range is noticeable in a choir where there are low basso profundo (bass), medium (baritone) and high (tenor) voices for men and contralto, mezzo soprano and soprano ranges for women and boys. A singer is labeled by the pitch range or frequency range he or she can work in most comfortably. Every performer should find a speaking range in which he or she feels most comfortable. A performer can often do this by producing his or her highest and lowest sounds, then by striking the mid-point to determine whether that is a reasonable level from which to build a range.

Most often one's pitch comes naturally, seldom changing from youth, except in boys during later adolescence. A boy has a chance to redefine his speaking range as he matures. A girl's voice may change less noticeably, but in most cases can be trained and improved. Frequently, pitch is the result of imitation, usually of one's elders. Thus, girls in particular may be influenced adversely and unintentionally by imitating a high thin voice of a relative or teacher. In such cases the pitch can be changed, if at all, only after a great deal of hard work through retraining. Once the pitch is properly established, the performer uses it as a tool for vocal emphasis in interpretation.

Range

Range is the extent of a performer's ability. In reference to volume it is from barely audible to deafening quadraphonic; to time and rate it is the unlimited subtleties one can devise in speeding up or slowing down the material; to style it is the versatility of a performer to play "8 to 80" years of age in straight or character parts; to pitch it means the scale from low to falsetto; to experience it refers to one's understanding of life and people. The total of variations a performer can get in the voice is incredible; the subtleties are great if a performer wants to develop them. The sum of these variations are considered his or her range. The greater the range, the more variations the voice has and the more useful it is. A performer can extend the range by practicing, as one would practice a musical scale with the hope of developing one's singing ability.

Volume

A performer increases and decreases the loudness of his or her voice to give to a sound force, emphasis and sufficient audibility so that the performer can be heard and understood. Generally, a performer uses just enough volume to do the job. Peggy Lee sings at whisper level for an intimate, romantic, subtle effect; Robert Daltry's frantic, deafening rock film, *Tommy*, screams a raucous extreme. Both performers graduate the volume according to the right moment in the song. Volume should be sufficiently loud so that a listener-viewer can hear comfortably without straining. If a politician wishes to stress a point, he or she typically uses volume. It is the most common way to tell an audience, "Now hear this!" A few years ago commercials were played hotter or louder on radio and TV stations than programs so that listener-viewers would be startled into paying attention. A performer uses volume as an interpretive tool for precisely the same reasons. Volume can be damaging to one's vocal cords; if used improperly as in some forms of cheerleading, for instance, the vocal cords bang together savagely until, over a period of time, a tissue buildup similar to a callous develops on the vocal cords causing hoarseness.[9]

Time and Rate

Time and rate can be confusing. Time refers to how long it takes a performer to deliver a syllable, a word, a sentence. For aesthetic purposes a performer senses precisely when to utter a sound, such as on the beat, after a laugh, before the action, and precisely when to pause, for pausing can add emphasis to a message. Mechanically speaking, a person delivers the lines to the second so that the commercial, the drama or the newscast will end appropriately. This may mean speeding up or slowing down the rate or pace at which the words are delivered. On the average there are about 120 to 140 words in one minute of copy. Many performers read slightly faster or slower, but they must read at a rate allowing them to finish on time or "on the nose." Some performers pencil in time cues on their copy every 15 seconds to assure them of perfect timing.

Variety

Variety is the use of the voice in an unexpected way: a change of pitch (raising pitch at the end of a sentence instead of lowering it), a change of time (slowly reading a line that ordinarily would be read rapidly), a change of volume (emphasizing phrases through loudness), a change of style (shifting from what an audience might expect, such as slick sophistication, to a stumbling, unprepared delivery). Variety includes most of the tones on an interpreter's palate and blends them into new implications. Variety should be motivated and not just mechanical or arbitrary. Sometimes a beginning performer will say to a voice coach, "You mean you want me to say the word louder?" "No," the coach replies, "just differently." So, the performer hunts for another meaning, another motivation—trying again and again to go beyond the usual interpretation to bring something new and exciting to the listener.

Style

Style is the performer's way of delivering the material, each performer attempting to be unique. A performer's style may be described as innocent, sophisticated, aloof, efficient, easy, mechanical, artificial, friendly, warm and so forth. Typically, whether the material is memorized or read it begins at a high energy level, tending to burst on the scene (without being out of context), progressing at a somewhat rapid rate, rising to a vocal crescendo, tagging the final line, pausing, then cueing the next segment of the program (or a commercial). The performer's final pose is then retained until he or she is positive the next segment is on the air. Common errors at the conclusion of a segment are prematurely "breaking" one's gaze, pose or position, and adding some inappropriate gesture (sniffing) or remark (anything unexpected which overlaps the next segment).

Different personalities, even newscasters who try to be objective, are bound to develop a style or an individual manner of presenting their material. Walter Cronkite reads the news as though it were part of a long narrative with jaunty moments of optimism and despair; Harry Reasoner reads his copy with a touch of warmth—everything will be all right—and a wry smile; John Chancellor has a slightly critical or scolding tone; David Brinkley's delivery is cynical, "what fools these mortals be"; Eric Sevareid is reflective, philosophical, precise, and a little weary; Dick Cavett is urbane, witty and intelligent; and Rona Barrett's gossip is chatty, rapid and sensational like her predecessors Hedda Hopper and Louella Parsons. Several who made their reputations in radio developed memorable speaking styles: Paul Harvey's exaggerated inflection is often comical, his timing for effect is superb—"G o o d . . . bye"; Arthur Godfrey is conversational and sentimental—"How are ya, how are ya, how are ya." Edward R. Murrow spoke with grave, dramatic impact, implying the public's responsibility to act.

Styles vary noticeably in weather reporting people. Some read the weather as a simple fact, some in a comic vein with lots of gags, some in a warm and folksy way including information about recreational activities and area get-togethers, some go into meteorological details and flight information. Sportscasters do the same thing with a lively, infectious jargonese implying they are intimately acquainted with all of the players. A few sportscasters have magnified their own characteristics to become personalities covering the sports scene. A dapper dresser, Heywood Hale Broun spins complex descriptive yarns about selected sporting events with the finesse of a connoisseur of fine wines. "Color man" Don Meredith played the role of a drawling country boy to Howard Cosell's perceptive criticisms of sports figures while Frank Gifford called straight play-by-play action of big time football.

Style is well defined for entertainers. If rock star Aretha Franklin, country singer Johnny Cash and romantic vocalist Andy Williams were asked to sing the national anthem, each would interpret it in a unique, individual and recognizable manner—that's style.

AMPLIFICATION

Amplification is magnification of the voice so that the audience can hear better. It can be done electronically or through voice projection. Projecting one's voice is not merely a matter of shouting or increasing the volume, although this sometimes accomplishes the goal. Projecting requires that the performer *think* where he or she wants the voice to reach and through thinking the performer sends it there. This technique is effective in an auditorium wherein the performer can project or think the message to the middle of the house or the balcony, and can elongate certain words as one might in theater so that they will carry the distance.

Usually in media, projection is not necessary beyond the minimum utterance for exciting or vibrating electronic equipment. The tiniest murmur can be amplified with the right equipment, and that equipment can be concealed in a performer's costume or at a distance. Amplification is what makes a recording session such fun. The entire range of a voice can be used from the lowest levels to the loudest, and these levels can be electronically re-inforced and extended, so that the performer's voice will sound even better, much better, than the performer could possibly do in live performance. In recent years this has forced performers, musicians especially, to transport their entire electronic package on theatrical tour in order to preserve what the public identifies as "their sound" which, in fact is a sound produced in a studio and sometimes cannot be reproduced live on stage without being supplemented, at least in part, by recordings. For example, "Up with People" has its vocalists accompanied by prerecorded background music for some local TV appearances. Often when a performer sings alone on a large stage or TV studio with no microphone in sight, he is prerecorded. Dancers, breathless after a strenuous routine, mouth words to prerecorded lyrics. The electronic manipulation of sound is a study in itself, and a performer should get involved in it.

In sound recording a performer stands or sits about a foot from the microphone, holding the copy in a position which will not greatly jeopardize the relationship of the mouth to the center of the microphone. Microphones have various characteristics in regard to sensitivity and size. The sensitivity of a microphone depends on its frequency range or ability to pick up the high and low pitch levels in a performer's voice. If a microphone cannot pick up the entire range of a performer's voice then the audience hears less than the performer is capable of doing. So, usually a performer gets, or perhaps owns, a microphone that exceeds the range of his or her voice, an instrument known to be reliable. These microphones may cost $300 to $400 apiece.

In a sense performers treat a microphone like a human being. They talk to it, loudly and intimately; they caress it; they joke with it; they treat it as though it were alive. They never (well, almost never) kick it, hit it, tap it or spit at it. They treat these wonderful instruments as their most useful tools, which they are. Extending from a microphone is an area called a *beam,* which picks up sound in an optimum way. The beam can be wide or narrow, rather long or short. It can be on one side (unidirectional), two sides (bidirectional) or on all sides (omnidirectional) in which case one speaks across the top of the microphone instead of directly into it. When a performer speaks directly into the beam of a microphone, he or she has maximum "presence" and is said to be *on mike.* (See, "Using Microphones.")

Microphones used in recording studios can be placed anywhere and can be of any size, thus allowing for maximum fidelity. In visual media, emphasis is placed on keeping the microphones out of sight, so they are smaller and often placed above the head of the performer at about a 45-degree angle. Many musical performances would simply be impossible if the microphones did not show, so they *do* show. To achieve maximum audio quality, many TV programs and feature films use prerecorded or post-synchronized sound; that is, performers pantomime to audio recordings so that the recording and the live studio image can be recorded on videotape. In films, performers reread or sing their parts to pictures of themselves projected on a screen; therefore, maximum fidelity and electronic assistance, like sound effects, can be mixed into the final sound track.

Whether or not a microphone is correct for a performer depends upon how it sounds in performance. Several fine microphones are made by various manufacturers. A performer may prefer the old RCA

44BX because he or she feels that the mellower qualities of the voice are preserved. Such a microphone may be suitable for radio but not for TV, because it looks too big and old fashioned. Television uses small lavalier or lapel microphones which have a more limited frequency range, sometimes limiting the attractive characteristics of a voice. Some performers, particularly singers, use a microphone as a prop; they even decorate them. Such equipment may not even be plugged in during the performance; instead, the performer's voice may be picked up on a microphone located over the heads of the studio audience. If a performer wants a flawless performance, he or she should learn to pantomime or "lip sync" to a recorded sound track. A fine recording is, of course, the optimum presentation of a performer's work and that is what an audience expects to hear. For performers appearing regularly on "live" programs—newscasters, home show personalities, public affairs hosts and quiz MCs—a microphone is fitted to them almost like a pair of shoes. It becomes part of them. Unfortunately community experts appearing on TV do not have the advantages of such a practice. They take what they can get, often without knowing the difference.

Along with the microphone is the volume control adjusted by the audio operator at the audio console in the studio control room. The audio operator's job is to be certain that the performer is heard and heard well—especially above the accompaniment, background music, audience response or whatever. The voice of many a delightful singer has been drowned out by a musical background not properly balanced by the audio operator, and many another has been helped by an operator who covered weak delivery with orchestration. These ideas are intended to suggest parameters for various kinds of performers and to indicate why top studios are expensive, employing the finest artists and technicians in the business.

5: Movement

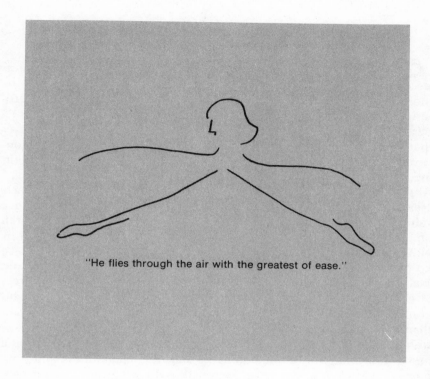

"He flies through the air with the greatest of ease."

A PERFORMER in visual media is defined as much by movement as by voice. Some research indicates that nonverbal cues may be more than four times as effective as language cues in transmitting attitudes.[1] One study claims that body language can take up as much as 93 per cent of one person's message to another. Dr. Cody Sweet believes that there are eight nonverbal communications: body language conveyed by gestures and postures, voice tones, physical appearance, clothing, touch and touching, use of space, surroundings, time and timing.[2] Anthropologist Ray L. Birdwhistell coined the term *kinesics* in the early 1950s to include the study of all body movement of communicative value.[3] During the ensuing 25 years a substantial collection of research on body movement indicates among other things that no gestures or movements have meaning in isolation, that a performer should make no extra or random movements to clutter and blur the message, and that the performer must make certain that his or her body reinforces or contradicts the spoken text in accordance with the subtext of the literature.[4] In visual media perhaps no movement is more important than a smile, assuming, of course, the smile is appropriate to the occasion. Smiling varies from a minimal grin to fully parted lips exposing most of the mouth. A smile conveys warmth, friendliness and confidence. A smile is a sign to the viewer that the program is under control, even when it isn't. For some people a smile must be practiced until it appears natural and genuinely expressive. To do this, you can:

1. Look in a mirror to establish a smile you like by observing different poses.
2. Practice the position of the smile until it can be made on command.
3. Thereafter, display the smile whenever it is called for, knowing it is attractive and pleasant, even though it may not be fully motivated because of stresses which you do not wish to reveal to the viewers.

A discussion of movement includes a careful look at the moving figure, reasons for movement, characteristics of movement and the elimination of involuntary movement. Relaxation and concentration are prerequisite to these considerations.

CONCENTRATION

Concentration aids a performer in controlling movement and in focusing attention on the message without interference from non-related activities and stress. Concentration allows a performer to become completely absorbed in what he or she is doing to the exclusion of everything else. Some individuals are much better at this than others. Some people can work while a radio or television set is playing. Others require absolute silence. "Ladies and gentlemen, because of the high degree of danger in this act, you are asked to remain absolutely quiet . . ." Such a statement is partly showmanship, but the performer undoubtedly has less chance of being distracted or losing concentration if an audience is quiet. In this instance the audience is polarized concentrating along with the performer. Many performers in live concert prohibit photographs. Peggy Lee once reprimanded a flash gun user—"Don't do that!"—without missing a beat in the song she was singing. The loss of concentration frequently causes forgetfulness, stammering, the delivery of the wrong line, or losing one's place on a cue card. "Quiet on the set" is called prior to shooting a film or scene for TV partly to avoid picking up unwanted noise and partly to assist performers with concentration. Concentration can be broken, too, if items, such as props, are misplaced or furniture is rearranged, thereby disrupting the performer's anticipated routine. Expert performers adlib around unexpected changes without notice by the viewers, but a wise performer checks his or her props and equipment before shooting a scene. A TV program or film may be made before a small crew or a capacity filled stadium, so the potential for losing one's concentration is great. A performer must play to the audience whether it consists of one viewer at home or thousands by maintaining confidence in himself or herself and the material and concentrating upon what is being said or done each moment.

RELAXATION

Relaxation is as necessary for movement as it is for voice control. A performer must learn to relax. Relaxation is not easy because of the personal strain that usually accompanies a performance in media. Tension can become so intense that a performer feels like exploding. Instead, this energy needs to be channeled into the performance, and released in just the right amounts to insure a swift pace for the program. Relaxation enables a performer to knowingly control the voice and body.

Typical exercises to achieve relaxation are based on tension. Tense and release one's body while breathing deeply is a common routine. This physical procedure is accompanied by the notion that a performer should clear the mind of all thoughts not directly related to the exercise. If a performer's mind is void of stress, the body will relax. The mysteries of relaxing for the purpose of mental and physical control have been studied for centuries by those who practice yoga.

A few simple exercises will help you to relieve tension:

1. Assume a basic stance with your feet together and your hands relaxed at your sides. Breathe deeply while practicing each of these exercises. Think only of relaxing in a favorite quiet, secluded place. Close your eyes and play soft music, if that helps you.

a. Drop your chin to your chest and slowly rotate your head in a circle. Inhale on one complete cycle and exhale on the other.

b. Raise your right shoulder as high as you can; lower it as far as possible. Repeat the exercise with your left shoulder.

c. Bend forward at the waist and roll the torso in a circular movement to the left, back and right, stretching as much as you can. Repeat the exercise in the opposite direction.

d. On a one-two count lift up on your toes, while stretching your arms toward the ceiling.

e. Bounce up and down in a rag doll fashion to enhance total muscular relaxation..

2. Sit on the floor with legs apart. Bend from the waist, extending the fingers as far as you can in the direction of the right foot, then the left.

3. Lie down on the floor and relax. Lift each limb, stiffen it and relax it.

4. Repeat each exercise several times. Do not hurry. Gradually build your stretching capability. The objective is to relax. You are not competing with anyone. You are relaxing your own mind and body.

THE MOVING FIGURE

Every movement has meaning. There are two kinds of movements: those which reinforce the message and those which do not. Those movements the performer needs give animation, interpretation, em-

phasis, clarity and style to the performance. Those a person does not
need blur the message the performer is attempting to convey. They
distract the viewer's attention, they sidetrack or short circuit the viewer.
Sometimes the movements call so much attention to themselves that the
viewer has lost the main intention of the message; thus, it is generally
assumed that a performer remains perfectly still until the performer is
motivated to move.

Position

Central to TV and film work is the moving performer and the cor-
ollary, the moving camera. The camera moves more often and further,
as a rule, then the performer; therefore, a performer must understand
that much of the time he or she is essentially static or motionless. The
static nature of TV was illustrated in a program for ABC hosted by
former New York mayor John Lindsay. Lindsay made six brief appearances. In his first pose he stood with his hands behind his back, in the
second he sat with them in front. Three views were closeups excluding
movement altogether.

A performer should be aware of body positions in relation to a
camera. An *open* position allows the director to get the best shots of the
talent, and so a performer tends to face or "cheat toward" the camera.
A performer begins a movement such as walking, opening a door or
handing an object to a guest with the limb farthest from camera.
"Cheating" creates the illusion of facing the camera. During an interview, for example, instead of two people facing each other as they
might in normal conversation, both slightly favor the camera lens in
their gaze and position. To the contrary a *closed* position limits the
director and yields attention to other performers. Positions are the
same as those in the theater except that they are in reference to the
camera lens: directly facing the lens, one-quarter turn right or left
away from the camera, profile, three-quarter turn right or left from the
camera and full back to the camera. "On camera" means the performer
is actively in the scene and is probably in camera view. At such times
the performer always conducts himself or herself as if in camera view.
Strictly speaking, a person is "off camera" whenever he or she is out of
camera view, even though they may be participants in the scene.

Naturalness

Children move naturally. As a person grows older, he or she becomes aware of social restraints. Social conduct imposes certain movements and gestures upon us. A person becomes conscious of the way he
or she moves. Self-consciousness retards the natural ease to which he or
she once was accustomed. Because of the self-conscious movements developed in adolescence and beyond, most performers must be taught

how to move so that they appear natural, yet graceful, before an audience. Common movement may be quite difficult: walking across a room, sitting in a chair, moving one's hand. Society has dictated what is considered graceful in these matters and the performer must learn what is accepted. Often a person's first awareness of his or her movement occurs when appearing before a group. Suddenly the person is pulled from the anonymity of the peer group and is singled out by being placed in the "spotlight." Fear may strike the individual, and he or she may be temporarily paralyzed or "frozen." Hence, the common expression, "I froze." In any event the person cannot move with abandon before the group until he or she relearns how to be natural in front of a group or on mass media.

Naturalness is the appearance of being at ease, warm, friendly and gregarious on-camera and on-microphone; awkwardness, shyness, embarrassment and deceitfulness are the antithesis. Naturalness comes from being oneself; a performer is whatever he or she values most. The catch is in knowing what is of value. Social experience and education help a performer determine what one is and what one wants to become. The Socratic philosophy "know thyself" is aptly applied here. Many performers never know themselves or what they want out of life.

Naturalness in a performer varies with age, experience and self confidence. Custom and education tend to dictate behavior. Education moves an individual in the direction of the norm, the socially accepted standard. Peers tend to force a person toward demonstrations of common practice in regard to appearance and action, resulting in the reduction, redirection and/or elimination of individual tendencies. Though some characteristics and idiosyncracies are superfluous, many great entertainers preserve and even nurture their unusual, atypical movements. Indeed some promoters of entertainers invent idiosyncracies for a performer, realizing that these personal details make performers, especially entertainers, more fascinating to the public and hence more likely to get publicity. Idiosyncracies are less acceptable in those who present information. A journalist is expected to be devoid of idiosyncracies in movement.

Posture

A performer hears the expression, "Stand tall" or "Stand your full height." This suggests that one should stand as though a string were attached to the center of the top of the head, and presumably it could lift the person directly skyward. So it should be with a performer's posture. The body should be aligned and balanced so that a plumb line from the ear to the ankle bone would divide the body equally with half of the weight on either side of the line, the hands and arms hanging relaxed at the sides.

Standing. Standing in place means the performer is exactly on the marks designated in tape or chalk on the floor of the studio. The performer's posture is correct and natural looking. No other movement distracts from the message. Frequently a performer tires and breaks stance by shifting his or her feet, drifting away from the marks and gradually out of the optimum light level. The performer should avoid twisting, swaying or leaning.

Sitting. Sitting gracefully requires the performer to feel for the chair or seat with one's leg, being certain that the chin, eyes and manner do not acknowledge the hunt. Then the body is lowered onto the chair with the thigh muscles keeping the back straight and lifted out again with the leg muscles, the back remaining straight. Whenever a performer expects to get up, his or her hands should not be allowed to anticipate the rise by moving forward. Legs may be crossed at the ankles or knees so that the body position remains open toward the camera. Long legs should be positioned as inconspicuously as possible by keeping the cross low and the legs together. When stooping, the back is kept straight with the foot further from camera slightly forward providing stability and balance. The body is then lowered over the heel of the foot nearer the camera. Kneeling also requires a straight back and smooth movement keeping weight on either foot.

Walking. In walking, the secret is to move the weight with ease. To begin the performer should lift the body and keep the weight on the balls of the feet. As one moves starting with the leg farthest from the camera, the toes are pointed straight ahead and not outward or inward which may result in a waddling effect. The legs are swung from the hip in an easy rhythm with relaxed and flexible knees. The performer takes moderate steps, letting the ball of the foot touch the floor a fraction ahead of the heel.

Climbing Stairs. In ascending stairs, the performer must look up, keeping the weight on the balls of the feet and using the thigh muscles to lift the body from one step to another. In descending, the performer glances down the stairs and then looks up, thus making no acknowledgment of each step. By leaning the body slightly back and retaining weight on the up thigh until the down foot is secure, the performer can transfer the weight quickly and evenly.

Falling. Falling can be accomplished without broken bones and bruises if the performer relaxes the body completely, keeping weight on the opposite leg from the side on which the fall is made and melting from the knees. To break a fall the performer must hit the floor with the calf, thigh, hip and shoulder successively. Falling should of course be practiced on mats to alleviate apprehension.

Bowing. In the United States bows are made from a modest nod of the head to a bend at the waist. European bows are deeper from the

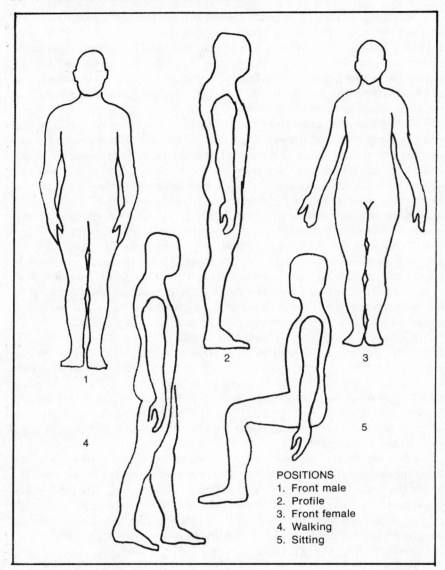

POSITIONS
1. Front male
2. Profile
3. Front female
4. Walking
5. Sitting

waist. Some performers in theatrical disciplines, such as the dance, curtsy to the floor. In every case the back remains straight.

Hands. Hands should be an integrated part of body movement and personality. They can hang like dead weights at the sides of the performer whenever there is no motivation for moving them. Every performer must find a comfortable position for hands and remember it when the hands have nothing to do. Common positions are hands at the sides, hands folded in front, hands folded in back, hands or thumbs in pocket(s), one hand at the side and the other clasping a wrist or arm, arms folded in front with hands buried (Ed Sullivan), arms folded with one hand resting against the face (Jack Benny), hands on hips. Laurence Olivier once remarked, "I've got an awful way of flinging my hands about which I detest and try to control it. But some times a part requires all you've got, weakness and all, and I just let it all happen and hope for the best."

Motivation is, of course, the key to using the hands. A few vocalists try working with a handkerchief; most of them depend on caressing a microphone. Other performers actually hold scripts they do not really need because they are using teleprompters for lines. Occasionally a performer must hold books, graphics, photographs and works of art. These objects are held in a predetermined position for good camera pick up. The angle of the item must allow for sufficient light without reflecting glare. Glossy photographs are usually tipped slightly toward the camera from the top edge. A performer must hold an item long enough for the viewer to know what it is and study it, if necessary. Only steady hands can do this effectively.

Balance

Animating a static pose requires balance if the performer is to have facile, fluid movement, instant bodily response and quick changes of direction. Establishing your balance may be more difficult than you suppose.

1. Assume an erect stance. March in place gradually raising knees higher and higher, or brush the right foot forward and backward several times, then the left; or kneel on the right foot and then the left, moving the entire body up and down several times.

2. Tape a straight line on the floor, then walk it like a tightrope. At first you may wish to use a rod or chair to assist you.

3. Squat to the floor, extending your arms forward. Slowly rise adjusting your feet to a secure stance. Note the position of your feet and body in a mirror. If the stance is attractive as well as balanced and comfortable, remember it, for it can be used as your basic standing position. Practice moving from this position by taking a few steps in various directions.

4. Walk directly to a chair. Sit in it. Practice moving around the set until you are absolutely secure in your movements, efficient in your direction and smooth in every gesture.

Animation

In one sense animation simply refers to movement of the face and body; in another, animation gives life or a quality to the movement by making it more interesting, exciting and impressive. Such movement has been formalized in an art form practiced for centuries called *pantomime*. Pantomime is associated with the acts of many great comedians from the silent screen's Charles Chaplin and Buster Keaton to television's Red Skelton and Carol Burnett. Pantomime is communicating ideas, emotions and narratives by means of bodily expression without words. A few basic principles are that the chest is the key to all bodily action, that positive emotions—courage, honor, love—are expressed through an expanded body with a high chest and head, free movement, and animated features, that negative emotions—greed, hate, fear, suffering—shrink the body and are expressed by a contracted chest, restricted gestures, tense movement and drawn features, that expression in the face precedes action with the thought first being detected through the eyes and then flowing over the body, that all action must be definite in thought and execution, and motivated.

In less complex terms, a person is said to "speak" with the hands or eyes which usually means that these movements are reeinforcing the message. Temperamental people are inclined to be highly animated, whereas reserved ones move subtly. In TV and film, animation varies greatly because the slightest gesture can be magnified on the closeup camera. This is in contrast to appearing in a large theater where the performer's gestures may be more difficult for the audience to see.

MOTIVATION IN MOVEMENT

Inasmuch as unnecessary movement wastes energy and may blur the message, a performer moves only when he or she has to: movement should have purpose, movement should catch attention, movement should tell a story, movement should convey emotion. In dramatic situations and comedy sketches movement should delineate character and explain character relationships.

Purpose

Movement should have purpose. Obvious movement—moving one's head up and down to read a script, turning to see a studio monitor, pointing to a chart, holding a dish for a demonstration—these actions are necessary to construct the visual message. A vocalist moves from the shadows into a pool of light in the center of the studio floor.

The purpose of her movement is so that she can be seen. She moves for a reason. She knows why she is moving; this is called *motivation*. A performer should move only if he or she is motivated.

Attention

Movement catches attention. The smallest movement will draw attention if a viewer sees it. In general, movements are obvious and intentional. The performer wants the viewer to follow his or her movement so that the viewer will better understand the message or appreciate the performer's ability. Movement can be analyzed as (1) capturing attention, (2) focusing attention or (3) redirecting attention. To illustrate: a performer stands beside a refrigerator on camera right. She opens the door with her right hand (capturing attention). She moves her right hand past food shelves calling attention to space and quantity (focusing attention). She closes the door and walks to the freezer side (redirecting attention). How distracting it would be if during the presentation the performer wiped her nose, looked off set away from the refrigerator or limped. These movements may seem absurd, but many performers have equally distracting movements which immediately draw viewer attention away from the product.

Narration

Pantomime, dance and sign language often tell a story in movement, but so does a salesman who points at a viewer and says, "I want to sell you a car." Most commercial messages and public service announcements have a simple, direct message. To illustrate: two boys are playing on a gym set in a park. A woman appears to take one of the boys home. The other child is left alone. Over a freeze frame of the lone child, an announcer says, "Johnny, doesn't have a home. Won't you give him one. . . ." In this instance preliminary narration in movement frames the message.

Emotion

Movement should convey emotion. Emotion is expressed when a football player throws a ball onto the ground with force and displeasure, when a rock star removes his clothes, when one clown hits another clown on the head, when a newscaster narrates with tearful eyes and quivering hands the death of a head of state or distinguished colleague killed in the line of duty, and on a myriad of other occasions. Emotion—conveyed through movement—is a wonderfully exhilarating tool for the performer, if he or she can control it. While one usually thinks of emotion in dramatic acting or dance, it is common in the delivery of sermons or the advocacy of a point of view. On one public affairs telecast, a woman opposing the Equal Rights Amendment for women turned her chair so that she would not be able to look at her opponent. Most movement is relatively controlled and the emotional level is subtle, because the emotion is secondary to conveying the message of information. This movement is supportive of the message. For example, a man takes a swig of soft drink, "Mr. Pibb is a thirst quencher." Pleasure in movement. A woman turns so that her long hair swirls around her head in slow motion, "My hair is so clean. Breck clean." Movement illustrating pleasure.

Character Delineation

Movement should delineate character. A common exercise in a performance class is to ask each student to walk across a room, a distance of 15 feet or so. Then the instructor asks the class to analyze what it saw: What is the person like? Is the person ambitious . . . fun to be with . . . dynamic . . . disagreeable . . . attractive . . . natural . . . stiff . . . nervous . . . slow . . . self important . . . friendly? Then the class may be asked: What was the position of the head? What was the eye level . . . high or low? Was the head tilted . . . steady? The arms—did they swing . . . Much? Did the fingers move? Was the walk straight . . . fast or slow . . . defective . . . self conscious? From such questions a class learns that every movement delineates character, and that every person is a "character." Careful study will enable a performer to improve his or her own image and in the case of entertainers such study will enable them to imitate people at all ages of life through dominant characteristics of movement.

Relationships

Movement should explain performer relationships. In a newsroom the placement of the reporters around, next to or near the anchorperson explains their relationship. This is especially noticeable in the live format where the anchorperson is in the center position and he or she turns to the right or left to acknowledge the weather person, sportscaster, contributing reporters or interviewees. This cluster approach is common on TV. The principle position—"the star" or anchor spot—is in the center and the lesser contributions are to the sides. No lead—newscaster, politician or entertainer—yields the starring position, if it is his or hers to hold because the audience must be continually reminded of the performer relationships. Such decorum is religiously adhered to on the Johnny Carson show where incumbent guests move over one space at a time to yield the single guest chair next to Carson. Performer relationships are obvious in a telecast of a message from the President or a national political convention: The President is the "star," taking center stage. The featured players are those introducing him or giving lesser speeches, the supporting players are the Congress or convention delegates, the incidental participants would be escorts, standard bearers and other walk-on roles. In an entertainment program the curtain call again illustrates the relationship of the performers: The star is in the center, featured players are recognized and nearby, supporting players are in the second row or at the ends of the front line, and incidental performers (dancers) are in the back row if on stage at all. In dramatic productions and comedy sketches performer relationships are more complex involving characters moving toward and away from each other to demonstrate attitudes, yield attention and reveal information.

CHARACTERISTICS OF MOVEMENT

Every movement can be defined and studied in terms of direction, strength, speed, duration, timing and grace. No movement should signal anticipated action to the viewers, but certain movements may cue the director. As mentioned earlier, perhaps the most important movement in TV is the movement of the lips. If this movement is extended broadly, curved slightly upward (direction), with sureness (strength) and quickness, held for a few moments (duration) after a remark or significant action (timing), and done with ease (grace), it is usually interpreted as a friendly smile. The smile itself has saved many TV performers from utter disaster. The smile aptly illustrates characteristics of movement which can be readily applied to broader actions. Every movement must be coordinated with every other if the performer is to have a harmonious overall appearance. Gymnastics, dancing and simple movements such as "step, clap, snap" develop coordination.

Direction

Direction in film and TV has to do with the relationship of the performer to the camera. A performer moves up or down, horizontally or vertically depending on the relationship to the camera. Typically, a performer comes into or out of camera view and moves toward the camera or away from it. Or, the performer can remain in a relatively fixed position, and the camera operator can move in relation to the performer. This is equally common. Once the general movement of a scene is determined by the director, called "blocking the action," the performer knows where to move during the production; but while shooting the scene, the director moves the cameras whenever and wherever he or she pleases in relation to the performer. The director may tell the performer "Don't worry about the cameras, we'll find you." For instance, on a discussion program or an interview. At this point it might be said the performer is at the mercy of the director. A third possibility is to have both the performer and the camera moving. This often happens: that marvelous crane shot revealing all of the dancers whirling on the floor as the camera moves farther and farther away from the performers, that tracking shot on the beach where the camera follow the lovers walking side by side. Direction, therefore, refers to the moving performer in relation to a fixed camera and lens, or a moving camera and/or moving lens with a static performer, or a moving performer and a moving camera and/or moving lens. Still more complex is the performer as a multi image on the screen showing various views traveling in different directions superimposed or on multi screens.

Strength

Strength is the degree of power in the movement. Strength of movement is largely psychological: How motivated is the performer? Must he or she reposition quickly, for instance? What is the emotional level of action? Emphatic or uncertain, how dominant is the physical presence of the performer—in sheer bulk (weightlifter), in agility (pole vaulter)? Strength is especially important in fight sequences. Here the illusion of contact without significant real impact is maintained by having actors rehearse the strength of the delivery of the movement without real physical contact—a fist to the jaw, that misses the jaw in reality, a Karate chop to the back of the neck, that stops prior to neck injury— the thrust of the move in each case is at full strength, but only the illusion of strength exists on impact.

Speed

Speed refers to the amount of time it takes a performer to move his entire body or any part thereof from one place to another. Fast action can speed up a performer's movement so much that the movement may resemble that of an old film. Normal movement is anything that appears to be associated with the movement one sees everyday, and slow speed is familiar to TV viewers because of instant slow motion replay in sports events. A performer judges his or her movement in the context of the total performance. Speed can be skillfully used to lend variety to a performance.

Duration

The length of a movement can be so painfully long that the audience tires of watching it, or so acutely short the audience misses the movement altogether. The right length is the amount of time it takes for viewer understanding, comprehension and aesthetic appreciation. The last flick of a hand may be the perfect touch to end a pas de deux; a gradual uplifting of arms in supplication may be the proper duration for stressing a point during a TV ministry; a child's dash down the aisle of a classroom to announce "no cavities" may give the right amount of excitement and focus to a toothpaste commercial; dragging a body across a floor in slow motion may provide the psychological impact required for a drama.

Timing

A performer controls movement so carefully that he or she knows when to be at an exact position on the floor, when to pick up a visual, when to turn from looking in one camera lens to another. In comedy and drama, entertainers know when to deliver a line to get a maximum laugh or when to cry for maximum emotional impact. These judgments on the part of a performer are collectively referred to as one's timing. Timing then is the ability of a performer to predetermine the moment he or she will move. See also Voice—Time and Rate.

Grace

Grace is the ease of movement and its appropriateness to the total action. Indeed, some movements are awkward; and they are appropriately so. A person moving with confidence, as though he or she had done the task many times before and yet is enthusiastic about doing it again, is thought of as graceful in a common way. Human beings have a natural grace in walking, standing and sitting that is quite acceptable if it can be preserved for media appearances. Sometimes a performer experiences intense self consciousness on camera which stiffens the muscles and produces a high level of nervousness which prohibits the performer from graceful movement and he or she looks uncomfortable. Nowhere is this awkwardness more apparent than in high school speech contests in which a student takes two steps laterally or vertically—one, two—to give the student, mechanically, a transition by means of movement. A performer's uneasiness can be eliminated by a clever director who reassures the insecure performer that he or she is going to do well. This may be the most important contribution a director makes for a performer. Robert Redford was asked, "What does Sydney Pollack (who has directed some of Redford's finest films) do for you as an actor?: "Sydney inspires confidence." Such confidence results in relaxed, graceful movement.[5]

INVOLUNTARY MOVEMENT

Common involuntary movement is at one's subconscious level. A performer does it without realizing he or she is moving. Common distortion of the face is the result of frowning, grimacing, sniffing, mouthing words, protruding lips for sexual effect, enlarging nostrils for dramatic effect, squinting, blinking, turning down the corners of the mouth, biting the tongue or lips, chewing without gum, picking or scratching the face, leaving the mouth open and licking the lips, among others. Unattractive positions and movements of the hands include clawed, stiff fingers, heaviness in the hands, playing with jewelry, paper or pencils, tapping or shaking objects, repeated gestures, rhythmic gestures and wringing the hands. Distortions of the torso are wriggling shoulders and hips, muscle spasms, heaving chest or abdomen, humped back, stiffness in posture and twisting or swinging in a chair. Distortions of the legs are swaying to and fro, foot jiggling and locking one's legs at the knees. Frequently these movements are caused by stress. Facial registration of disgust or disappointment is particularly detrimental and should be kept off camera. Controlling involuntary movement is accomplished by

    1. Recognizing the offending movement by seeing it on videotape or being told about it.

    2. Knowing what action you will take to avoid it.

    3. Remembering the offending movement when you are under stress on-the-air.

    4. Keeping the offending movement at your conscious level until it has been completely eliminated.

6: Talent

Agent: "He tells funny stories, too."
Producer: "But can he act?"

Intuitive Ability
Imagination
Discipline
    Ambition—Competence—Dependability—Longevity

Kinds of Talent
    The Dominant Performer (Personalities; Entertainers; Actors and Actresses)—The Dominant Message (Journalists; Announcers; Presenters from other Professions)

TALENT IS DEFINED as whatever ability a performer possesses naturally. By definition nearly everyone has talent: "a gift of gab," "a winning smile," "sex appeal." For a performer to be considered talented, however, he or she must recognize and use these abilities—fluent speech, putting people at ease, being sexually enticing—for the purposes of exhibition. Talent is a natural combination of abilities that the public wants to see and/or hear to the extent it is willing to pay for the opportunity.

INTUITIVE ABILITY

Intuitive ability is manifest in several common descriptions—musical, vocal, artistic, intellectual and mechanical ability. Some people are fortunate in having ability which they have developed early to a high degree—a child prodigy who has played classical piano since the age of five; a young Tom Edison who has been a science fair winner; a superbly skillful youngster who can design and sell clever items she makes out of scraps around the house; a high school athlete who has been offered scholarships to the top universities; a dancer who at age 12 has performed for a professional company; an intellectual genius who is invited to join advanced study programs. These people are talented, and their abilities were recognized at a young age. Often these youngsters are misfits, introverts who have difficulty in working or playing with their peer groups in school; yet, if their talents are properly cultivated, they may become the performers sought after by the media.

Improving one's ability is the task of educators. An individual's unknown ability may be discovered as much by fate as by design. The abilities of most people go unnoticed, because most people are preoccupied with learning career skills that will enable them to participate in the obvious work force. The lack of time and money are big inhibitors of talented people who find that they are well beyond their youthful years before they can pursue the work of a performer. The perfecting of one's ability and the establishment of contacts to exhibit it may take years to develop. Nevertheless, this process can be accelerated through obtaining an education at good professional schools, colleges and universities.

Latent ability is untapped ability that will probably never surface, because the social pressures surrounding the normal desire to seek a place in society will not allow sufficient opportunity for nurturing such ability. Occasionally a superior coach, talent scout, producer or teacher may spot latent ability, develop it for a considerable period of time and have it flower to some extent. For the most part, these talents in everyone are beyond the reach of present day development. Recognizing that there is such a slim chance for a person's performing ability to be developed, the Soviet Union set up schools which repeatedly test people in an attempt to discover scientifically, and somewhat mechanically perhaps, superior ability. Those who pass the tests are sent to schools of physical culture, dance and elsewhere to become outstanding Russian performers. In the United States the method of development is much more haphazard, but the results are perhaps more effective, for a performer must persevere, flourish or die, in the commercial marketplace which is directly responsive to public acceptance.

IMAGINATION

An attractive blonde did precisely what she was told on camera. She had her visuals in order, her script was ready. She produced her part of the program thoroughly. To all appearances she should do very well in mass media. When it came to planning future programs, however, and the details of her role in them, the director had to come up with clever ideas for her to use. In other words, the attractive blonde had inadequate talent for the job. She could not fuse her past experience with current ideas to form a new, original, exciting, fresh program. She lacked imagination. She was always asking, "What do you think I should do next?" Then she would ask, "How do you think I should do it?"

An active, vibrant imagination is part of a performer's intuitive ability. Imagination springs from the innermost self, a creative region wherein the artist or entertainer, thinker, or scientist or journalist seeks the truth and makes his or her appeal to the public. Joseph Conrad has described this region so admirably:

A work that aspires, however humbly, to the condition of art should carry its justification in every line. And art itself may be defined as a single-minded attempt to render the highest kind of justice to the visible universe, by bringing to light the truth, manifold and one, underlying its every aspect. It is an attempt to find in its forms, in its colors, in its light, in its shadows, in the aspects of matter and in the facts of life, what of each is fundamental, what is enduring and essential—their one illuminating and convincing quality—the very truth of their existence. The artist, then, like the thinker or the scientist, seeks the truth and makes his appeal. Impressed by the aspect of the world the thinker plunges into ideas, the scientist into facts—whence, presently, emerging they make their appeal to those qualities of our being that fit us best for the hazardous enterprise of living. They speak authoritatively to our commonsense, to our intelligence, to our desire for peace or to our desire for unrest; not seldom to our prejudices, sometimes to our fears, often to our egoism—but always to our credulity. And their words are heard with reverence, for their concern is with weighty matters; with the cultivation of our minds and the proper care of our bodies; with the attainment of our ambitions; with the perfection of the means and the glorification of our precious aims.

It is otherwise with the artist.

Confronted by the same enigmatic spectacle the artist descends within himself, and in that lonely region of stress and strife, if he be deserving and fortunate, he finds the terms of his appeal. His appeal is made to our less obvious capacities; to that part of our nature which, because of the warlike conditions of existence, is necessarily kept out of sight within the more resisting and hard qualities—like the vulnerable body within a steel armor. His appeal is less loud, more profound, less distinct, more stirring—and sooner forgotten. Yet its effect endures forever. The changing wisdom of successive generations discards ideas, questions facts, demolishes theories. But the artist appeals to that part of our being which is not dependent on wisdom; to that in us which is a gift and not an acquisition—and, therefore, more permanently enduring. He speaks to our capacity for delight and wonder, to the sense of mystery surrounding our lives; to our sense of pity, and beauty, and pain: to the latent feeling of fellowship with all creation—and to the subtle, but invincible, conviction of solidarity that knits together the loneliness of innumerable hearts to the solidarity in dreams, in joy, in sorrow, in aspirations, in illusions, in hope, in fear, which binds men to each other, which binds together all humanity—the dead to the living and the living to the unborn.[1]

It is like a bottomless well from which more ideas flow than a performer has the opportunity, time or money to carry out. Imagination can be encouraged, stimulated, challenged, prodded or suppressed depending on the working conditions or learning environment in which it is exposed. A good school will let a performer articulate whatever ideas he or she has, however daring; and, whenever possible, will help the performer see those ideas materialize in productions. But, first, the performer must dream the impossible dream, and then decide how to produce it. All top notch performers have the imagination to dream dreams; a few find the wherewithal to produce them. To improve one's imagination, a performer:

1. Dares to think *anything* he or she wishes.
2. Remembers that those thoughts may be very valuable someday.
3. Knows what is happening in media by viewing, listening and reading.
4. Gathers ideas from art galleries, exhibitions, lectures, sports events and entertainments of all kinds.
5. Tries new experiences through people and activities.
6. Plays games of improvisation and story telling that relate to media.
7. Keeps a notebook of blank paper which he or she continually fills with ideas and sketches, however crude or incomplete they may seem to be at the moment.

DISCIPLINE

Many people would like to perform, but far fewer are willing to work at it. It seems so easy for the other person to look so good. Artists of great skill practice every day. Concert pianist Van Cliburn practices every day, Olympic champion Dorothy Hamill must skate every day. Perfecting a talent exacts extreme discipline. The greater the artist, the greater the discipline. Discipline is a way of life for most dancers, actors, writers and other professionals. It is folly to suppose that a person can be an adept performer unless he or she works at it every day. A commercial announcer, a newscaster, a singer must practice every day. Russian ballet star Mikhail Baryshnikov has said that because of the toil and sweat, sometimes he hates to dance—in fact, quite often.

Occasionally a novice is heard to say that he would like to be a "part time" announcer, as if announcing were something one could pick up on a moment's notice. With few exceptions, it is not possible for a person to be an announcer on the spur of the moment. Such people have not kept their voices in practice nor their ability to move before cameras equal to or surpassing the ability of available disciplined competition. Aside from certain instances of type casting, practiced fluency in reading, clear enunciation, physical maintenance and familiarity with audio equipment requires continuous attention.

Talent that has been in hiatus for a decade or more (while having a family, for example) should not be encouraged to resume study for performance. Professionally, this person opted for another type of work years ago and is unable to retrace his or her steps—the main reason for inability to make the transition to professional performance is lack of discipline. The characteristics of discipline are ambition, competence, dependability and longevity. In other words, a performer with even modest talent, a burning desire to be on media, a tireless effort at doing what is asked whenever and wherever the occasion arises day after day, one who allows performance to be first in his or her life, has a stronger chance of success than those talented people with less ambition and discipline. Many performers have been down on their luck, but they keep up with their lessons and maintain themselves mentally and physically. These performers often bounce back time after time. In all probability this steadfast attitude will sooner or later pay off, because relatively few people are willing to work hard enough to be performers.

Ambition

Ambition is the desire one has to be a performer. Some performers will perform if coaxed, but this is a low level of ambition, and there are very few performers who are so exceptional that the public will coax them for long, largely because there are so many others eager to perform. A higher level of ambition is the performer who studies but has several things he or she can do well, and performance is just one of them. Multi-talented people may have enough drive, but probably will not focus it sufficiently to be successful as a performer. A third level of ambition is the performer who does nothing so well as perform. To this person performing is his or her life. This person will sacrifice anything, and sometimes anybody, to perform. Many famous performers fall into this category. These people will gamble their talent on any chance that seems big enough to promote their performing interests. To them, success is just on the horizon. There is always hope. Where they played, what they did, what plaudits they received are the big moments in their lives. These performers are obsessed with show business and/or journalism. Thousands of people spend their lives on the hope that one day they'll make the big time, and even if they don't, they are content in the trying. A fourth category of ambition is the overwhelming talent who follows a media career that is of secondary importance in his or her life, family or something else being primary. Usually this performer has already established a reputation and may be wealthy or may have some relationship with the media, such as being married to the station manager or being an offspring of the producer of a series, that will guarantee access to media.

Competence

Competence is the minimum level of ability. A competent person will get by, and with hard work on his or her part and that of a sup-

porting crew may readily compete in the main stream of public attention. Competence, especially if coupled with ambition, is the basic contribution of many performers to media.

This is to say that many performers are capable, but may not be
exceptional. These people frequently provide the basic announcing,
newscasting and hosting for radio and television stations throughout
the country. They have no desire to leave their hometown communities. They are familiar with what their friends, neighbors and those in
the area prefer on media—and they deliver it to the local audience in a
manner that a professional outsider might be years in learning. Many
stations, particularly some large ones independently owned, have over
the years sold stock to some staff members who are performers: the
promotion director may be the lead on a children's program, the news
anchorperson may be a stockholding vice president of the company.
Competent people like these may do the performing tasks from reasonably well to very well indeed, while retaining this status through versatility, financial investment or some kind of staying power other than just
performing ability.

Dependability

Dependability sometimes is more highly prized in a performer
than unusual or exceptional talent. Naturally, a manager does not want
to have to choose. Both talent and dependability are desirable. A dependable person who is competent, but perhaps not so highly gifted,
may endure longer than a more talented colleague. Dependability
means having the work in on time and working in anticipation of extenuating circumstances. The key to dependability is commitment. A
performer who agrees to appear and then meets that obligation every
time regardless of illness, bad weather, family disaster, personal pleasure or unexpected circumstances is often sought after because of his
or her high dependability. Such a commitment is part of the discipline
of a performer. A dependable performer is prepared for all eventual-
ities, and this is only possible if the performer can anticipate any circumstances that may arise.

Under the pressures of TV and radio, a performer is counted on
to provide so many seconds or minutes on the air. If this performer
defaults, the producer must not only find a substitute but may also lose
the cost of the original session in which the performer was to appear.
Once an art museum director refused to meet his commitment to a TV
series. "What will I do for a program?" the producer complained. "Go
dark," was the response. But, the public has come to rely on mass
media, and the producer felt obligated not to default, and so he found
someone else.

Dependability, further means that while a producer depends on
performers, performers depend upon themselves to get the job done,

even though they may accept gratefully the assistance of staff and crew. When a performer steps into a spotlight, he or she is the one who usually takes the credit or the blame for the quality of the program.

Longevity

Frequently someone says, "I could do as well as he does. How did he get the job?" The answer, commonly, is that he stuck it out through good times and bad, low salary and high, criticism and praise, and adroitly kept on the good side of management. That performer is a disciplined professional in that he has stuck to the business and, as in most businesses, opportunity usually arrives if one is not too impatient.

Audiences are capricious; they seldom know what they want. Often they simply want change, and so performers find work in media unstable. One day a performer is a hit, the honoree of several awards, but before the ceremonies are over, his or her program series is cancelled. Once again the performer must draw upon his or her abiding discipline as a performer, believing that tomorrow or soon another opportunity will come along. Trends and styles in media are usually short-lived and constantly changing. Program ideas spiral forth tending to repeat scripts, music, routines and so on every few years. A performer must be ahead of the trends, always striving for improvement and freshness.

Until recent years fewer women performers were on TV or radio. One of the reasons was that some women dropped out of broadcasting to marry or raise a family; thus their years of longevity with the company were terminated. Staff turnovers, new program formats, new sponsors, new voices and faces are a few of the reasons an opportunity to perform will open up—and someone with longevity, well liked and known to management frequently gets the nod.

KINDS OF TALENT

There are, in general, two kinds of talent: one kind draws attention to itself and the other draws attention to his or her message. The latter category includes journalists, announcers and presenters from other professions. Very often the names of these people are not remembered by the public, but their messages are. By contrast, personalities and entertainers may or may not deliver memorable material, but they themselves may be remembered by the audience, and that audience may clamor for a great deal more personal information about the performer. These artists tend to develop themselves as a resource: for instance, with their voices they make funny sounds (George Carlin, Victor Borge), or they play instruments with great skill and showmanship

(Liberace, Gene Krupa, Louis Armstrong). Such people present themselves in a unique way to the public primarily because of the fortunate development of obvious and latent intuitive ability. Purveyors of information depend upon intellectual skills to gather, assemble and present that information. Such work requires judgment, analysis, perspective, human understanding and sometimes a philosophy regarding the relationship of men and women to the universe. Purveyors of information must be able to deal in weighty matters.

The Dominant Performer

Personalities and entertainers must be dominant whenever they are in the spotlight. Some of these people may, in fact, be rather low key in their personal lives, having low visibility and genuine affinity for anonymity. Most of them, however, are rather flamboyant people because, other reasons notwithstanding, it is good business. If a person elects to be a media personality or entertainer, he or she should expect to lead a public life, wherein every aspect of the performer's life is subject to public knowledge, discussion and approval. Some media people like to be "on" all of the time. They like people around them. If someone is willing to pay attention, they are ready to perform. They constantly seek encouragement. They feed on praise, which heightens their ability to perform. They work at fever pitch, and have faith in their talent in spite of adversity. Many tend to be adventuresome in their personal lives and easily adjust to a rather rootless, transient life. They frequently do what they innately feel is right without clear explanation, rather than follow the guidance of their advisors. They are often poor managers of their financial affairs. Many live on emotional energy, which they seem to have in abundance. These performers often experience an emotional range beyond that of most people. These characteristics—abandon, consummate skill, controlled emotional extremes, concentration, daring—make a performer exhilarating to an audience.

Personalities. A so-called "personality" is anyone who exhibits unique characteristics. Often personalities in show business are masters of ceremonies, hosts, quiz masters and panelists. Arthur Godfrey, Jack Paar, Dick Cavett, Merv Griffin and Dick Clark are a few who come to mind. These performers tend to specialize in being themselves. They are not journalists, although on occasion some may read news; they are not entertainers, although some may sing, dance or tell funny stories from time to time. They are interesting people who often have unusual experiences that they are willing to share with an audience; but typically they bring out the experiences of their guests on talk shows or facilitate the smoothness of quiz programs by being efficient catalysts. By the mid-1970s game shows took up an estimated 40 per cent of all weekday television. While recognizing the enjoyment an audience gets from vicariously experiencing the winning of prizes and matching skills, the program hosts themselves must be credited to a large extent for the increased popularity of these series. (You can watch seven hours, one show after another, five days a week.) Tom Kennedy, of *Name That Tune,* Dennis James, of *The Price Is Right,* and Gene Rayburn, of *The Match Game,* are a few of the dozen or so TV game show hosts. While prize money may be the principal attraction on some program series (*The $128,000 Question*), frequently money is of no importance (*What's My Line?*). A key factor from an audience viewpoint is that the game show personalities are always fun to be with. For the most part these performers can do many things with more than common ability, and they are well versed on many subjects so that they can talk about almost anything on the spur of the moment. They also capitalize on dominant characteristics that contribute to each performer's style, such as an intimate delivery, emotional display or involvement, intellectual prowess, wit, sincerity and charm.

Entertainers. Singers, dancers and variety artists are obviously entertainers. Anyone who arouses our emotions in a pleasureful way might be considered an entertainer. These performers usually develop a physical skill to an extraordinary degree and then display that skill with emotional interpretation. The extent and quality of one's talent, sufficient for claim as an entertainer, cannot be easily measured, if at all. Frequently the artist cannot tell how much ability he or she has. This judgment is left to critics and public response. Even then publicity and opportunity, called "the breaks," have a great deal to do with whether a performer develops as an entertainer. It appears, however, that extraordinary talent will be successful. At least there are numerous testimonials documenting the notion that economic conditions do not suppress superior talent. Media demand so much talent that scouts are constantly looking for exceptional individuals. What is strenuous for most performers is obtaining the money and time that it takes to mold rough material into a superb performance. Fortunately for the public, some performers and their families sacrifice for years to produce an entertainer. Those talented people who are already living in a media environment, such as children of entertainers, have a distinct advantage in getting started. Of course only the public can determine a performer's degree of success and longevity.

Actors and Actresses. An actor's or actress's name may be better known than his or her material—the performer is dominant over the message, for the script or play is used as a vehicle by the performer as a display of talent. A good case could be made for those hundreds of performers who act somewhat anonymously. These people are the strength of the industry which may call upon them consistently for years without ever elevating them to star status. For the performer who wishes to be a star must dominate the material. Eventually Carroll O'Connor must be better known than Archie Bunker, the fictional role he played in *All in the Family,* and Henry Winkler must survive his role as Fonzie in the *Happy Days* series. Perhaps more difficult to establish will be the identities of each of *Charlie's Angels*—Farrah Fawcett-Majors, Kate Jackson and Jaclyn Smith.

The number of people seeking work in the acting profession is legion. Actors and actresses may be variously classified as those who would like to get work but never do or have not as yet; those who have occasional bit parts and walkons; supporting players; those with minor roles but established names; those with major roles but not necessarily well known to the public nor remembered by it; those who are stars, and superstars.

The Dominant Message

If a message is dominant enough, it makes no difference who delivers it so long as minimum credibility exists. "Bobby was hit by a car" is just as believable from a lisping child who may have seen or heard about the accident as it is from the evening newscaster. The journalists, announcers and presenters from other professions whose messages are dominant over their personalities bring judgment, responsibility and perspective to a message.

Journalists. Media have gone through a period of *news readers* who may or may not have been journalists. Readers are attractive people who tend to be personalities more than journalists. Frequently these readers neither gather news nor edit it; they perfect the delivery of a prepared script. Many newspaper and wire service journalists brought their investigative and reporting abilities to radio in its early days, but the advent of TV tended to modify all this as the appeal of the visual image—the newscaster, presenting the material—drew larger audiences than the news itself. In recent news programs auditory and visual concentration has shifted to the coverage of real "actors," (i.e., citizens) with narration provided by an unseen reporter. This de-emphasis on the newscaster's physical appearance has shifted to that person's ability to gather and research the news—that is, one who has a strong journalistic sense rather than one who simply displays an attractive voice, appearance or manner. Of course, it is reasonable to assume that stations can get attractive appearance and journalistic expertise in a single performer. The better present-day news team typically consists of aggressive, good-looking anchor-persons who know news; efficient contributing reporters who specialize in certain areas of the news such as city hall, police or transportation; a sportscaster who has a virile look (he often plays in competitive sports for fun and charity) or, in the case of a rare woman sportscaster, has feminine charm; and a weather person who emphasizes human qualities such as gentleness, warmth and humor. Each member of the news team is in contrast to the others, but taken as a whole they work well together.

Announcers. Commercial announcers specialize in interpretation of copy. Their chief objective is to motivate the public to buy products and services. Ed Herlihy, the voice of Kraft Foods products, once recommended that a commercial announcer should have a pleasant voice, a good well-rounded education, a certain amount of voice culture, and fourth, he or she must be an extrovert.

> This, I would say, is downright essential. The announcer, being a salesman, must sincerely like people and he must, without being too obvious about it, make them realize that he likes people. I have known introverts who made the fringes of the Big Time, but there they stop. If you are contemplating a career in announcing, or any other form of salesmanship for that matter, analyze yourself for these qualities. If you class yourself as an introvert, try something else. As I said before, I've known people of that type who had every other ingredient for success at "hosting" on the air. They did well, up to a point, and then failed. They were trying to fool themselves that they genuinely liked people, and obviously at the same time they were trying, perhaps even unconsciously, to fool the public, and that never works.[2]

Numerous well-known personalities, artists and unknown, ordinary-looking folks have made commercials. A commercial announcer is usually hired because, in the opinion of the agency producer or client, his or her look and/or sound will effectively sell the product or service. *Mash* star Alan Alda sells Polaroid, Betty White of the *Mary Tyler Moore Show,* Spray 'n Wash. The selection is admittedly a guess, based as much on intuitive decision as scientific research. The commercial announcer represents an entity which is offered to the public primarily at the emotional level, because emotion is more persuasive than logic. Absolutely nothing about the announcer should turn the listener-viewer away from the product or service. Comparatively, this suggests that some announcers are rather bland, nondescript performers; and this is true, particularly for station or staff announcers. A staff announcer specializes in making announcements that will inform the public without having the public become interested in the announcer as a person. A staff announcer also fills in for performers who are on vacation or ill without competing for the absentee's job. Reading copy clearly without overly coloring the voice, objectively without prejudice, yet energetically, efficiently and directly is skill in itself.

Presenters from Other Professions. Politicians, executives, physicians, educators and clergy are among those who must exhibit a talent for performing from time to time. Often they exhibit this talent on media. Although these people are respected primarily for their knowledge of a particular subject and, therefore, may not be so attractive or polished in media usage, the infrequency of their appearances and the genuineness of their appeals command an audience. A few years ago inept media utilization by such nonprofessionals was readily excusable. Today's leaders, however, are beginning to use media effectually. They realize the public identifies them and their causes by means of a positive media image.

Leaders in all fields show concern for their appearances in media. Skillful leaders manage to filter out the undesirable aspects of their images so that these things will not harm them or their causes in the public view. President John F. Kennedy was highly adept at showing his most favorable side to the public through media. A president's relationship with the press is just about as difficult as any other aspect of the presidency. His choice of a likable press secretary who has an affinity for media is all important. In business and industry the same combination of company president and public relations head is critical to the public's understanding of a company. A good public relations person will establish a favorable public image for a company by performing skillfully on media and by making certain that the company president does likewise. The business world is amazingly inept at using media. Most large companies such as petroleum, steel, insurance and banks compound their weak public images by having unattractive representatives. Often these representatives are dedicated in-house employees who convey the impression on media that the welfare of the public ranks second to the profits of the company.

A challenge for improvement in this respect was offered recently by Henry C. Ruark, a consultant and writer specializing in the learning media field and former first national director of information for the National Audio Visual Association:

> All too often, the American business executive walks into a TV situation . . . not in-house, but TV-news, interview, or public spotlight . . . without proper preparation. And, all too often, that exec ends up looking rather forlorn and foot-tangling, too, since being on-camera in-house with a script is far removed from being on-your-own among the wolves.
>
> What can you do? If you have any hand at all in TV-ing for your organization, give your man a chance to practice, practice, practice, in similar open-ended, public-atmosphere circumstances. Set up a critical group not afraid to fire hard questions; get your exec to give you *topics,* not *cues;* and frame him up to have to an-

swer unexpected and unfriendly queries. If he's smart, he'll understand and enjoy the process. You may help him to save an important image . . . *his.*[3]

In addition to public relations an important role for the performer
in business and industry is instruction via closed circuit television. Once
again the performer must combine technical knowledge with media
finesse. Suitable teachers are sometimes drawn from existing staff. Occasionally they are hired from outside, because plant employees teaching other plant employees can go just so far. The plant manager may
think he can present an edict to employees which they will obey, but he
had better re-evaluate that idea and rely on those better suited to
media instruction. The day may come when outside professional actor-
instructors will use company in-house media to teach employees how to
operate equipment and explain the virtues of the business. Some of this
is already being done, because media professionals are being hired to
read copy prepared by industry officials for audio visual programs on
employee orientation, company rules and procedures and safety.

Physicians are leaders in society today. They have power, prestige,
and money. They are trying to maintain a favorable public image while
there is mounting public pressure to control medical care. The medical
community attempts to convince the public of its progress in research
and good intentions for the public well being. In TV drama the role of
the physician generally is romanticized by his or her selfless effort to
aid the community, but the experience of the public in reference to rising high costs of medical care suggests a different public view. The
public accepts the professional skill of a physician, but increasingly
rejects the godlike role some physicians prefer to maintain, especially in
a time when paramedical fields and socialized medical services are
closer to reality. Some physicians have a talent for presenting their
work to the public in heroic proportions. During the Guatemala earthquake of 1976, an American doctor residing there made a greatly favorable impression by serving the needs of the victims and by teaching
the natives how to take care of themselves through paramedical assistance. A few seconds of newsfilm did a good deal to remind the public
of what medicine used to be all about—healing the sick. In this instance, a physician became a performer representing himself and the
nobler aspects of the medical profession.

Educators have to do more in the future to convince the public
that their institutions are worthy of burdensome tax support and private funds. This means that university administrators and faculties will
have to use media to state their needs so that the public can understand
those needs and react by telling legislators what they want from education. In the area of TV teaching, lectures are as old fashioned as the

"talking head" in news. Students prefer participating in discussions, seeing and doing. They do not want teachers to lecture endlessly. One reason educational TV was so poorly received in the 1950s was that some teachers were as dull on TV as they were in the live classroom. A media presentation requires more work and preparation than a live classroom presentation, and it requires a person who can compete with the media professionals that today's students see and admire. For years teachers have preferred to believe that a practicing teacher is better able to teach on TV than an actor. Research indicates this claim is nonsense. If given the proper materials or script, an actor could teach as well as anyone.[4] The trend, nevertheless, is toward having effective use of TV by teachers who have the charisma and the ability to perform on TV themselves.

Recognizing that the use of media is one way to get into the apartments and homes of those who do not attend church, the clergy has experimented with ways of making services more widely appealing. Spectacular productions from stadiums, cathedrals and public squares, large casts with huge choirs, audiences in the thousands, contemporary musical arrangements of religious songs that cater to fundamental, foot-tapping rhythms and, in some cases, lavish costumes, ritual and decorum have all contributed to public acceptance of religious services.

But the most dramatic change has been in the clergyman or woman appearing as a performer. Today's pastor is often young and attractive or distinguished and mature, surrounded by youthful participants, colorful settings, fast-paced activities and guest celebrities. An outstanding illustration is Oral Roberts. Dr. Roberts is the force behind Oral Roberts University in Tulsa, where elaborate religious programs are produced on campus in excellent facilities. Each major telecast is professionally designed with a popular, commercial variety format consisting of Roberts, members of his family, especially his son and his son's wife who sing, their friends, university students and nationally known guests. The program is mounted in an elegant setting, usually showing familiar locations such as street scenes, home and church, although the church itself is often suggested more than constructed. During the telecast Roberts takes a few minutes for his sermon in which he alone is featured. The subtle but clearly evident religious nature of the program is delicately balanced with its entertainment values.

Although the established traditional religious community has attempted to use media effectively for years, Roberts and Rev. Billy Graham are probably the principal leaders on television who have attempted consistently to broaden their work to include a mass media following of diverse religious backgrounds. Remarkable exploitation of mass media has been accomplished for shorter duration by Katharine Kuhlmann and leaders of Eastern cults. Of course, Dr. Martin Luther

King promoted the Black Movement through the utilization of mass media during the '60s with a mixture of religious fundamentals and political potency. Media clergy have come a long way from the single-person lectures of Catholic Bishop Fulton J. Sheen in his successful TV series of over 20 years ago. Despite the changes in presenting religious messages outlined above, the rather long personally delivered sermon is still commonly presented on media. The foremost example is radio's longest running series, *The World Tomorrow*, in which Garner "Ted" Armstrong, son of the program's originator, relates current events with Biblical prophecy.

7: The Intangibles

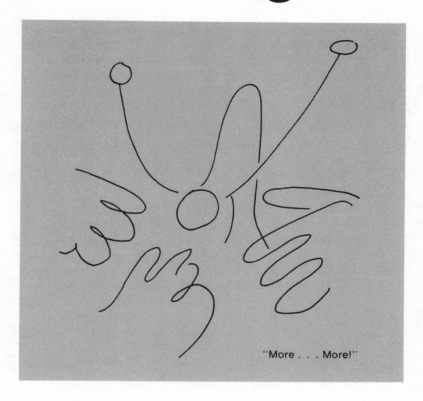

"More . . . More!"

Charisma
Credibility
Traditional Values
Sex Appeal
> Audience Acceptance—The Sex Image (Male Images; Female Images; Bisexual Images; Techniques)— Communicating Sexual Enticement Through Media

Sensationalism
> Risk versus Winning—Capitalizing on Disaster and Human Tragedy—Nudity and Promiscuity

The Violence Syndrome
Timeliness
A Combination of Talents

WHAT MAKES A STAR? No one really knows. After reading many biographies of famous performers, one thing is certain: the magnetism of a star is neither transferable nor completely describable, because the power of a star rests not with the star alone but in combination with the fertile imagination and sensibilities of the listeners and viewers. A performer becomes a star only in proper context. Stardom is not something an agent, producer, coach or someone's mother can superimpose on one who is not basically talented. A star in the heavens, though existent at all times, is appreciated only in the context of evening; the brilliance of a human star is evident only in the context of unusual accomplishment and/or recognition within his or her era. A star is recognized by mass appeal at the box office, radio and TV ratings, income, and by the quality of the performer's work as judged by peers, critics and the public. In general, celebrities might be categorized as well-known, famous and stars.

There are many "stars," a few are great performers. A great performer is remembered because of the significance and quality of that person's contribution. Usually a great performer is, first, linked with history, participating in events of great impact—such as Bob Hope entertaining soldiers during World War II, Korea and Vietnam or Edward R. Murrow reporting the battle of Britain and the McCarthy investigations in the 1950s. Second, a great performer is unique in appearance, voice, movement and/or decision making such as harsh-voiced Harry S Truman who decided to campaign for president by whistle stop, or Rudolf Nureyev who intriguingly blends personality, sexuality and movement in the ballet. Third, a great performer captures public imagination and keeps it, like super MC Ed Sullivan or comedian Jack Benny who were enthusiastically received by the public for decades. Fourth, a great performer gives to the public an original contribution of intellectual (Winston Churchill, Eric Sevareid), artistic (Lena Horne, Vivian Leigh) or physical (Mark Spitz, Bruce Jenner) magnitude. Fifth, a great performer is consistently excellent (Orson Welles, Lucille Ball), rising at times to extraordinary heights.

A great performer is such a powerful human communicator that he or she radiates messages whether in the spotlight or out. Most stars cannot help sending messages—they hope someone out there in the vast unseen public will appreciate them. Unlike a painter, sculptor, writer or composer who absorbs messages, retains them, interprets them and re-expresses them in the form of an entity—a painting, statue, manuscript or composition—great performers cultivate themselves to the extent that every aspect of their beings are attuned to the origination and distribution of emotional and/or intellectual messages which, when focused, reach perfection in public exhibition.

Thus, it is in this ever-changing milieu, this human and historical context, that a performer seeks his or her fortune: the brilliant collisions of talent, preparation, opportunity, history and public appreciation propelling the great performer to sometimes dizzy heights that allow that individual to glitter across all media—or to collapse like a sagging balloon never to rise again.

CHARISMA

Charisma is the ability of a performer to intellectually and/or emotionally reach and touch or stimulate and enchant another person—and in media, perhaps millions of persons. Some performers are more effective "live," some are more effective in media. Some performers have greater charisma in intimate settings, some before throngs. A performer's charisma is conveyed by his or her act. A performer appearing before multitudes often has an overt act such as Elton John who utilizes loud music, colorful costuming and flashy movement.

We like some people and some we don't. The people we like have personal attraction for us—that's charisma. Charisma is sometimes called "magnetism," for it enables a performer to attract the public. Charisma is a hypnotic, powerful fascination that an audience has for a performer. Charisma is innate, a performer is born with it. True, the characteristics of charisma can be enhanced through training, but basically it is *naturally* within a person in varying degrees. In most people, charisma rests at a rather low level, but it is certainly a characteristic of one's friends and neighbors. In everyday discourse, for instance, most people nominally arouse those with whom they come in contact, but they do not stimulate them to an extraordinary level. A performer distills this power and exhibits it under optimum circumstances and does so in an acceptable, pleasurable way so that the public is continually enchanted. Even if the public becomes disenchanted, however, the performer with charisma is likely to return in time to public favor as the irresistible prodigal or black sheep: Richard Burton, Frank Sinatra. The public cannot resist charisma.

Typically, a performer's charisma plays upon a specific response in another individual. Thus, the public may be enchanted by a performer's haunting, pathetic, depraved, silent scream for help as he sings the blues and, yet, may be absolutely repelled by the performer in every other way. Whether emotionally or intellectually appealing, a performer instinctively relates to the audience in an enticing manner, assertively and purposefully arousing the audience. Eisenhower, a rather short man with a round face and a big grin, radiated the kindness of a warm, understanding father figure. Truman, dapper, self-assured, earthy independent who pumped the air with his right hand when delivering a speech, drew great affection from the public for his honest, scrappy, forthright conduct of public affairs. Both presidents had a great deal of personal charisma.

Charisma is charm, a spell that is believable, at least during the course of the performance and often beyond, accounting for the tendency of the public to associate a star's role as a performer with his or her personal life. Gunther Gebel-Williams said in an interview: ". . . many peoples say I have charisma. And nobody knows what is charisma. I don't know. [It's] personality and everything, you know, and [it makes me] look big in my cage. And they see me outside and say, 'Oh, you're so little. You look so big inside,' you know. I think, uh—peoples see something in me when I'm working."[1]

Media enhance charisma. Qualities that bring a performer to public attention are refined and amplified, such as the light, whimsical appeal of Red Buttons, the gentle, romantic adolescence of Richard Thomas as John-Boy in *The Waltons* series, or the heroic concern for the average citizen shown by Randolph Mantooth as star of TV's *Emergency* squad. What is the magnetic appeal of Ryan O'Neal whose media image is aloof, sullen, spoiled yet handsome; or of Glenda Jackson, staunchly independent, liberal, an ambivalent mixture of a sophisticated lady and a tramp; or of Mick Jagger erotic, bisexual, free to do as he pleases, hard working and frail as a steel cable? These qualities, as amplified in media, appeal to the secret desires of great segments of the public and constitute charisma. Every performer has certain qualities an audience likes to watch. The desire of the performer to exude these qualities and for the public to receive them is a shared experience between the performer and the public—that communication or shared experience constitutes charisma.

CREDIBILITY

A young child watching TV asks his mother, "Did this story really happen?" "No," she says, "it is make believe, and those people are actors." Within a short time, the child will be able to judge the credibility of a TV performer for himself. He will eventually adopt a wary attitude, for example, if he finds that toys shown on TV do not live up to the announcer's claim. He will learn which adults to believe, and why— this is credibility. To purveyors of information credibility is essential; yet, recent events have reduced credibility for doctors, lawyers, politicians, military officers and many others because of public disenchantment with people in professions who once were trusted to work for the public good. The bond of trust which the public extended to professions and to business somewhat indiscriminately has been dissolved in favor of a specific trust in the performer: O. J. Simpson for Hertz, Joe Namath and Muhammad Ali for Brute, Carol Lawrence for Maryland Club Coffee, among others. Unfortunately, in recent years many well-known public figures have disappointed us greatly—"let down" the public, as it were.

Unlike purveyors of information, entertainers are expected to be somewhat capricious, unstable, to prevaricate or, at least, stretch and embellish the truth, particularly about their personal lives and achievements. Indeed the press releases of entertainers claiming a long list of superlatives—"marvelous," "best of the year," "fabulous"—are seldom accurate.

This is not to say that entertainers are not believed. The basis of a credible image on mass media for anyone is a look, a voice, a manner that conveys honesty and rationality. Credibility presupposes at least a modicum of intelligent judgment. Sometimes, in fact quite often, a performer can be rather unsophisticated in language, appearance and/or manner, and yet be believed by the mass public. Country and western stars, from Will Rogers to Loretta Lynn, are well known for this. The greatest asset a politician can have is credibility based on public trust. Georgia Governor Jimmy Carter's media believability—his honest look, his reasonable replies—swiftly elevated him from statewide to national attention during his campaign for the presidency in 1976.

To the public, of course, trust in an individual and trust in his or her media image may be different, but not inseparable. The confidence that a politician may generate while sitting in a voter's home drinking tea and discussing the issues of the day, shaking hands or delivering an after-dinner speech creates an illusion that the voter is in some way close to the politician. This impression must then be conveyed through media so that it can be disseminated to vast audiences. The politicians' speeches are written in simple, easy-to-understand terms. Public officials, furthermore, dress conservatively, unless they wish to use an item of clothing for image identification (such as a bow tie). Politicians move gracefully, smoothly and swiftly as though they are in a hurry to meet as many people as they can. Though warm and energetic, they may or may not go in for physical upkeep (facelifts, diets and so on), but they usually keep physically fit and sometimes boast about it—for example, rarely wearing an overcoat even in cold weather. Politicians learn to smile on cue and to be aggressive in shaking hands, such scenes being very popular on media.

TRADITIONAL VALUES

Heroes and heroines, both real and fictional, exist at different levels. All of them preserve to some degree society's noblest traditions and values. The performers who portray these figures in dramas or who are, in fact, these leaders in sports, politics, medicine and so forth serve as an inspiring embodiment of society's noblest traditions. And, because of media, they do so frequently and with great impact. Among a hero's or heroine's noble attributes are

1. A consistent knowledge of and pursuit of what is right and good.
2. An unlimited degree of self sacrifice.
3. An inextinguishable love and understanding of human beings, collectively and individually.

Over the past few decades the media have depicted these heroes and heroines in the throes of an increasingly complex universe confronted with overwhelming terrors. Such a universe preserves the stratification of heroes and heroines familiar to us since ancient times. Simple stratification consists of, first, god-like, super-heroes and heroines with nuclear, atomic, genetic, or bionic characteristics; second, less powerful, extraordinary mortals—police, firemen, professional people and sports stars among others; and, third, ordinary human beings who act bravely under unusual circumstances (Rocky). All of these performers serve in media, and often in their personal lives, as an inspiration especially to youth.

In today's universe the forces of evil often appear to be inundating the forces of good on the one hand and, on the other, in an effort to depict the world "as it really is," heroes and heroines (more often than villians), are depicted in shades of imperfection. Thus, the hero or heroine is presented with a double threat—the legions of evil and his or her own deficiencies. Survival in this world, somewhat paranoid over crisis, becomes even for heroes and heroines more of a challenge and a more admirable attainment. Despite the controversy over violence in media, it must be encouraging on the whole to have these heroes and heroines consistently meet and outwit the foulest of villians and, thereby, reaffirm traditional values of society.

SEXUAL APPEAL

Sex appeal holds an inordinately prominant place in our current society and it is, therefore, important to anyone who utilizes media. Characteristics of sex appeal to men and women vary somewhat, with men seeming to rank visual over auditory enticement and women the reverse. Both notions, are, realistically speaking, largely fantasy of course, but then, media are not reality even in their naturalistic moments. Media are illusion, media are light and shadow, media are impressionistic.

Audience Acceptance

Inasmuch as sex appeal changes considerably with maturation, a brief profile of audiences will aid the performer in judging how to be sexually attractive to different age levels. Audiences of all ages respond to sexual enticement. Children of age six or seven begin observing adult sexual behavior closely. They like to "role play" through dress-up, use of make-up and imitation of adults in language and action. Child performers, on the other hand, have often found media success because of behaving like adults—that is, worldly beyond their years (Tatum O'Neal, Butch Jenkins). Performers should realize that children are extremely observant of sexual references, and that while children may enjoy these references, their parents may object vigorously.

Generally, a teenage audience appreciates the excitement of visual and vocal display, provided that it doesn't go so far as to thoroughly embarrass the teenager in public. If this point is reached, the teenage public may adopt a pseudo blasé attitude and pretend boredom. Teasing, hinting, and suggesting within a romantic sex setting are usually more successful. An audience of young single adults tends to respond more to sex visually and aurally, especially if presented in a light, playful vein. After football superstar Joe Namath made an amusing appearance on TV advertising panty hose, several athletes appeared in ads for men's colorful, bikini underwear. Young married couples tend to like a serious note with women, particularly, looking for marital partners who are kind, steady, loving, understanding and having permanent values appropriate to a continuous relationship. The performer's sexual appeal for this age level is based on ambivalence— implying the wish to get married to the "right person" and settle down, yet still maintaining a fleeting quality of abandon, recklessness or capriciousness. Sex appeal in media performers is insubstantial and ephemeral, and does not lend itself to the constant dependability of monogamous marriage. Thus, performers often keep their own marriages secret, change partners or, at the very least, flirt extensively with audiences. For example, Elvis Presley and Tom Jones, married or not, kiss women and mop their brows with clothing which is later distributed as a souvenir, as part of their act.

A young sex idol may or may not be able to make the transition to mature life and still maintain his or her audience sex appeal. Many child stars illustrate this difficulty—Frankie Avalon, Fabian, Eddie Fisher. During early middle age when young parents are deeply involved in raising their own children and making ends meet financially, the curiosities of sex and romance are dissipated in some members of this audience. Sex appeal intensifies again in the later middle-aged audience which now has grown children and is able to afford more expensive entertainments—Las Vegas attracts a mature public—and the maintenance necessary for the illusion of youth. In other words, this age group has the time to be interested in revitalizing its interest in sexual enticement. This is the period in which middle-aged performers are likely to recondition themselves in body, clothing and manner. A new media image may be quite rejuvenating for a performer and the audience, both coming to a time of deeper appreciation for each other. The public seems to approve of an older person who takes the trouble to cleverly maintain his or her physical appearance. This zeal for preserving a healthy, young look prevails in many people, especially performers who often manage to survive handsomely for many decades, never retiring even though they tend to slow down. Lawrence Welk, Helen Hayes, George Burns, Marlene Dietrich, Dr. Michael DeBakey and many elder statemen have all maintained themselves and their media images through careful personal upkeep and illusion, to the benefit of the public.

The Sex Image

A performer's sexual image is undoubtedly related to physical attractiveness. A pretty girl, a good looking guy have one ingredient for sex appeal; but this is far from enough, for a performer must appear to be attainable and, by reasons of personality, desirable. A performer, therefore, builds sex appeal on these ingredients: a pleasing image, communicating sex through media and the illusion of being available. The latter is accomplished through fan clubs, gossip magazines, media interviews, telephone conversations, public appearances and the distribution of miscellaneous paraphernalia. Sex images are creations; they are designed.

Male Images. The dominant male images are the self-made man—a rugged, free, adventuresome, captivating, usually wealthy, "macho" individual—and the decent guy next door—dependable, marriageable, clean-cut, charming, the backbone of civilization. The former never rests, his business is international, intriguing and often violent. He is self-contained and occasionally super-human: The Six Million Dollar

Man, Agent 007, Batman, Superman, TV cowboys (*Gunsmoke, Bonanza, The Virginian*), detectives (*McCloud, Perry Mason*) and physicians (*Ben Casey, Medical Center*). He uses a woman for his own sexual gratification and cares little for her satisfaction unless the lack thereof demeans his own self-assessment of his sexual prowess. The latter is a regular guy, attractive, perhaps handsome, who will be successful, especially if he gets some help from a woman (*Rich Man, Poor Man*). He may be religious, often has a family and likes parenting (Pat Boone); he may be warm, generous, intelligent (Robert Young as *Marcus Welby, M.D.*). Older men who are less physically attractive may be sexually attractive because they convey an impression of doing the best they can, usually with female assistance, in a complex world. For instance, Peter Boyle as the balding lead in *Joe* or Bob Newhart in his TV series. This fellow is less worldly and experienced, but he retains a youthful charm and awkwardness (James Stewart). Naturally these characteristics are projected in mixed proportions for each male performer, but most men and youths fall into one category or the other at the time they are considered most viable sex images. To a large extent looking "sexy" is a matter of design more than happenstance. To illustrate: according to uniform manufacturers athletes are "very fussy" about the fit of their uniforms. "They all want custom tailoring and tight pants." "I can't condemn a player for wanting to look sexy," said Charles O. Finley. "Maybe the females will come out to the park more."[2] In recent years double knit uniforms, flyless pants, striped waistbands, and pullover tops have found a place in baseball, along with the unique style of such crowd pleasers as Willie Mays and Mark "the Bird" Fidrych.

Female Images. The principal female images to their male counterparts are the breathtakingly beautiful, self-confident, sexually Platonic goddesses who dwell in media fantasyland, often helping an inadequate, although handsome and charming, male (Elizabeth Montgomery as Samantha in *Bewitched,* Barbara Eden as Jeannie in *I Dream of Jeannie,* Lynda Carter as Wonder Woman and Diana Prince in *Wonder Woman*), and the girl next door who is an ideal marital partner. Most women portrayed in media are of the former category. They are indestructible females (Barbara Stanwyck in *The Big Valley*) who are at least as durable as males. They make their emotional suffering known outwardly as did Greta Garbo, but their internal fortitude consisting of great common sense, integrity, an unflinching set of values, overwhelming optimism and confidence in their capabilities enable them to rectify the troubles of their family, friends and, if need be, the world eventually to reign supreme (Sada Thompson as the mother in *Family*) whether they are soap opera heroines or those incredibly gorgeous sex symbols whose images reside forever on the media's Olympus (*Charlie's Angels*).

The other popular female sex image—the girl next door—is often vulnerable. She makes mistakes, she's zany (Lucy, Mary Tyler Moore, Rhoda, Laverne and Shirley), but in quieter moments she can be loving, kind, sincere, bright, gracious, understanding and absolutely devoted to her boyfriend or husband. Barbra Streisand plays this role in many of her films. Older women are especially steadfast. Some women, when older, may lose their physical attractiveness by getting heavy or looking matronly, but they remain sexually viable because of a deeper commitment which they often have for an aging male companion whom they support, whether or not they approve of his actions (he may be an alcoholic, gambler, philanderer or desperado). Their faith or love for him may continue until he casts them out by looking for another woman, often younger or wealthier (Simone Signoret in *Room at the Top*). If, however, a woman takes a young lover, he may be characterized as naive or opportunistic, but she is frequently the more emotionally complex, intelligent, worldly and powerful of the two (Warren Beatty as Paulo and Vivian Leigh as Mrs. Stone in *The Roman Spring of Mrs. Stone;* the 17-year-old son on *Family* falls in love with a female cinematographer twice his age).

Bisexual Images. Duality in male and female sex images has always existed. Until recently, society usually expressed extreme disfavor with bisexuality. However, with emergence of the unisex concept generated in part from women's liberation and greater public tolerance of homosexuals, bisexuality has become more prominent and will continue to be so as years go by. Men have frequently played female roles in media, and on stage it is a tradition for men to do so as in Shakespearean plays; women have likewise played male parts. But an image in which a male or female actively reverses sex roles, other than in comedy like Flip Wilson's "Geraldine," must be played with great strength so that the principal sexual identity of the performer will not be blurred. For example, John Davidson could appear as a female impersonator in *The Streets of San Francisco* without jeopardizing his male image. Bisexual relationships expressed overtly or implied by performers have a place, for they touch upon deep ambivalance in the sexual composition of the public itself.[3]

Techniques. Performers purposely create broad sexual appeal for both sexes. This is to say that both sexes want to be attractive to both sexes, although normally and popularly a heterosexual relationship is dominant. Beyond the descriptions mentioned in earlier chapters on appearance, voice and movement, a performer emphasizes those areas of the body which convey sexual promise—typically and obviously:

1. Through tight clothing—both sexes wearing clothing to reveal cleavage, the shape and placement of nipples, buttocks and genitals.

2. Through movement that draws attention to sex organs by means of undulation, body position, and intimation through walking and dancing.

3. Through voice by means of innuendo, double-entendre and inflection that conveys the suggested availability of the performer for sexual activity. The best opportunity for a performer to convey this enticement is in fictional roles, but this image may be extended to interviews and public appearances, especially for entertainers, as a performer's media image and actual life become inseparable. For example, a Hollywood reporter touched and held the hand of a young TV star during the course of an interview.

4. Through nudity by appearing in various states of undress—once called "cheesecake" for women and "beefcake" for men. In silent films, Rudolph Valentino frequently appeared nude from the waist up for at least one scene and Gloria Swanson got in and out of several baths. By the mid-'70s complete nudity for performers was quite common in cinema and not infrequent on television.

Communicating Sexual Enticement Through Media

Sexual enticement in media combines two basic characteristics—warmth and energy, that is, being "nice" to everyone so that everyone will be interested in the performer as being physically capable and, indeed, eager for sex. After energy and warmth, other characteristics have less universal appeal. Power, for instance, in some performers, even arrogance, will be appealing to some people in an audience but not to others. Gentleness, even sweetness, will have a mixed response, and so a performer concentrates upon enticing everyone, so to speak, without turning anyone away, which results in presumably favorable audience feedback. To illustrate: while the Six Million Dollar Man may be expected by mass audience to consort only with young, beautiful women, he (his image) should not suggest that he is unavailable to older, less attractive women. Often female performers are seemingly attracted to mature, and sometimes powerful, men but they (their images) should not be altogether unavailable to younger men.

Daring is sexually attractive and has wide appeal. Daring to an older audience may be interpreted as foolishness, and so there is a limitation. Sexual daring is not necessarily the same as physical daring exhibited, for example, by a TV detective, although physical daring may reinforce the attractiveness of the TV detective (Baretta). Sexual daring is illustrated by the young rock star who suggests by unbuckling his pants that he is going to expose himself in public or by the movie ingénue who wears a see-through gown, goes braless or without under garments. In another kind of daring, performers who do something illegal, whether or not as part of their fictional characterizations—such as petty theft, smoking marajuana, gambling money or their lives—may be sexually attractive.

Sexual identity is an appealing characteristic. The public responds best to a clear, positive, simplistic sex image: a man who looks and acts like a man or a woman who is sufficiently feminine. With some exceptions, a performer's sexual identity should be unmistakable. The sexual appeal of a male ballet dancer is far greater to a mass audience if he dances without feminine characteristics. The infusion of female movement by male dancers has probably done more to harm public interest in the ballet than anything else. In recent years mass media have tended to force dancers into more positive sexual orientation in regard to their public images.

It is fundamental to suppose that everyone likes to think of himself or herself as sexually promising to one or both sexes. Sex appeal is based more or less on the notion that the performer, if given the chance, would seduce everyone in the audience. The larger the number of people who think they want to be seduced, the more influential the performer. While social mores tend to lessen the obviousness of such an appeal for politicians, clergy, teachers and others, sex appeal in some of them is still there and, though perhaps latent, is a powerful instrument in getting and holding public attention. A priest, who projects a "sexy" media image, as it were, can be a highly potent propagator of the faith. In advertising where 90 per cent of the effectiveness of an ad may be to get audience attention, some research indicates that as much of 50 per cent of advertising uses sex to sell things.

SENSATIONALISM

A sensational act results in tremendous publicity for the performer within a short time span, such as a so-called "overnight sensation." This means that the performer has received worldwide news coverage or headlines: "Lindburgh Flies the Atlantic," "Man on the Moon." A sensational act is frequently so impressive that witnesses believe they have experienced one of the great moments of their lives, perhaps of history. A sensational act shows human beings overcoming extraordinary circumstances or exhibiting extraordinary abilities or charcteristics. In the noblest tradition these acts, if uncalculated, produce heroes; more commonly, however, these acts are calculated or contrived. A performer may hope to be the right person in the right place at the right time, but significant historical events will not cross the paths of most performers. They must, therefore, take a calculated risk to obtain attention, such as by gambling their lives or well being. Thus, they must create the illusion of being sensational, such as by becoming very skillful through extremely hard work—often at something that few other people would want to do—for example, a magician using dangerous wild animals in a magic act like Siegfried and Roy, "The World's Greatest Illusionists." Sensationalism in a lesser form, still very effective, is the exhibition of a deformity, such as a side show attraction. Sensationalism can exist or be induced by taking chances and winning against great odds, by human disaster and tragedy, by extreme novelty, deformity and the bizarre, and by extraordinary artistic, scientific and/or intellectual achievement.

Risk versus Winning

The reality or illusion of risking life and limb at any price is a device centuries old. Whether going over Niagara Falls in a barrel or Snake Canyon in a jet cycle, the element of extravagant risk is the same. High wire artists, sword swallowers, movie stunt people, auto racers, certain skiers and divers, wild animal trainers and war correspondents are some of the performers who gain attention through personal jeopardy. The public enjoys seeing pugilistic matches: human beings against nature or against themselves. Fighting with swords, chains, fists, clubs and guns are skills that have been demonstrated for ages as entertainment. Today's arena exhibition in the boxing ring, the football field, motocross, hot rod racing or Kung Fu contests is less likely to be destructive and, yet, with the bullfight, the performer (the *Torero*) carries out the ritual to the death, a descendant of bloody earlier exhibitions. Today there are more humane rules and protective shields such as helmets, expensively designed equipment and machines like sleek cars that surround performers. These people are bound to get a certain amount of publicity and money from exhibiting themselves to the extent that the person who performs these unusual deeds becomes a marketable property in his or her own right; that is, his or her person becomes valuable.

Winners are marketable. A winner accomplishes something unusual, and the public is often willing to view the winner live and/or in media. A beauty contest winner, an Olympic medalist, a home team football star, an extremely wealthy person who made money with little or no assistance, a vote-getter with an unexpectedly large plurality, a scientist who is identified with conquering a disease or anyone who has won against great odds, including the handicapped, are examples. Distinguished claims like those in the *Guinness Book of World Records* may in themselves give an individual performer status. Olympic medal winners Sonja Henie, Johnny Wiessmuller, Jesse Owens, and Cathy Rigby all became media celebrities. Media have made performers out of some astronauts such as Frank Borman for Eastern Airlines, the former

Princess Luciana Pignatelli Avedon for beauty products, and fashion designers Messrs. Blass, Cartier, Pucci and Givenchy for Lincoln Mark IV automobiles. These people have demonstrated extraordinary success, sometimes at personal risk.

Capitalizing on Disaster and Human Tragedy

Journalists feed on disaster and human tragedy, often at great personal risk to themselves. It is estimated that a journalist's career might be advanced five years or more if he or she can be assigned to a war zone, because the frequency of getting a story on the air increases tremendously, and the reporter is almost always visually and/or vocally involved. If a journalist is to gain and hold public attention, the reporter must be involved in "hot" or important news stories, preferably sensational ones. "It's easier to get to the top than it is to stay there," CBS correspondent Dan Rather has said. Nearly every network newscaster who is recognizable by the general public was brought to national attention by reporting a major story—Edward R. Murrow, the battle of Britain; Charles Murphy, the Kennedy assassination; Morley Safer, the Vietnam village burning.

Nudity and Promiscuity

Sex is sensational, and some performers are skillful in promoting themselves through sex. Nudity and promiscuity, especially among the wealthy and famous, do a great deal to attract the public. When Brigitte Bardot was in her prime, news photographers were always trying to take pictures of her in the nude. Misapplied sex scandals—that is, those not designed to promote someone's career—have ruined the careers of some performers, or at least diminished them so substantially that they were never able to regain public enthusiasm. This was true of the sex scandals in the movie industry during the early 1920s and of certain Congressmen in the '70s. Performers should use nudity and promiscuity as tools to advance their careers, if they depend on sex to build their images. The movements of Hoochie Koochie dancer Fatima at the turn of the century, the nearly nude fan dancing of Sally Rand and the verbal innuendoes of Mae West during the '30s, the plunging necklines of TV's Faye Emerson, suggestive antics of Eddie Cantor in the '40s, and the pelvic undulations of Elvis Presley during the '50s are just a few examples of the performers who have been partially censored or barred from mass media only to enhance their public demand. By the mid-1960s emphasis shifted from prohibition to exhibition of nudity and promiscuity in sexually-arousing performers. Partial nudity began appearing in some dramas and documentaries, some dancers depended on more explicit movement and sheer leotards, and some musicians like Jimi Hendricks overtly converted microphones and musical instruments into symbols of sexual enticement. Robert Fletcher's male costumes for the American Conservatory Theatre's 1976 production of "The Taming of the Shrew" (PBS) flaunted a jock strap pouch which Marc Singer as Petruchio aggressively strutted before TV cameras, thus adding a new vitality to Shakespeare.[4]

THE VIOLENCE SYNDROME

Violence in its many facets—from pathological sadism to mass devastation, from minimum visual display (a puff of gunsmoke and the bad guy falls) to the execution scenes in *Taxi Driver*—fascinates the public. The American public is entertained by an endless parade of violence in mass media, patronizing those programs and idolizing those performers who appear on them: *Kojak, Petrocelli, Starsky and Hutch, Police Woman, MacMillan and Wife*—15 or more program series with violent heroes and heroines each season. By the mid-'70s approximately one-third of all network TV programming concerned police or criminals. Why the public is so tremendously enchanted by violence is the subject of on-going examination and research. The performers themselves have certain characteristics which appeal to the public rather consistently. These performers are strong, physically and mentally; they are in full control in moments of disaster. They are invulnerable—the public knows they must return next week, and though hurt will not die. They are ingenious in outwitting their adversaries; no challenge is too great. They are almost without compassion, usually disassociate their exposure to violence from sentiment. Therefore, a little blood or a lot of it, a small wound or a big one, a body intact or one brutalized is, after all, just another body, and there are a lot more where they came from. The supply of human corpses exceeds the number of investigators to the point that they are simply decorations of the environment in which the performer demonstrates his or her endurable qualities—supreme confidence, elegant strength, incisive decision-making and, most of all, virtual indestructibility. International film and TV stars Charles Bronson and Clint Eastwood portray relentless assassins who exterminate human targets with the admirable precision of master craftsmen. Thus, for the performer the death of the target and/or the assassin merely signals the end of the play. What is important is the parade of intriguing qualities that the performer exhibits to the public before the play's ultimate climax, for these qualities are then associated with the performer, the good ones outweighing the bad according to the intentions of the performer, scriptwriters and promoters.

TIMELINESS

Some performers have an accurate sense of timeliness. Their material is in sympathy with the mood of the public. They express the deep, internal feelings of the public by bringing them to the conscious level. The TV series *All In the Family* has brilliantly done this. The performers created characterizations clearly enough to enable the public to identify with them in vast numbers. *Mary Hartman, Mary Hartman* is likewise attuned to the times as it lampoons the day-to-day melodramatic experiences portrayed on soap operas. Performers who are participants in programs which are so timely often become famous themselves, although the characters they portray may be even better known: "Archie" Bunker (played by Carroll O'Connor), "Maude" (Beatrice Arthur), "Rhoda" (Valerie Harper), "Mary Hartman" (Louise Lasser). Predecessors of these TV series were the critical, satirical comedians of the 1960s such as Lenny Bruce, Mort Sahl, Godfrey Cambridge and the Smothers Brothers who seized upon the timeliness of their observations using an earthy manner, four-letter language, folksy urban humor and at times the smart "in thing," audience abuse, which is carried to extremes in the comedy adlibs of Don Rickles. Once that period of public introspection waned, however, the comedians had to turn to something else, and they often found that difficult because of being so strongly identified by the public with a certain period.

Timeliness is more than delivering topical gags or sketches about current events, however beneficial these might be; timeliness may be happenstance, such as a reaction to the previous period of entertainment. Rock and roll, for instance, was as much a reaction to the melodic, whistle-able, understandable tunes of the previous decades, as it was a furthering of the fast tempo dance crazes. Timeliness is being a minority or female performer when the public is in a mood to view their acts. A timely performer personifies the era, whether or not he or she understands it.

A COMBINATION OF TALENTS

A performer may have many abilities. After becoming well known in one area, he or she has a platform from which to present other abilities. The public refreshes its interest in the performer, because he or she reveals new personality dimensions. Very often these secondary abilities do not shine to the same extent as the original talent, but they are acceptable. For instance, many actors on occasion try singing, although they may be rather weak singers. The attempt does not reduce the public's respect for their primary ability (Jack Palance, Kirk Douglas). Frank Sinatra, with a declining career as a vocalist during the late 1940s and early '50s, gave a stirringly dramatic, non-singing performance as Angelo Maggio in *From Here To Eternity,* re-establishing his reputation as a major star and then going on to new heights as a singer.

Less well exploited is the performer who has intellectual interests, such as Peter Ustinov, a playright as well as an actor. Performers who show interests in social causes—Robert Redford, land conservation; Bing Crosby, wild life preservation; Marlon Brando, Indian rights; Jane Fonda, anti-war campaigns—sometimes touch upon other interests that the public finds attractive, and these enterprises help to sustain the performer especially when he or she is not working. Medical telethons and sports tournaments keep the names of certain performers alive even though they may have little to do with them. Many performers go back to school to broaden areas of interest that they neglected while trying to pursue their profession. Many travel, and some engage more or less actively in other businesses when their peak popularity declines. A few have accepted appointments in government (Pearl Bailey as representative to the United Nations, Shirley Temple Black as ambassador to Ghana) or have been elected to public office (California Governor Ronald Reagan, United States Senator George Murphy). Journalists must be extremely versatile, knowing a little bit about a lot of things though specializing in content areas such as local politics, science, the arts, sports or weather. They often appear in fund raising events for community activities, thus expanding and enhancing their celebrity status. For instance, celebrity tennis and golf.

8: Abnormalities

"The truth is, doc, I enjoy my problems."

Overcoming Physical Disabilities

Medical Treatment (Speech; Sight: Glasses, Contact Lenses, Blindness; Hearing)—Reshaping the Body (Abdomen; Breasts; Buttocks and Thighs)—Reshaping the Face (Face-lifts; Complexion; Nose; Teeth; Hair)

Emotional Control

Self-Confidence—Frustration—Psychological Aptitude—Nervousness (Pre-performance Nervousness; Nervousness During Performance; Post-performance Nervousness)—Forgetfulness—Methods of Relief (Stimulants; Depressants; Meditation; Commonsense)

Many performers suffer from physical handicaps. Loss of sight or hearing, facial deformities and missing limbs are more commonplace than one might suppose. Artificial ears, eyes, noses, jaws, teeth, breasts, thighs, buttocks, upper arms, shoulders, knees, hands and elbows are some of the available prosthetic devices. For every ten women who have their faces lifted two or three men have cosmetic plastic surgery. Where surgery is indicated, the author advocates it, after having seen the advantages to students who have had noses, chins, breasts and teeth repaired. Most performers disguise their handicaps; a few capitalize on them. British plastic surgeon Dr. Ivor Feldstein predicts that politicians will be the one occupational group most likely to take advantage of cosmetic surgery in the future. In 1972, Georgia's lieutenant governor Lester Maddox acquired a new hairpiece, eyeglasses, dental plate and a hearing aid. "If nothing else breaks down," said Maddox, "I'll be in pretty good shape." Maddox ran for president in 1976. That same year Alabama governor George Wallace ran an intensive campaign for the presidency despite being confined to a wheel chair. Wallace frequently reminded voters that such a limitation did not prohibit President Franklin D. Roosevelt from winning office four times.

Performers suffer from untold internal and external limitations. Alec Templeton, George Shearing and Stevie Wonder, though blind, have displayed their musical talents with great success. Patricia Neal, crippled by a stroke, triumphed over this handicap to act again; years earlier Arthur Godfrey, despite being severely injured in an automobile accident, became a household word on radio and television. Performers are jeopardized only if their talent is diminished by the handicap or if they cannot physically or psychologically express themselves because of the handicap. Thus, it is critical for performers to channel their talents, so that they can maximize their abilities whatever they are. Handicapped or not, the drive to be a performer must come from the talented individual. It is not easy for anyone to be successful as a performer, and for the handicapped person it is especially difficult, because few station owners, producers and agents will bother with handicapped people when they can place or use others so much more readily. The handicapped person has to show that he or she is worth the added attention required.

In the last analysis, a performer must consider two things: Is the handicap apparent to the public, and is it so severe that the performer cannot function? If the answer is "yes" in the first case, the handicapped performer will probably want to disguise the handicap or make it more obvious and capitalize on it. If the answer is "yes" in the second case, the handicapped performer will probably want to develop related talents—compose music, for example if playing the piano is physically impossible, for he or she must make the rational judgment that it would be futile to pursue the first choice.

OVERCOMING PHYSICAL DISABILITIES

Frequently handicapped performers do not like to appear on television, because they are self conscious. Some of them do find a place in radio or other media where the performer is less visible. Blind children, especially those who have never been able to see, learn a great deal from media and are quite willing to participate. The determining factor is usually the parents. Both reluctant parents and children should be encouraged to appear on television, for the public becomes more tolerant through such exposure. The handicapped should be placed in situations which emphasize their skills, rather than their deficiencies. They should be attractively clothed and, for instance, if customary to a blind child, he or she should wear dark or smoked glasses, so that no visual deformity detracts from the overall personality of the individual or from the message. All handicapped persons should be shot with great care by the director so that they appear as attractive or acceptable as possible.

People with palsy, muscular dystrophy, multi-handicaps and other visual and oral disabilities are unique. Their disabilities can be severe, but their media appearances can be outstanding. One instance that comes to mind is an interview with poetess Vassar Miller. Ms. Miller is severely limited in the movement of her head, neck, arms and body—in fact, she could utter only a few words. The interviewer asked Miller questions that required very short answers. Then the interviewer read some of Miller's poetry while the director superimposed a tight closeup of Miller's expressive face as she reacted to the words she had written, but could not speak. The result was a moving portrait of a fine writer.

On the other hand, one of the least effective ways of presenting a handicapped person in visual media is to raise funds for the performer's affliction. Too often this exposure is embarrassing, and designed in part, moreover, to promote the reputation of a celebrity. Children are frequently the pawns in these fund drives, being asked to praise, hug or show appreciation to the stranger (celebrity) emceeing the telethon show. Exhibition of terminal cases is maudlin. Emphasis would be better placed on films or tapes showing the afflicted children in therapy, utilized in research or other forms of constructive progress.

Medical Treatment

It is assumed that a physician will be consulted in regard to the discussions that follow. Competent plastic surgeons, for example, may be found by calling your county medical society. The point is that very often performers do not have to suffer from deformities or handicaps, if they receive proper medical attention—preferably applied early in their careers. Although cosmetic surgery has become much more popular in recent years, it is still a long way from being universally accepted or, indeed, affordable to the general public. Rio de Janeiro, with more than 500 doctors, specializing in plastic surgery, has emerged as the plastic surgery capital of the world. Plastic surgeons estimate that just about any upper class Brazilian woman past 40 has undergone some form of aesthetic surgery; moreover, in recent years, about 20 per cent of such operations have been performed on middle-aged men.[1]

Speech. Many speech defects are clearly physical. They are usually associated with a malformation in the mouth or elsewhere in the speech anatomy. Most of such defects—cleft palate and lips, improperly formed jaws, missing teeth, improper closure, nodules on the vocal cords—are detected early in life, and are corrected today through modern techniques. Thus, many problems of lisping and faulty language reproduction are eliminated. While the organic problems may be eliminated by a physician, the functional disorders in learning how to use articulators to produce proper speech may require the services of a speech therapist. One of the most baffling speech disorders has been stuttering. The precise cause is unknown, but it is believed to be emotional, at least in part. Several highly successful performers have speech defects, and have overcome them or have effectually capitalized on them. Mel Tillis, a singer, songwriter, comedian and TV personality is known as an entertainer who stutters except when he sings. In 1976, Tillis was voted "Entertainer of the Year" by the Country Music Association.

Sight. A few performers work without glasses or contact lenses, even though they need them. They memorize where to stand, and they know their lines. It has been said that Rudolph Valentino's black-eyed seductive look resulted partly because he could not see well; and various women have gone before cameras barely able to find their marks. Although poor eyesight can be a detriment in such cases, usually it is not. One attractive, myopic news anchorperson, who cannot wear contact lenses, has a prompter mounted on her desk. She can read the news without glasses and yet retain contact with the audience by looking directly into the camera lens.

Glasses. If vanity permitted, almost every performer would wear glasses or contact lenses. Glasses add an element to the face; indeed, some glasses are very attractive and become a recognizable part of the individual. Elton John is supposed to have hundreds of pairs; some years ago MC Allan Ludden looked quite scholarly hosting the *General Electric College Bowl* in dark-rimmed glasses; after years of reporting without them, anchormen Chet Huntley and Frank McGee subsequently always wore glasses on camera. Glasses, rimmed or rimless, plain or glittery are often prominent during awards programs. One reason for not wearing glasses is that they obscure expression in the eyes, a main asset for actors. Another reason is lighting—the glass and rims cause unattractive reflections, lines and shadows on the eyes and face. Some newsmen are in the habit of peering just under or over the rims, resulting in a weird half-pupil effect. So, if possible, avoid glasses. Notice, for instance, that the principal announcers for those commercials advertising eyewear seldom wear glasses themselves during the commercial. If, however, glasses are part of a performer's appearance like John Denver's and have been for many years, as they were part of President Lyndon Johnson's, then by all means wear them (Johnson switched to contact lenses during his presidency).

Contact Lenses. Contact lenses are preferable to glasses, because they are less noticeable and require little special lighting. Occasionally contacts are hard to wear under bright TV lights, causing excessive tearing and eye irritation, but this can be eliminated by asking the director to change the direction or to lower the intensity of the lights. A performer must be strongly motivated to wear contacts in order to build up an initial tolerance for the hard lenses; they can be bothersome until they have seated themselves properly on the eyes. Soft lenses, now in wide use, are fragile but easier to wear. Contact lenses come in various colors and can be used to intensify the natural color of the eyes or, in some cases, change it. The main thing is to get a good fit from a competent, optometrist so that the contacts can be worn imperceptibly. Inasmuch as they come in various sizes, from just barely covering the pupil and iris to covering the entire eye, some contact lenses may be noticeable in camera closeups. No performer should tolerate a wide-eyed, blinking, watery appearance from an improper fit.

Blindness. Blindness does not prohibit a person from appearing in mass media. Some exciting performers have been blind or partially sighted—Sammy Davis, Jr., for instance. Some politicians and radio personalities are blind. Radio serves the blind community handily. Blind disc jockeys have to memorize the audio console, and become very efficient in operating it. For a TV appearance, a blind person should seek the help of a sighted person who will manage the details of grooming. A "sharp looking" blind performer is an inspiration to everyone. Dark glasses are symbolic—an audience wants to know whether a performer is truly blind—but colored, even glittery ones, are in vogue. Ronnie Milsap wore glittering yellow ones for the 10th annual Country Music Association's TV awards program (1976). Carefully tied neckwear and well-maintained clothing give the blind performer energy and style. This type of person already has audience appeal, for the mass media image of a blind person is sincere, honest, usually handsome, intelligent and having super sensitivity in the remaining senses. James Franciscus portrayed such a blind lawyer in TV's *Longstreet;* and in that same tradition a Houston police officer, blinded in the line of duty, promoted the police department through frequent TV appearances.

Hearing. Hearing aids are so small, and can be concealed so readily within the ear and covered by hair, that they are not noticeable. An important (and often degrading) image-stereotype implying incompetence or aging exists for those performers who wear them, therefore, most performers do not reveal that they wear such aids. A few entertainers, like singer Johnny Ray, do wear one obviously and admirably for the purpose it was intended.

Reshaping the Body.

Cosmetic surgery on the body principally concerns two areas: the breasts and the buttocks, occasionally the abdomen.

Abdomen. Sometimes sagging muscles and a protruding stomach may be strengthened or reshaped through surgery.

Breasts. Breasts can be made larger or smaller, or altogether reshaped and reproportioned. To increase breast size, the insertion of a transplant (costing from about $175 to $200) can often be made through an incision under the breast which will not be noticeable. The surgical work for this procedure may cost another $750 to $1,500, and swelling may last as long as three months. Some women have resorted to silicone injection to enlarge their breasts, but this is considered dangerous. Reducing the size of breasts, or reshaping sagging ones, may be a more complex operation causing more noticeable scarring and possible damage to nerve endings, but this risk may be relatively unimportant compared to the desirable results of the operation.

Buttocks and Thigh. These parts of the body can be successfully reshaped. Portions of the thigh, and medial and latter buttocks, such as caused by "riding breeches" deformity, can be cut away. The cost of this operation is roughly estimated at $1,500.

Reshaping the Face.

While no decision requiring surgery should be made casually, some considerations are improvement of features, accessibility of physicians and medical facilities, and expense. Because the face receives the most attention on media, it is the area that many people would like to change.

Houston television personality, Marvin Zindler, has undergone plastic surgery: "Now, if I didn't have the face I have, I wouldn't have the job I have. Television just ain't going to have you around if you are ugly. I know that from experience. It's a fact of life." During the first surgery in 1955, Zindler insisted on tranquilizers and local anesthetics:

> With Marvin fully conscious and giving muffled suggestions, the doctor inserted a scapel in each nostril and cut all the skin away from the formative cartilage areas of the nose. The nostrils were then stretched and expanded to several times usual size with a special instrument to allow for larger surgical tools in the nasal area. Working inside the nose with surgical clippers, the doctor cut out a canoe-shaped portion of the cartilage that had formed the hump. Then with assorted tools resembling chisels and gouges, the doctor hammered away, pulverizing the supportive cartilage and bone. Once this was fragmented, a new nose could be shaped in much the same manner as modeling clay.
>
> Delicate scalpel work was performed to excise the skin from the nose, separating it from underneath in an expanding arc towards the cheeks. Once the base of Marvin's new nose was formed with the deft fingers of the doctor, the excess skin could be "ironed" outwards with the fingers. It soon shrinks into place and grows again to the fleshy part of the face. The inside casing of the nose cavity was sewn back into place. The result: a new nose, a relaxed mouth, and no cuts on the outside of the face.
>
> To strengthen the receding chin, the doctor pulled out the lower lip and made a long incision between the lip and the lower gum. Further deepening cuts exposed the bone of the chin itself. Cartilage from a medical bank was inserted and fastened in a carefully shaped fashion about the chin portion of Marvin's skull. Then the flesh was replaced, stretching enough to cover the implant.[2]

Facelifts. The mature performer may consider a facelift. Gary Cooper admitted he had a facelift before his last movie. Creased skin between eyebrows, sagging folds around eyes, jaws and neck can be stretched to the hairline where excess tissue is removed and incisions are relatively unnoticed. The operation can be performed under local anesthesia. According to one New York plastic surgeon, Dr. William

Thomas Keavey, it is easier for a woman to attain the hollow-cheeked Greta Garbo look than the young, plump-faced appearance of Marilyn Monroe. The face becomes somewhat slimmer with years, and skin tucks at the ear level, supplemented by some behind the hairline, will restore the nice taut look that accents the bones and slenderizes the cheeks. "The skin is not as elastic the second time, so it will hold much longer, perhaps indefinitely," said Keavey. "Also, if there were unsuccessful scars the first time, they can be hidden." His own suture technique generally follows natural folds and curves of the skin, rather than making a straight line, which the eye is quick to notice.[3] Although swelling may take a month to six weeks to completely subside and the face may be a year "settling," many performers such as comedienne Phyllis Diller believe it is worth it.[4] "When you look so much better, you feel so much better" is a common reaction. A facelift without redoing the eyes costs from $1,500 to $2,500.

Complexion. Perhaps the greatest physical asset a performer can have is smooth, clear skin. More than 80 per cent of adolescents, however, are affected by acne; the trouble begins about age 12, reaching its peak at 16 and then tapering off and disappearing during the early 20s. Although about 20 per cent of these young people have severe acne, physicians have treated it successfully with vitamin A acid and benzoyl hydroxide, and in recent years major clinics have been established for the treatment of acne. Performers who have severe problems should get treatment as soon as possible, so that facial tissue will not be scarred. Damaged skin requires surgical techniques wherein the face is sanded to remove the outer layers of the skin so that a smoother layer will replace it. Often this procedure is unable to restore a smooth surface to the face, especially where pock marks and ridges of damaged tissue exist from improper treatment, such as squeezing pimples. Experimenting with the skillful application of make-up, a slightly defocused lens on closeups and careful lighting—perhaps with intense light from behind and soft light from in front of the performer—will soften the complexion defects that are noticeable to an audience.

Damage to the complexion may be caused by allergies rather than acne. Allergies to food and various factors in a performer's environment such as make-up, fibers in clothing, animals and many other things may cause skin irratations that are often mistaken for acne. Lanolin and certain other ingredients are common causes of allergies for some performers, but a complete line of non-allergenic make-up is available. Some food dispensed in vending machines and eaten by performers during rehearsal breaks may also cause allergies: chocolate, nuts, cheese and milk are among them. Too much sun and one's own perspiration can be detrimental to the skin. Competent medical advice from qualified physicians is the best way to remedy these problems.

Nose. A common alteration of the nose is a reshaping of the cartilage or bone at the bridge to straighten the nose and give it a smaller
appearance. The patient is totally sedated under local anesthesia, while
the surgeon performs this operation by inserting instruments up the
nostrils. The surface skin is not broken. This procedure costs from
$750 to $2,500, depending upon what alterations are necessary. An example is reshaping of the nostrils. Singer J. P. Morgan once said that
plastic surgery on her nose and chin changed her life.

Teeth. The public expects reasonably good looking teeth. Crooked
teeth should be straightened. Frequently this is done in adolescence.
The procedure consists of wiring the teeth so that they will gradually
straighten over a period of a few months to a few years with the patient
returning to the dentist periodically for adjustments in the braces. No
one likes to have this done, regardless of age, but attractive teeth are
essential to a performer. This cost ranges from a few hundred to a few
thousand dollars.

For obvious reasons, noticeable gold and silver fillings, dark and/or
chipped front teeth are not suitable for TV and film closeups. An exception to having her teeth repaired is actress Gene Tierney: "When I
went to Hollywood they wanted to straighten my teeth, but my father
and the country's leading orthodontist had written into my movie contract that they were never to be straightened or capped because changing them would have affected my mouth, my smile and even my facial
bone structure, probably causing more problems than would have been
corrected. It seems to have been an advantage in a time of glossy, look-
alike glamour. I was myself, and believe me that was rare."[5]

Usually, faulty teeth are capped. The procedure consists of grind-
ing the natural tooth to the shape of a small *post.* The post is then fitted
with an enamel-looking artificial tooth, or cap, that matches the color of
the other teeth and extends under the gumline so that the edge does
not show. The cap is a permanent replacement for the deteriorated
tooth. The cost for each cap begins at about $125. An entire set of caps
may cost from $4,000 to $25,000, depending on the dentist, the complexity of the undertaking and the location, the higher rates tending to
be in Hollywood. Often performers cannot afford such an expense,
and so they can sometimes have this work done at dental schools,
where dental students do the work under faculty supervision. Under
these circumstances the performer pays for little more than the cost of
materials.

An Atlanta dentist, Dr. Ronald E. Goldstein, president of the
American Academy of Esthetic Dentistry, has developed an economical
method of cosmetic contouring of teeth. "We start out by etching the
teeth with buffered acid which roughens the surface of the teeth. And

then we end up by applying a thickened resin, which can be used to alter the shape or shade of the teeth, creating an attractive veneer. Sometimes teeth are crowded or misshapen. Such conditions can be alleviated to some extent with cosmetic contouring. Here we try to create an illusion of straightening."[6]

Hair. Hair is a sign of youth. Many men lose their hair at an early age, but women seldom do. Four common ways to enhance one's hair are by means of wigs, hairweaving, transplants, and implants. Ironically, some women buy wigs and hairpieces as casually as they purchase new clothes, but men generally consider such purchases unmanly. Nevertheless, male performers, particularly if they are sex attractions, buy natural looking toupees of various shapes, sizes and colors. Among them are William Shatner, Burt Reynolds, Johnny Mathis, Larry Hagman and Charlton Heston. According to Ben Z. Kaplan, Universal Winners, New York, a realistic toupee is made by crocheting the hair into a sheer netting or lace, which is then gummed into the scalp with a double faced tape and liquid adhesive at the hairline and a little below. When done properly, and with additional make-up, it is undetectable. "Many movie stars continue to wear this type to the present day. However, it is such a headache to put on and take off that some of the old-timers like Fred Astaire and John Wayne, have taken up a more modern type of hairpiece which can be applied in about 20 seconds." A recent type of wig making is hair weaving. This method involves tying an artificial hair to your own hair. Whether or not the hair grows out of your scalp, you have to be able to clean and maintain it.[7]

Educators, doctors, salesmen, politicians and others—about a million U.S. males—wear hairpieces now made available at high quality for approximately $100 to $500 each. There is no reason for a man of 40 to look a great deal older if a toupee will help his career and personal adjustment. Numerous individuals, such as those who intend to enter politics, should consider this before they define their media images. Some young men lose their hair during their late 20s. If such a loss occurs, a performer should invest in a hair restoration program, so that the transition from natural to artificial hair will be hardly noticeable.

Besides the use of transformations, hair transplants are becoming increasingly popular. This method consists of removing hair under a local anesthetic from where it is plentiful to a bald area. Frank Sinatra allegedly spent $25,000 to have this done. In another case, a man paid $1500 to have 200 transplants. A hairpiece may be worn while the transplant grows to normal length.[8] Some persons have tried hair implants, a method by which hairs are stapled to the head. This procedure may cause considerable pain and the possibility of infection.

EMOTIONAL CONTROL

A performer's emotional control may be developed by having: (1) self-confidence; (2) a highly capable production staff and excellent facilities; (3) a pleasant environment with complete freedom to experiment and work; (4) an encouraging audience; and (5) minimum frustration. A performer's production staff, environment and audience feedback are discussed elsewhere. Building self-confidence and reducing frustration require some attention here.

Self-Confidence

Some performers are obsessed; they perform at all costs. Being so driven, they fall into periods of deep despair when their careers are doing poorly or when they *think* they are not going well enough. Frequently, performers are not good judges of their own progress and during these times some performers may seek psychiatric consultation, if they can afford it. The frustrations of performers can be monumental, resulting in mental disorders, suicides, or a dependency upon dementing forms of temporary relief in alcohol and narcotics.

By contrast, many of today's very successful performers follow their careers simply because they have aptitude for them and they enjoy them. Their aptitudes were discovered while they were in school through examinations conducted by psychologists in the school's guidance program. To these individuals performing is rather like any other job. They do it as long as they are able, and the public wants them. Eventually they expect to go into a second career with, perhaps, equal enthusiasm.

To the obsessed performer, performing is life itself, as romantically depicted in *The Red Shoes*. To the career performer, it is a part of life, contributing to a larger and more important whole. A performer's philosophy toward his or her career is fundamental to emotional stability. Some people become performers because fate has given them leadership roles which must be expressed through media. For instance, some social advocates and minority leaders have found themselves on radio and TV out of necessity—the good of the cause—rather than by personal choice. Then, there are those performers, who absolutely hate to be in front of a group or on media, but for whom destiny has dictated that they be in the spotlight at least temporarily.

So, it might be said that performers have at least three distinctly different dispositions toward performing: they are obsessed, career-minded or reluctant.

For most performers, emotional control is derived from several factors. First is to know your objectives—usually to please and serve your public, to make money and to satisfy yourself. All of these objectives are worthwhile, but you must realize that you can only fulfill them in varying degrees at any given time, and not necessarily at the high levels of your own expectation. Nothing can give a performer perspective like experience—the more the better. To most performers a little experience is dangerous, because some performers draw too many inferences or conclusions from too little experience. Too much quick success can be just as stifling as too little. A career that lasts is usually built on a variety of successes and failures, and the determined performer survives all of them. Personal determination—"I know I can do it"—coupled with that rare degree of personal daring or abandon form the hard core of a performer's personal confidence. Experience, determination and abandon can withstand the shock waves that build a successful career. Experience is generated by accepting any opportunity that comes along, doing the best you can each time. Eventually the opportunities will multiply and become more complicated. Practicing to perfection, so that you are prepared for anything, adds immeasurably to your emotional control. Experience together with your determination—your desire to perform, your uncompromising attitude, your obsession, if you please—results in a state of abandon. Abandon, of course, is that lofty level of attainment at which performing becomes relaxation, enjoyment and high self-esteem.

Frustration

Self-confidence is thwarted by frustration. The sources of frustration for a performer seem endless. They can be categorized roughly, however, and recognized for what they are: first, personal frustration, in which one's innerself asks those nagging questions—"Can I do the job?" "Is my talent up to what is expected of me?" Second, environmental frustrations, in which the facilities are inadequate or the performer's associates have a non-professional attitude over which the performer has little or no control (staff antics, derogatory remarks, tension in the studio), or have lack of technique or organization (miscueing, floor noise, unnecessary interruptions, chaos). Third, conflict frustration, in which the performer's efforts toward perfection are misunderstood and he or she is considered difficult to get along with. Then, too, a performer may have personal inner conflicts (fear of criticism, fear of being different, fear of not being accepted by other professionals) that the production staff must contend with. Many of these frustrations reside with the performer for his or her entire career. To overcome them you will learn:

(1) To accomplish your objectives despite the obstacles, because you are going to be a "survivor."

(2) To perfect everything you can before you enter the studio,

knowing what effect you want and getting others to help you achieve it.

(3) To control greater portions of your medium—the performance, the editing, the directing and so forth.

(4) To surround yourself with associates who will make you look good.

Psychological Aptitude

There is no way to predict whether a person has what it takes to become a performer. A person may have physical skill and artistic ability, and yet not have the psychological desire to perform. Many young people demonstrating a certain amount of ability are encouraged by friends and relatives. Few are serious about performing until they consider whether to study it or to accept a job. Most people realize that getting a job as a performer is a risk. Many performers tend to come from the ranks of those who risk nothing, because they are poor in the first place, and those who are wealthy. Those who are in the middle income bracket, those who are likely to go to school, come from families who are afraid of the risk, and they naturally discourage members of the family "from getting their hopes up" or they seek forms of assurance of success such as aptitude tests. Some schools, placement services and professional testing centers can provide useful guides to maximize a person's chances of success in any occupation. But after all of the test results are in, only the performer can tell whether he or she has the drive to perform, having been encouraged by the test scores or dissatisfied with them.

Nervousness

Nearly every performer is somewhat nervous before, during or after a program. "Those butterflies (in your stomach) develop teeth like crocodiles," Paul Newman told the audience for Jimmy Carter's "Inaugural Eve Entertainment Special."[9] The questions are, "Is the performer's nervousness detrimental?" "Does this nervousness constitute a health hazard?" Most performers know whether their nervousness is extreme. If the face becomes exceedingly flushed, the heart flutters, breathing is heavy or dizziness develops, the performer may want to consult a physician.

The flush of excitement associated with an eagerness to do a good job is normal!

Pre-performance Nervousness. Nearly every performer is nervous prior to going before cameras, microphones or live audiences. Nervous energy takes many forms. Some performers show extremes in behavior. Commonly they experience loss of appetite, nausea, minor rashes, headaches, slight fever, dizziness, fatigue, instability, loss of control of limbs (such as hands that shake, knocking knees), chattering teeth, laryngitis, and hives. Some performers are sullen, irritable, moody and inclined to cry. Others chatter constantly. "I get very nervous when I do a show like the Emmy Awards," Johnny Carson once said. "I pace and keep pulling up my pants." And, dancer Rudolf Nureyev told Dick Cavett: "Every night is opening night . . . I get nervous every night. A dancer's nightmare is to be on stage with street shoes or with some part of the costume missing or miss your entrance or see the wrong person on stage."[10] Director Vincent Minnelli once said that Fred Astaire lacks confidence to the most enormous degree.[11] The School of Television and Commercial Speech, New York, recommends that performers disguise their nerves in these ways:

1. "Hard Back" your script to avoid shakes. (i.e., keep the script stiff)
2. Carry water in a bottle to avoid "dry mouth."
3. Take a breath, and start to talk "on the breath"!
4. Read the first line looking at audience.
5. Hold your script UP, and "in a line" with your audience. To see it, SHIFT *YOUR EYES* ONLY!
6. Avoid nervous habits, such as keeping time with your head, or your pencil, or your hand.[12]

Nervousness during the Performance. The more successful performers are relieved of their nervousness once the performance is in progress and the audience has expressed favorable satisfaction through laughter or applause. The circular response for this performer is at times so overwhelming that he or she is urged on to new levels of achievement as hitherto pent up nervous energy is released in proportion to audience reaction. This performance is attained only before a live audience which exudes its energy in empathic response to a performer, thus stimulating the performer beyond all previous expectations, as discussed earlier.

Judy Garland once began a stage performance by confessing her nervousness. The audience applauded enthusiastically as she sang her opening songs. Seeming to gain confidence in herself as she went along, the actress built the emotional intensity of her act by weaving her wistful, fragile, nervous instability into her performance. By the time she ostensibly ended her show with "I Was Born in a Trunk," the audience was electrified; and, when at last encore she sang "Over the Rainbow," it was emotionally overwhelming. Unquestionably this performer used a common weakness—nervousness in performance—to great advantage. Performing before a live audience is greatly reassuring to those in variety, comedy, quiz and other audience participation programs.

If a performer is thoroughly prepared and yet nervousness persists during the performance, he or she is probably losing concentration by not being sufficiently immersed in the action of the program. Absolutely quiet working conditions may help, along with encouragement from the other performers. If a performer adopts the mental attitude that he or she has something of importance to give an audience, this sharing of something important may enhance the abandon that a performer must have.

Post-Performance Nervousness. Post-performance nervousness manifests itself in releases of energy that cause mildly abnormal behavior. The performer may become very joyful, ravenously hungry, giddy, light-headed, unusually loving and gay. Some performers are "let down," resulting in mild melancholy. Although their performances may have been well received, they are now "spent," exhausted, prone to weep, withdrawn and generally depressed; but a good night's sleep or an invitation to do a new show revitalizes them with amazing speed.

Forgetfulness

Some of the reasons for loss of memory are temporary amnesia, a disruptive environment that may destroy a performer's concentration, and aging. Older people sometimes become forgetful: long speeches are more difficult to remember. Mass media programs can usually be taped in short segments so that remembering long roles or musical compositions is unnecessary. Those performers who force themselves to remember tend to keep in practice, and they seem to be less likely to forget. Almost all of the reasons for temporarily forgetting are related to environmental happenings that surprise, bewilder, confound or in some way short-circuit a performer's thinking process: a prop put in the wrong place, a miscue by someone else in the cast, a surprising emotional reaction to something within the set, or an influence from something or someone outside it, such as a member of the audience. Memory loss is more noticeable in fully scripted plays, speeches or readings that are memorized and then taped before a live audience as though they were being performed in the theater. On one occasion a young man was cued before live TV cameras. Sweat began appearing on his brow. He stared blankly and opened his mouth, but no words came out. He was literally scared speechless, a fear many performers have experienced at least once. The challenge is to recover with some finesse. The TV floor director immediately moved nearer to coach the talent, but the young man failed to respond. Finally after several seconds delay another member of the panel adlibbed the opening. The young man, sufficiently prompted by this time, completed the program without a flaw. Cue cards, prompters and pieces of the script placed around the set are helpful, and so is a quick wit to cover a forgotten line, delivered either by the performer or by another member of the cast.

Tomfoolery among cast or crew members is an attempt to make a performer forget on the air. Performers who manage to retain their composure during such antics are considered real "pros." A media performance is subject to so many mistakes under normal circumstances, however, that most professionals do not tolerate nonsense while they are working.

Methods of Relief

Emotional limitations may be very complex, involving the deep psychological make-up of the performer—for instance, a fear of performing itself, or of audiences, or of any number of real or imagined disabilities, or feelings of insecurity or inadequacy. A rational understanding of the cause of a performer's fear is necessary to dissolve the emotional disturbance, and some of these matters can not suitably be discussed here. For those emotional upsets that most performers experience before, during or after a performance, however, some suggestions for relief are in order. One method is hypnotic association, described by Dr. William S. Kroger in his book, *Clinical and Experimental Hypnosis.* "Network nerves untreated will continue, as does stage fright even in our greatest stars who may have years of experience." Dr. Kroger says he gives the person an image with five senses to induce concentration and relaxation. For instance, "You have them imagine the beach, with the hot sun, feet touching the sand, now walking in the breakers, near the waves, taste the salt spray, take a deep breath and inhale the breeze." According to Dr. Kroger, "A lot of people go on talk shows thinking, 'beach scene, beach scene.' "[13]

Stimulants. Some performers need to be stimulated for a performance. They are usually lethargic from overwork or emotional strain during the rehearsals, so they need to be "up" for the performance. Caffeine-heavy drinks such as coffee or coke and drugs that prohibit sleep are simple remedies, and for some people fairly effective. Sugar gives quick energy to some people. A brief nap (20 minutes or so) is wonderfully revitalizing to many performers.

Some performers also take potent narcotics called "uppers." Initially, the end (a top performance) seems to justify the means—taking the dangerous drugs—but in the long run this rationale doesn't seem to work. As Robert Hegyes, co-star of the *Welcome Back Kotter* series, has said: "As with anything in life, you have to accept the responsibility of your actions. If you just want to experiment with barbiturates, heroin or speed, know that the end of the line is death. But to anyone who is interested in expanding his mind, don't experiment without researching the drug you think you want to take. Know what it is, what it can do to you, and the laws prohibiting it. . . . I have never—nor will I ever—performed under the influence of marijuana. It just isn't true that it enables a person to act or sing better."[14] Several lives and the careers of marvelously talented people have been ruined by addiction to drugs which are eventually mentally and physically debilitating.

Depressants. Performers use depressants to calm them down before, during and after a performance. The degree of relief required indicates the method. Nervousness is normal, as discussed earlier. A few asprin tablets or phenobarbital, Valium or Librium, taken as prescribed by a physician, can be helpful in relaxing the performer. Of course, it is better to rely on simple rememdies: a quick nap, a few moments of seclusion, a cup of tea or hot milk, even a reassuring conversation with a friend can produce the same results. Alcohol permits some performers to give a less restrained, freer performance. Sometimes this works very well. In the long run, however, alcohol can be debilitating and addictive, leading to ruin and possibly death. So, it is a risk. Because of its wide social acceptance and availability, alcohol is the most popular form of emotional relief available to a performer. Potent narcotics are also available by prescription or illegally. While euphoria may have a short-term benefit, the devastating effect on a performer's body and talent is generally considered not worth the involvement.

Meditation. In recent years several performers have turned to meditation, which is essentially of two types: one focuses the mind on the performance at hand and the other voids the mind of any thought at all. Meditation is practiced by some performers for about 20 minutes, once or twice a day, as a routine for living a better, more productive, more creative life and, therefore, offering the public a better performance. Advertisements for one form of meditation—transcendental meditation—claim that Peggy Lee, the Beach Boys, Clint Eastwood, 10 per cent of all major league baseball players and many other prominent professional people practice it. "I've learned that the best way to achieve good work is to concentrate on the work and not let artificial pressures bug you," says Mary Tyler Moore. "Don't concern yourself with reaction. Concern yourself with your own action." Both she and her husband, producer Grant Tinker, became meditators during the mid-1970s.[15]

Commonsense. Self analysis will go a long way in providing emotional relief and control. This method requires little or no explanation. First of all, decide why you want to be a performer: Is it to present an extraordinary talent to the public? It is to be of service to the public? Is it to make a great deal of money? Is it to become famous? Is it to satisfy yourself—to be able to say you have performed well? Second, you will calm your fears and bring emotional relief as you gain experience, confidence, determination and abandon. Third, you will have increased emotional control after you develop a willingness among your staff to enhance your performance, not just for money but also for the pride in a job well done. Fourth, you will feel emotionally at ease in a working atmosphere that provides you the tools to do the job and a professional attitude on the part of everyone to do quality work. And, finally, you will be emotionally satisfied by the response you get from an appreciative audience. Whatever time, energy and emotional duress you have experienced will seem worthwhile, when you enjoy a ground swell of public approval.

Part Two

THE PERFORMER'S ENVIRONMENT

9: The Studio

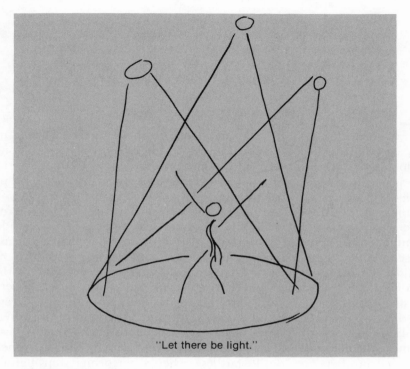

"Let there be light."

Types of Studios
Radio Studios (Turntables; Reel-to-Reel Tape Recorders; Cassettes; Cartridges; Telephones; Emergency Monitors; Mobile Units)—Recording Studios (Recordings)—Television Studios (Television Cameras; Switchers; Videotape Recording; Studio Monitors; Projection; Television Remote Units)—Film Studios (Film Cameras)

Communication With the Performer
Cueing Radio Performers—Cueing Television Performers—Cueing Film Performers

Personnel Relationships
Producers—Directors—Floor Crews

Using Cameras
Direct Audience Contact—Indirect Audience Contact

Using Microphones
Presence—Microphone Characteristics—Techniques

Typical Settings   Complex Settings

T O A PERFORMER studios are merely places where a performance can be originated, recorded or transmitted under controlled conditions indoors or relatively controlled conditions outdoors. A TV or film studio is mostly space surrounded by lighting instruments, scenery, properties and equipment that will transmit and/or record pictures and/or sounds. A performer's primary function is to relate to the microphones, cameras, staff, crew, and a possible live studio audience, while simultaneously communicating information or entertainment to a vast unseen public. Paradoxically, a performer standing in a pool of light amidst the paraphernalia of a large studio (and some are mammoth) can find the experience lonely, frightening and frustrating. A performer learns that it is difficult to get instructions from the floor crew or director working beyond the edge of light; the studios are often cold; instructions for the performers are frequently changed at the last minute; the live audience is impatient; the pressure is on the performer who has nowhere to hide. Regardless, when a performer steps before the microphone and/or into the light, he or she fulfills the efforts and indeed the hopes of the producer, director, production staff, financial backers and the public that has paid one way or another for the occasion.

TYPES OF STUDIOS

Of the four kinds of studios—radio, audio recording, television and film—all require sound recording equipment; TV and film also have video recording equipment. The better understanding a performer has of the operation of a studio, the better his or her performance may be, although, in fact, a number of successful performers know next to nothing about studios and equipment. There is a lot of equipment, it is constantly changing and its use is highly sophisticated. Performers are expected to know the fundamentals of studio operation and the design and use of equipment, but they should not feel intimidated by equipment or technical personnel. A performer is expected to apply basic knowledge of studio operation to further learning on the job, the staff at each station or studio taking pride in itself for "being a little different" and, in its opinion, better than elsewhere.

Radio Studios

A radio studio is a small acoustically treated room with a microphone in it. At one end of the room is a large window. Beyond the window in a second room, the *control room,* the performer can see the director and audio engineer. Both of them may give the performer technical instructions and encouragement. As the performer speaks or sings into the microphone, sound waves are generated. These waves are converted into an electronic signal that is carried to an *audio console.* The console ranges in length from a one-and-a-half foot portable unit for remote broadcasts to an eight-foot engineer's control board that is located in a master control room and used for complex productions. The functions of an audio console are to strengthen the signal, regulate the volume by means of small levers or dials called "potentiometers" ("pots" for short), "mixers" or "faders," and to send the amplified signal to the recording apparatus or transmitter. The producer-director-engineer (and they may be the same person) listens to the performance on headsets or over a control room speaker and decides when the sound quality is adequate for recording or transmission.

A radio studio can be very small; a few large ones, symbolic of radio's heyday of dramatic productions, still exist. Its size depends on its function; a studio operated by a single performer should be so intimate that everything the performer needs is within an arm's reach. A good many disc jockeys across the nation work in such surroundings. One end of a mobile home or van is often converted into a radio studio and used as a remote unit at fairs and shopping centers. Radio studio equipment includes turntables, reel-to-reel cartridge and cassette tape recorders, telephones and microphones. A performer should know how to operate each of these items. The performer is encouraged to consult a radio production book for a definitive explanation of equipment operation, but a summary follows:

Turntables. For years turntables revolving at 16, 45, 33⅓, and 78 inches per second (i.p.s.) were the industry standard; performers learned how to efficiently change discs. This one-two-three technique consisted of having (1) the record precued with the stylus (i.e., needle) backed up about a quarter of a groove, (2) the disc jockey starting the turntable, and (3) quickly turning up the volume. If incorrectly timed, a "wow" resulted from a record not up to speed. Clever DJs and sound technicians could cue notes, phrases, lines and sounds anywhere on the disc with great precision. In recent years discs have become obsolete; instead, the DJ is a cartridge jockey.

Reel-to-Reel Tape Recorders. Central to a radio (or recording) operation is the reel-to-reel tape recorder. Tape comes in various widths, but ¼-inch is most common. Standard thickness of the tape is 1.5 mils, and it is usually wound on a 1200-foot, 7-inch reel. Depending on the capability of the machine, tapes are played at slow speeds of $^{15}/_{16}$ (recording books), 1⅞ or 3¾ (news actualities) for voices, 7½ (ordinary radio recording) and 15-inches per second (high fidelity FM) for music. Tape recorders can be single track or monaural, two tracks or stereophonic, or four or more "multi" tracks. Performers seriously interested in audio production gradually learn how to use tape recorders at their various levels of sophistication.

Performers work with reel-to-reel tape recorders in the production of commercials, newscasts and other programs that require editing. Reel-to-reel audio units allow for precise editing done by hand or electronically. To edit an audiotape by hand, a performer locates the beginning and the end of the portion he or she wishes to keep and merely cuts it out of the rest of the tape. One of the slicker ways of splicing an audiotape is to use a cutting bar which is slotted horizontally to hold the tape firmly and diagonally to allow for a neat cut. (A vertical cut results in a more noticeable audio interruption.) If the tape is to be added to another, a short piece of mending tape overlaps the join on the shiny side of the tape, the audio information being carried on the dull (oxide) side. No gap should exist between the ends of the tape at the join, if the continuity is to have a minimum jump in the program material.

To edit electronically, a performer uses the record and erase capability of most units by finding the portion to be eliminated, erasing it as skillfully as possible, and then rerecording that segment. Precision timing is really critical; but after a great deal of practice, a performer can electronically "drop in" a segment without damaging the foregoing or following portions of the tape, nor cutting it. An efficient performer can edit a tape in seconds. Some complex radio programs such as documentaries and dramas have scores of edits before a final master tape evolves.

Huge reel-to-reel long playing tapes are used by highly automated FM radio stations on which announcers read infrequent commercials, brief news items, station IDs and other requirements.

Cassettes. Cassettes are plastic boxes enclosing a miniaturized reel-to-reel audiotape unit. Cassettes are played on specially designed machines by running the tape from one reel to the other, usually left to right. The cassette can be removed from the machine, turned over and played on the reverse side. A series of heads enable a cassette unit to record, erase and play back. Cassettes are very popular because the recording unit can be as small as a purse. For example, the small, por-

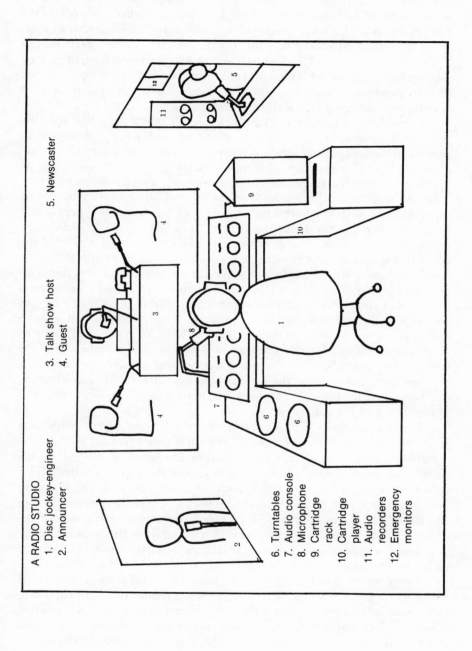

A RADIO STUDIO
1. Disc jockey-engineer
2. Announcer
3. Talk show host
4. Guest
5. Newscaster

6. Turntables
7. Audio console
8. Microphone
9. Cartridge rack
10. Cartridge player
11. Audio recorders
12. Emergency monitors

table, lightweight Sony TC 110A cassette tape recorder, which costs about $120.00 is, according to Bob Wright, news director of KLOL-FM, Houston, "the work horse of the industry." Recently, a similar, more sophisticated model was put on the market—Sony's Superscope TC 110B—for about $350. Though acceptable for voice recording, cassettes using narrow-width tape and playing at speeds of 7½ i.p.s. are too slow to produce sufficient quality for music. Generally, the quality of cassette recordings is below that of discs.

Cartridges. A cartridge ("cart") is a small plastic box like the cassette. Inside, however, a continuous loop of audiotape is designed to play its information once, then stop automatically and recue for immediate replay. The machine that plays cartridges has various slots or openings in which a single cartridge is inserted. The performer pushes a button to activate the machine and a second button, often remotely controlled, to start the cartridge. A series of lights lets the performer know whether it is cued and ready (green) or playing (red). Many cartridge machines can record, erase and playback, and the tape loops come in various lengths running a few seconds to five minutes.

Telephones. Radio performers are rather dependent on the telephone. Listeners call station DJs and reporters call in news items. Studio phones allow several lines to come into a studio, usually one or two for local calls and one for long distance. The performer is able to switch from line to line, to put a caller on hold, to record calls and to delay conversations for the purpose of deletion of obscenities. The DJ can speak to the caller over the normal telephone receiver or through a tiny speaker mounted to the studio console. The entire conversation can be picked up on a microphone, so that listeners can hear both the performer and the caller.

Radio reporters, often at the scene of an event, carry wires and jacks that can transfer information from their tape recorders directly to a public telephone and on to the station. One such Y-shaped device consists of a single wire which is inserted into the tape recorder and a split wire at the other end which attaches to two posts in the listening end of a telephone receiver, after the plastic screen is removed. If an induction coil is placed over the receiver and connected to a tape recorder, it will transfer information without removing the plastic screen.

Emergency Monitors. Police, sheriff, fire departments and other law enforcement agencies grant permission to news departments to listen to emergency dispatches. Reporters hear these calls on a battery of speakers or monitors, one for each agency. Frequently more than one call comes in at a time. With a little experience a reporter can subconsciously select important calls. Based upon these reports, one sends the station's mobile unit (which may also have a monitor) to the scene, or telephones hospitals, appropriate departments and elsewhere for the story. Monitors are relatively inexpensive but valuable equipment.

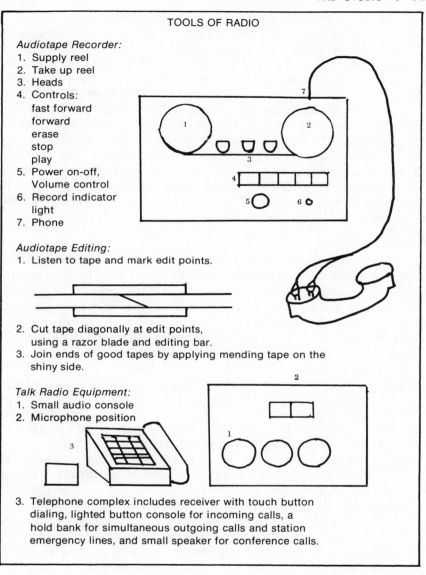

TOOLS OF RADIO

Audiotape Recorder:
1. Supply reel
2. Take up reel
3. Heads
4. Controls:
   fast forward
   forward
   erase
   stop
   play
5. Power on-off,
   Volume control
6. Record indicator
   light
7. Phone

Audiotape Editing:
1. Listen to tape and mark edit points.

2. Cut tape diagonally at edit points,
   using a razor blade and editing bar.
3. Join ends of good tapes by applying mending tape on the
   shiny side.

Talk Radio Equipment:
1. Small audio console
2. Microphone position

3. Telephone complex includes receiver with touch button
   dialing, lighted button console for incoming calls, a
   hold bank for simultaneous outgoing calls and station
   emergency lines, and small speaker for conference calls.

Mobile Units. Aside from portable tape recorders, radio's other principal portable facility is a mobile unit. It may be used on air, sea or land. Some stations own several mobile units, and news employees often equip their personal cars with a two-way radio. Thus many units are available to cover sprawling urban areas. Mobile units are equipped with two-way communication and with monitors for emergency calls.

Many refinements are available. For example, a version of the walkie-talkie can be carried into a burning building and keyed to trigger a transmitter in an idling mobile unit which in turn emits or boosts a signal to the station. A newsman can report directly from within the disaster area without returning to his vehicle. Mobile units are expensive. Small stations do not rely upon them greatly, but large news departments do. Mobile units can be a hindrance; when covering riots and other disturbances, units have been wrecked. Crowded traffic conditions also tie up the unit when it is needed most. Other kinds of mobile units are used. Helicopters are particularly helpful in surveying traffic conditions and widespread damage. Boats are necessary where maritime traffic is heavy and water conditions are of interest to the community. News departments often own their own land transportation, but they lease units for sea and air.

Recording Studios

A recording studio is similar to a radio studio except that it has no transmission capability. Numerous recording studios in the larger cities are used for making commercials for agencies and tapes for local musicians. One recording studio, for instance, consisted of two rooms—a control room with an audio console and another with only a microphone, a chair and a music stand. This studio was rented by advertising agencies to record audio tracks for commercials.

In a studio that specializes in recording music, however, each element of the performance is recorded on a different soundtrack on separate audiotape machines. Thus, if a group consists of a vocalist on Mike 1, backup singers on Mike 2, lead guitar on Mike 3, second guitar on Mike 4, drums on Mike 5 and an organist with effects on Mike 6, each (or some) performer in the studio could be isolated from the others by means of sound absorbing panels or "gobos," allowing for each sound to be recorded separately on one of six different tracks. Members of the group hear each other over headsets. As the recording is being made the group's producer tells the engineer to alter the sound input of any one of the microphones. Several recordings are made throughout the session. Later the best moments from all tracks will be combined or mixed into a single perfect master recording from which discs and cartridges are produced for distribution.

Recordings. Although sound recording for mass media began with Thomas A. Edison's development of the phonograph in 1877, radio broadcasting and sound-on-film did not emerge significantly until the mid-1920s. TV and audiotape came into distribution during the mid-'40s and videotape in the mid-'50s. The next decade saw refinements adding dimension and fullness to sound recording: high fidelity, monaural sound yielded to two-channel stereophonic sound wherein dupli-

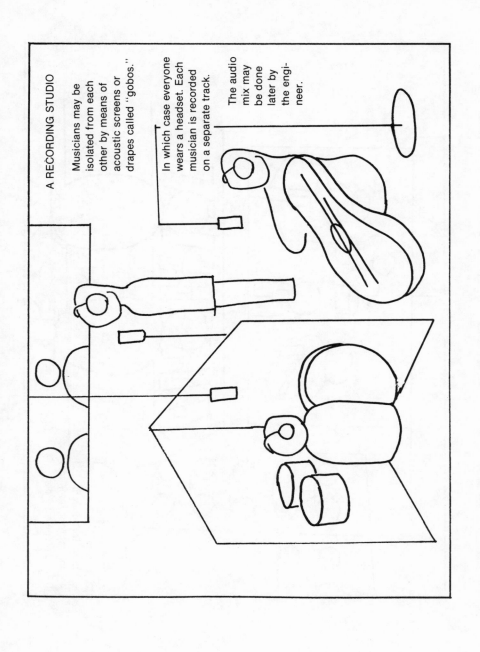

A RECORDING STUDIO

Musicians may be
isolated from each
other by means of
acoustic screens or
drapes called "gobos."

In which case everyone
wears a headset. Each
musician is recorded
on a separate track.

The audio
mix may
be done
later by
the engi-
neer.

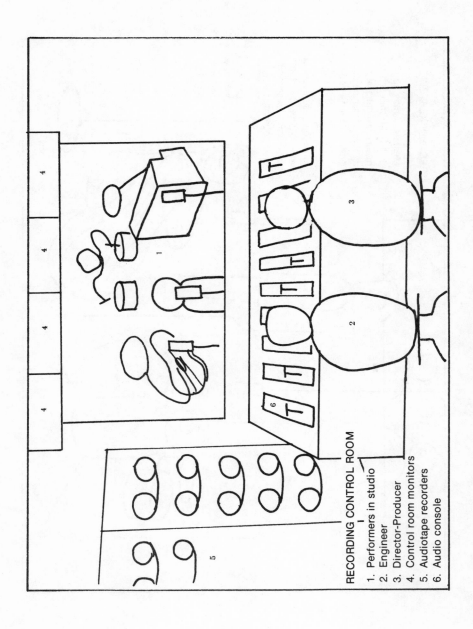

RECORDING CONTROL ROOM

1. Performers in studio
2. Engineer
3. Director-Producer
4. Control room monitors
5. Audiotape recorders
6. Audio console

cating and non-duplicating information originates and is played back on two speakers. Sound pick-up and play-back units have multiplied to four ("quadraphonic") or more.

Complex systems suggest complex utilization, especially in music. To the performer this has meant a richer variation in his or her artistic achievement. The fidelity of the recording process coincided with experimentations in unusual handling of sound through electronic enhancement—amplification, synthesizers, electronic reinforcement; the infusion of oriental sounds with occidental music; reaching for dissonance, dimension, volume, incoherence, intense, raucous rhythms and an integration of major kinds of music such as C&W, MOR, classical and rock. These new uses of sound have cross-pollinated all areas of mass media. News consists of emotional sound fragments as well as verbalized coherent reports; music consists of emotional grunts and groans as well as understandable lyrics; and a TV performer's rock concert hits a stage or movie house like an earthquake. It's as though an artistic pre-school child discovered that there's more than a Big-8 box of crayons, that there's anywhere from 48 to enough wax for every variation in the rainbow. The range in recording quality and content today is stunning. For the artists who find an original amalgamation of sounds like the Motown or Nashville sounds, the rewards are staggering. Prospecting for such a find takes place in humble garage studios as well as in large professional ones.

Television Studios

A TV studio is a large room with microphones, lights and cameras. A performer must be aware of the placement of the microphones, and the carefully lighted areas designated on the studio floor in chalk or masking tape. These designations are *marks*. A performer must move only through these areas in order for camera operators to properly align the shots. Being off one's marks, even slightly, can make a substantial difference in the light level or composition of the shot. A performer sometimes resents being so restricted in movement, but the less there is to light and mike, the better quality the lighting and audio may be. A typical studio does not have enough sound equipment or lighting instruments to cover the entire floor, and electronic subtleties in TV are multitudinous. For instance, if the cameras do not match (an engineer's problem), the performer may look great on one camera but poor on the other; if the light level drops below camera minimum (a lighting problem), the performer may be in deep shadow or transmit the wrong color; if the microphone isn't in the right place (an audio operator's problem), the performer may sound as if he or she is speaking from another part of the studio.

TV programs may be classified as "live," that is when they are on the air; "live-on-tape," meaning that they are recorded without editing; or "recorded," meaning that they are probably edited. Each format has its value. The material in live programs like the news is usually perishable and may have little replay value. Live-on-tape programs have spontaneity—like some audience participation shows, public discussions or sports programs—with little editing required. The content of these programs may be perishable, also, but they are videotaped for replay at a more convenient time. An edited program is extremely popular with performers, because the content is closer to being artistically and technically perfect and will be replayed perhaps for years. Frequently, the only live portions of a newscast are of those people who anchor it. To be competitive a performer's work must be perfect, and electronic engineering has made that possible. The only deterents are money and time; the performer's company may not be able to purchase enough studio time to reach perfection; thus, a performer settles for something less. A high-priced studio is expensive, because it has the most experienced, creative artists available to do every task. Studio costs range from about $100 to over $1,000 an hour.

Television Cameras. A TV camera looks like a box mounted to a pole or tripod. Cameras function at the performer's eye level much of the time. The internal workings of a camera are extremely complex, requiring constant adjustment and maintenance. Black-and-white cameras are adjusted by focusing on a gray scale or line chart; but color cameras are frequently adjusted by focusing on a chart of color bars or on the complexion of a model; i.e., a "stand in" or "color girl."[1] If the skin color looks natural, the rest of the TV picture is likely to be acceptable. Engineering adjustment begins an hour or more before air time. Instruments in master control tell an engineer when the cameras are ready for operation. To the performer these technical adjustments are boring; but they are absolutely necessary if the performer is to have optimum appearance to the public. So, any adjustments that require the presence of the performer or the accompanying visuals are well worth the time and inconvenience.

Cameras, their mounts and lenses move according to simple commands from the director or camera operators. The principal commands for moving the camera and its mount are "dolly," which means move toward or back from the performer or object; "truck," which is moving the camera mount right or left; and "arc," which is moving right or left in a curve. "Boom" or "crane" up or down elevates the camera overhead. Cameras on tripods are almost impossible to elevate; but those on pedestals move up or down hydraulically on command, "pedestal" up or down. The principal commands moving the camera itself, without moving its mount, are "pan," which moves the camera horizontally right or left; and "tilt," which moves it vertically up or

A TELEVISION STUDIO

1. Performer
2. Cue card holder
3. Floor Director giving cue
4. Audio Operator in control room
5. Technical Director
6. Director
7. Back light
8-9. Fill light
10. Key light
11. Floor light
12. Teleprompter
13. Tally lights
14. On-air lens position for turret mount
15. On-air lens zoom mount
16. Cue cards
17. Microphone
18. Monitor

down. The variable focus "zoom" lens is on most TV cameras today. These lenses have a sweeping capability from a wide shot covering a panoramic landscape to a closeup of an outfielder catching a ball. Older cameras use a turret lens system wherein three or four fixed focus lenses, giving a long, medium and closeup shot, are rotated to the on-air position as required by the director.

At the back of a TV camera, sometimes on the studio floor, and in the control room are monitors or tiny TV receivers which allow the director, camera operators and engineers to adjust focus, lighting, composition and field of view, among other things. Because of the complex nature of the TV medium, a director has to be careful that the content of the program doesn't get lost in the complex technical process of getting it on the air. A performer can help a director without imposing on his or her authority by calling attention to the images the viewers must see and when they must see them.

Switchers. Somewhat comparable to the audio control board is the *switcher.* This electronic control panel consists of several buttons that execute changes from shot to shot. These changes can be instantaneous, called a "cut," of longer duration, called a "fade," or of overlapping scenes known as a "dissolve." A variety of electronic transitions, termed "wipes," enables the operator, the *technical director,* to use various geometric configurations like squares, circles and bars. Additional effects can be inserted into the TV picture electronically, such as a tiny window that can move around on the TV screen. Colors, distortions, numbers, lines of type and computerized designs can be added and/or deleted. A performer does not have to know how a switcher works, but he or she should know what effects are available, so that they can be utilized to enhance the program.

Videotape Recording. Videotape looks like audiotape except that videotape is wider—½-, ¾-, 1- or 2-inches—and the videotape recorders (VTRs) are much bigger and more expensive. The broadcast standard for videotape is 2-inches, but industry and the professions depend heavily on the other gauges. Videotape carries both sound and picture and can be electronically edited, having flexibility similar to film. Some performers like to be familiar with the operation of videotape equipment. Videotape recorders can record, erase and play back. Operation of the machines is basically simple, but it takes a great deal of practice for one to electronically edit on machines that have that capability. The operation of VTRs is done by a specialist. Videotape is fairly durable and can be re-used. In some ways editing videotape is difficult, because a performer must depend on electronic scanning rather than viewing frames as in film. Recent videotape editing machines have made it possible for a performer to view his or her work "frame by frame," however.

Studio Monitors. A television monitor is a voiceless viewing screen. Often it resembles an ordinary television receiver. One or more are usually positioned on the studio floor or at the news desk, within easy view of the performer. They enable the talent to see film clips for voice-over-picture narration, presentations from other cities or remote units. Whenever a newscast calls for a prerecorded segment, the anchor watches it on the monitor. If an emergency occurs or if the picture is substandard, the reporter knows what the viewer saw and adlibs necessary information. A performer should make certain that the monitor is within easy viewing range, especially if he or she is required to identify small objects.

Projection. Moving picture film, slides and opaques originate from *telecine,* in a projection room adjacent to the control room. In projection, various motion picture and slide projectors are arranged so that they beam pictures into a small vidicon camera which, through a mirror system known as a *multiplexer,* may handle two or three film or slide projectors. A performer should be acquainted with projected materials: moving picture film, transparent slides and opaques. Each requires a special projector. (See "Preparation of Visuals.")

At a preplanned moment during a program, frequently a newscast, a projector casts a photographed image on the screen behind the talent; hence, the term *rear screen projection* (RSP). Up-to-date pictures received in a newsroom over a photowire may be rephotographed and mounted as 3¼ by 4-inch lantern slides. These slides are inserted in a still projector located in the studio behind a large screen serving as background for the newscaster. Several slides—primarily of people, significant events, maps, scenes, animation, even moving pictures—may appear during a single program. Rear screens vary in size from a normal television receiver to a large motion picture screen. Much of what appears to be rear screen projection may actually be produced electronically through the switcher in which case the performer is said to be "keyed" or "inserted" over the background scene. This electronic technique is very attractive for musical numbers (moving shapes and designs), dances or dramas (complex scenery) and news (buildings, arenas). Although the making of RSP slides and electronic effects is left to the production staff, the performer will be involved in the selection of these effects and should be aware of their availability. Special staging is also required: the performer must avoid wearing blue, for example, because this color is blanked out during the keying, thus allowing the background image to replace any blue image.

Television Remote Units. In an effort to cope with the immediacy of radio, television news departments have turned to "instant" electronic news gathering (ENG). The ENG truck contains a portable camera and audio system which is driven to the scene and quickly set up for relay-

TOOLS OF TELEVISION NEWSFILM

Camera:
1. Load camera.
2. Set shooting speed (24 fps) and footage indicator at 0.
3. Focus Lens.
4. Determine f-stop using exposure meter.
5. Shoot film.

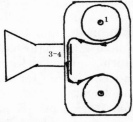

Exposure Meter:
1. Set ASA
2. Determine light intensity on subject by means of indicator needle.
3. Set dials accordingly.
4. Observe position of dial at $1/60$th of a second (24 fps).
5. Note f-stop number opposite $1/60$th.
6. Adjust lens on camera accordingly.

Editing Equipment:
1. View film and mark edit points.
2. Cut film into scenes and note content of each scene.
3. Splice scenes in order by cementing at join.

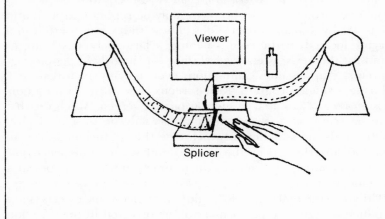

ing information to the station, thus enabling the reporter to broadcast from the scene before the event is over. To the performer, instant news gathering requires the same relationship to a camera and (hand-held) microphone as anywhere else. Preparation is accelerated, however, and the subtleties of controlled studio lighting and other cosmetic niceties are sacrificed. Occasionally transmission is uneven and the performer finds he or she must do an unexpected amount of adlibbing.

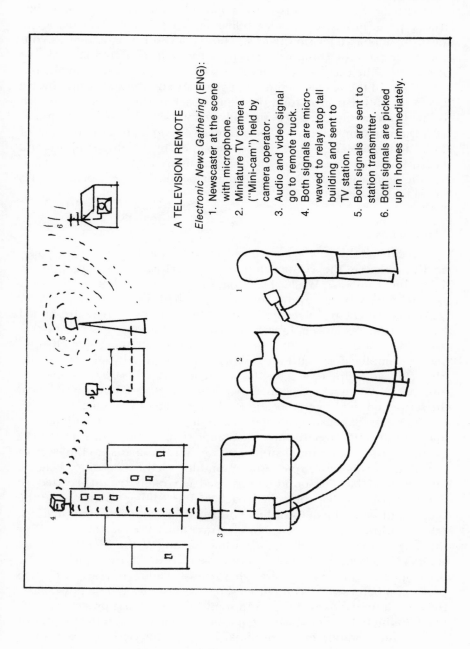

A TELEVISION REMOTE

Electronic News Gathering (ENG):

1. Newscaster at the scene with microphone.
2. Miniature TV camera ("Mini-cam") held by camera operator.
3. Audio and video signal go to remote truck.
4. Both signals are micro-waved to relay atop tall building and sent to TV station.
5. Both signals are sent to station transmitter.
6. Both signals are picked up in homes immediately.

Scheduled events of magnitude—entertainments from theaters, concert halls, casinos, sports palaces and fairgrounds, and some public affairs programs—are broadcast live or recorded on videotape by means of mobile television trucks. These television remote trucks contain every piece of equipment essential for putting a complex telecast on the air. The cab area of a modest-sized truck contains a small control room. In the rear is engineering gear, and on the roof a microwave link is set up for transmitting the signals back to the station. Inasmuch as the director is in the truck, the only action he or she sees is on monitors. Directors must rely on expert camera operators to pick up shots of the action. The larger vans are accompanied by a utility support van. These units may be capable of using as many as 25 cameras on nationally significant telecasts such as major political conventions, parades and sports coverage.

Film Studios

In cinema the performer's problems are basically the same as those in TV: What is the relationship of the performer to microphones, lights and cameras? While TV programs are often shot in relatively long segments from several minutes to a half-hour or more, or recorded on videotape in segments of various lengths, movies are filmed in brief segments lasting a few seconds to a few minutes. For some feature film productions getting the equivalent of one and one-half minutes of completed screen time a day compares with 16 minutes of finished TV videotape time a day for say, *The Electric Company*. Scenes for movies are not shot in sequence. A performer does all of the action in the script confined to one location before moving to another location.

The less expensive newsfilm cameras record sound and picture magnetically and directly onto a magnetic stripe which looks like a very narrow ($3/32$nds of an inch) audiotape which is laminated to the edge of the film. This is *single system* sound-on-film (SOF) recording. Feature films require that the sound be recorded separately from the video, so that it can be better controlled back in the editing room where the sound and video image will be conformed or "married" into a single release print. For big expensive feature films the performers, after shooting, reread all of their lines while looking at the silent film. The actors voices, sound effects and music are recorded on several, separate tracks in this post-synchronization process. Then, they are mixed to perfection before conforming to a single release print. The possibilities for the manipulation of image and sound in the editing process are virtually unlimited, which means that a performer through the artistry of the production staff can substantially exceed his or her own human ability. This is *double system* sound-on-film recording.

FILMING ON LOCATION
Lovin' Molly,
filmed near Bastrop,
Texas.

1. Actress Blythe
   Danner sits on
   porch.

2. Tracking shot
   is taken by
   cinematographer
   and director
   beyond the trees

3. If necessary, sound effects, voice and
   music are added back in the studio where
   the actress, musicians and technicians
   synchronize the audio to the picture.

Film Cameras. Moving picture cameras are not the same as TV cameras, although to the public the result is similar. The terms "videotape" and "film" are frequently confused. A film camera has virtually the same flexibility in size, mounts and operation as a TV camera. Instead of having a video engineer, experts in film processing develop the pictures. Film is a strip of still pictures that, when projected rapidly, creates the illusion of movement, if the pictures show images in similar positions for brief periods of 8 or more pictures per second. Standard shooting and projection for sound-on-film movies and all film for television is 24 frames per second.

A film camera is constructed like a box and mounted on anything from a person's hand to an elaborate crane. Inside the camera, one roll of undeveloped film stock is gradually wound on an empty spool. Along the way a series of pictures is recorded one by one behind the camera lens and an opening in the camera housing called the "aperture." A sound track may be recorded directly on this film, such as in the single system optical recording or it may be recorded on a magnetic stripe either simultaneously or a great deal of film is shot silent with sound tracks being added later. Camera lenses are identical to those used in TV. Sixteen and 35 millimeter (mm) lenses for TV and film cameras are interchangeable on some camera models, and their functions are the same in regard to the regulation of light (f-stops), focus, depth of field and field of view. Details of film cameras will aid those performers who want to be broadcast journalists, although often the performer-reporter and the film camera operator are two different people.

Film stock comes in various gauges—8mm, now obsolete; Super-8mm, widely used by amateurs and some professionals; 16mm, used by newsfilm crews, advertising agencies and local film production companies; 35mm, the standard gauge for feature films; 65mm and higher, used for expensive wide screen feature films for theatrical release. Of course, each gauge requires compatible equipment; i.e., 16mm film stock is shot, edited and projected on 16mm equipment.

COMMUNICATION WITH THE PERFORMER

When a performer arrives at a studio, preparation is complete. The script is memorized or on cue cards, the blocking has been rehearsed or is at least generally understood; therefore, the performer simply gets acquainted with the performing area and, when appropriate, special costuming or make-up. If no technical problems arise, a rehearsal(s) and airing or taping follow as soon as the director can possibly do them. To meet this schedule, the performer gets a series of check points or *cues,* orally before the airing or taping, and visually during the performance.

Oral and visual cues are given by the director or his/her representative. Cueing is precise but informal, unless the circumstances are complex. A performer must know who is giving the cues, where the person will be, and how visible the cues will be. Once cued, a performer reacts instantly and does what is expected. Ordinarily cueing is simple; however, in TV and film a performer works through an intermediary—usually the floor director—to talk to the director. Consequently, cueing can be misunderstood or late. In such cases, if the instructions to the talent are simple, the director may resort to the studio intercom (i.e., loudspeaker), but if they are complex, the director will come into the studio to converse directly with the performer.

A reporter, however, is connected to other members of the television production team through his floor manager and/or through a headset. The headset enables a reporter to listen directly to instructions from the control room. Many news people feel much more secure wearing a headset. In radio, where the visual aspect is eliminated, large foam rubber pads attached to the headset cover the entire ear, so that the newsperson can listen carefully to the sound quality as well as the various elements of the production. Inasmuch as audibility is all that is required of a television newscaster's headset, modern headsets, like those manufactured by the Telex Corporation, have inserts for the ears and are not very noticeable to viewers. Most intercommunication systems are controlled by the director who receives messages from the studio, projection, videotape and other locations. Of course, the newscaster hears this conversation.

Cueing Radio Performers

Typical oral cueing for a radio program in the studio consists of the director-engineer advising the performer: "One minute to air . . . 30 seconds . . . Stand by (10 seconds) . . . Take it (cue)."

Most radio programs have an amazing amount of prerecorded material—commercials, discs, features and syndicated items—therefore, the performer may walk in and out of the studio several times while the program is on the air with recorded portions. The live part of the broadcast continues with the performer taking cues from the control room or the clock. Performers may also cue the director-engineer when they, for example, want the theme music to sneak under closing remarks. One way of doing this is for the performer to gesture for increased volume in clear view of the director-engineer. The speed and vigor the performer uses in the gesture will cue the director-engineer in regard to the pace. With a little practice such cueing is instantly understood.

A large percentage of programming from some stations occurs on remote location. Contacts with reporters are maintained by means of a *pager* or *beeper* which the news person carries everywhere. On a signal from the pager the reporter telephones the station or calls on a two-way radio in the mobile unit. In New York City an area relay system is being developed in which the reporter can speak into a microphone from the scene, the signal being relayed to the station from a permanent transmitter located in that part of the city, thereby bypassing the necessity of using a telephone or car radio.

Cueing for a complex program at a radio station is discussed more readily from the director's viewpoint. This is typical contol room procedure:

To talent over the intercom: "Level check, please." The engineer adjusts the "pots."

To talent over the intercom: "30 seconds to air."

To talent, 10 seconds to air: "Stand by—quiet."

To engineer (in the control room): "Hit theme. Music to background."

To announcer (in announcer's booth): "Cue announce." The announcer reads the copy.

To engineer: "Music up." (It plays for a few more seconds so as to establish the sound.) "Sneak music out."

To talent (gesturing from control room): "Stand by and cue."

Talent performs. (During the broadcast the director gives whatever additional hand signals are essential. He may smile or gesture that the program is going well. He watches the time carefully. In long programs talent prefers cues at 15, 10, 5, 4, 3, 2, 1, and ½-minutes.) Talent finishes.

To engineer: "Theme. Fade to background and cue announce." The announcer reads the closing copy.

To engineer: "Theme up and fade out."

Everyone remains silent until the director indicates that the program is over. Speaking over the intercom: "That's it. Thanks, everybody. That was fine."[2]

Cueing Television Performers

Typical oral cueing prior to the beginning of a TV program is announced by the floor director: "One minute to air (or tape) . . . 30 seconds. Quiet in the studio . . . 10 seconds. Stand by. (A countdown may begin: "Five, four, three, two, one—) Cue."

At the 10-second "stand by," the floor director raises a hand with the flat of the palm toward the talent or points an index finger toward the on-air lens. On cue from the director, spoken over the FD's head-set, the floor director points directly at the performer, who responds instantly. Most visual cues concern timing—the minutes or seconds remaining before the program is over, wrap up, stretch, or speed up. Some deal with movement—the floor director waves the performer from one camera to the on-air lens of another, especially if the talent cannot tell from the tally lights which camera is on the air; or the performer, by placing the palms of the hands on a desk in front or on top of his or her thighs, may indicate that he or she intends to stand. Some have to do with content—if a floor director taps the palm of one hand with the index finger of the other, this signals the talent to go to a spot announcement or commercial; if the FD assumes the pose of looking through a lens while cranking a camera, this means "go to film;" or if the FD points to an item on the set, this means go to that item. For the most part, so long as the performer remains on his or her marks, sticks to the script or program outline and performs as the program was rehearsed, cueing is minimal.

At its conclusion, the talent does not move until the floor director announces that the show or taping is over: "That's it. Good job. Thanks alot," or until the cameras have obviously broken to another set. A common error for a novice is to move, especially move one's eyes from the camera lens, or grimace prematurely. Such action might ruin the take.

Cueing Film Performers

In film making the director, often sitting a few feet from the action, gives the cues, but in big or complex scenes, cues may come from assistant directors: "Ready on the set . . . Quiet . . . Roll film . . . (Camera operator calls: "Speed," indicating that the film is up to recording speed). "Slate" . . . (A production assistant runs in front of the camera and identifies the scene. The camera continues to roll for a few seconds of black). Action!" During the film very few, if any, cues are given by the director. If the scene doesn't go well, it is reshot. Much of the sound will be dubbed later in a sound recording studio, rather than in a movie studio or on location.

If a flaw develops in the production, the director will stop the performance, referred to as a "take," by saying, "Cut." A discussion of the scene follows. Soon thereafter the performer will hear: "Okay, once again from the top." The scene including the cueing procedures is repeated until the performance is acceptable. Numerous takes may be required; a half dozen or less is par, except for complex scenes in dramas or commercials. Performers, incidently, should never assume the flaw is their fault, because it probably isn't. More likely it is a technical error.

HAND SIGNALS

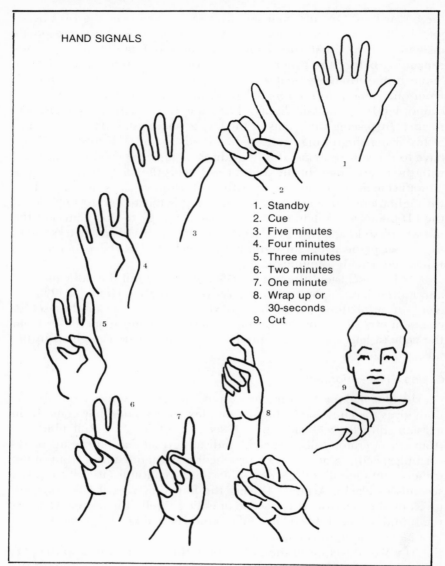

1. Standby
2. Cue
3. Five minutes
4. Four minutes
5. Three minutes
6. Two minutes
7. One minute
8. Wrap up or
   30-seconds
9. Cut

PERSONNEL RELATIONSHIPS

If a performer becomes a star, it is because he or she has over-whelming talent, ambition, the expertise and cooperation of other per-formers and countless people on the production staff. A performer is well advised to be reciprocally cooperative and generous. If the staff

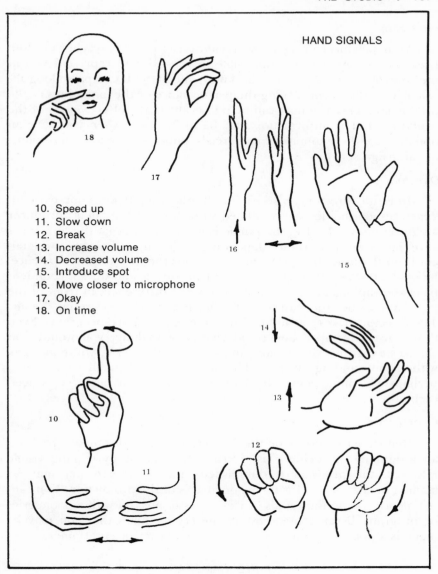

HAND SIGNALS

10. Speed up
11. Slow down
12. Break
13. Increase volume
14. Decreased volume
15. Introduce spot
16. Move closer to microphone
17. Okay
18. On time

likes a performer, it often gives an extra measure of devotion to make that performer look good; but if a staff dislikes a performer, the reverse can result. For instance, as a performer *you* may not need a rehearsal, but keep in mind your crew does; and, if you are too big to stand in for yourself, then hire someone to do it.

Producers

Your producer or agent, in some cases a relative, teacher or close friend—someone who is responsible to you—should represent you in the control room. A person who knows media well, can pass along invaluable feedback concerning the performance or the limitations of the production. The producer can help to evaluate the effectiveness of the studio crew. This information may be useful later when you have an option as to where to make commercials, public service announcements or campaign spots.

Directors

In radio, directors *per se* are for all practical purposes non-existent. Their responsibilities are combined with those of the talent, producer and/or engineer. In TV, the public is hardly aware that the director is alive, his or her importance depending largely upon how great the talent is on the tube. If a performer questions the director's competence, he or she does so through an agent or producer, and does it confidentially and diplomatically. Do not try to settle differences in front of the crew. Remember the director calls the shots while you are on the air. The director makes the audio-visual choices on all live programs. Even if you are videotaped and could change something, you would find changes expensive. In cinema, and occasionally in TV, you may work with an outstanding director. This will be a highlight in your career, perhaps a turning point. Great directors and great performers need each other.

Floor Crews

Remember everyone on the floor crew counts. If someone fouls up an assignment by being noisy during the take or by making visible mistakes, the program is diminished, and the performer may be blamed by the viewers for the inadequacies of the production. You cannot afford having thousands of viewers associate you with a poor series or program, because ineptness in the crew implies that you may be inept as a politician, minister, teacher, newscaster or entertainer.

USING CAMERAS

The camera shows everything in its field of view. Whether a performer is scratching a leg or adjusting a microphone or making an unpleasant expression, the camera will show it—perhaps to thousands of people if it is on the air. Performers must assume that they are on the air all of the time during the airing or taping of a program, therefore, they never do or say anything that could not go over the air.

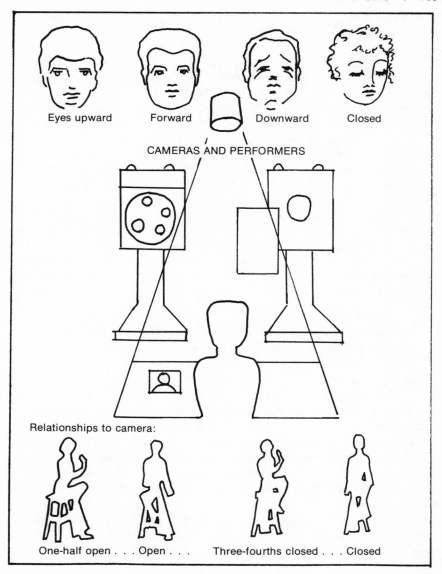

Eyes upward   Forward   Downward   Closed

CAMERAS AND PERFORMERS

Relationships to camera:

One-half open . . . Open . . .   Three-fourths closed . . . Closed

Cameras are frequently big and clumsy, especially commercial ones. They move slowly from set to set. Nowadays the zoom lens adds fast and fluid variation from a wideshot covering the entire set to an extreme closeup of the performer. No matter how many lenses are visible, a camera has only one that is "hot" or on the air. This hot lens is in a different position on different cameras depending on the model. The performer should be certain which lens is hot. Often cameras have tiny lights indicating they are on the air, they are called "tally lights."

Direct Audience Contact

Performers who wish to address an audience directly look into the on-air lens, just as though they are speaking to a close friend. News-casters, politicians, teachers and entertainers frequently look directly into the on-air lens. Any other position, such as glancing down to read a script, is interruptive, distracting and sometimes breaks com-munication completely. To some extent an audience accepts the read-ing of notes, because of the tradition of lecturing and public speaking from notes. The illusion of fluid conversation, either adlibbed or read from prompters without interruption, is better direct communication between the performer and the audience. This means looking directly into the camera and, when necessary, discreetly changing one's gaze from one camera to another, by looking directly into Camera One, then down at a script, and up into Camera Two. Peripheral vision allows the performer to see the floor director wave the performer from one camera to another.

Indirect Audience Contact

If a performer is addressing someone on the set, the public acts as an observer to the scene. Except for some panel discussions, perhaps, the viewers are less involved. Frequently, interpretive work such as readings, singing or acting allows the viewer to participate in an experi-ence vicariously and indirectly. An actor's emotions and interpretation of a role are observed by the public, but the public is not a direct parti-cipant. Instead, the performer either speaks directly to another per-former on the set as in a play or speaks to a focal point arbitrarily fixed in the black depths of the studio. Although camera operators move as the director dictates, the performer pays no attention to their place-ment. Few vocalists sing directly to a camera lens. Most of them sing to a studio audience or to an imaginary focal point. Often the point is about 10 feet off the floor and in direct line with a bright light called a "key" light. This light illuminates the face of the performer and it tends to add a sparkle to the eyes by making them water slightly.

USING MICROPHONES

A performer is concerned with a microphone's frequency range, coverage, size, placement and use. Unless a microphone is used as a prop, like those jeweled ones some entertainers hold while they lip sync to their latest recording, a performer prefers not being encumbered by one. Microphones are, after all, unattractive. Dark or shiny, they obscure a performer's expression, attach to clothing or limit the area in which he or she can move. Microphones are not playthings, of course, they are expensive, necessary tools of the trade. Two principles should guide the performer: select a microphone that is right for you and never use more microphones than you need. Naturally these principles will have to be carried out in cooperation with the studio engineer. And, of course, never rattle your script.

Presence

The term *presence* refers to the degree of fidelity which a sound has. It is the notion that this sound is what an audience would hear if it were in the same room with the performer and listening under optimum conditions. So, engineers do their best to convey optimum presence through media transmission and recording. A performer's knowledge of recording equipment and its proper utilization will help immeasurably to give an audience optimum presence. Ultimately, presence is a subjective judgment made by the producer, director and/or performer. Usually a normal conversational voice is pleasing. No effort need be made to project the voice, but then it should not be abnormally soft either. Speak as though you were talking to someone in the control room or operating the camera; that is, someone about 10 feet away.

Microphone Characteristics

Each microphone has its own characteristics. The principal microphones a performer uses are the *dynamic* or pressure microphone, which tends to favor the high frequencies; the *ribbon,* which favors the low frequencies; and the *condenser,* which gives the truest frequency response. The dynamic microphone is the least expensive and most rugged. It comes in various models. It is omnidirectional, meaning that it picks up sounds from everywhere whether the performer wants it to or not. The ribbon microphone is much more selective, having a narrow beam extending fore and aft in a bidirectional pattern. The condenser microphone is often used on musical productions, because of its omnidirectional pickup that can be made unidirectional. Condenser microphones cost about $350 to $1,500, whereas good dynamic microphones can be purchased for less than $100.

The smallest microphones are the size of a tie-tac that may be clipped on a suit or dress. Somewhat larger is the two-inch lavalier, which hangs around the performer's neck on a lanyard or clips to clothing. About six inches in length are the hand-held microphones which can be mounted on stands or in brackets suspended from overhead booms. An addition to the uni-, bi- and omnidirectional pattern for microphones is a heart-shaped pattern known as a *cardioid.* A "super" version of the cardioid, about 18-inches long and casting a rather narrow pickup pattern some 10 to 15 feet is called a "shotgun," which is mounted on the balcony of a theater and aimed in the direction of a performer who is on the stage. In recent years wireless microphones attached discreetly to a belt enable performers to work within a 25-foot radius of the receiver-transmitter, thus relieving the performer of an unattractive microphone cable. Their frequency as well as their range, however, is limited.

Microphone Techniques

Keeping in mind that a microphone is a relatively delicate and expensive item, a performer tests it by simply speaking into it, using the same volume and pitch of voice that he or she intends to use on the air and maintaining an appropriate distance from the mike. Tapping, whistling, blowing and yelling into a microphone for testing purposes are not only unnecessary but may permanently damage the instrument. Ribbon microphones are especially sensitive to mistreatment; the key element, the ribbon, stretches permanently if abused, reducing the frequency range. The engineer will adjust the level of a microphone on the console accordingly, so that every performer's voice blends with the rest of the program. If a performer is at a loss for words when the engineer asks, "Level check, please," simply read the script or count until the engineer has heard enough to adjust the pots. Do not stop and start capriciously. A performer's voice registers on the console's meters only when he or she is speaking. In general, a performer, especially in a unionized market, does not move microphones; this is the audio engineer's job. Besides, moving a microphone may jeopardize the sound quality or the aesthetics of a shot. If a performer is not comfortable with a microphone, this should be discussed with the floor director or director. Testing a microphone takes only a few minutes.

A performer works four to eight inches from the screen of a dynamic microphone and speaks across the surface of it, depending upon how much he or she wants low frequencies to register. The closer the performer gets to the screen, the better the low frequencies will register; but breathing and plosives in the English language will begin to be heard as "pops." Condenser and cardioid microphones also use the pressure principle, but when their pickup patterns are uni- or bi-directional, they are used like a ribbon microphone, that is, a performer speaks or sings directly into them.

Some suggestions for microphone placement may be helpful:

If you must have a microphone around your neck, place it under your clothing—tie or scarf. If clothing muffles the sound, your engineer will tell you. Fasten your lavalier. If it moves, it may hit buttons or jewelry; even swinging over the surface of a shirt may be noisy. A

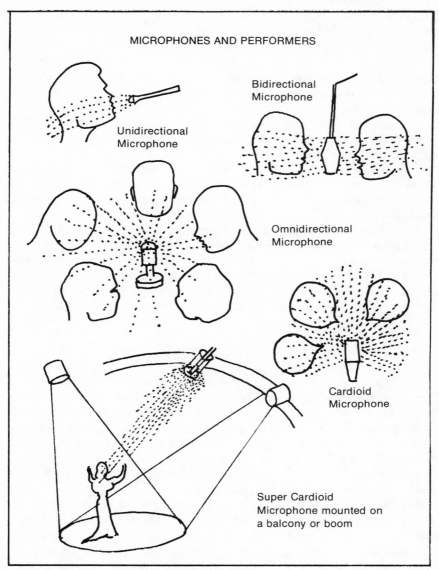

MICROPHONES AND PERFORMERS

Unidirectional Microphone

Bidirectional Microphone

Omnidirectional Microphone

Cardioid Microphone

Super Cardioid Microphone mounted on a balcony or boom

jacket or patterned blouse helps women, particularly, to draw attention away from the microphone.

If you must hold a microphone while standing, remember the long cable will show. To minimize its visibility when you are standing, attach it to your belt, being certain to leave enough slack so that it will not pull on your clothing. Nothing looks worse than a performer wrestling with a long microphone cable or being trailed by a long black cable resembling a rat's tail. Preplan so that you have ample cable to go wherever you must during the performance.

If you are working with a microphone stand, remember it is easy to kick, causing a resounding thud. If the microphone is suspended on a boom or overhead, avoid the performer's tendency to move out of the beam.

In general, if you are singing or speaking, one microphone, preferably unseen, should be enough. If you are a newsmaker, a battery of microphones may be necessary to accommodate each reporter with an actuality, but this is really the same as one microphone to one performer. If you use a musical instrument, mike it separately. If you are part of a round table discussion, one good omnidirectional microphone is adequate. If you are on a panel—seated in a straight line—probably one microphone for every two or three people is necessary. Do not attempt to pass the microphone, because it will be noisy. If you are in a musical group, all principal singers and instruments must be miked separately. If you are in concert, however, the orchestra may be picked up on one microphone suspended in the center of the auditorium, and you will probably have a personal microphone.

TYPICAL SETTINGS

A simple setting consists of the background and floor, scenery or furniture, set decoration to make it look finished, and lighting. Properities ("props") are items the performer must manipulate during the presentation. A *cyclorama* is a drape, often made taut, or plaster wall ("hard cyc") usually white, gray or blue that encloses much of the set. Most performers look good in front of a blue cyclorama.

Furniture can be troublesome. Some things a performer should watch for are furniture that dwarfs the performer, that relaxes the performer to the extent that he or she looks slovenly on camera, that is too attention-getting by being too colorful or complex in design, that obscures the performer from the audience such as a large desk tends to do. Molded plastic chairs with straight backs, shallow seats, moderately padded, of medium gray scale in color are common. They should be armless so that you can get close to your guest, and both feet should touch the floor when you are seated. Most chairs are too low, too deep, too bulky, too cushioned, too hard; consequently, stools are often used. The stools should be of the right height to give the performer a strong vertical line.

In reference to set decoration, the performer should be certain the flowers, papers, books, ashtrays, sculptures, paintings and miscellany do not call attention to themselves. Nor should they appear at odd places through optical illusion—plants placed behind a performer may appear to be growing out of his or her head, or on a newscast a figure on a rear screen projection may be pointing into the newscaster's ear. A bowl of light flowers in front of dark clothing may be undesirable, just as metal objects may cast unattractive reflections on the performer.

For the most part these problems are the responsibility of the production staff, but the performer should be aware of them. Most sets are disappointing, makeshift, tacky, even dirty and discolored to look at. Do not worry about this. Check what the setting looks like on camera. It will probably look fine when lighted properly. Don't worry about the space you have, some of the finest programs are done with virtually no space. For some years David Brinkley was in a relatively small studio at WRC-TV, Washington, D.C. He worked behind a rather tired looking stand, but on the air this set for *The Huntley-Brinkley Report* was very impressive. During the first half of the 1970s Harry Reasoner anchored his part of the network news from behind a small desk in ABC's basement studio in New York.

COMPLEX SETTINGS

Complex settings and multi-settings are used for dramas and variety programs. These settings are usually built inside a studio but may be built on location. In any case they are essentially background that aids the performer and adds impact to the program. Performers are relatively oblivious to a setting except for the part of it in which they work. In drama, settings provide reality to the performance, and so they re-enforce the performer's emotional awareness of the character's environment. For instance, a naturalistic setting may help the performers in *Roots* to develop a stronger feeling for their roles. Likewise, a subjective treatment of a setting for a mystery may intensify a performer's acting. Overwhelming sets, flashing lights, glittering drapes and moving objects do assist a musical program; (1) if the performer is static, (2) if there is a long period in a song when an action cutaway is needed, (3) if image association will re-enforce his or her appearance, such as a cut to the performer running through woods, making love or other tasks that could not be done during the song, or (4) if the performer isn't a strong singer in the first place and the audience needs to be diverted. Several performers who are known in some other field— drama, sports—are helped by this technique.

A delightful setting was built for the "Pedro's Plant Place" sequence from *The Electric Company*. This setting, an interior "box" set, consisted of a door, two floor-to-ceiling bookcases, a large window with

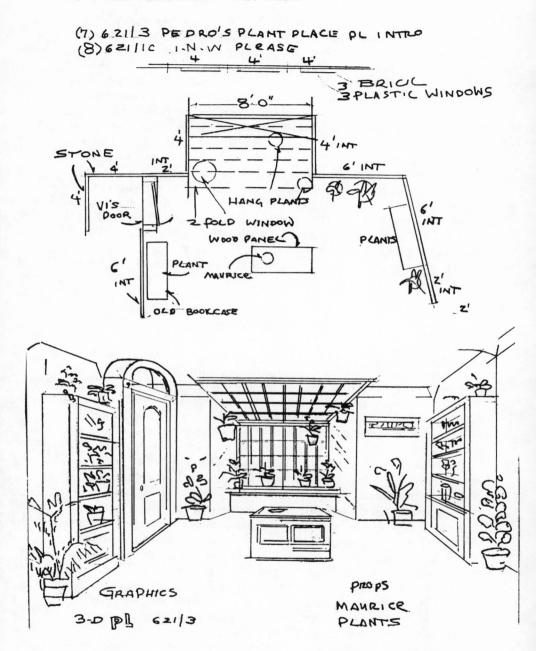

(7) 6 21/3 PEDRO'S PLANT PLACE PL INTRO
(8) 6211C I.N.W PLEASE

3 BRICK
3 PLASTIC WINDOWS

8'0"

STONE

INT 2'

4' INT

6' INT

HANG PLANTS

2 FOLD WINDOW

WOOD PANEL

PLANTS

6' INT

2' INT

VI'S DOOR

6' INT

PLANT

MAURICE

OLD BOOKCASE

2'

GRAPHICS

3-D PL 621/3

PROPS
MAURICE
PLANTS

a skylight and, of course, several plants. The action took place in the middle of the room where Pedro has a conversation with Maurice, a talking plant. "This set was more complicated than usual," said David D. Connell, vice president for production, Children's Television Workshop. "It was used over and over again in a series on the formation of sounds."

In another instance, the stage of the Ed Sullivan Theatre in New York provided multi-sets that served as changes in background for host Howard Cosell. (See Chapter 12, page 248)

10: Preparation

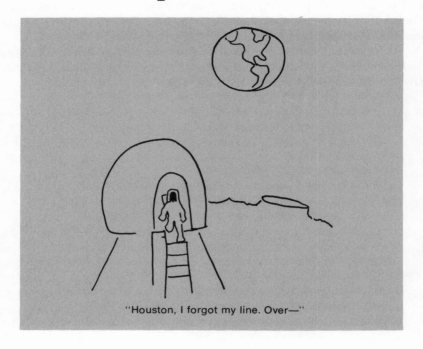

"Houston, I forgot my line. Over—"

Live Performance
Memorization (Electronic Memory)—Reading (Scripts; Video Prompters; Cue Cards)—Extemporaneous Presentations (Mental Outlines)

Recorded Performance
Live vs. Recorded Performances—Correcting the Recorded Performance (Typical Editing Procedure)—Working with Pre-recorded Materials (Pre-recorded Soundtracks; Pre-recorded Video)

Preparation for Guests
Gathering Background Information—Contacting the Guest (Pre-rehearsal Meetings)—Preparing Excessive Material

Preparation of Visuals
Filmed Materials (Moving Picture Film; Slides; Photographs)—Graphics (Charts and Graphs; Drawings; Three-dimensional Objects)—Demonstrations

THE ARDUOUS WORK of performing is the preparation. Well prepared performers are secure. They know what they are doing and how to do it. This knowledge is the result of study, practice and experience on the job. Like the proverbial iceberg, preparation is the mass and depth below the surface, and performance is its majestic peak. The greater the iceberg beneath the water, the greater the peak above. Preparation is a lifetime occupation of gathering ideas and experiences, selecting and discarding, assembling, combining shapes, depths and nuances by objectively and emotionally observing life's passing parade. Preparation is an amalgamation of all that life has to offer. Everywhere performers look, there are bits and pieces of material they can apply to their presentation. If a person is a unique performer, part of the reason may be that he or she is uniquely prepared. Such a person's experiences or outlook may be different from what others experience, feel or believe.

Performers reshape the world for themselves and the public. Every kind of background and interest is valuable to media in one way or another. Those specializing in information usually have interests in government, economics, sociology, anthropology, physical and natural sciences, history, journalism and the fine arts. Entertainers become deeply involved in drama, art, music, speech, cinema, broadcasting, dance and physical education. Some who study media have previous experience or employment in weather service, agriculture, teaching, police and fire departments, computer operation, insurance, home making and management. Preparation requires much time spent without praise, alone in seclusion, reading and rehearsing for hours and hours. Serious performers like to do this work; those who are not serious do not want to do it. While a few people can get away with minimum preparation for a short time, most performers require years of study. That is the reason so many professional performers are relatively old before they become prominent. They need time to prepare, to mature, to understand what they are doing. Such seasoning takes years, and the gestation period is often on the sheer speculation that one will succeed, for success is never guaranteed in any occupation.

LIVE PERFORMANCE

A live performance is exciting, because the public is seeing and/or hearing the program at the moment it is going on; thus an original experience is created both for the audience and the performer. They share a moment that will never be seen or heard again. Mistakes may be present, but empathic intensity may be present too. A live performance is thrilling, frustrating, terrifying and risky—you could bomb. You could forget, become confused, stumble, make a fool of yourself . . . and you could be tremendously successful. The net result is that a performer is more than a little scared before a live performance. Nevertheless, some performers work better before a live audience, because they require immediate empathic response to stimulate them. This is particularly true of those in comedy, sports and music. After all, many situation comedies, dinner "roasts," sportscasts, quiz programs, religious rallies, political conventions, beauty contests, concerts and "award" presentations are held before live audiences, even though they may be videotaped for later broadcast. In all of these events there is an element of the unexpected—something may happen on stage or in the audience that is not planned, such as the kidnapping and shooting during the Olympic games in Munich in 1972.

To a performer every show in a sense is live. The audience ranges from a small studio crew to a large audience in the studio to a vast unseen public of listeners and/or viewers the size of which a performer has difficulty comprehending.

Memorization

If a performer could present a continuous flow of fascinating conversation or perpared copy without referring to notes or a prompting device, that would be ideal. Ronald Reagan attempted to do this in his network TV appearance on March 31, 1976, in which he explained his qualifications for being president and his plans for the nation if elected. Performers try to do this by reading extensively, becoming familiar with the backgrounds of guests they interview, and by keeping up with complex issues and changes throughout the world. To use expensive media time wisely—supporters may pay about $100,000 for the airtime—every second must be planned. Every word in a speech, a commercial, a drama must be exact. This requires an accurate memory. In some cases—commercials and editorials, for instance—the substitution of a single word could destroy the idea being advocated in the spot, or could place the station in legal jeopardy or could ruin the reputation of an innocent person. So, memory must be exact. This perfection can be obtained either through exact performer recall, reshooting and/or editing.

   Memorization comes easier for some people than for others. Here are some of the reasons: (1) some performers concentrate better than others, and therefore mentally arrange ideas in the script quickly; (2) they have a fondness for verbal expression and language; (3) they hear with a finer discrimination of sounds; (4) they tend to have a photographic recollection of the printed page. One procedure for memorizing material is to grasp the major ideas first, then look up the pronunciation of any difficult words, phrases or ideas. Third, take note of meters, rhyming or other euphonic aids. Fourth, read the material aloud several times experimenting with inflection, reciting the material line by line building your recall. Fifth, recite the entire piece, aloud if possible, over and over until it is verbatim. Sixth, perfect your interpretation. Seventh, test yourself by repeating it anywhere, anytime. Know the material flawlessly. Security in memorization is absolutely essential if the performer is to relax into the delivery reflecting a deep, subtle interpretation and professional level of confidence.

   Some other techniques which may be helpful are: to write down the difficult passages because this will give you visual re-inforcement; to work with friends or an audio tape recorder that will feed you cues; to move according to blocking instruction while you are delivering your lines; and to memorize prior to bedtime when presumably your mind at rest will retain the material more readily.

   Electronic Memory. Some new devices and methods are being developed which provide an electronic memory for a performer. One device, for example, consists of a tiny tape recorder and a wireless hearing device. The performer's script is recorded in advance on the tape recorder and then replayed during the performance. In effect the performer simply recites what is heard on the tape, delivering lines about two words behind the dictation. This device has some drawbacks, but the performer is never at a loss for memory when it is carried along. Thus, a stand-up news report could have the fluency of absolute memory without really memorizing it. Some time is needed to record the material. Pacing the material is always a problem and a disaster could occur if the recorder went amuck.[1]

Reading

   Reading with fluency, interpretation and style takes much practice. Reading requires *instant* word recognition for meaning and pronunciation. It also requires pacing, and, if the audience is to respond, conveying an understanding by the audience of what the performer has read. The performer, therefore, must truly communicate with the audience.

   Scripts. Many performers depend on reading a typed script. Performers who move to TV from radio, wire services or newspapers and teachers, ministers and politicians commonly read from scripts. These scripts, held relatively high and in an easy-to-read position, are usually typed in big, black bold letters, double- or triple-spaced, with paragraph indentations, few lines to the page and no divided words or interrupted phrases where possible. Performers often type their scripts across the page, although many in television type on only one half of the page, allowing the other vertical half for director cues and notes on visuals. These cues may be essential for performers who must know where film, slides and other visuals will come in the program.

While markings on scripts are kept to a minimum, they indicate where a performer can rest during the reading. For instance, periods, semi-colons and commas are enlarged to indicate rest stops where a performer can breathe, if necessary, at the end of sentences and phrases. Words and phrases requiring special emphasis are underlined. Some inflections—a rise or lowering in volume or pitch—may be noted by curved lines above words or at the end of sentences. These notes are especially helpful if the performer has gotten into the habit of a monotonous delivery and wishes to break it. All new or foreign words should have English respellings to aid pronunciation. Each piece of copy is clearly marked. Continued speeches should be noted with "More," indicating that there is a carry-over onto the next page. Pages are usually numbered in one upper corner and/or identified in the other corner by a key word (slug), such as "accident" or "city hall." Insofar as possible be certain that the same slug is used to identify news stories on the director's and crew's scripts. Clear identification avoids a lot of confusion and saves a great deal of time. All abbreviations should be noted, understood and, if more helpful, spelled out. Color coding pages is helpful: yellow might be the "to read" copy, light green the prerecorded commercials. Few stations do this however. The final script should be as clean and unconfusing as possible.

When reading, a performer's peripheral vision allows him or her to see a few words in advance. This helps assure fluency. By pulling the unread sheets on the reader's right over the read sheets on the left, the copy is moved inconspicuously. Occasionally performers reading copy around a stand microphone will drop the pages silently to the carpet for quick disposition after reading them. A performer always checks the order of the pages just before air time.

Common errors in reading include slurred words, halting delivery, excessive sweetness, unexpected extremes in volume, noticeable breathing, failure to look up sufficiently from the script, energy-less or too sober in delivery, stumbling, without smoothly regaining composure, clearing the throat on microphone, questions read to guests, and an inability to read copy smoothly without rehearsal; i.e., "cold." If an item is misread, a performer rarely goes back to reread it unless the error changes the meaning of the content.

A MARKED SCRIPT

PAGE_____ 275 H

STORY___ MIAMI FIRE

Date/Show____/ 30 SEC.

REP_____ CM____

Slug Line:
for story
identification.

O.C. [Newscaster is on camera.]

LOOK INTO ON-AIR LENS

FIRE SWEPT THROUGH A 60 YEAR OLD MIAMI HOTEL THIS MORNING/ LEAVING AT LEAST SEVEN PERSONS DEAD AND 13 OTHERS INJURED. //

SIL VTR VO 25 [Newscaster reads over 25-second videotape.]

WATCH TAPE FOR VISUAL CUES

Marking Techniques:

1. Underline for emphasis to indicate continuous reading.

2. Enlarge punctuation to enhance timing.

3. Respell words for pronunciation.

4. Add symbols to improve style:

   a. " ✓ ➚ " indicates a rise or fall in inflection.

   b. " ∿∿∿ " indicates reading may be difficult.

   c. "/" or "//" indicates a pause or point of rest in the reading. The virgule is easy to see.

5. Note instructions for cueing.

FIRE OFFICIALS SAY ARSON IS STRONGLY SUSPECTED IN THE BLAZE. AN EMPTY CONTAINER/ THAT HELD A FLAMMABLE LIQUID/ WAS FOUND IN THE REAR OF THE HOTEL AVONDALE/WHERE THE (AV·ON·DALE) FIRE STARTED. POLICE EARLIER TODAY QUESTIONED THREE PERSONS/ INCLUDING TWO HOTEL EMPLOYEES/ IN CONNECTION WITH THE CASE. THEY'VE BEEN RELEASED AND THE INVESTIGATION CONTINUES.

Reading time of story.

MORE

PRODUCER

Video Prompters. Video prompters are mechanical devices attached adjacent to the on-air lens of TV cameras revealing the script line-by-line to the performer through a lighted prism that magnifies the type. The close proximity of the videoprompter and the on-air lens creates the illusion that the performer is telling memorized material directly to the viewer. Over the years journalists, entertainers, politicians and others have tended to use video prompters more and more—but they can be used only as long as the camera is relatively close to the performer (about 7 feet) and easy to read.[2] Any squinting or other signs of strain showing on the performer's face nullifies its value, and so a video prompter works best for static situations or those within a close radius of the performer. Teleprompter is a commercial brand name commonly associated with any device of this general description. Prompters are also built into lecture stands and desks, allowing performers to read copy from a projection of the script.

Cue Cards. Cue cards, sometimes called "idiot cards," carry a performer's lines or key words in bold letters on large sheets of cardboard or paper. They are held near the on-air lens by a production assistant, sometimes referred to as a cue card holder. Such cards are difficult to handle because they bend easily, may be large and long, and depend upon legible printing by hand or type to be effective. The production assistant must change the cards quietly, keeping them in the right order and pointing, if possible, to each of the lines being read on the air. A difficult problem is getting the cue cards close enough to the lens so that the performer can create the illusion of memory instead of obvious reading. Many professionals are very skillful at reading cue cards, depending greatly on peripheral vision and a well-placed production assistant. Occasionally when the system fails, the performer is forced to acknowledge the cue card holder while on the air.

Extemporaneous Presentations

Thorough preparation of oneself on the topics most likely to be discussed on the program is necessary for extemporaneous presentations. One of the big challenges for those working in political affairs, for instance, is keeping up with government to the extent that performers can talk with congressmen and other officials about late breaking events on the spur of the moment. This requires background and a substantial knowledge of current events. Finding the time for such preparation can be difficult. In fact, too many radio hosts of talk programs are unprepared and must "wing it," not because they want to, but because they do not have time to adequately prepare for the broad range of topics facing them on talk programs nearly every day. The strain of being unprepared is evident in an actual conversation held immediately before one such radio program:

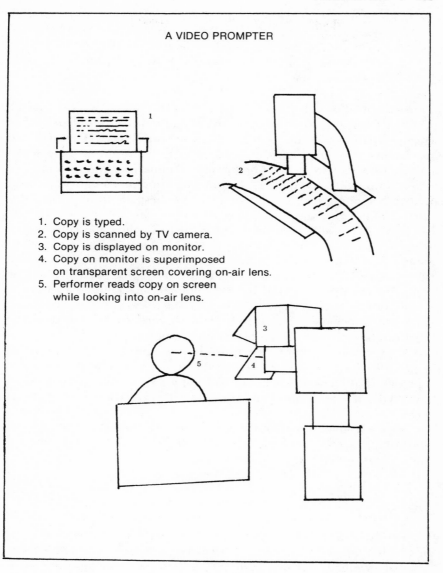

A VIDEO PROMPTER

1. Copy is typed.
2. Copy is scanned by TV camera.
3. Copy is displayed on monitor.
4. Copy on monitor is superimposed on transparent screen covering on-air lens.
5. Performer reads copy on screen while looking into on-air lens.

Host: "Why are you here?"
Guest: "I'm not sure. To discuss the movie, I guess."
Host: "Oh."
Guest: "I saw this movie a couple of times and was asked to talk about it."
Host, glancing at a review in *Newsweek:* "I haven't seen it."

Guest: "I'll outline the plot, talk about the director and cast, and we'll discuss some of the more controversial points, okay?"
Host: "Good. Then we'll take calls from the listeners."
Guest: "I've never heard the program. How long is it anyway?"
Host: "An hour."

Mental Outlines. For extemporaneous discussions and interviews a performer clusters his or her thoughts on a dominant simple structure which provides coherence and direction for the subject. The principal approaches are: *chronological* (consisting of background, present status and the future); *topical* (including items of similar classification such as: in regard to a film, its content, cast, direction and impact); or *importance* (that is, beginning with the questions of greatest significance then discussing others of descending importance).

Journalists are fond of discussing topics in their most up-to-date form knowing that broadcast media have little or no time for background; so the barest background information is given to viewers and listeners to enable them to understand the report. Applied to a subject of insufficient funds for spraying to eliminate mosquitos, for instance, the important questions are: What does this mean to human beings? What are the chances for disease? How hazardous are the diseases? What can be done? What has been done? and so forth.

A topical approach may be applied to selecting plants for an apartment by discussing plant size, required care or price. The chronological approach is often used when interviewing guests—What are you doing now? What has led up to your success? What are you planning to do next?

A simple mental outline like these will give the performer organization and security, and the audience direction and perspective—in other words, something it can remember.

RECORDED PERFORMANCE

The freshness and excitement of a live performance being created for the first time is desirable in all forms of performance. Early TV was "live"; it gradually became "canned" or recorded on film and kinescopes. Later, videotape was used on the one hand to carefully record and edit some programs, and on the other, to create an illusion of "live-on-tape" unedited spontaneity for certain programs. Current trends in TV production—new videotape techniques, instant replays, mobile mini-cameras—suggest that the freshness of live-on-tape TV is as prominent now as it ever was. In recorded programs imperfections can be eliminated and inaccurate statements corrected. Even though editing may be expensive, there is no question a performer can control a recording and, thus, the performance.

Actors, politicians and other professional performers who need to protect their reputations cannot afford to have their work appear at anything less than its best, particularly after the public has come to recognize a standard of quality in the performer. Those who wish favorable public recognition must appear always at their best. To make this possible utmost care and control are exercised in recording for mass media which, of course, will as quickly reveal a performer's deterioration as well as excellence.

Although local public affairs programs are videotaped, as a rule they are not edited, and so performers must recognize that fact when they do the program. Some programs are pre-recorded in advance of airing; others, especially those of opinion or newsmakers, are recorded while playing on the air. These programs may be syndicated or excerpted for news programs. A comment on *Face the Nation,* for example, may appear later in the day on a local news program. Newsmakers frequently want to omit statements from a pre-recorded program—those very statements that give the program life and drama—but producers rarely allow them to preview the tape in advance. Sometimes, too, opinionmakers appearing in live TV misspeak. Journalists often capitalize on such errors in judgment in an effort to reveal the genuine nature of a person to the public. Politicians are particularly vulnerable to misconstrued statements or those reported out of context. For instance, President Ford was forced to admit his misstatement concerning Soviet domination over Eastern European countries during the 1976 debates. Some journalists, interviewers and personalities make their reputations by surprising guests with the nature of their inquiry on the air. To avoid embarrassment, a performer must insist in advance of the taping upon previewing and possibly editing the tape. In reality, producers rarely allow this to happen unless the celebrity is in extraordinary demand.

Live vs. Recorded Performances

A live performance perishes the moment it is aired. Most programming on radio is perishable. It may be recorded for legal purposes, but these recordings are never heard again unless litigation should arise, and within months they are destroyed. In effect, the performance was broadcast live and that was the end of it. Certain programs or segments, such as feature materials, interviews or discussions may have longevity, may be repeated and/or syndicated. For the most part, however, programs at the local level are so tailored for a specific community that this rarely happens. A few celebrities have syndicated radio features, but most talk and news programs are perishable.

In TV and cinema the situation is quite different. Both media depend on the re-release value of the material for supplementary income, because they frequently do not make enough money on the original distribution to recover initial expenses. A feature film must gross two or three times what it cost to make in order to break even, according to Eric Pleskow, president of United Artists. A TV series, which makes no money on the first public showing, depends upon network reruns and/or syndication to make a profit. Series like *I Love Lucy, Star Trek* and *Bonanza* will make money for the performers, owners and percentage holders indefinitely. In other words, some performers can draw "residuals" or income for much of their lives from a successful TV series or film.

Besides residual value, the performance can be corrected, as mentioned elsewhere. But recording gives performers a kind of immortality. Performers can look their best and remain that way, preserved indefinitely on tape or film. This creates an unusual phenomenon in reference to longevity, for so long as the series plays the public thinks of the star as being active to an extent at least, and the star tends to remain ageless (Jack Lord in *Hawaii Five-O*).

Correcting the Recorded Performance

A recorded performance can be corrected by excising portions or by re-recording the entire performance or any part of it. Both audio and video can be corrected individually and separately—that is, an audio track can be erased and new audio laid in without disturbing the already acceptable video portion, and vice versa. A good videotape operator can make these changes imperceptibly. Words are often removed or "bleeped out" of certain programs, and almost all films originally made for theatrical release are edited for TV, if not for discretionary purposes or legal jeopardy, then for timing, so that there is enough time during the scheduled period to get in commercials.

Typical Editing Procedure. Correcting audiotape, videotape or film can be tedious. In TV particularly, a performer spends considerable time waiting for electronic corrections; therefore, it is useful for a performer to understand what takes place while editing videotape. The procedure is as follows, with the director in the control room watching monitors and the performer in the studio:

> *Director:* "Roll to record . . . We are recording. This is a take. (The floor director tells the talent what is happening.) Color bars (so that the engineer can adjust color cameras) . . . Go to black (so that no information from one part of the tape is confused with another) . . . Slate (to identify the scene) . . . Black . . . Cue talent. Fade in (Camera) One."

The performer performs. If, after a few minutes a mistake occurs (i.e., "makes a fluff," "blows a line") . . .

Director: "Cut. Stop tape. Videotape (operator), recue and put in an edit point (i.e., an electronic tone) at such and such a place."

The tape is recued and the tone is recorded.

Videotape Operator: "Ready. Roll for 10-second cue (to edit point)."

Director: "Standby. Roll to record. (Tone sounds at edit point). Cue talent."

The performer, on a cue from the floor director, picks up the dialogue at the edit point and continues.

This procedure takes about ten minutes, depending upon how efficiently everyone works. Sometimes it is much quicker to redo the entire segment from the beginning or "from the top." In radio and film, the scene is redone (or at least enough of it is redone) to enable the radio producer or film editor to correct the error. Film and radio editing procedures are of little concern to most performers because they are seldom around when they are finally edited. In TV, however, the performer frequently waits until the editing is complete.

Working with Pre-recorded Materials

Nearly every radio or TV program is partly recorded. A performer learns to integrate the pre-recorded materials into the entire program, and to do this efficiently and smoothly. Pre-recorded audio materials include actualities, voicers, interviewers, discs and commercials. Visuals include film, slides and videotape.

Pre-recorded Soundtracks. Singers promoting hit records and newcomers who aspire to the same attention will want to synchronize their lip movement to a pre-recorded soundtrack while making a TV appearance. And they should, so long as the performer can be convincing with lip movement. This technique assures the performer excellent sound quality. On one occasion, a pantomime was done so cleverly that after a rehearsal an agent wanted to sign up the striking redhead who sounded like Eartha Kitt. Of course, she was doing a pantomime to Miss Kitt's recording with such skill the agent was unable to detect that she was not using her own voice. Teen parties and dance shows featuring artists promoting their records are well known for using pre-recorded soundtracks. When a performer is alone on a huge stage without a microphone—Perry Como singing, "When you are far away from me . . ." or Andy Williams, "Moon River . . ."—a pre-recorded track is used. When a singer-dancer goes through a strenuous routine, finishing a dance and singing with complete breath control, the track may be pre-recorded.

TV and radio news people use pre-recorded reports: "Now here is a report from John Doe in New York . . ." Sometimes the newscaster will say: "Here is a report taped earlier today." Occasionally a TV anchorperson will show a slide and run a comment by the person shown in the slide: "I had this telephone conversation with the coach in Florida minutes ago." The point is, the segments were audiotaped earlier, and the public is unaware the reporters left the studio long ago. Programs may simply carry the disclaimer: "Portions of this program were pre-recorded."

Pre-recorded Video. Videotapes, slides and films are examples of pre-recorded video. Often news people read copy accompanied by these visuals. Usually the newscaster or sportscaster selects slides and films either obtained that day or from a stock file, gives them to the director and shows the director where they are to appear on the program. The performer hopes the director gets them on the air on time and in the right order. Usually the director does. A sportscaster may also read copy against a short film naming, for instance, major players and plays. This film is, of course, running silent and the sportscaster is recreating play-by-play action for the viewer. The present trend is definitely away from seeing a reader on TV and more toward having as visuals either live reports at the scene from miniaturized mobile TV camera units, or pre-recorded reports on videotape or film. A news program, therefore, may consist of a live anchorperson alone in the studio introducing pre-recorded segments including weather and sports.

PREPARATION FOR GUESTS

Much programming originating from local stations involves a guest performer: a subject expert, a personality or various groups. In all-talk radio an hour or two may be devoted to guests and/or listener call-ins in each quarter of the day. Local TV's morning, home, noon, celebrity and talk programs and the network's *Today, Tonight* and *Tomorrow* program series all depend greatly on guests. In such a format, the interviewer or moderator asks the pertinent questions and guides the program by responding to signals from the floor director. In these cases interviewers have the principal responsibility for the program and may, in fact, serve as producers, as discussed in a later chapter.

Gathering Background Information

Performers must be prepared for the guest, preferably by having a biography on the guest and an outline of the subject matter. Printed biographies on local guests may be available if they are well known in the community. More likely the information will have to be obtained from the guest over the telephone or in a preliminary conference shortly before the broadcast. Minimum information includes the guest's name, occupation and/or title or relationship with the topic— Why is the guest worth listening to on this topic? Further information includes educational background, employment history, honors, related and personal data, and travel. The interviewer picks out what is more valuable for the public. While some interviewers do not care whether they know anything about the guest in advance of the program, others like to know as much as possible. Occasionally friends, relatives and business acquaintances can provide this information but usually the guest provides it. An interviewer may also maintain a personal bio-graphical reference file on people in entertainment, authors, scientists and newsmakers, some of which may be obtained from a newspaper morgue.

As to subject information, the interviewer depends on things he or she has heard from vague sources, and then documents these leads or rejects them based on research done at libraries, government offices, on-the-scene interviews and observation. Current publications, special news services, prolific reading, and attendance at events aid the inter-viewer in discussing a broad range of topics with guests. Fortunately, topics of great public interest get media attention and this exposure will supplement an interviewer's knowledge. The gathering of elaborate background information during elections was explained by Catherine Mackin in 1972:

> NBC is using a new system this year, and I think it's a sound one. They assigned four of us to cover the state primaries, and I drew Florida, Indiana and California. I went in and lived six to eight weeks in those states, and it will be a tremendous help now since I already know the party officials and some of the delegates. It makes for a more comfortable feeling going in.[3]

Contacting the Guest

Although for some celebrities an interviewer/producer must work through the guest's agent, in most instances the interviewer calls the guest directly: "I am hosting a program. Will you be on it?" Most peo-ple are delighted, even celebrities, especially if they have a project or cause to promote. Having general consent, the interviewer arranges a mutually satisfactory time to discuss the topic and to get somewhat acquainted. Frequently, however, broadcasting does not permit this because the number of guests is too high. In that event the interviewer meets the guest prior to the program. Local citizens are usually quite easy to work with, unless they are embroiled in controversy and believe that an interview could be harmful. In these cases the interviewer must reassure the guest, discussing the procedure for the program and the opportunities the guest will have for telling his or her point of view. The interviewer should also be as flexible as possible in regard to scheduling so that the guest cannot decline for technical reasons. When dealing with celebrities, there are greater variations. Some celebrities are extremely responsible and willing, others are not. They are used to being paid and flattered. Insofar as possible the interviewer should try to do both. In general, giving guests the "red carpet" treatment pays.

An interviewer is always slightly apprehensive about the arrival of the guest(s). Will the guest cancel? Will the guest arrive on time? Many guests do cancel, and the interviewer must be prepared with alternative material. Nevertheless, most guests show up and on time. Often celebrities have agents with them to arrange appointments and limousine service to expedite a tight schedule. A good agent will be certain that the guest arrives on time, although that may be mere seconds before the show.If you are particularly desirous of having someone and uncertain about whether that person will show up, offer to pick up the person yourself at the hotel or residence. Tell the guest exactly when to be ready and then show up slightly early. Allow for a few minutes of flexibility in case of heavy traffic on the way to the station and the possibility that the guest will not be ready on time.

Prerehearsal Meetings. At an advance meeting, in the car on the way to the studio or upon arrival of the guest at the studio, the main points of the interview may be covered in *decreasing* order of importance. Some guests will not want to answer what you *must* ask, and so you will hold off asking those questions until you are on the air, or you discreetly probe to find ways to get the answers to the questions. Be assured that people who are in public attention expect you to ask the most important questions and know that if you do, you are doing your job. They have answers prepared already. Whether they will give your listeners more specific information depends upon your skill, and the confidence they have in you. Most people will tell "everything" on camera or they will appear to do so. The folks around town, however, are much more innocent in regard to media, and they may tell more than is good for them. Your program will benefit from this candor initially, but your acquaintances in the community may soon become wary of you if you have been too crafty. There is a delicate balance you will want to maintain. People want to look good in media, but at the same time you must steadily seek the truth of a situation, the resolution of an issue or the inner drives of a personality.

Some caution should be observed so that the subject and/or the guest is not exhausted prior to the broadcast or filming. This is a real danger. Non-professional performers tend not to say the same things, even the good things, on the air that they said in the snack bar moments earlier. If they do, they lead with, "As I was saying earlier . . ." which is a dull response at best. So, when on camera an interviewer should peak the guests' responses by asking questions phrased differently. An interviewer, furthermore, does not provide a verbatim list of questions nor the order in which they will be asked, because a newly phrased question is likely to get a fresh response and generate a livelier discussion.

For many, being on media is a strange and unsettling experience. This may be the first time the guest has ever heard his or her voice and looked at himself or herself other than in a mirror. The guest will see an "image," and much of the time the image will be a disappointment unless the camera operators and director have carefully designed the video and audio to emphasize the attractiveness of the guest. So, the guest is nervous, and the interviewer must put the person at ease. To do this, the interviewer greets the guest, at the door of the station if possible, and makes the guest feel at home. The interviewer briefs the guest on the layout of the station, noting where the rest rooms are located, and introduces key production personnel. The guest is advised not to worry, to be natural and to pay no attention to camera movement or crew, and to observe the time cues and other signals. This conversation can take place in a snack bar or conference room. Some guests relax with coffee, candy or cigarettes, although such items may not be welcome in the studio. If a guest brings along members of the family or friends, see to it that they are properly taken care of, and separated from the guest so that the business of the program can continue. On local programs make-up is frequently not applied to guests, even though they would look better if they were made up. Stations usually have a common make-up supply for guests. Some guests are unfamiliar with make-up, so a performer and/or a production assistant should apply it routinely to the guest. Generally, if an interviewer wears make-up, the guest should too. Familiarization with the studio, staff and procedure will put guests at ease, or at least as much at ease as possible.

Preparing Excessive Material

Massing more than enough material is rarely a problem. The more you know, the better you will be as an interviewer. You can guide the conversation along more constructive channels, add depth, new insight, and the guests will be very impressed that you have taken the time to be so familiar with their work. They will be genuinely flattered. Even big stars are flattered. A rule of thumb is to prepare 10 questions for every minute you are on the air. You may not need them. Yet, on the air an interviewer finds that some of the questions unexpectedly merge into one; some answers that were supposed to be long are short and vice versa. Celebrities acquainted with media talk endlessly. Once three students were on a discussion program with architect F. Buckminster Fuller. Fuller spent the entire program answering a single question from one of them. Under somewhat similar circumstances, comedian Joe E. Brown recited his entire biography while student discussants patiently waited for him to give them a turn. Brown, intuitively concerned about the pacing of the program, paused fleetingly for questions. When they did not materialize fast enough, he simply continued his breathless narrative.

Non-professional interviewees do not respond with consistency, and so the interviewer may end up delivering a monologue on the topic, the guest falling to near-silence or an occasional "yes" or "no." At times like these an interviewer is glad to be over-prepared. Some news and sports situations place performers in periods when long adlibs are necessary to provide continuity while nothing else is going on. Baseball games and golf tournaments require quite a bit of fill material, for instance. An interviewer hopes to avoid a situation in which the guest says, "Have you read so and so" or ". . . just like so and so," and the interviewer does not know the reference. Of course, the interviewer may hedge—"Why don't you brief our listeners" or "Perhaps you'd tell us what you mean by that term"—or the interviewer may confess, "I don't know." This is embarrassing if the references are current common knowledge which a sophisticated person in media is expected to know.

PREPARATION OF VISUALS

Performers often prepare visuals for informational television programs and films. If the visuals already exist, it is a matter of identifying and locating them. A performer's guest usually provides these items; but the performer must be able to decide whether they are appropriate for media. Visuals fall essentially into two categories: filmed materials including moving pictures, slides and photographs; and graphics including drawings, charts and graphs, and three-dimensional objects. Visuals do a great deal to make a presentation stimulating; therefore, they should be purposefully built into a program. Some television stations hire artists to draw scenes during a trial, so that the TV presentation will have more visual impact. The principal guidelines for all visuals are:

1. Keep them simple.
2. Have action and/or words in the center of the screen.
3. Have clearly defined images.
4. Be sure visuals are relevant to the topic.
5. Have enough visuals for good pacing.
6. Emphasize one point for each visual.

7. Use the horizontal aspect ratio—four units wide, three units high.

8. Generally use color, remembering that black and white can be effective.

9. Be consistent in the design and style of the materials.

10. Present complex information in a series of simple steps by means of visuals.

11. Use illustrations rather than words or data.

12. Be accurate.

Filmed Materials

Moving Picture Film. Entire films and segments of films, called "film clips," are available from some guests, stock footage at the station, promotion and public relations firms, and local libraries. Sixteen millimeter film, shot with or without sound, is standard for the television and advertising industries. Occasionally Super-8 film can be used by stations, closed circuit and cable television companies. Many news departments are heavy daily users of 16mm film. A few stations have libraries for storing this film, which is used on later documentaries and feature telecasts. Effective media presentations on travel, animal life, underwater photography, and medicine are a few examples of programs with filmed segments. Whenever action is important, moving pictures are required. A performer should try to keep films and/or rights to the use of them. Several television and film celebrities own their own films or videotapes of their programs which they can syndicate or re-edit for rebroadcasting. No one can predict the value of such properties.

Slides. Color 35mm slides are inexpensive, quickly produced, portable and add immeasurably to any media presentation. Every performer would be wise to purchase and know how to operate a 35mm camera, particularly if he or she is working in informational programming. Here are a few additional suggestions concerning slides:

1. Limit all words to about six lines with no more than six words per line.

2. Use bold easy-to-read lettering. Letters are usually white.

3. Proofread all slides.

4. Avoid repetition, but have duplicates if necessary.

5. Mark each slide indicating the order and position of the image; i.e., upright and obverse side.

Large slides are used in some instructional media (2-by 2-inch) and for rear screen projectors. These slides are usually made by the company.

Photographs. Photographs are seldom used on television or film. When they are, they are mounted on heavy, dark cardboards allowing for wide borders. They are stacked on easels, and so consistency in size, preferably 8 by 10-inches, is desirable. Sometimes they are taped or pinned to large menu boards. The photographs themselves should have a matte finish which is obtained through printing or spraying. Glossy photographs reflect studio lights.

Graphics

Graphics are informational and decorative. For instance, old theater programs, sports posters, original art and three-dimensional objects enhance any discussion. They are worth the effort in assembling them.

Charts and Graphs. Charts and graphs are forms of visual reinforcement, and they are probably more effective and memorable than tables or data. Charts and graphs are used largely for comparisons. They are most effective when the bar, pie or column graph is limited to about six bars, wedges or columns. A line graph should be restricted to no more than three or four lines. High contrast designs which are simple and easy to understand are essential.

Drawings. Drawings require the same guidelines as all visuals. Original drawings should avoid extremely high contrast materials (black ink on white illustration board) unless these materials are sprayed so as to shift them to a medium gray scale. Black ink on a medium gray scale green or blue poster board is recommended for drawings.

Sketch artists and entertainers use chalk, crayon and easel to complete a drawing during the course of an interview or the telling of a story. Often the drawings are faintly pre-sketched so that the talent can quickly trace them during the program. This technique is especially effective in telling stories to children.

Instructors may use blackboards for illustrating their lectures or sales presentations. Much of this material is semi-complete before the presentation, because there is not time to finish it otherwise.

Three-Dimensional Objects. Statues, paintings, automobiles, boats, sports equipment, camping gear, cooking utensils, antiques, plants and rockets are a few of the items a performer may show on media. These objects must be identified, taken to the studio and returned safely. Often the guest is of great assistance in the handling of these items and should be encouraged as long as the director knows what items are in the show. The director will suggest modifications if necessary. Three-dimensional items are excellent as background for the performers, as stimuli for movement (performers can get in and out of some of them) and as items for manipulation.

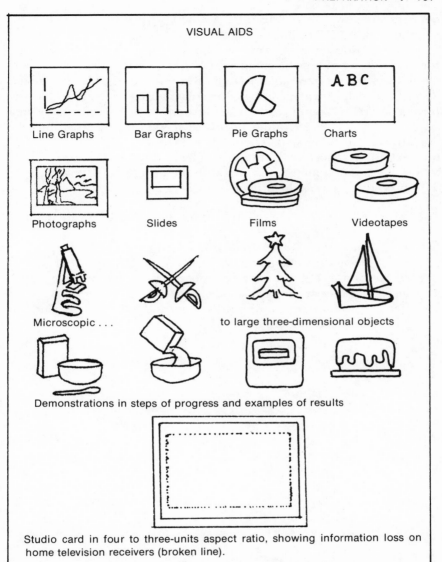

VISUAL AIDS

Line Graphs   Bar Graphs   Pie Graphs   Charts

Photographs   Slides   Films   Videotapes

Microscopic . . .   to large three-dimensional objects

Demonstrations in steps of progress and examples of results

Studio card in four to three-units aspect ratio, showing information loss on home television receivers (broken line).

Demonstrations

Most demonstrations are procedures for doing or making things. They involve action and a variety of visuals, and so they are excellent for media. Demonstrations may be routine (how to care for animals in your apartment) or dramatic (the slashing of a melon placed on a person's stomach). Demonstrations are best when they mix entertainment and information (how to juggle).

A demonstration is prepared in steps of completion, because a performer seldom has time to complete the task and repetitive work is boring to the viewer. One cannot bake a cake, sew a dress, change the oil, decorate a wall, instruct, construct or create an entire entity. The performer, therefore, outlines the procedure the viewer would follow in a series of steps. The performer begins each step, telling what must be done to complete that step. Then, he or she goes to the next step, and the next, until the project is complete. The finished product(s) is shown to the viewers, who may be satisfied with the result and motivated by it. This procedure may be helpful:

1. Introduce the participants and the objective of the demonstration.

2. Show the materials that are needed to complete the project.

3. Have the demonstration prepared in steps of progress.

4. Go through the complex procedures, when possible, advising the viewers of the problems.

5. Conclude by showing the results and telling where one can get further information.

11: Rehearsals

"Just one more time."

Typical Rehearsals
No Rehearsal—Abbreviated Rehearsals

Complete Rehearsals
Preliminary Rehearsals—Camera Rehearsals (Initial Camera Rehearsals; Dress Rehearsals)

REHEARSALS ARE PRACTICE SESSIONS for the performers and members of the crew. The more complicated the program, the more rehearsals a performer can expect; indeed, rehearsals may be regarded as stepping stones to perfection. The amount of time spent in rehearsal varies with the station or production company. Small local stations have little or no rehearsal; large production companies and network studios have many rehearsals. Of course, these are not occasions for practicing basic skills. Performers develop these skills in speech, acting, dance, communication and other classes.

When rehearsals begin there are certain guidelines, responsibilities and privileges, established in the theater, that pertain to mass media. As a performer, you are entitled to:

1. An advance schedule of rehearsals and performance dates, including time, place, and a general idea of what is expected on each occasion.

2. Concise and courteous direction from the director.

3. Freedom to develop your role to the best of your ability, so long as you work within the concept of the director.

4. Consultation with the director if you do not understand the concept.

5. Cooperative assistance from the cast, production manager and crew.

6. A reasonably quiet and orderly atmosphere during rehearsals and performance. It is difficult for a performer to work when there are noise and commotion in the studio, although practically speaking this is often the case.

7. Director's notes and comments on your performance throughout the rehearsal period insofar as time permits.

8. A share of whatever praise or criticism the production receives, regardless of the size of your role.[1]

In return, your responsibilities are:

1. To be present and prompt for every rehearsal. If an unforeseen event prevents this, you must inform the floor director or director immediately and work out satisfactory arrangements for a substitute rehearsal, or replacement. An unforeseen event does not include a social engagement that arises unexpectedly.

2̸. To give your director complete and courteous attention and the rehearsal complete concentration. When you are not on camera or microphone, you should be learning lines, working on your role or practicing lines with other performers not required on the set. This is done while listening for your cue.

3. To advise the floor director of your whereabouts during the rehearsal, never leaving until you are officially dismissed by the director or floor director.

4. To maintain a cooperative and positive attitude toward the whole company.

5. To remember a performer in final rehearsal is probably not as important as (1) getting the program done on time, (2) meeting union requirements, (3) making broader artistic decisions, (4) maintaining client relationships, and settling other unanticipated problems. The performer, therefore, should pay attention, perform as required and remain silent.

The discussion that follows refers primarily to TV, because radio programs are rarely rehearsed in a group anymore (a newscaster may read the script aloud prior to the program) and films are rehearsed and shot in segments. If the film director is dissatisfied with the scene, it may be reshot the next day. But in TV the circumstances are different. Actor Jack Klugman has said that, "your performance comes out of your rehearsal . . . you select what is best . . . you strive for perfection . . . I hate television . . . you don't have a chance to select . . . you're under such time limits."[2]

TYPICAL REHEARSALS

A performer should expect the director to say there is no time for rehearsal; the expression is, "We'll have to wing it." Under such stringencies, a performer should try to get openings, closings and transitions rehearsed, because these areas cause the most problems. If that fails, the performer studies the program format, the requirements of the guest(s), the phrases to be used, the movements that will be necessary to show graphics. Much of this preparation can be done before the performer arrives at the studio. A wise performer anticipates extenuating circumstances and prepares in advance for them.

No Rehearsals

Rehearsal at a local station is minimal. That (or those) of radio newscasts or public service programs consist of whatever the talent wishes to do, such as read through the copy once or twice before going on the air. Often the talent reads copy "cold," that is, without rehearsal. If the talent is excellent at sight reading, the public is not the wiser, but if the talent is not so capable, errors in pronunciation, enunciation and the like will become immediately noticeable and consequently the performer's public image suffers. In a small operation it is essential that each person, especially the performer, turn in work of high calibre because there is no one around to constantly evaluate and urge professional standards. The performer must assume these responsibilities.

Abbreviated Rehearsals

A form of abbreviated rehearsal is one that rehearses the opening of the program, all important transitions, such as movement from one set to another, and the closing of the program. A strong, well-rehearsed, well-delivered opening and closing, together with a confident, winning smile from the performer can overcome in public acceptance whatever technical errors that occur, such as a microphone going dead temporarily or a film breaking on the air. Careful rehearsal of these elements can save a program from disaster. A performer must know exactly how the program begins, how it ends and what the physical transitions are, so an abbreviated rehearsal is the answer.

COMPLETE REHEARSALS

The complete rehearsal is really a series of rehearsals necessary for the shooting of a TV program, feature film or, in the 1930s and '40s, a complex radio script, in its entirety at one time. Dramas, variety programs and comedies presented before a live studio audience have complete rehearsals. The rehearsals are designed to give a sense of continuity to the entire program for the benefit of the performers and crew. Of course all performers are expected to be punctual, because they know rehearsals are expensive, and there is never as much time to rehearse as one would like to have.

Preliminary Rehearsals

As a professional, the performer applies all of his or her abilities to develop the finest characterization or dance or musical presentation or comedy sketch imaginable. These efforts begin to take shape in a rehearsal of the program probably conducted in a large empty room without equipment or crew. The first rehearsal is an occasion in which everyone in the cast sits down with the director to read the script aloud. This read-through rehearsal is not complicated, but the performer should receive from it an understanding of the role he or she is playing and how that part relates to the total production. Long variety programs, shot in segments, frequently do not require a performer appearing as a guest, or "cameo" appearance, to rehearse anything except his or her segment. This segment, nevertheless, is sufficiently rehearsed to bring it to the same level of perfection as the rest of the program.

During the second rehearsal the talent walks through the part. In other words the movement is "blocked," as in theater. Unlike theater, however, the space is usually smaller and the movements more precise, because the director must plan the composition of the shots according to the movement and positions of the performers.

By the third session the performer, being a "quick study," has mastered the lines or music and remembers the blocking and director's comments. The rehearsal consists of a seemingly endless series of stops and starts of each scene. The objective is to reach near perfection for each scene before it is put in a TV, film or radio studio. These developmental rehearsals will minimize the expense of studio production time. The rehearsals could go on and on consuming several days at long hours. The director decides when these rehearsals are adequate, and this decision is made in accordance with artistic judgments and the budget.

These pre-camera rehearsals are the more important ones because the director gives undivided attention to the performers. Later, when everyone is in the studio, the director becomes preoccupied with the crew and numerous technical decisions, resulting in less time devoted to the performers. The dominant impression of a role, the warmth of the working environment, the confidence in decisions, the nurturing of subtle, latent expressions, all are developed during these vital rehearsals. The director is the biggest single guide and aid to the performer, and so a performer is fortunate indeed to work with one of the top media directors.

Camera Rehearsals

While pre-camera rehearsals may take weeks, on-camera rehearsals in the studio will probably take a few hours, a few days at most. The cost for a TV studio may be as low as $100 an hour with crew; the production cost of a feature film may be as much as $8,000 an hour. Detailed preparation and rehearsals, as previously discussed, are made prior to setting up in a studio. If everyone has prepared his or her part thoroughly, known as "doing one's homework," the on-camera rehearsals should go smoothly.

Initial Camera Rehearsals. The director, having worked sufficiently with the performers, adds technical reinforcement to a program in the studio. This is a very exciting time. Specialists move quickly to complete costumes, lighting, scenery, sound effects and music. Each person adds an artistic and/or technical contribution to the program. If miscued, anyone could shatter the impact of the program. So, the director blends all of the diverse elements into a grand unified production by means of a series of on-camera rehearsals ending in the final "dress" rehearsal.

Even though a director may have previously called "technical rehearsals" for the crew without performers, the performer must understand that the director's attention is necessarily divided once everyone is assembled in the studio. These rehearsals can be difficult for a performer, because there may be long, long periods when he or she must wait to perform without knowing the reason for the delay. Everything can be in order in the studio, but sheer chaos may reign in the control room—the videotape recorder may have gone out, the special effects generator may not work properly, the audio pickup from the studio may have static, the music may be pretaped at the wrong speed. Presumably the director will relay the cause for the delay and estimate when it will be resolved, but often the director and crew are just so busy the message is forgotten. At moments like these the professional performer shows his or her stamina by waiting out the delay, performing on cue and performing well.

In addition to electronic difficulties, there may be various technical errors: lighting is too bright or not bright enough, make-up is wrong for the role, the boom shadow is in the shot. There may be script errors noticed at the last minute—a fact needs to be updated, the script is too long, the slide order does not correspond to the order in the script. There may be performer problems—the anchorman does not know how to pronounce a foreign name, the microphone cable is trailing behind the vocalist, the star just tore her dress, and that widely publicized guest everyone counted on missed his flight out of Atlanta and so a standby film is being cued up. Each tick of the clock costs money, probably lots of it. Tempers get short. Somehow those beautiful subleties that everyone planned in early rehearsals are not quite so lovely or important. The cast and crew, now tired, after long hours of emotional and mental strain, take a short break before the final dress rehearsal.

Dress Rehearsals. Dress rehearsal is a complete run-through. Everything the performer plans to do (except possibly that ultimate burst of on-air performance energy) shines forth on the dress rehearsal.

Dress rehearsal should be like the on-air production with only the finest last minute touches being added or altered; ideally nothing need be changed. Some directors tape the dress rehearsal, hoping that by some miracle it will be air quality, so that they can keep it and concentrate on some other part of the program. Sometimes they are lucky; most of the time, they are not. Every time a director stops a tape for the least thing, remember that it takes about ten minutes to rescue the tape and restage the segment. A performer can become exceedingly unpopular if he or she stops a taping session by saying, "Stop tape. I blew my lines." The decision to stop a tape should remain with the director, for the director must ultimately re-edit, cover up or eliminate the error. In any event the dress rehearsal should run as smoothly as possible and without interruption.

12: On the Air:
MEDIA PROFESSIONALS

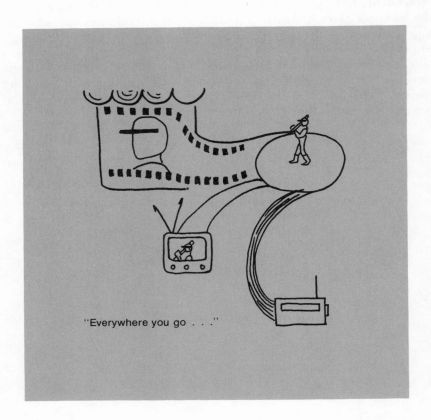

"Everywhere you go . . ."

The Performer As a Producer/Writer
Script Outlines
    Adlibbed Continuity (Disc Jockey Continuity; Talk Shows;
    Contests; News on-the-Scene; Sports Play-by-Play)—
    Interviews—Discussions

Complete Scripts
    The Single Performer—Entertainers (Actors; Comedians;
    Dancers; Vocalists)—Information Specialists (Announcers;
    Newscasters; Sportscasters; Weathercasters)—The Large
    Cast (Documentaries; Dramas; Variety Programs)

T HE LAST SURGE of energy heightens the final take of the performance. To many performers it may not make a great deal of difference whether the performance is live or recorded, because the nervous energy is still there, the insecurity, the desire to do your best. As you take your place, the studio lights seem brighter and hotter than they were in rehearsal, the mike cable is shorter than you remember it, your clothes are tighter, you're uncomfortable in your chair, your contact lenses bother you, your throat is dry. You check everything under your control; you check your script for the nth time; you can't remember the opening lines. Suddenly, the floor director signals, "Stand by . . . Quiet . . . Cue!" With confidence, abandon and a greater awareness of your being than you normally have, you burst forth to give the public a few moments of emotional and intellectual stimulation that no one else in the world can give in quite the same way—no other newscaster or actor or comedian or teacher or politician or minister—just you.

Network and syndicated programs such as dramas, comedies and variety series for TV are shot in their entirety before live audiences about 5:30 in the afternoon and again about 8:00 that evening. The better scenes from both performances are edited into the final recording for distribution. Some quiz series may be shot at the rate of two or three programs per day. Network news originates from New York studios daily.

By contrast, many other complex dramas, documentaries and variety programs are shot in segments. These segments require a similar series of rehearsals, but the performer may never see more than the segment being shot and may never see the complete production. Performers sometimes admit in interviews that they have not seen their latest movie or TV appearance or heard their latest album, because they have not seen or heard the final editing and assembling of all of the segments. NBC's purchase of *The Godfather,* re-edited into a 10-hour version, suggests the tremendous complexity of the editing task. Once the performance is "in the can," that is, on tape or film, it can be edited in any way the director chooses; thus, a performer's lament—"My big scene ended up on the cutting room floor"—becomes a possibility.

Local live performances for disc jockeys, newscasters and others often become routine; that is, consistently slick, certainly not dull. The entire team of participants becomes acquainted with every subtlety of the program. The performer gains increasing confidence in the crew and vice versa. A production chief once said of a new anchorman, "Give us six weeks and he'll look really good. We'll get a better mike to bring out the nuances in his voice. We'll adjust the lighting, make-up, camera angles and pace of shooting so as to bring out his low key, warm, friendly, conversational delivery. He'll look and sound great." And he did. With cooperation from the crew a performer soon looks and sounds better than he or she ever imagined. In the same spirit the performer will have the finesse to cover an occasional technical breakdown or error in judgment in the otherwise smooth flow of the program.

THE PERFORMER AS A PRODUCER/WRITER

To some extent performers must serve as their own producers. To increase the chance of being on-the-air, performers assemble everything necessary to make the performance possible. Sometimes this includes money or obtaining sponsors for the program. Meeting influential people by attending and/or participating in charity drives, fund raising for public television stations or other worthy causes can give the performer recognition. Whether a performer is producing a segment lasting only a few minutes or a complex one-hour special, the procedure is identical: First, an idea is developed that fits the program. Second, a script showing audio and visual requirements and dialogue evolves after various rewrites. Third, audio visual support is assembled, including scenery, props, graphics and other production elements. Fourth, rehearsals are conducted under the supervision of the director. Fifth, the presentation is filmed, taped or broadcast live. Sixth, the performance is candidly evaluated so that a new, improved presentation evolves when the cycle begins again.

On-the-air performers follow an established structure for their presentations. This structure is called a "format." The format is the overall concept for the program which may outline anything from a verbal extemporaneous briefing for the performer to a detailed script. In general, the more expensive the program, the more detailed the script and its production. For the most part programs are built in segments. Each segment within a program may have its own outline making the segment itself an entity. Single appearances, interviews and/or discussions may have formats that are part of a larger program format. For example, *The Electric Company,* produced by the Children's Televi-

sion Workshop, consists of interviews, discussions and single performances which are recorded individually and then assembled segment
by segment into a half-hour program. Outlines for documentaries and
dramas are called "scenarios." Scenarios are scene by scene outlines of
the action. The point is that performers must have material to rehearse
and present on the air. Often this material, sometimes referred to by
entertainers as an "act," is provided by speech writers, copywriters,
playwriters, screenwriters and composers; however, many beginning
performers must provide their own material. A performer, therefore,
who wants to be on the air must assume from time to time the responsibilities of a writer and/or producer, the two responsibilities being virtually inseparable. Ironically, the beginning performer who may be
starving between dates and the superstar whose work is so unique that
he or she must supervise the concept and the execution of the material
so that it is "just right" function to some extent as writers and producers as well as performers. During the frantic years in between, while
struggling to the top, someone else may provide the material because
the pace demands quantity for frequent exposure rather than the ultimate concentration on quality demanded by a superstar.

SCRIPT OUTLINES

Virtually every program that is worth doing has a script of some
kind. In order for someone other than the performer to gather the materials necessary for the programs, to get it on the air, to obtain talent
for it—indeed, to sell it to sponsors—some form of script must exist.
This script may be brief however, consisting of a list of items to be covered during the program, time cues for station breaks and spots, the
principal ingredients being provided from prerecorded sources (discs,
audio and videotapes, films), from contributors outside station or company control (guests, contestants, teams) and from remarks adlibbed by
professional entertainers or journalists. A typical minimum script,
sometimes called a "run down," consists of an opening statement, necessary transitional cues during the program and a closing statement. In
other words a few lines getting the program on the air, a few getting it
off and sufficient dialogue to cue upcoming elements.

Adlibbed Continuity

The ease with which a media professional adlibs his or her remarks
may take years for a novice to acquire. Extemporaneous response using
just the right word choice or movement, degree of humor or sympathy,
pacing, understanding of the situation and psychology of the other
performers involved separates the distinguished performers from the

merely adequate ones. The adlibbed situation makes more demand upon the performer's educational background, range of interest, accuracy of information and ability to recall it, emotional composure and finesse in mastering any situation which may arise from the unexpected while he or she is in the spotlight. The demands are so great on the adlibbed performer that the few who are successful are in great demand and may be highly paid. Adlibbed continuity is evident in five principal formats: disc jockey programs, talk shows, contests, news on-the-scene, and sports play-by-play.

Disc Jockey Continuity. The format for a disc jockey program consists of patter and playing records. The music selection depends upon the listening preference of the audience to whom station clients want to sell products and services: rock and roll (R&R), or top tune, country and western (C&W), middle of the road (MOR) or easy listening, soul, rhythm and blues, jazz, religious and classical. Many DJs begin working in their teens as part-time performers on small radio stations. They learn to talk freely with the public and to spin records or cue cartridges efficiently. Novelty, high energy and an attractive manner in keeping with the mood and interests of young people are essential for the top tune DJ with a target audience under 35 years of age. Surveys conducted by trade magazines and a tabulation of call-in requests keep DJs aware of current trends. Comedy by means of kidding the audience and oneself is a great asset, because the top-tune DJ has to balance bouncy good humor and cleverness without being too cute, trite or off-color. The top-tune DJ talks just enough to maintain personal identity and a "bright" station sound. Typically this means the DJ is limited to one or two remarks between records, if that much. Copy usually isn't written out, although ideas may be, along with old standbys such as time and weather. DJs on top-tune programs have strong personalities that are unusual and fun to listen to. Inasmuch as the station's music director or program director has probably selected the music in advance, an excerpt from a DJ's script merely shows a list of those preselected recordings.

While the broadcast lifespan for a top-tune DJ may be about four years in one market, the MOR, classical or C&W disc jokey has potentially greater longevity. In fact, some of these performers become fixtures in the community, gaining considerable respect as they mature and become better known in the listening area. The pace is slower, the depth of patter is somewhat more complex, and may be based on personal research, observation or knowledge of music over a longer period of time. The success of a DJ is as much happenstance as design. Many DJs are fairly astute observers of the contemporary scene. They are aware of trends, problems in the community, both favorable and unfavorable actions of community leaders, and have the ability to comment in an amusing way—sometimes harshly criticizing to the point of being threatened by a legal suit and sometimes making a good many people laugh while irritating no one. A DJ is welcome company in everyone's home, at least for a little while. A good DJ is exceptionally inventive, usually has a keen sense of sound production and how radio can be used to express his or her unique form of lunacy, romance, good sense, candor, knowledge of music or simple companionship for the lonely. Sometimes a two-person DJ team spurs a lively counterpoint between partners who complement each other in background and expertise, and enjoy working together. Mark Hudson and Irv Harrigan (assumed names) on KILT, Houston, are regarded as "one of the hottest talk duos in the country." They have a prerecorded opening for their morning drive time show. That's followed by 16 zany ("If it moves steal it, if it doesn't rip it off") bits (i.e., funny sequences). A few DJ techniques include talking over the final bars of records to speed pacing, tight cueing, antics such as shouting and yelling, feigned disagreement while playing the role of the underdog to management or society, giveaway contests, soliciting audience input, and personal appearances.

Talk Shows. Practically every radio and television station in the country lists some kind of talk show as part of its public affairs commitment to Federal Communications Commission requirements. Nearly 5,000 radio and TV stations are listed in talk show directories.[1] Some of these talk programs consist of interviews and discussions with known personalities and, therefore, have a partial script. "The giant talk machine's insatiable appetite for guests is fed by a behind-the-scenes apparatus that helps hosts, on the better shows, seem omniscient about their guests' pasts, hobbies and the contents of their latest book. In most cases, hosts have never met their guests before nor have they read the book they are about to discuss. *Today* hosts . . . for example, may have looked through an author's work before air-time, but the hard reading is left to staff members who then come up with synopses of the material, including suggested questions. Similar digests of a guest's present and past, based on staff preinterviews, also are provided."[2]

A rarer form of talk program is the listener call-in, consisting of an ongoing dialogue between a moderator and callers on a given topic, usually selected each day by the moderator and/or program producer. Call-in formats require elaborate and expensive telephone equipment installations that are not found in music stations. Typically several hours a day, usually in two-hour blocks, are assigned to listener participation. Listeners express their opinions anonymously and the moderator may adlib a response, either seriously or humorously, depending upon the program concept. For the most part talk programs are entertainment and the moderators are entertainers. The range of topics is so great that the moderator must have a rather broad background, being well informed, widely read, interested in contemporary issues, probably opinionated and articulate. Talk programs succeed because the moderator becomes a personality with a large listening audience in the 18 to 49 age range—that is, the preferred age range of most consumers. The program, therefore must be skewed toward this age bracket, although input from the elderly and children is not discouraged. Aside from topic selection, some of the problems facing the moderator are discouraging "regular" callers who would call every day, derogatory remarks reflecting racial or religious bias, and legally prohibited comments. A producer in the radio control room may initially answer all calls, screen them, and transfer the appropriate ones to the moderator for response on the air. Even so the moderator on occasion will have no choice but to cut off the caller. In any case, the moderator must have a receptive style which encourages people to call in, by allowing them sufficient time on the air to express their views fully. If the moderator decides to discuss an issue with the caller, he or she must do so adequately to peak audience response and interest without seeming to be arbitrary or unfair. In the eight years Alvin Van Black had a talk program on KTRH, Houston, he estimates that he talked to 70,000 individuals. "I keep a running tabulation of about 30 callers a day. That's 150 a week, 7,800 a year. In the early years of the program, I used to take more calls. I know one talk host who tries to take 15,000 calls a year."[3]

Contests. Contests fall roughly into two categories: quizzes, which depend upon the ready recall abilities of the contestants, and games, which mainly seek laughter at almost any price. Many of these popular programs were transferred with little or no format change from radio to television. The most popular quiz show in the early days of radio was *Dr. I.Q.* "I have a lady in the balcony" became a classic line introducing a contestant who would win silver dollars for correct answers. Irene Beasley was hostess for *Grand Slam,* an audience participation program based on a bridge game motif. Clifton Fadiman hosted *Information Please* in which a panel of experts was challenged by people at home who sent in questions. Radio's *Take It Or Leave It* was a key program because it was hosted by such personalities as Jack Paar, Phil Baker, Garry Moore and Eddie Cantor. *Take It Or Leave It* provided the format for *The Sixty Four Dollar Question* which became *The Sixty Four Thousand Dollar Question* on TV during the fifties, starring Hal March, and the *One Hundred Twenty Eight Thousand Dollar Question* in the seventies. TV's early viewers also enjoyed musical quiz programs such as Bert Park's *Stop the Music.* Fun and game shows like TV's *Dating Game, The Newlyweds* and *Let's Make a Deal* are descendants of radio's *Bride and Groom* and *Blind Date. Blind Date,* which originated in the 1940s, starred Arlene Francis. Both Ralph Edward's *Truth or Consequences* and Art Link-letter's *People Are Funny* were transferred intact from radio to TV during the '50s.

Jack Barry's career illustrates how versatile a performer may have to be: creating, producing and performing. Barry graduated from college with a degree in science and economics. Failing to get a job as a bandleader, he joined his father's handkerchief manufacturing business, which he gave up for a staff announcing job at a station in New Jersey. In 1946 he created and sold the radio version of *Juvenile Jury,* which he hosted. Shortly afterward he developed another solid hit, *Life Begins at Eighty.* Barry then formed a partnership with Dan Enright, and together they produced *21, Concentration,* of which Barry was the first host, *Tic-Tac-Dough* and others. In 1969, Jack Barry Productions joined Goodson-Todman, thus uniting some of the most successful game show innovators in the business.

Bill Cullen, of *I've Got a Secret,* once recommended to TV emcees and panelists: "Be fair, just, friendly. And, at all times, maintain a sense of humor about yourself and the world. People will welcome you to their radio sets and their TV screens. . . ."[4] Some of the principal characteristics of hosting is an ability to adlib. Most TV game and quiz programs have a highly energetic, gregarious, extroverted personality as host. The hosts and hostesses enjoy people and people enjoy them. They demonstrate a great deal of self confidence and often come from a background of personal salesmanship, quick wit, ready smile and extensive knowledge of many subjects. Somehow, as an emcee, they skillfully dominate the program while sharing the spotlight for a little while with the guest. Game show hosts work from a format that requires flexibility and continuous management by the host, because he or she must expedite the basic rules of the game within a time limit that allows each contestant an equal opportunity to win the prizes. Information necessary for contests includes the overall format, a precise statement of the rules, all questions and answers precisely phrased, "vita" on each guest, and a fairly standard opening and closing for the program. Adlib remarks, therefore, supplement the program structure by maintaining a smooth-flowing, light, fun-filled conversation with individual participants and the studio audience.

Bob Barker, perhaps the highest salaried master of ceremonies on the air, estimates that he has interviewed about 50,000 persons in the nearly 20 years he has been in broadcasting. From more than 4,000 *Truth or Consequences* shows and 1,000 segments on *The Price is Right,* he regards himself as an instant psychoanalyst. He has but a few seconds to size up a contestant, put him at ease and come up with an observation or a quip to provoke an interesting response:

"I have a choice of directions on how to go with each contestant," he explained. "Sometimes it's current events, sports, marital relationships or a joke. . . . I warm up the audience on *T or C* and pick the contestants before we go on the air, which makes it easier for me. On *Price Is Right* I see them for the first time on camera and have to make quick decisions. The audience has to be taken into consideration too. Each crowd has a personality of its own. I lay a few lines on them to see what they respond to. Some audiences will howl over a joke on booze, others don't react at all."[5]

News-on-the-Scene. Upon arrival at the scene, the reporter, called an "outside" reporter, is expected to organize thoughts quickly. A simple chronological or topical order works well: What happened? Why? What are the consequences? For radio, the story must be a concise narrative and sound compilation. These stories are developed from original news sources like police monitors located in the station, telephone tips from listeners, wire services, newspapers and other media competition, and by calling police and fire stations and hospitals, known as "making the rounds." The outside reporter is often in a mobile unit at the time a story breaks, and must be directed with all haste to the scene by someone at the station using a locator or *key* map. At the scene the radio reporter gathers the information and reports it as:

1. a "voicer," by simply reading the story over the telephone.
2. An "actuality," by feeding a tape recording of a participant or witness.
3. a "wrap around" (or "donut"), by combining a voice open and close with a tape.
4. a "Q & A" (questions and answers), by conducting an interview(s) at the scene.

For television there must be visuals as well as sound. The camera operator and the outside reporter must be of one mind as to what they are looking for: essential visuals to tell the story, plus background for fill footage to amplify the story and to provide necessary transitions for smoother editing. Typical stories are preplanned, semi-planned according to a routine, or unanticipated. For unanticipated events a reporter, drawing upon all of his or her skill, does the best job possible and hopes the story is successful. Preplanned stories include meetings and speeches before which the reporter often receives an agenda or text of the speech. The reporter reads the speech and picks out the highlights, records them and prepares a story based on those quotations. Two examples follow:

CITY COUNCIL MEETING

COVER SHOT OF CITY COUNCIL	City Council discussed a new bond issue today. Etc.
MEDIUM SHOT OF CITIZEN SPEAKING TO COUNCIL	Some citizens were for it; others were against it.
INTERVIEW WITH CITY COUNCIL MEMBER AFTER MEETING	One council member said:
CLOSEUP OF REPORTER	Reporter tells what options may take place.

AUTOMOBILE ACCIDENT

LONG SHOT OF FREEWAY	A truck and car hit on the 610 Freeway today.
MEDIUM SHOT WRECK	A police officer ticketed a driver for speeding.
AMBULANCE LEAVES SCENE	The other driver was taken to the hospital. He is in fair condition. This is (reporter) at the scene.

Sports Play-by-Play. Network scripts may likewise be written out or adlibbed from play-by-play observation, outlines, topic guides or note cards about players. For long events such as golf, baseball or football, calling play-by-play action requires a wealth of game information that the sportscaster has avidly memorized. A few sportscasters have encyclopedic memories about sports. Some sportscasters build audience participation radio quiz programs around their ability to recall sports facts. Formats for most live play-by-play sports programs are similar:

COVER SCENE	We're at stadium, field, pool, golf course, where Team A meets Team B or player so and so takes on someone else.
CLOSEUP SPORTSCASTER	I'm principal play-by-play sportscaster. With me is color or feature commentator.
CU COLOR COMMENTATOR	Commentator says something. Brief update on team records. Roll cue (word cue) to break.
TEAMS ENTER FIELD	Cheers from audience.
COMMERCIALS	COMMERCIALS ON TAPE
LONG SHOT FIELD	Opening action.

The sportscasters are little more than established visually on TV. Their voices carry the continuity. The performers on camera are the players. At half times and other break periods interviews may be conducted with celebrities and players, but much of this feature material is pretaped and included as fill during anticipated slow moments in the event.

The envy of every aspiring sportscaster are those who call play-by-play for the networks. A typical game was the Astro Bluebonnet Bowl, played in the Astrodome on December 29, 1973, and telecast by ABC. Keith Jackson did the play-by-play and Bob Grosscup provided color. Both men were somewhat similar in style—crisp, clear, medium pitched voices, shouting at times but generally easy in manner. The press boxes are located on the fourth level of the Astrodome. They consist of a series of small booths; the one for ABC was about 8 feet wide and 14 feet long. At one end two metal stools were lighted sufficiently for the brief initial appearance of the sportscasters; at the other was a camera with a zoom lens which was focused on the field most of the time. After all, as Howard Cosell has said, "Your show is in the arena." At the "open," Jackson adlibs essential remarks to establish the teams and location. Grosscup, who has been purposefully leaning out of the picture, is introduced with some amusing remarks by Jackson. Grosscup reads his notes about the players. Within two or three minutes everyone's attention is directed to the field, and the sportscasters are never on camera again. Six cameras cover the game: four are at booth level and two are on trucks on the field. The audio commentary requires three key persons in addition to the sportscasters: the spotter, who knows every player extremely well; the statistics person, who has the records ready in an instant; and an assistant director, who feeds promotional information and coordination details to the sportscasters. Immediately in front of these five is a work table, on which are a spotting chart, a statistics chart and a color chart listing all of the players with personal notes on each one. There is also a telephone, a desk microphone, a small calculator and two monitors—one in color and one in black and white. Jackson and Grosscup have microphones hanging on the front of them in special mounts so that their lips almost touch the screens as they speak. They wear large soundproof headsets during the game, but not when they are on television. With an ease and finesse only experience can bring, the two sportscasters adlib back and forth by "feel" and "look." After attempting to enliven the final minutes of the telecast, a somewhat exasperated Keith Jackson told those of us in the booth: "I'm so sick and tired of watching routes—That's gotta be the longest seven minutes of the month."

Another typical job for a TV sportscaster is re-creation of on-the-scene coverage wherein the sportscaster adlibs over a piece of silent video. The sportscaster, having seen the game or having read a prepared cue sheet, knows the action and the players. Usually this report is condensed to a key moment in the game shown as part of the daily sportscast. Frequently longer commentary is done in sports programs having the sportscaster and the team coach call play-by-play of a replay of the highlights of the game. Anyone aspiring to be a sportscaster will

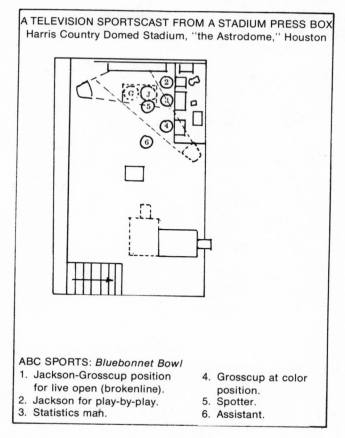

A TELEVISION SPORTSCAST FROM A STADIUM PRESS BOX
Harris Country Domed Stadium, "the Astrodome," Houston

ABC SPORTS: *Bluebonnet Bowl*

1. Jackson-Grosscup position for live open (brokenline).
2. Jackson for play-by-play.
3. Statistics man.
4. Grosscup at color position.
5. Spotter.
6. Assistant.

find calling play-by-play or reading copy against sports films is excellent practice. College and professional football teams are especially efficient at documenting every game they play, For example, it is the responsibility of the home team to film, summarize and distribute to every other professional team under the authority of the National Football League the complete action of every game. The "Game Summary" includes date, location, weather conditions, officials, player lineups, scoring summary, final team statistics, final individual statistics, first half summary, a play-by-play summary for each quarter with the time indicated for major action and defensive statistics.

In the early 1970s the George Foster Peabody Award went to Curt Gowdy as "television's most versatile sportscaster." Gowdy's career began when he was a youngster playing basketball and practicing on his own as an announcer. In 1944 he got a job for KFBX in Cheyenne for

$18 a week and was soon hired by KOMA, Oklahoma City. After six years he joined the New York Yankees broadcast team as an assistant to Mel Allen. In 1951, he became the lead announcer for the Boston Red Sox. Fifteen years later he left to do the NBC *Baseball Game of the Week.* "I haven't done radio play-by-play since I left the Red Sox," he said, "and I miss it." It's the most fulfilling job in sports. You're like a wild bird. You can just take off and soar. You can talk about the weather or the fat lady in the stands. You can paint a picture of that game. You're not chained to a monitor or a big crew. It's you and your adlib ability and a pencil and a scorecard."[6]

Interviews

An interview is essentially a conversation between two people, the interviewer asking the questions, the interviewee answering them. A press conference, however, is also a form of interview in which three or four persons may ask questions in turn of one or two respondents. The format requires the interviewer to provide an opening statement familiarizing the audience with the topic, to introduce the guest by name, title and/or relationship to the topic, and to begin the conversation with a major question, often the one the interviewer believes most people would like to ask.

As a practical matter, interviewers tend to specialize in show business, politics, science or education, and even then a small staff is busy researching this information, providing the interviewer with a biography and a list of questions. Throughout the interview the interviewer watches for time cues, apportioning the conversation accordingly. About 30 seconds from the end, he or she may summarize briefly, thank the guest by mentioning his or her full name and title, and promote the next segment of the program.

Conduct with the guest mentioned earlier—that is, the public relations responsibility, determination of the format and producing are all part of interviewing—may fall to one person if the program is low budget, which it usually is. The job of producing includes getting appropriate visuals, charts, art objects (even automobiles or boats), sports equipment, furniture, backdrops or other pieces that a station would not normally have in stock or could construct. Of course, the guest usually provides these items, but the interviewer must select which items for the guest to bring—which animals, which magic tricks, which flower arrangements. One of the reasons an interview series depends on the same setting (typically two chairs on a riser, against a background, often consisting of a lighted cyclorama) is to reduce expensive time in staging and lighting. The interviewer tends to share responsibility for damage to items borrowed for the program and, occasionally, for transporting them.

The key to interviewing is for the interviewer to listen to what the guest is saying, and to know enough in advance about the guest to develop further questions from that dialogue. Most interviewers maintain an aura of fairness which the guest is led to trust in answering difficult questions. "I go into an interview with an open mind, not an empty one," David Frost told NBC's Tom Snyder. "I don't know why I got the opportunity to interview President Nixon. Perhaps it is because I interviewed all of the political candidates in 1968 and most of the world leaders."[7] Johnny Carson, interviewing Beverly Sills, led into a difficult topic by saying: "I know you don't want to dwell on this, but it was in the papers . . ." To which the irrepressible Miss Sills responded, "You're very healthy except for a slight touch of cancer." "Usually my first questions are throw-away questions," Barbara Walters has said. "I don't pounce on the guest with the big, tough one. When I do get into difficult areas, I may say something like, 'I know you are an honest person and that you would like to answer in your own honest way the things that are being said about you.' Or I may say, 'There are those who say such critical things about you as . . . and I know you would want to respond to that in your own way.'"[8]

You should be aware of overworked words, phrases and expressions:

"You know." "Ah." "Well." "Okay." "I see." "Best of Luck." "Interesting." "Anything else you'd like to say." "Today" and other references to time: "I see we're just about out of time." Telephone numbers. Repeating a guest's answers. Most crude expressions such as "got bombed" for "was intoxicated." "Yes, sir" and other excessively formal phrases or terms of address. "As I said before the show" and other forms of repetition. Asking questions during the last thirty seconds: "In 30 seconds tell me . . ."

AN INTERVIEW FORMAT
Solar Energy[9]

VIDEO	AUDIO
SILENT VIDEOTAPE OF THE SUN. HOSTESS BEGINS VOICE OVER:	Energy! Where will we turn for new sources—oil becomes more and more expensive; gas is becoming scarce; coal is a pollutant; nuclear energy is a political bombshell and raises questions of health hazards. The sun—solar energy—may be part of the answer to this growing dilemma.
CU OF HOSTESS.	With me today to discuss the implications of solar energy are two very qualified individuals.

CU GUESTS.

Dr. Alvin C. Hildebrandt, chairman of the Department of Physics, at the University of Houston, and his associate, Dr. Lorin Vant-Hull. To date, they have received over $400,000 in continuing grants from the National Science Foundation to pursue solar energy research. And, together with their colleagues in the Physics Department, they have established themselves in the forefront of solar energy research.

1. Dr. Hildebrant, can you briefly explain the background and purposes of these grants?

SLIDES: 1. Heliostat (single mirror)
2. Backside heliostat
3. Artist's concept of many heliostats
4. Ball
5. Tower

2. Dr. Vant-Hull, how does one harness solar energy and convert it into a useful form for mankind?

SHOW MAP

3. What about geography in converting solar energy?
Do you need the sun 365 days a year?
Is this a practical energy source for northern climates?

SLIDE: Sunset.

4. What happens if the sun goes down?
Are you out of business when we have cloudy days?
Can you store energy in great amounts and indefinitely?

5. There's been a lot of controversy surrounding nuclear energy. How safe is solar energy comparatively speaking? What's the comparative cost to users?

6. How far into the future will it be before solar energy significantly affects our energy situation?

SLIDE: Experimental station in France
(Show after it is mentioned).

Are there plants producing solar energy now?

I'd like to thank my guests, Dr. Alvin C. Hildebrandt, chairman of the Department of Physics, at the University of Houston, and Dr. Lorin Vant-Hull, co-recipients of solar energy research grants, for being my guests today.
I'm Ellen Williams.
ROLL CUE TO NEXT SEGMENT.

Discussions

Conversation on media is cheap, and so it often rambles on without direction and is promptly forgotten. Ideally, it should be selective. Discussion groups, wherein there is great diversity of opinion, are especially prone to wander without strong leadership from the moderator. The following procedure is very useful if applied properly:

1. The moderator should define the topic, limiting it to an aspect that can be reasonably discussed within the given time period.

2. The moderator should select the discussants carefully through individual private conversations prior to the program rather than simply by reputation. The moderator would then know the areas in which the discussants agree and disagree.

3. The moderator should invite those persons who best articulate differing facets, especially opposing points of view (which does not simply mean one proponent and one opponent). Sometimes views are so potentially explosive that the moderator may opt for inviting discussants of singular views to express them without confronting each other on the same program. These sessions can often enlighten the public without as much emotional distraction. Of course, the dramatic values of the discussion may be sacrificed as well.

4. The moderator, during the program, directs the attention of the discussants to those specific points on which they have strong views, thus excluding all other material. Such discussions are focused and much more interesting to the public.

5. After the program, the moderator may have to hurry around thanking the guests, particularly if they streak off in opposite directions at a high emotional level, because the moderator should diplomatically preserve an impartial position throughout the entire discussion and beyond.

COMPLETE SCRIPTS

Most of the broadcast day on radio has a complete script: news, commercials, station continuity, promotional and public service announcements. Disc jockey continuity and talk programs are the exceptions. On television, all major programs—drama, variety, comedy, news, documentaries, features, commercials, PSAs, promotional spots, station continuity, and most programs for education, industry and medicine—have complete scripts. Exceptions were noted earlier as requiring script outlines. All features films have complete scripts except those adlibbed TV programs shot on film that do not require a full script.

The Single Performer

The single performer frequently has the responsibility for producing his or her own segment of a program. Among the many different kinds of single performers who may serve as producer/writer are actors, comedians, dancers, vocalists, advocates, announcers, educators, executives, newscasters, politicians, religious leaders, sportscasters and weathercasters.

Entertainers

Actors. Some actors (Orson Welles, David Hemmings, Vincent Price) have found short readings and play-length monologues (Hal Holbrook as Mark Twain, James Whitmore as Will Rogers) successful. Usually an actor's material is written by someone else, and he or she performs it. The actor must read a great deal of material and select those items that are exactly right. Actors tend not to be very versatile on media. They are "type cast" to play juvenile or mature, straight or character roles. Movies are especially inclined to type cast. In selecting material an actor or actress should first consider whether the character is close to his or her age and/or behavior pattern. Second, whether he or she can be convincing as this character. Acting takes insight and an exceptional intellectual and emotional understanding of human beings. Some actors and actresses are not very realistic. They think they can live up to vaudeville's boast of playing "8 to 80" when in mass media they cannot. A *tour de force* is seldom required of a performer, but Cicely Tyson played a role in which she appeared to age in TV's "The Autobiography of Miss Jane Pittmàn," and Dustin Hoffman was similarly outstanding in the movies' *Little Big Man*. Make-up, especially the use of latex, changes in voice and physical attitude are essential in making such portrayals convincing. Sally Field demonstrated extraordinary versatility as a multi-split personality in "Sybil."

A useful exercise, if nothing else, for the aspiring media actor is to have prepared a monologue or dramatic reading of about three minutes. This material can be presented on a moment's notice as a showcase for the actor's work. Typically, however, an actor or actress is expected to read a scene from a script with little or no preparation. Both the actor and the director are at a disadvantage. As director David Lean has said of screen tests, "If the actor is even 25 per cent good, and I have a hunch he'll do well in the part, I'll take a chance on him." Actors often get a start in media by being extras in films or TV programs. A non-union extra for a film, usually shot on location, may be solicited by a newspaper advertisement. The pay is about $20.00 a day and lunch. Extras are costumed by the film company, told precisely what to do, and must be prepared to stand around and wait a long time for the moment before cameras. Professional extras joining the Screen Extras Guild become eligible for network TV programs and feature films shot primarily in Los Angeles and New York. One graduate of the University of Houston who did this was earning over $50 a day (union scale) for appearances on such TV series programs as *Happy Days, Baa Baa Blacksheep* and the Disney film, *Pete's Dragon.*

Comedians. Comedians, especially beginners, must write their own material. They cannot afford writers who will study their style and develop materials for them; therefore, they must write as well as deliver their own material, much like some singers. On Fridays before the show, Chevy Chase, Lorne Michaels and a few writers culled newspapers for Chase's "Weekend Update" on NBC's *Saturday Night.* The professional life of a comedian depends on material. Many comedians have vanished more for lack of fresh material than for anything else. Much comedy is topical and therefore perishable. A few routines become classics like the "cleaning woman's fantasies" of Carol Burnett or the oriental impersonations of Buddy Hackett and, consequently, bear repeating. Comedians stockpile gags, sketches and routines, using them over and over, freshening them up whenever possible. While one-line gags are the stock in trade of monologists, every comedian has characteristics that he or she rigidly defines and presents as a continuing gag— dialect, obesity, stinginess, amorous tendencies, ethnic, family, mental or physical ineptitude. In other words, comedians base their acts on certain continuing themes or personality traits. For example, Milton Berle steals gags, which itself has become a "running gag" throughout his career. Some comedians, used to one-line gags, adlibbing, independence from a cast and freedom of movement on stage, find blocking for TV cameras and precise memorization of lines inhibiting and difficult. Nevertheless, they tolerate TV because of the tremendous visibility they get which tends to reinforce their audience on tour dates. The difficulty a comedian may have in obtaining an acceptable TV format is illustrated by Don Rickles. Rickles, who essentially works alone, outrageously berates those around him. After previous TV failures, Rickles appeared in *CPO Sharkey,* a light comedy series in which he showed his superiority to a group of naval station recruits.

Dancers. Dancers who work in the theater must restage their dances for the camera. Generally TV studios are much more limited in space than film studios. A 10 by 10-foot square is not uncommon. The choreography must be understood sufficiently by the director, so that he or she can get all major movements *and* good closeups of moments when the dancers are posed. To do this, the director rehearses the dance sufficiently to be acquainted with it. A dancer can provide a

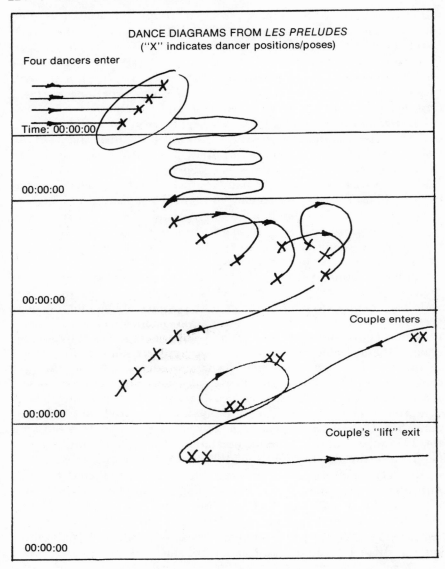

DANCE DIAGRAMS FROM *LES PRELUDES*
("X" indicates dancer positions/poses)

Four dancers enter

Time: 00:00:00

00:00:00

00:00:00

Couple enters

00:00:00

Couple's "lift" exit

00:00:00

diagram of the movements which serves as a script to remind the director of those instances when there is a shot advantage.

Another common method of scripting is for the dancer or choreographer to list all of the principal movements, as illustrated in this sequence from *Les Chapeaux:*[10]

VIDEO	AUDIO

Scene: Exterior of two hat shops.

1. Thief enters from left looking for someone.
2. Countess enters from right looking for someone.
3. They meet, embrace, exit different directions.
4. Angot's Apprentices (3 girls) enter from left.
5. Derain's Apprentices (3 girls) enter from right.
6. Boy (Angot's son) enters from right
7. All Apprentices & Boy dance together. One of them hangs boy's knapsack on a hook on the Hat Shop that is Camera Right.
8. Girl (Derain's Daughter) enters from left.
9. Boy & Girl dance. Apprentices in background.
10. Mme. Angot enters from left.
11. M. Derain enters from right.
12. Derain & Angot hide their apparent affection for each other, as Boy & Girl back of them "smooch."

Vocalists. It is not enough for a singer to know several songs. These songs should be organized in an order that produce a 20 to 60 minute act, as in a nightclub. Averaging 2½ minutes for each song, that amounts to from 8 to 24 songs. The act should include some variety such as a comedy monologue or dance routine. This material need not be complicated, but it should be very well done. Each song should be arranged in a way that expresses the unique talent of the vocalist. A typical act might begin:

> Announcer (off camera): Ladies and gentlemen,_____!
> Vocalist sings a fast song to get audience in a lively mood.
> Vocalist greets audience: "Thank you very much. It's wonderful being here." The vocalist is warm and friendly in a few remarks and moves immediately to the next song, something slower. "My next song is a favorite of mine. I hope you like it, too."
> Vocalist without a break sings a third song.
> Vocalist does a medley of songs and/or dance routine with two or three songs, including some comedy numbers.
> Vocalist sings a dramatic number or perhaps an original composition. This may be the high point of the show.

Vocalist thanks the audience for being so nice and ends with a lively tune, preferably with a high volume finish. At its conclusion there is a fade to black or other transition.

A vocalist in a TV or feature film concert sings two or three pre-planned encores, including a powerful dramatic finale. There is a fast fade to commercial followed by program credits with full volume orchestra and much applause.

The vocalist pulls from the basic act, described above, one or two numbers for short TV appearances and expands the material if in a position to do a longer program. Usually a single performer does not appear more than about half the time on an hour-long TV program. The remainder of the program is taken up with guests, patter, dances, sketches and other routines in which the vocalist walks on and off briefly to preserve continuity for the program without becoming overexposed.

Many young people are involved with music at an early age, and so it is common for them to play instruments, sing and even compose music individually and in small groups. Original scores for local TV and films are challenging, and musicians are usually glad to get the experience with media. One or two musical compositions a year are produced by students for University of Houston productions, such as the films *Farewell to All the Ghosts and Goblins of Circumstance* (1974) and *The Second Door* (1977).

Many popular song writers—Paul Simon, Joni Mitchell, Neil Sedaka and Stevie Wonder—both write and sing their own songs. "I would like to be known and respected for my songs," says Melissa Manchester, "but that's a hard thing to say because those kind of things either happen or they don't. It's not something you can go after. You write for yourself. And then you meet many, many people who think that you wrote for them. And that's nice. It's nice to know people are connecting with what you're feeling. It's nice to know that you are, in fact, communicating and touching people."[11]

Information Specialists

Announcers. The term "announcer" has been applied to several performers; however, the announcers referred to here have essentially two functions: commercial announcers who sell products and services and/or staff announcers who read spots, IDs and station miscellany, providing continuity throughout the broadcast day. Announcing for media dates from the early days of the phonograph when speakers announced selections on unlabeled cylinders, the antecedents of discs, but announcing as a skill was not seriously defined until the mid-'20s, when the announcer was supposed to visualize "a little family group" assembled around the loud speaker of a radio. Early announcers were mainly actors, orators or even engineers who found themselves doing more than simply testing and maintaining equipment. The techniques for live platform appearances in theaters were, however unsuitable, transferred to radio. It was not until 1931, after having spent many months in the hospital listening to radio while recovering from a very serious auto accident, that Arthur Godfrey, an experienced radio announcer, recognized the major fault of most announcers—they were talking to a group, rather than to an individual. Godfrey adopted a style of speaking to only one individual, and that is what he visualized while broadcasting.

Women likewise made their debut on radio during the early 1920s, but listener polls quickly restricted their efforts as announcers. One station polling 5,000 listeners in 1926 decided 100 to one against women announcers. Ten years later when a few women did appear on the air, they gave the weather and the billboard for evening programs.[12] This practice is still common although some inroads have been made in other announcing tasks, such as emceeing talk shows and selling products and services.

A commercial or staff announcer works from copy. Announcers primarily deliver the sense of a message in a persuasive way. Announcers complement the product, such as a handsome Orkin man implying "I'll be right over" to provide more than exterminator service or a sophisticated woman recommending an "Aviance Night"; or they personify the average consumer of a product, such as the enthusiastic housewife and skeptical husband selling Glade "air conditioner air conditioner." Some announcers document the product by citing statistics, for example Frank Blair for Bayer asprin, or they bring attention to the product—especially if the product is unglamorous, such as the zany "fruits" selling Fruit of the Loom underwear or a seductive model dressed as an owl for White Owl cigars. Visualization linked with product identity is extremely important, because a purchase is often based on a consumer knowing *little* about the advertised product but *nothing* about the unadvertised competition on the shelf in the supermarket. It follows that the announcer's personality should be compatible with the merchandise, and he or she should communicate the value of the product in a memorable way. These performers are chosen on appearance and/or voice from the files of talent agencies. In recent years celebrities have made several commercials. Among them are Laurence Olivier and Candice Bergen for Polaroid, Henry Fonda for GAF products, Gregory Peck for Travelers Insurance, Peter Sellers for Trans World Airlines and Bing Crosby for Minute Maid orange juice. Most spots are written and produced by advertising agencies.

Local radio stations are inclined to produce many commercials of their own. The procedure is for the local sales person to get the account from a local retail merchant. A writer at the station then drafts appropriate copy for the supermarket, department store or automobile dealer and submits it to a station disc jockey for reading on-the-air.

Local TV stations may devote many hours a day to producing spots for local clients. These spots may be run on all of the TV stations in town. These spots are probably cast and produced by a local TV advertising agency. Disc jockey comedy teams may spin records and adlib comments about sponsors based on a simple fact sheet about the product. A farm reporter may mix his farm news with products and services that he personally endorses, the entire program consisting of a flow of conversation wherein the advice given in commercials is barely perceptible from the news content. Occasionally a business report will blend with a commercial promoting a bank such as a daily tip on economic trends. In each case the copy is written by the performer.

Whether a commercial is written by the performer or someone else, the copy enables the commercial announcer:

(1) to introduce himself or herself;

(2) to polarize the listeners and/or viewers;

(3) to introduce the product simply, easily and clearly, leaving no questions in the mind of the listener or viewer;

(4) to repeat the main points insofar as time permits;

(5) to advocate the purchase of the product because it will be satisfying and easy to get.

In these two examples the bank copy has a part for a man and an announcer. The second spot requires a man, a woman and an announcer:

AGENCY:	Weekley & Penny, Inc., Houston
CLIENT:	Houston National Bank
MEDIUM:	30-second TELEVISION
TITLE:	Home Wrecker #HNB 1/30-77 (1 voice plus announcer)

VIDEO:

Middle-aged, casually dressed
man outside against pastoral
setting. He is talking to
"someone" who at this point is
the camera.
His delivery should be very
soap-opera melodramatic.

AUDIO:

MAN: I'M NOT BLAMING YOU.

YOU WERE WITH ME STARTING OUT ...

AND THEN THE KIDS.

IT'S JUST ... I'VE OUTGROWN YOU.

(Big gulp, lump in throat, tear in eye)

SO ... THIS IS GOODBYE

Camera angle changes 180˚ and we see Man is actually addressing an old, rundown <u>house instead of his wife</u>.

ANNCR(VO): HOUSTON NATIONAL BANK KNOWS YOU NEED MORE ROOM NOW. BUT WHY BREAK UP A HAPPY HOME. GET A HOME IMPROVEMENT LOAN FROM ONE OF OUR PERSONAL BANKERS.

Man Hugging house.

MAN: I ... I HAVE SOME WONDERFUL NEWS.

Logo. Houston National Bank
       Member FDIC

© 1977 Weekley & Penny, Inc.

AGENCY: Weekley & Penny, Inc., Houston
CLIENT: Friendswood Development Company/Kingwood
MEDIUM: 60-second RADIO
TITLE: Shopping #KWD 7/60-77   (2 voices plus announcer)

SFX:	Pots and pans rattling (under)
WOMAN:	NOW WHERE'S THAT SALAD BOWL?
SFX:	Back door opening in distance.
MAN:	(off mike) RUTHIE, I'M HOME.
SFX:	Back door closing. Footsteps coming to mike.
WOMAN:	HI, HONEY ...
SFX:	Kiss
WOMAN:	WHEN'S YOUR BOSS COMING OVER?
MAN:	OH, ABOUT FIFTEEN MINUTES ... WHAT ARE WE HAVING?
WOMAN:	STUFFED PEPPERS .. (suddenly realizing) AND I FORGOT THE PEPPERS.
MAN:	(voice and footsteps going off mike) OKAY, DON'T PANIC, YOU KEEP HIM COMPANY.
SFX:	Back door opens.
MAN:	I'LL BE BACK SOON.
SFX:	Car starts and boldly screeches off (fades under)
ANNCR:	THIS ISN'T THE WAY A QUICK TRIP TO THE STORE HAS TO BE.
MUSIC:	Segue from screeching car
ANNCR:	NOT WHEN YOUR HOME'S IN THE LIVABLE FOREST.

```
SINGERS:        LIKE THE OPEN AIR
                EVERYTHING IS THERE
                IN THE LIVABLE FOREST
                KINGWOOD

ANNCR:          LIVING IN KINGWOOD.  IT MEANS LIVING WITHIN FIVE MINUTES OF A MAJOR

                SUPERMARKET.  WITHIN FIVE MINUTES OF A BANK.  WITHIN FIVE MINUTES

                OF MODERN STORES -- EVEN A FLOWER SHOP.  AND IT'S ALL HERE NOW.  MAYBE

                YOU SHOULD BE TOO.

SINGERS:        LIKE THE OPEN AIR
                EVERYTHING IS THERE
                IN THE LIVABLE FOREST
                KINGWOOD

ANNCR:          US 59 NORTH TO KINGWOOD DRIVE.
```

© Weekley & Penny, Inc.

Newscasters. The majority of radio and TV anchorpersons and contributing reporters who read news copy on the air rewrite it from on-the-scene reports, wire services, printed publications, and reports from media competition. According to the Associated Press, the primary objective in writing for the air is to be clear at all times, phrasing copy to prohibit stumbling or tripping.[13] Few anchorpersons do outside-or on-the-scene reporting. A so-called five-minute radio newscast without commercials and PSAs runs about three and a half minutes. The radio newscaster gathers, rewrites and reads the news many times a day, instantly updating late breaking events. Audio support, such as audiotapes, are provided by the newscaster, especially at small stations. A typical five-minute radio format follows:

Time in Seconds	Topic	Information Source
10	Headlines or Teaser Story	Newscaster
	Commercial	Agency or local copywriter
	Commercial	Agency or local copywriter
20	Local Story	Newscaster with telephone update or
20	Local Story	newspaper or on-the-scene or moni-
20	Local Story	tors with telephone update
	Commercials	
20	National Story	Wire service. May have telephone up-
30	National Story	date or pretaped network update
20	National Story	
20	Stock Market	Wire service
20	Feature	Wire service or possible local item
	Commercials	
20	Sports	Wire service or local newspaper or tele-
		phone or monitoring other stations
10	Weather	Weatherwire or local weather bureau

Brian Hill, of KLOL(FM), Houston read the following news copy over the air on July 15, 1977:

15jul77bh

SAYING HE COULDN'T STAND THE HEAT, STATE SUPREME COURT JUSTICE DON
YARBROUGH GOT OUT OF THE KITCHEN TODAY. THE JUSTICE, INDICTED ON
CHARGES OF FORGERY AND PERJURY RESIGNED HIS HIGH COURT BENCH SHORTLY
BEFORE NOON TODAY.
YARBROUGH TURNED IN HIS RESIGNATION AFTER LEGISLATORS REFUSED TO
POSTPONE HEARINGS CONCERNING HIS FORCED REMOVAL.
STATE ATTORNEY GENERAL JOHN HILL HAD THIS COMMENT ABOUT TODAYS DEVELOP-
MENTS.
TAPE: Q: A LOT OF TIME.
ONE STATE LEGISLATOR, HOUSTONS CRAIG WASHINGTON, DOESN'T AGREE WITH
HILL. HE SAYS YARBROUGH WAS TREATED UNFAIRLY.
YARBROUGH STILL FACES THE FORGERY AND PERJURY INDICTMENTS AND A 100
COUNT DISBARMENT SUIT FILED BY THE STATE BAR.

15jul77bh

OPTIMISM FROM THE WHITE HOUSE TODAY.
CARTER FOLKS SAY NORTH KOREAS UNUSUALLY LOW KEY COMMENTS CONCERNING
THE U S ARMY HELICOPTER DOWNED BY NORTH KOREAN FIREHAVE RAISED HOPES
FOR THE EARLY RETURN OF THE ONE CREWMAN IN CUSTODY AND THE THREE MEN
KILLED.   REPRESENTATIVES FROM BOTH SIDES WILL DISCUSS THE INCIDENT
AT THE PANMUNJOM TRUCE VILLAGE BEGINNING AT NINE THIS EVENING HOUSTON
TIME.

15jul77bh

TODAY, AS NEW YORK CITY RECOVERED FROM THE EFFECTS OF THE BLACK OUT,
MAYOR ABE BEAME AND POLICE COMMISSIONER MIKE CODD WENT ON A WALKING
TOUR OF ONE OF THE HARD HIT AREAS OF BROOKLYN.

AS THE MAYOR PICKED HIS WAY THRU THE RUBBLE OF ONE STORE HE WAS MET BY
A DISTRAUGHT BROOKLYN BUSINESSMAN WHO HAD BEEN WIPED OUT BY THE LOOTING
CROWDS.

HE TOLD THE MAYOR THE POLICE JUST STOOD BY AND DID NOTHING WHILE LOOTERS
CLEANED OUT HIS STORE IN BROAD DAYLIGHT.

<u>TAPE:</u>   Q: HOW WE CAN HELP YOU.

15jul77bh

THE C I A TOLD THE SENATE MOMENTS AGO IT HAS UNCOVERED NEW INFORMATION
ABOUT THE EXTENT OF THE SECRET C I A DRUG TESTS CARRIED OUT ON
UNSUSPECTING AMERICANS BETWEEN 1953 AND 1964.

AT CHIEF CARTERS DIRECTION, HEAD SPOOK STANSFIELD TURNER HAND DELIVERED
A LETTER TO SENATOR DAN INOUE SAYING THE C I A CHIEF WILL VOLUNTARILY
TESTIFY ABOUT THE NEW MATERIALS BEFORE THE SENATORS C I A OVER SIGHT
COMMITTEE AS SOON AS POSSIBLE.

MR CARTER TOLD PRESS TYPES TODAY HE THINKS THE MATTER IS RATHER SERIOUS.
THE DOCUMENTS DEAL WITH, AMONG OTHER THINGS, A KNOCK OR "K" DRUG THAT
INVOLVED ADVANCED CANCER PATIENTS, A POSSIBLE IMPROPER PAYMENT TO AN
UNNAMED INSTITUTION AND POSSIBLE ADDITIONAL CASES OF DRUGS BEING SECRETLY
TESTED ON AMERICANS.

THE DRUG TESTS CARRIED OUT UNDER THE CODE NAME MK-ULTRA ENDED TEN YEARS
AGO ACCORDING TO TURNER.

15jul77bh

CHARGES OF DISCRIMINATION AGAINST MEXICAN AMERICANS, ACCORDING TO ONE
TEXAS SOUTHERN UNIVERSITY OFFICIAL ARE UNFOUNDED.
EARL BEAN OF T S U'S SCHOOL OF LAW EXPLAINS THE PROCEDURE FOR
ADMISSIONS.
TAPE: Q: RULES AND REGULATIONS.
TWO STATE SENATORS, INCLUDING HOUSTONS JACK OGG, SAY THEY FREQUENTLY
RECEIVE COMPLAINTS OF ANTIHISPANIC BEHAVIOUR DIRECTED AT T S U.

15jul77bh

THE CARTER ADMINISTRATION HAS ENDORSED LEGISLATION TO ESTABLISH NO
FAULT AUTO INSURANCE NATIONWIDE.
SUCH A PROPOSAL HAS NEVER RECEIVED WHITE HOUSE BACKING BEFORE.
THE LEGISLATION HAS PROVISIONS FOR SERIOUSLY INJURED ACCIDENT VICTIMS
TO OVER STEP THE BOUNDS OF NO FAULT AND SUE OTHER MOTORISTS FOR
LIBILITY.
NO FAULT INSURANCE IS CURRENTLY IN EFFECT IN 16 STATES.

15jul77bh

THE TEXAS WATER QUALITY BOARD HAS GIVEN THE GO AHEAD TO A 24 THOUSAND
DOLLAR STUDY OF THE HOUSTON SHIP CHANNEL.
THE STUDY MAY EVENTUALLY SAVE HOUSTON MILLIONS IN POLLUTION CONTROL
DEVICES AND MEASURES. THE RESEARCH WILL BEGIN IN AUGUST.

15jul77bh

PRESIDENT CARTER SPENDS THIS WEEKEND AT CAMP DAVID IN MARYLAND.
NEXT WEEK HE GOES SOUTH TO SPEND ONE NIGHT IN THE HOME OF ELIZABETH
COOPER IN YAZOO CITY, MISSISSIPPI. MRS. COOPER SAYS SHE'S GOING TO
BE WORKING HARD TO GET THE PLACE IN SHAPE FOR MR CARTER.
TAPE: Q: WELCOME MAT OUT (LAUGHTER).

15jul77bh

FOR WEEKS DICK HERSHEY HAS HAD A PROBLEM WITH DEER POACHING ON HIS
BACK YARD BOULDER COLORADO GARDEN.
NECESSITY BEING THE MOTHER OF INVENTION, HERSHEY CAME UP WITH A
BRILLIANT IDEA AFTER A FRIEND TOLD HIM DEER ARE SCARED TO DEATH OF LIONS...
EVEN IF THEY'VE NEVER SEEN ONE.
SO WITH THE HELP OF A FRIEND WHO WORKS FOR THE DENVER ZOO, HERSHEY
ARRANGED TO PICK UP..NO NOT A LION..BUT LION MANURE TO SPREAD AROUND
HIS GARDEN. THE CABBAGE LETTUCE AND CARROTS ARE DOING JUST FINE THANK YOU!

Tom Jarriel, of ABC Television News, Washington, D.C., provided a
copy of his afternoon *Newsbrief*. This frequent telecast consists simply
of the newscaster and slides:

TJ/ tlb 7/5/77

Good Afternoon......

video/box.....Panamanian born Luis Robinson will

be arraigned today on charges of

murder and kidnapping. The U.S. Navy

seaman surrendered to police last night,

He released

~~halory~~ his last hostages unhurt

after allegedly killing two people and

wounding two others during a nine hour

bus hijacking at JFK airport.

The Pakistani army has placed the

VIZ
Pakistan
Map

country under martial law after

imprisoning Prime Minister Bhutto in an

apparently bloodless coup.

VIZ
Brezhnev

Soviet leader Brezhnev has told

U.S. ambassador Malcolm Toon that

American foreign policy is damaging

Soviet-American relations.

The Vatican has urged American

VIZ
Vatican

bishops to seek government money to

support parochial schools.

- more -

page 2

VIZ
Pipeline Map

The Canadian Energy Board has recommended an eight billion dollar pipeline to bring Alaskan natural gas to the U.S. and Canada.

And Researchers at MIT report

VIZ
Sickle Cell Anemia

discovery of a compound that could help treat sickle cell anemia.

For further details watch the ABC

VIZ
Newsbrief

Evening News.

Barbara Walters, co-anchor of the *ABC Evening News,* has summarized the role of the performer as a TV producer: "You really have to have . . . the ability to know what makes a story . . . the ability to write it up . . . the ability to go out and work with the film crew and put the story together . . . the ability to deliver it on the air." [14]

While a network reporter may have one story a day, most reporters have three or four. Whether covering one story or four, each local news reporter repeats a similar work pattern. Lynn Sherr described her daily routine while a reporter with WCBS-TV:

Normally you go out and shoot your film on the same day as you use it. I come in at 9:00 or 10:00, depending on what my hours are. I'll get an assignment—be somewhere by 10:00 or 11:00—and go out with a film crew; come back by 1:00 or 2:00. The film goes in to be developed; you start talking to the associate producer and figure out how you're going to put the piece together. The film comes out of the soup; you go back into film editing; screen the film; figure out how you're going to structure it; go and write the script; go back with the film editor, putting it all together. By then it's 4:30 or 5:00 o'clock, if you're lucky; go and write live open or close; 5:30 you get made-up and 6:00

o'clock you're on the set. . . . The producer decides who is on set live. It's a question of how many bodies they want on the set; how many bodies they'd rather have on film. You ask before leaving, "Do you want me on the set or do you want me to do a film close?" Sometimes the 11:00 o'clock producer will ask for a film close, although I do live on 6:00 o'clock, so he can recut it and use it on the 11:00 o'clock show. . . . I sometimes go 14 or 15 hours a day. And you have to look nice, of course, which takes even more energy."[15]

Sportscasters. Sports is a special form of reporting. It attracts a great many young men and more and more women. A sports summary usually consists of news items, scores, interviews, and commentary. Local sports reporting is mostly included in interviews reflecting player, coach and management opinion. At the network level the sportscaster has become as much a personality as the players, and in many cases as well known, because his or her exposure is consistently greater. Some unique sportscasters are visually attractive (Frank Gifford), vocally distinctive (Howard Cosell) or brilliantly perceptive (Heywood Hale Broun).

Scripts for local sportscasters are written. They include major stories of the day, feature interviews and scores. The sportscast below is a segment from the late evening half-hour news program on KPRC-TV, Houston. In it Sports Director Bill Worrell gives live reports, scores and voice-over-videotape stories from the studio. Another reporter (Anita Martini) conducts a live interview from a remote location (The Summit):

SWC BASKETBALL (LIVE) SWC SLIDE	SONY "B" ROLL 10pm 3-4-77 BW. ①
SWC SLIDE (KEYED) U. HOUSTON 94 TEXAS TECH 83	THE HOUSTON COUGARS USED A BIG FIRST HALF TONITE TO BEAT TEXAS TECH 94 to 83 AND ADVANCE TO THE FINALS OF THE SOUTHWEST CONFERENCE TOURNAMENT. ANITA MARTINI HAS A LIVE REPORT FROM THE SUMMIT:

■ LIVE CAMERA _____ #1 SONY....	(AS SOON AS ANITA STARTS HILITES, RUN THE FIRST SONY "HILITES") ANITA INTERVIEWS GUY LEWIS...(ONCE

#2 SONY......	GUY STARTS TALKING, RUN SECOND SONY "B" ROLL)
	        INSERT: GUY LEWIS
	             U.F. HEAD COACH
	ANITA FOR SHORT WRAPUP AND THEN ENDS WITH "ANITA MARTINI WITH THE BIG TWO INSTANT NEWS CAMERA, FOR BIG TWO SPORTS")

10

②

CAM	THE COUGARS VERSUS ARKANSAS TOMORROW NITE AT THE SUMMIT.... BY THE WAY, CHANNEL TWO WILL CARRY THE BIG GAME TOMORROW MORNING BETWEEN NUMBER ONE RANKED SAN FRANCISCO, AND NOTRE DAME. TIPOFF IS SET FOR 11:30 TOMORROW MORNING.
AEROS SLIDE	

15

③

AEROS SLIDE (KEYED) AEROS 2 WHALERS 3	THE NEW ENGLAND WHALERS SCORED TWICE IN THE FINAL PERIOD TONITE, TO EDGE THE HOUSTON AEROS 3 to 2. MARTY HOWE AND JOHN TONELLI SCORED FOR HOUSTON, BUT THE WHALERS RALLIED DOWN THE STRETCH.

	THE AEROS HEAD FOR CINCINNATI AND CHANNEL TWO WILL TELEVISE THAT GAME SUNDAY AT ONE O'CLOCK.	
BLANK SLIDE		:05

④

BLANK SLIDE (FULL)	ELSEWHERE IN THE WHA....	
WHA SCORES	INDIANAPOLIS LEADS SAN DIEGO	
	IN THE SECOND PERIOD....	
SAN DIEGO 1 2 (2) INDIANAPOLIS	2 to 1 —	
BASKETBALL SLIDE (FULL) (SCORES)		:15

⑤

BASKETBALL SCORE SLIDE (FULL)	IN THE NBA TONITE:
NBA SCORES	BOSTON NIPPED DETROIT AT THE BUZZER.....
BOSTON 94 DETROIT 92	GOLDEN STATE LEADS PHEONIX AT THE HALF....
PHOENIX 48 GOLDEN ST. 56 (H)	BUFFALO BOMBED NEW ORLEANS.....
NEW ORLEANS 91 BUFFALO 95	
SAN ANTONIO 135 N.Y. NETS 121	
WASHINGTON 99 ATLANTA 100	SAN ANTONIO MOVED TO WITHIN A ½ GAME OF THE HOUSTON ROCKETS, BY CLOBBERING THE NETS....
	AND ATLANTA EDGED THE BULLETS 100 to 99...MOVING THE ROCKETS TO WITHIN 2 GAMES OF FIRST PLACE.

MALONE, MOSES   SONY SOUND   6pm   *1:45*

                                                                                          ⑥

ROCKETS SLIDE (KEYED)   ▬ HOUSTON ▬▬ PLAYS

                                         MILWAUKEE TOMORROW AFTERNOON

                                         AT 2 O'CLOCK IN THE SUMMIT....

                                         THE EARLY STARTING TIME DUE

                                            TO THE FINALS OF THE

                                         SOUTHWEST CONFERENCE

                                         TOURNAMENT.....

                                         WORRELL V/O
(1:41)
                                                        Rocket
SONY SOUND UNDER *:21* AND IT WILL BE A CHANCE FOR ▬▬▬▬ FANS

                                         TO SEE THE MOST IMPROVED PLAYER IN THE

                                         LEAGUE....HOUSTONS' MOSES MALONE. NUMBER

                                         21 HAS COME ON THE LAST SEVERAL WEEKS TO

                                         LEAD THE ROCKETS NEAR THE TOP OF THE CENTRAL

                                         DIVISION. WEDNESDAY NIGHT AGAINST THE LAKERS,

                                         MALONE HAD 26 POINTS AND 19 REBOUNDS...AND

                                         COMING AGAINST KAREEM ABDUL JABBAR. ROCKET

                                         COACH TOM NISSALKE WON'T COMPARE MALONE WITH

                                         JABBAR. *(21)*

SONY SOUND UP *:24*   (OUTCUE: "IS JUST GRAVY")
                              INSERT: TOM NISSALKE
                                      HOUSTON ROCKETS COACH

                                         WORRELL V/O

SONY SOUND UNDER *:10* MALONE SHOULD BE JUST A JUNIOR IN COLLEGE....

                         HAVING SIGNED RIGHT OUT OF HIGH SCHOOL THREE
                         YEARS AGO. AND HE IS JUST NOW DEVELOPING A
                         SHOT, WORKING WITH ASSISTANT COACH DEL HARRIS. *(10)*
SONY SOUND UP *:33*   (OUTCUE: "THAT WHAT I'M WORKING ON")
                              INSERT: MOSES MALONE
                                      HOUSTON ROCKETS

                    (MORE—MORE)

MALONE, MOSES   (PAGE TWO)   SONY SOUND

⑦

WORRELL V/O

SONY SOUND UNDER `i/5`   MALONE'S ROCKET TEAM ATES CREDIT A LOT OF
                        THEIR SUCCESS TO THE YOUNG GIANT....AND IT'S
                        EVIDENT, AS HE ACQUIRES MORE CONFIDENCE, SO
                        DOES THE TEAM.
                            THE ROCKETS GO FOR WIN NUMBER 35
                        TOMORROW AFTERNOON IN THE SUMMIT....AND MOSES
                        MALONE WILL BE FRONT AND CENTER ⑮

                BLANK SLIDE (FULL)   `:/0`

                                                                      ⑧

BLANK SLIDE (FULL)   BOB ZENDER SHOT A 67 TODAY
CITRUS OPEN   TO TAKE THE SECOND ROUND
   136   LEAD IN THE CITRUS OPEN GOLF
BOB ZENDER   TOURNAMENT. ZENDER'S 136
   137   TOTAL IS ONE UP ON BILL
BILL ROGERS   ROGERS AND JOE INMAN.
JOE INMAN

NFL SLIDE   `:/0`

                                                                      ⑨

NFL SLIDE (KEYED)   A FEDERAL JUDGE HAS GIVEN
                                      HIS APPROVAL TO THE NEW FIVE
                                      YEAR CONTRACT AGREED TO BY
                                      THE NFL PLAYERS AND OWNERS.
                                          NOW ALL THAT IS LEFT, IS
                                      FOR THE RANK-AND-FILE
                                      PLAYERS TO VOTE THEIR APPROVAL,
AND THAT'S EXPECTED NEXT
WEEK.

Weathercasters. Weather interests nearly everyone, especially if the coverage area is likely to have violent weather from time to time. A weather report consists of information provided by the nearest United States Weather Bureau or a weather wire service. The weather person need not be a meteorologist, but this background can be useful in interpreting and expanding the meaning of data. Some stations maintain rain gauges, thermometers, barometers and even radar scanning equipment. Some radio stations in coastal cities use a helicopter or small seacraft for observation.

The key to weathercasting is the personality of the performer. With everyone in the market basically reading the same report, the audience has little choice in content, so its selection of a performer is based on personality. The style of some weathercasters may be a straightforward factual approach, some depend on humor or rapidly delivered gags, and others on personal warmth and tidbits about local events such as club meetings, picnics and social activities.

Network weather reporting is confined to national weather forecasting provided by the U.S. Weather Service which predicts trends nationwide, ranging from a few days to a week. Natural disasters and regional weather problems are frequently reported as news or feature news and not strictly as weather.

The weather is usually presented as part of a news format. It is often sponsored separately, and therefore, at many stations takes on a character of its own. Weather personnel are not considered a part of the news staff at many stations. Some weather personalities are highly paid, receiving salaries equivalent to a news anchor. The weather person is actually on the air about three and a half minutes per telecast, but may have to report weather on a sister radio station. A common weather format may consist of two minutes of national weather followed by a minute and a half of local weather:

	ROLE CUE TO WEATHER PERSON FROM NEWS ANCHOR.
	WEATHER PERSON:
NATIONAL WEATHER MAP MAY BE FULLY PREPARED IN WHICH CASE WEATHER PERSON SIMPLY USES A POINTER OR IT MAY BE SEMICOMPLETE, IN WHICH CASE THE WEATHER PERSON ADDS WEATHER SYMBOLS TO THE MAP.	GENERAL STATEMENT ABOUT THE NATIONAL WEATHER. SPECIFIC STATEMENTS ABOUT THE MAJOR STORM SYSTEMS, HIGHS AND LOWS. SEVERE WEATHER IS GIVEN CONSIDERABLE ATTENTION.
	A COMMERCIAL INTERRUPTS THE WEATHER REPORT. UNLIKE MOST NEWS PERSONNEL, A WEATHER PERSON MAY ENDORSE THE SPONSOR.
THE WEATHER PERSON GOES TO A REGIONAL OR LOCAL WEATHER MAP.	REGIONAL CONDITIONS ARE DESCRIBED, ALONG WITH MAJOR INFLU-

LIGHTED DISPLAY BOARDS, FILM SHOT BY SATELLITES, RADAR SCANS AND SO FORTH ARE ADDED AT THIS POINT.

ENCES ON EXISTING CONDITIONS. PREDICTIONS RANGING FROM THE NEXT 24 HOURS TO THE NEXT 7 DAYS ARE MADE.

WHEN APPROPRIATE, HUMOR, HUMAN INTEREST ITEMS AND OTHER PLEAS- ANTRIES ARE INCLUDED IN THE WRAP- UP.

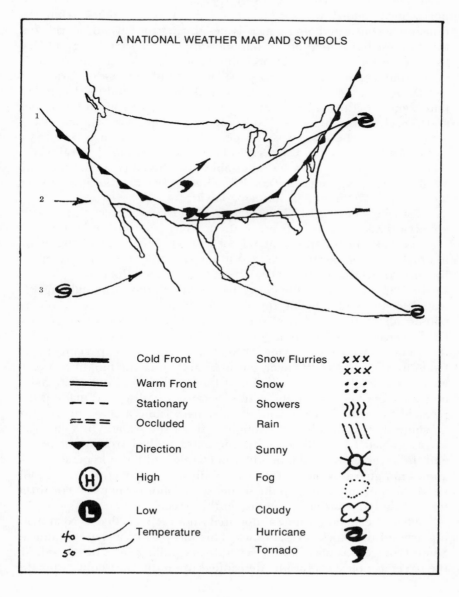

A NATIONAL WEATHER MAP AND SYMBOLS

▬▬▬	Cold Front	Snow Flurries	✗✗✗ ✗✗✗
═══	Warm Front	Snow	•••
– – –	Stationary	Showers	⟩⟩⟩
⇌═══	Occluded	Rain	\\\\
▼▼▼	Direction	Sunny	☼
Ⓗ	High	Fog	⬭
Ⓛ	Low	Cloudy	☁
40 50 ~	Temperature	Hurricane	⟩
		Tornado	⟩

The Large Cast

If a performer is a member of a large cast, participation is dictated by the number of scenes in which the performer appears. These scenes are shot in minimum time and out of sequence if preserved on film or videotape.

Documentaries and Features. The ambition of many reporters is to make long news documentaries or special investigative or feature reports. Such reporting is rare at network and local stations. While stations were concerned about such issues during the 60s and early '70s, this interest has waned and economic support for such programs has likewise declined, but it will probably cycle around again as the need arises, and so a budding young journalist should not be discouraged.

Dramas. Originating a TV drama is difficult beyond the local amateur context because dramas are for the most part expensive, complex and therefore produced on videotape or film in large studios in Los Angeles or, in the case of soap operas, may originate live from New York City. TV and film dramas may be shot on location. Typical scenes from two motion pictures are an establishing shot, a chase, a party and a fight. They are from *The Thief Who Came to Dinner,* shot in Houston, and *Lovin' Molly,* filmed in Bastrop, Texas.

For one scene in *The Thief Who Came to Dinner,* director Bud Yorkin set up his cameras in front of the modern administration building of the Houseton Independent School District. The name of the building had been temporarily changed to indicate that it was a museum of fine arts from which Ryan O'Neal, playing a super thief, was going to steal a huge diamond. The entire block surrounding the building was closed to the public during the shooting. Nearby was a large van containing all of the costumes, such as those for the museum guards. Other vans carried equipment, a power supply and food. Action for the scene consisted of having O'Neal walk across the parking lot in front, up the stairs to the main entrance and enter the building. Meanwhile six or eight extras walked past the building and out of it. Assistant directors helped cue the extras, because the distances made it impossible to hear or see anyone in the main camera position. By late morning the sun was bright enough to shoot the scene. On a cue, two extras walked from left to right, one extra walked from right to left and three came out of the building (a couple and a single person) past a museum guard, while O'Neal walked directly to the entrance. It took nearly all morning to set up the scene. It was shot perhaps two or three times. It lasted less than a minute on the screen.

That afternoon a camera mounted on a car recorded O'Neal driving around the block several times. This was part of a chase sequence. Some footage was also shot of several cars pulling over to the side of the street as police cars wildly descended upon the "museum" after the robbery. The total running time for these two scenes was probably under two minutes.

On another occasion, Yorkin staged a ballroom scene inside the Marriott Motor Hotel where everyone was staying. This scene was supposed to suggest that O'Neal was at the party while another house was being robbed. The action consisted of the arrival of the guests—all Houston socialites—dressed in silver, blue and white, a brief conversation by the party host and hostess and a little dancing involving eight couples, including O'Neal and his co-star, Jacqueline Bisset. On a cue, the merrymakers moved across the ballroom floor, greeted the host and hostess and formed into a kind of square dance. All of this activity was recorded on one dolly-mounted camera and a shoulder-pod-mounted camera. Boom microphones picked up the sound. Of course, the socialites donated their fees as extras to a charity but later in the day the best costume depicting the space age theme of the party was awarded a prize.[16]

In *Lovin' Molly,* directed by Sydney Lumet, on location in Bastrop, Texas, Beau Bridges and Conrad Fowks spent much of an afternoon practicing a fight scene to be staged under artificial lights that night. The action took place outside a white frame building that served as a dance hall. In this scene the two actors leave the dance hall and begin fighting in the parking lot. Those at the party hear the scuffle and come out. Again, the running time of the scene is short, but the preparation on the part of the crew and actors took most of an afternoon and that night.[17]

Variety Programs

A variety act can be just about anything a performer wants it to be. Comedy, music and information are the principal acts. Professional writing in these areas is highly sophisticated but it, too, began at some point in time, and a performer should not forget that. The following illustration indicates how a novice develops his or her ideas for a variety format.

In an effort to revive live television in New York, ABC originated an hour variety format during 1975–1976 season from the Ed Sullivan Theatre. The show was *Saturday Night Live with Howard Cosell.* This is the format for show #8, aired on November 8, 1975:

1. ACT ONE
    a. VTR: Carrillo Bros. cold opening.
    b. VTR: Titles with announcer voice over.
    c. Guest billboard with announcer voice over.
    d. Cosell entrance. He introduces "Chicago" routine.
    e. "Chicago" with Verdon, Rivera, Korthaza.
    f. Chicago talk.
    g. Lead in commercial #1.

2. COMMERCIAL #1
3. ACT TWO
   a. Cosell talks about New York.
   b. Remote tease of Carrillo Bros. from Nassau Coliseum.
   c. Introduction of Bill Crystal.
   d. Bill Crystal monologue.
   e. Lead in commercial #2.
4. COMMERCIAL #2
5. ACT THREE. This was cut.
6. COMMERCIAL #3 & STATION BREAK
7. ACT FOUR
   a. Introduction of Roy Clark.
   b. Clark sings "Kansas City."
   c. Clark and Cosell do a comedy bit with "Foggy Mountain."
   d. Clark sings "Yesterday."
   e. Lead in commercial #4.
8. COMMERCIAL #4
9. ACT FIVE
   a. Introduction of Senator Edward Kennedy.
   b. Kennedy and Cosell talk.
   c. Lead in commercial #5.
10. COMMERCIAL #5
11. ACT SIX—REMOTE OF CARRILLO BROS.
12. COMMERCIAL #6 & PROMO
13. CLOSING
    a. Goodnights with Clark playing.
    b. Promo of next week.
    c. Credits.

Both the afternoon dress rehearsal and the evening live telecast were presented before a live theater audience. The Ed Sullivan Theatre has a proscenium stage with an apron that extends toward the audience. About one-third of the house is used primarily for production. The remaining two-thirds is occupied by the audience. One side of the house is mirrored so that the audience appeared to be larger. Because of the five cameras, microphones and numerous crew members, no television show can be seen without interference from the main floor, and so large television receivers are suspended from the ceiling of the theater to provide visual continuity for the audience. The audience plays a major role in variety programs by adding life and excitement whenever intense overhead lights and flashing applause signs prompt it. In this instance a great deal of tension existed because of the appearance of Senator Kennedy—there was widespread concern among the house staff that some disaster might befall him. The audience for dress rehearsal was seated by 2 p.m.

2:00   Preliminary audience warmup.
2:30   Rehearsal begins. Some participants were in matinee theater

performances, so their segments were pretaped for the rehearsal only. Rehearsal went smoothly.

4:15 Break for 45 minutes; audience leaves; performers leave.

5:00 Director Don Mischer and others adjust shots on Clark segment and set boom. Technical details and changes are discussed with crew, which had assembled at edge of the stage. "We're basically winging the picking sequence," the director said. He checked the view from each camera and called the shots for camera cues. " 'Yesterday' is really going to be gangbusters—any questions."

5:45 Crew buffs floor.

6:15 Director Mischer assembles crew for last minute changes and calls out shots for "Chicago" sequence inasmuch as stars could not be present for dress rehearsal. The director talks through the script; he is very nice to the crew, maintaining a pleasant working relationship: "I think we have a chance of making a nice neat show tonight, not as sloppy as last week's."

6:50 The director finishes and the crew takes its place informally.

7:00 Ushers clean the theater and fix the reserved seats.

7:07 Kennedy's family arrive. (Outside a large crowd has gathered.)

7:20 A barbershop group (two banjoes, tuba and trumpet) warms up audience.

7:54 Director calls for camera positions and boom. Lights go up on stage and the audience.
Janet Leigh, Jack Cassidy and Pat Lawford arrive. They are introduced from the audience during the program.

7:56 Producer Rupert Hitzig warms up the audience, followed by Howard Cosell and Roy Clark. They leave the stage.

7:58 Two-minute countdown begins for program talent, crew and audience. ". . . one minute . . . 20 seconds . . . stand by."

8:00 Open on Carrillo Bros. Voice over picture.
Cosell begins: "Later tonight you will see the most fantastic high wire act, live from The Ringling Bros. and Barnum and Bailey Circus . . ."
Split screen of Carrillo Bros. climbing to the high wire.
". . . The incredible Carrillo Brothers who defy death on a single strand of steel cable high in the air above the Nassau Coliseum.
And now . . . in the vernacular of the circus . . . on with the show!"
Theme music continues.

A TELEVISION VARIETY PROGRAM FROM A THEATER
Ed Sullivan Theatre, New York

Saturday Night Live, ABC TV
1. Cosell at open.
2. Cosell with entertainers.
3. Cosell talks to audience.
4. Cosell interviews Kennedy.
5. Verdon-Rivera song-dance.
6. Clark's song.
7. Circus remote—rear screen.

Announcer voice over: "Tonight . . . Roy Clark . . . Gwen Verdon . . . etc."

8:10   Each performer appears live; the stage crew changes sets with amazing speed, the supervisor counting down each shift in scenery. Performers know their marks, read their cue cards and watch for their cues from a floor director who wears white gloves so that they can see his hands easily. Each performer wore make-up including Senator Kennedy.

A variety format is extremely complicated; therefore, it must be well organized. These shows are usually very expensive, costing upwards of $200,000 for each program.[18]

13: On the Air:
COMMUNITY EXPERTS

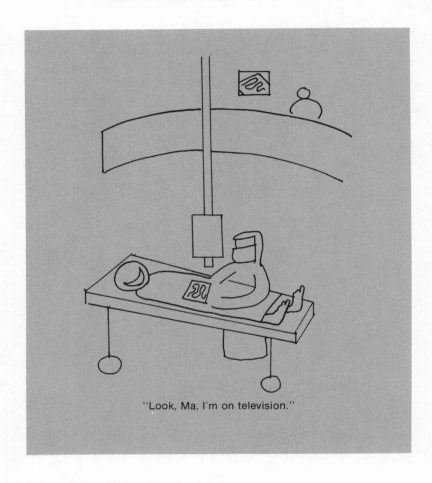

"Look, Ma, I'm on television."

The Community Expert in Media
Advocates—Educators—Executives—Family Members—
Medical Personnel—Politicians—Religious Leaders

A "COMMUNITY EXPERT" may be anyone who achieves public recognition through media. However potentially dangerous this notion may be, there are many instances of unknown persons gaining instant recognition because of an appearance on media. Although the person may or may not be a bona fide expert on a subject, the media may asign expert status anyway. Several celebrities have complained about demands that they function as experts in subject areas they know little about. By contrast, some persons of little or no expertise achieve a degree of status through skillful use of the media. From time to time too much media attention is devoted to empty-headed individuals who have neither genuine knowledge nor support for their cause. Thus, a power struggle may exist among genuine and alleged experts for, in most cases, media recognition improves an individual's status within the community. The physician, the lawyer, the business executive, the teacher, the citizen advocate who receives media recognition becomes, at least locally, distinguished.

THE COMMUNITY EXPERT IN MEDIA

The list of community experts who frequently use media is longer than the following discussion permits, although the principal categories are believed to be included. Certainly those who demand media attention because of the need for social reform have developed many skillful ways of gaining public understanding and sympathy. Educators, having experimented extensively with broadcasting and films for instructional purposes, have a long and complex experience with media. Religious leaders were also among the early participants to recognize the importance of media in disseminating their messages. While some politicians were individually active in media over the years, the major awakening took place after the Kennedy-Nixon debates of the 1960s. Now all politicians are avid users of media. Within the last decade business executives and medical practitioners, especially physicians, have begun using media to project a professional image, raise funds and strengthen in-house communications. Even the opportunities for members of the family to appear in media are remarkable. On-the-street interviews for radio, crowd scenes for movies and testimonials for television announcements are some of the reasons the family, like the other community experts, is a growing source of media performers.

Advocates.

Politicians, ministers, editorialists, public relations experts and minority leaders are examples of advocates endorsing a party, a religious belief, a point of view, an industry or a special interest group. Frequently they resort to public lectures, for better or worse, with few or no visual aids. In part they want to be seen as much as they want to discuss the topic. The politician usually appears in a home or office setting and reads directly into the camera lens. Sometimes the public is bored with this approach, especially if it exceeds 20 minutes. Political speeches run from a few minutes to a half hour and are ideally scheduled on media between strong entertainment programs. The complexity of the message (a presidential discussion of a world crisis, a lecture on a theological philosophy), the maturity of the audience (adults pay attention longer than children), the receptivity of the audience (an established performer or a welcome message) are the main factors. For instance, a long speech, poorly delivered, can be eagerly accepted by a devout public that already admires the performer; and the personal dynamics of the advocate are important factors in developing this material. Current trends in all advocate categories are toward less individual delivery, often referred to as the "talking head," and more toward a greater mixture of audio visual sources (pictures, slides, films, videotapes, and in radio, sound effects) with action.

Advocates usually find themselves in two situations: either on a newscast or a public affairs program. The newscast is in the form of a press conference, a speech or a statement to a reporter. The public affairs format is an interview or a discussion. The press conference or speech usually takes place at a formal meeting held in a hotel or auditorium, but the statement to a reporter is often on-the-scene such as in a hallway or public building, on a street or at home. Public affairs programs are staged in a TV or radio studio. While members of the press are often anticipated and welcome, frequently advocates meet them unexpectedly and must decide instantly whether to discuss delicate matters such as legal decisions, funding procedures, personnel problems. Industrial and personal disasters come at times when the advocate may not be sufficiently composed to make an appropriate statement. At these times experienced community experts are conveniently, and rightly, "unavailable for comment." Advocates should keep in mind that they do not have to say anything to the press nor do they have to give the press access to personal or private property. Advocates may feel it is better to ask reporters politely, but firmly, to leave or await a statement after the expert has consulted with other members of the group or with legal counsel. For the most part advocates like media coverage because they want to tell their views to the press and thereby receive public attention.

The most important reason advocates are on media is to influence the public favorably—vote for me, learn this, fund that, believe in this, buy that. Media are especially helpful in getting the public acquainted with the new and the unknown. Some of the following suggestions may be useful to advocate groups:

1. Select a spokesperson who is highly likable; one who in the opinion of outsiders has very positive charisma. If the public likes the spokesperson, it will be more receptive to the cause.

2. Keep the less effective, less likeable, advocates in the group away from public view. They may harm the cause.

3. Establish, if possible, the positive values of the organization before the more controversial ones are presented.

4. Concentrate on the organization's benefits to individuals and, thereby, attempt to develop a large public constituency.

5. Surround the spokesperson and the organization with symbols of accomplishments that have helped people in the past, pick the location in which to make the statement.

6. Research public reaction to positions the group may advocate, then work from issues of greater public support to lesser support.

7. Anticipate public questions and response and develop reasonable answers that are honest and responsible. Substitute party line, religious doctrine, company policy statements or institutional quotations by more readily understood replies oriented to a broader cross section of human beings.

Radio and television stations have a few professional advocates of their own. These individuals are usually station executives or senior news personnel. A station's endorsement of an individual or a position concerning a public issue is the result of the careful deliberation of the station manager, the news director and an editorial writer. Station advocacy can be frequent and trivial or infrequent and important. Occasionally this unique task is taken on by a single individual. In developing her three editorials and two commentaries for her three shows each day, news commentator Dorothy Fuldheim said:

I lean on subject matter geared to the national and international scene rather than to the local scene. When I do a local story, I very often take a whack at city council. But my temperament and my interests are of wider scope than local. Everybody thinks I have a research staff. I don't have anybody. I even take my own telephone calls. I have sort of a prehensile mind. Give me a fact and I'll just hold on to it. It is as though I have a storehouse up here. I remember the facts. I read all the time. I read a great many scientific publications because this is the century in which science and politics dominate.[1]

An aspiring news commentator, who may or may not advocate a position, should remember that most people would like to sound off with their personal opinions, but few of them will have the opportunity. The professional commentator clearly articulates depth of research, perspective and an outstanding grasp of problems of public interest. Eric Sevareid, Howard K. Smith and David Brinkley are some of the network's finest commentators.

Educators. Aside from instruction, discussed earlier, administrators and teachers use media in a variety of ways—to promote the institution, to disseminate policy, to raise funds, to discuss issues, and to advance public understanding of the values of education. Media images have humanized the roles of administrators and teachers in recent years, although the images of an educator as a prototype of high moral, personal and intellectual standards lingers. Formally produced radio and TV programs and films dealing with some aspects of education are legion, and these materials have been distributed under the guidance and sponsorship of school systems. The educational process beyond formal courses and institutions has been substantial. It is estimated that by age 18 a person has spent 18,000 hours in front of a TV set, compared to only 12,000 hours in school. Programs dealing with cooking, travel, animal life and most documentaries bring enrichment to listeners and viewers and are indeed educational in the larger sense. These programs answer in the negative the question, "Are formally trained teachers essential to instructional programs?" Nevertheless, these programs are frequently developed by authorities on education. Many fine TV performers appear in the role of an educator: Julia Childs, Marlin Perkins, Jacques Cousteau, Bill Cosby, and the casts of *Captain Kangaroo, Sesame Street* and *The Electric Company.*[2] Scripts for *The Electric Company* are developed by professional writers and then performers are hired from agencies or casting calls.

CHILDREN'S TELEVISION WORKSHOP

THE ELECTRIC COMPANY
Show #621
Air Date 3/8/76

---

1. *SHOW OPENING AND I.D. #621*

---

2. *TEASE*

EST. TIME- 2:00   3. *PEDRO'S PLANT PLACE—PL INTRO*

TALENT: Jim as Maurice
                Luis as Pedro
SCENIC: Pedro's Plant Place

FADE IN ON MAURICE. HE IS ADDRESS-
INGLY CAMERA DIRECTLY NEXT TO HIM
IS A STYROFOAM "PL"

NOTE: THE FOLLOWING DIALOGUE FOR
MAURICE IS TO BE SPOKEN IN
MAURICE'S STYLE, I.E., INCEP-
CIPHERABLY. IT HAS BEEN WRITTEN
OUT ONLY TO GIVE JIM AN INDICATION
OF WHAT ATTITUDE TO HAVE AND TO
LET HIM IN ON WHAT THE HELL'S
GOING ON.

MAURICE

Hello, kids. My name is Maurice. I guard
Pedro's Plant Place. Right now though,
I'd like to tell you about p-l . . . or pl.

LUIS

(ENTERING) Maurice, what are you
doing?

MAURICE

Talking to the kids out there.

LUIS

Maurice, they can't understand you.

MAURICE

They can't?

LUIS

No. (TO CAMERA) How many of you out
there understand what Maurice says?
(LUIS WAITS A BEAT FOR A RESPONSE.
NOTHING) See! Nobody knew what you
were talking about. Very few people can
speak plant language.

MAURICE BEGINS CRYING

LUIS
Awwww, Maurice, don't cry. (A LITTLE
COMFORTING IN SPANISH; THEN:)
Look, a lot of people speak a language
others can't understand. It's okay.

MAURICE
(THROUGH TEARS) But, I wanted to tell
the kids about p-l.

LUIS
You wanted to tell them about the "pl"
sound? There's another way, remember?

MAURICE
Oh I get it. . . . I know what you want me
to do.

MAURICE MOVES HEAD STAGE LEFT
AND PULLS HEAD ACROSS SCREEN
(LEFT TO RIGHT FOR A DIAGONAL WIPE
[DIANA WILL DO IN EDITING]) AS LUIS
NODS APPROVAL. (IT WILL LOOK LIKE
HE'S PULLING THE OLD SCENE OUT
WITH HIS MOUTH.)

---

4. *FILM: PL WITCHES*
   Time- :58 EUE 60

---

5. *VT: EB: PLUMS*
   Time- :12 TTP#17

---

6. *VT: PL LIMERICK: PLATTER OF PLUMS*
   Show 2 Item 16 Time- 1:11 R-30 A&B

---

7. *VT: EB: PL #2*
   Time- :05 TTP#5

---

8. *VT: THE APARTMENT—PL*
   Show 369 Item 15 Tk- 1 Time- 2:20 R-420 A&B

Catherine Atwater Galbraith described some of the difficulties encountered by her husband, John Kenneth Galbraith, in filming the series, *The Age of Uncertainty,* for the BBC and PBS:

An inaugural filming took place at 9 A.M. late autumn 1974 in the Winthrop House Senior Common Room at Harvard University. The subject was John Maynard Keynes and how his ideas had come to Washington by way of Havard, familiar history to my husband since he had been part of it. But now he was finding out how film stars earn their money. He had flown in from a meeting late the night before and had dragged himself reluctantly from his bed. He hoped to conceal his fatigue, but at noon he returned to the house even more tired, complaining, "They had me repeat the same paragraph all morning long, walking, sitting, standing, turning, putting my hand on the doorknob, picking up a book, and after the seventh time they decided the first was best."

Scriptwriting began in earnest in January 1975. We were in Switzerland, and Adrian [BBC producer-director Adrian Malone] came over. He explained that the Winthrop House filming had been a rehearsal. "But, Professor, we learned a lot from studying that film. You must never film when you are tired. How you do your part will make the difference between success and laying a gold-plated egg. You will have a day of rest before each filming session. You are to accept *no* other commitments." Rest, however, would not mean enforced idleness, the Professor always had to see the location firsthand and then to rework his script.

"Professor, you are not an actor," Adrian said. "You are not good at walking around. You are much more effective at rest, in close-ups. The gesture is in your eye. The action is what goes on in your head. That is what we must get." . . . Because he is so tall, my husband had always felt he had to minimize his gestures. His style is deliberate and wry, detached, concerned—but with amusement. He needed to write out his script, to be word-perfect.

"Keep in mind, Professor, that you are not preparing a lecture. You will be speaking to one or two people in their home, and if they aren't interested, they will turn you off. You'll talk to the camera as though it were somebody. Think what you want to say and how you want to say it. Don't worry if it is too long; remember it will be altered anyway once you have seen the filming location." Scriptwriting became perpetual condensation and distillation not only before but during filming.[3]

The Age of Uncertainty began in the summer of 1973. After 170 hours of running time were reduced to 13, the series appeared on the BBC in the winter of 1977. It cost approximately $2 million.

While budgets for educational programs originating in New York and London may be in the millions of dollars, these budgets and these programs are the exceptions rather than the rule. Numerous education-instruction-information types of programs are produced annually with meager budgets. Over the past 15 years the author has produced hundreds of programs using commercial television and radio facilities without ever having a budget in excess of $100. These programs include complicated one-hour specials featuring ballets restaged for television, swimming exhibitions from a local country club, homecoming from a college campus and a Christmas variety special. Formats such as these provide excellent vehicles for aspiring community talent. The educator serving in the capacity of a producer-performer-writer (and whatever else is needed) will find that most radio and television stations are very cooperative if the idea for the program is carefully planned, feasible and inexpensive. Two or three educators working in concert are ideal, but often one person ends up being the major driving force behind the project. A television or radio special can be generated by educators at any level from pre-school to university. The procedure is the same for everyone:

1. A concept is initiated.

2. An outline for the program or series is developed.

3. Talent is tentatively solicited and so are production materials.

4. With the production likely, the station is contacted.

5. Arrangements are made to use the station's facilities, and the station agrees to air the program.

6. The script is written and the talent is confirmed at the same time. Auditions and rehearsals are conducted, if necessary. Often the producing is more coordination, because each performer or group rehearses on its own.

7. A week or two before the airing or taping, the director assigned by the station discusses the program in detail with the producer-performer. Thereafter, the educator will find a lessening of responsibilities as the director assumes more of them.

8. During the final hours before the program the educator needs to concentrate on performing, and so the producing responsibilities are assumed by others to a great extent.

9. Somehow chaos yields to an amazing amount of coordination, cooperation and enjoyment as the complex program comes off much better than expected. The educator-performer benefits from the experience and from greater personal recognition, plus the thought that he or she has provided a vehicle which allowed the appearance of many talented, local performers.

Christmastime places an unusual demand on local talent. The hour-long format for "The Gift of Christmas" required about 400 performers drawn from a local university and several elementary and secondary schools. A local television station presented the program as public service and so did not charge for the remote pickup. Other program costs were incidental:

THE GIFT OF CHRISTMAS[4]

VIDEO	TIME	AUDIO
OPEN: FADE IN A LINE OF PEOPLE CARRYING LIGHTS. CHOIR GATHERS IN FRONT OF CHAPEL	7:00 P.M.	HOST: (VOICE OVER SILENT PICTURE) On a silent night, a holy night—over 2,000 years ago, the world found faith in a child. Each year it renews that faith at Christmastime. MUSIC: FADE IN "COME ALL YE FAITHFUL."
STUDIO CARDS OF CHAPEL, TITLES	7:00:10	HOST: The Department of Speech and the Office of Religious Activities at Texas Christian University present "The Gift of Christmas." Our special guests are the choirs of the schools of Fort Worth.
HIGH SCHOOL CHOIR	7:01:45	SONG: "CAROL OF THE BELLS" (1:35 SECONDS)
HOST	7:04:00	HOST: WHAT IS CHRISTMAS. (2:15)
HIGH SCHOOL BELL CHOIR	7:06:15	SONG: "DECK THE HALLS" (2:15)
COMBO	7:08:55	SONG: "WINTER WONDERLAND" (2:40)
VIDEOTAPE OF BALLET AND PAINTINGS	7:16:25	VTR: (7:30)
HOST	7:16:35	HOST: TRANSITION TO NEXT SEGMENT (:10)
ELEMENTARY CHOIR	7:18:20	SONG: "JINGLE BELLS" (1:45)
FIRST READER	7:21:50	READER: VISIT FROM ST. NICHOLAS (3:30)
HIGH SCHOOL GIRLS' CHOIR	7:25:10	SONG: "JESU BAMBINO" (3:20)
SECOND READER (GIRL)	7:29:25	READER: GIFT OF THE MAGI (4:15)
QUARTET	7:31:25	SONG: "GOD REST YE MERRY GENTLEMEN" (2:00)
THIRD READER (BOY)	7:35:25	READER: A CHRISTMAS CAROL (4:00)
STATION BREAK	7:36:45	STATION BREAK (1:20)
HOST	7:37:15	HOST: TRANSITION TO NATIVITY (:30)
ANOTHER HIGH SCHOOL CHOIR	7:40:00	SONG: "COME TO THE MANGER" (2:45)
NARRATOR, NATIVITY, ANGEL	7:42:15	NARRATOR: "And it came to pass . . . good will toward men." (2:15)
VIDEOTAPE OF HARP	7:45:50	VTR: HARP SOLO (3:35)

NARRATOR & SHEPHERDS	7:46:50	NARRATOR: "And it came to pass . . . as it was told unto them." (1:00)
MIXED CHORUS	7:50:20	SONG: "AS LATELY WE WATCH" (3:30)
NARRATOR & WISEMEN	7:52:50	NARRATOR: "Now when Jesus was born . . . they departed another way." (2:30)
UNIVERSITY CHOIR	7:56:30	SONG: "THE CONCLUSION OF THE SCHUTZ CHRISTMAS STORY" (3:40)
HOST CLOSE	7:57:50	HOST CLOSE OVER CARILLON: "JOY TO THE WORLD" (1:00)
VTR: CREDITS OVER CHAPEL	7:59:30	SONG (VOICE OVER): "O HOLY NIGHT" (1:40)

Executives. Industry spokespersons have at least three functions: (1) company public relations, (2) instruction and development of in-house audiovisual presentations, and (3) coaching line and executive level management. From time to time the highest ranking company executive may appear on TV as a public relations gesture; more frequently lower level personnel appear in films, videotapes and slide presentations.

Company public relations consists of public and in-house visibility. The range of objectives varies from simple greetings to the public on holidays to the sometimes complex reasons behind rate increases or the company's failure to comply with standards for pollution control. Experienced executives often adlib from an outline prepared by a public relations official. This message is dominantly positive and optimistic; so much so in past years that the executive and the message have lost some credibility. Top executives are wary of the stereotype image of an executive—stodgy, inflexible, rich, out of touch with the public—and shrewd public relations officials avoid the appearance of company executives who in some way might jeopardize the company image. To wit, if the chief officer of the company already looks too comfortable or has a manner that seems unsympathetic with the public need, that official may jeopardize the company's claim for a price increase. Relatively few corporate executives appear in media on any regular basis. When they do, their functions are: (1) to extend simple greetings, (2) to react to newsworthy emergencies, (3) to disseminate in-house policy often by way of closed circuit television. Top executives of smaller companies assume a fourth task: salesperson. If the company president is also a top salesperson, then he or she is likely to appear with the notion that the public will believe that the top person at the company is intimately acquainted with its operation and is concerned personally about customer satisfaction. The executive salesperson has been effective in numerous TV commercials particularly for automobile dealerships. The president of the dealership or a member of the family may appear on TV or radio in an attempt to offer the public warmth, concern, honesty and credibility. Similar strategy is used by major companies in commercials wherein principal performers are bank vice presidents inspecting building construction sites, farmland or oil rigs, and airline executives carrying luggage. By contrast, a series of spots for Western Electric have rank-and-file employees creating the impression that the company is made up of likable human beings ("Hello, America").

Besides commercials, corporations run non-sales spots called institutional advertising. These spots promote the image of the company in general without selling a specific product or service. Philanthropic groups inform the public of their activities and needs by means of public service announcements (PSAs). These are similar to commercials except that they concern public or private agency or charity identification, information and/or fund raising. Most charities and agencies do not have much money, if any, for PSAs; and so they often welcome almost anyone to make a spot for them gratis or at cost. Stations are reluctant to pay staff to make these spots, but they are glad to have locally produced PSAs from the charities themselves. PSAs, therefore, can be especially helpful to the beginning executive/performer who writes and performs on behalf of such organizations. The procedure is for the performer to study the material available concerning the organization and to draft copy as an example of what could be produced. Then the draft copy is taken to the organization which agrees to the draft with whatever corrections are necessary, and authorizes funds. With this approval the performer goes to the public service director at the broadcast station to ask whether the station will run the spot if it is produced. Frequently the public service director at the station will approve the spot if the level of production is reasonably sophisticated and if the station commitment is little more than airtime. With the assurance of the sponsoring agency and the station, the performer plans the production in detail by writing the final script in which the performer will have, of course, a leading role.

A few additional points should be made in reference to instructional programs for business and industry. The best performers for in-house instruction are often current employees. They know the job, they like the recognition, they are less expensive than outside performers. Still, a script and considerable coaching may be necessary by the personnel training staff. Inexpensive audio-visual programs are slide shows wherein employees demonstrate their tasks on-the-job by appearing in a slide collection. One small restaurant chain wanted a series of training programs on how to wait on tables. The high turnover in waiters and waitresses indicated that a slide program showing correct procedures, proper hygiene and manners would be less expensive than training new employees through live techniques.

Videotapes and films are better instructional media if action is indicated. While an employee can provide a convincing visual image, frequently the same employee does not have an adequate voice to explain the procedure, in which case an outside performer, such as a local radio announcer, may be hired to record a narrative over the visuals. Thus, the audio visual training aid has a combination of credible visuals and a well articulated audio track. While commercials and programs for the general public need to be sufficiently sophisticated to compete for national TV and radio audiences, in-house production should utilize strong employee prototypes rather than more sophisticated outsiders. The level of empathy may be greater and, therefore, the learning may be more complete and faster.

Family Members. Members of the family are frequently willing, and often *un*willing performers on media. Sometimes they are experts on discussion programs or they give testimonials in commercials. Often they are eyewitnesses to events or they are participants in misfortunes. Because of the power of media, family members need to be careful about making rash statements that may be used against them at some later date. Accidents, crimes and public controversy may involve members of the family through the media's distribution of statements which seemed innocent and/or "factual" at the time. For instance, when an automobile accident occurs, it is not uncommon in a large metro area to have six wreckers, a photographer, several reporters and spectators all arriving at the scene before the ambulance and police. Many of these people may be asking questions of the involved parties and witnesses. In general, family members should provide statements only to legal authorities and no one else. Under no circumstances should they assign fault to anyone, because fault often must be determined by complex legal procedures. Furthermore, the emotional strain and/or physical injuries to the person involved may be such that his or her response is not sufficiently lucid. This is particularly true of deeply emotional events relating to crime and disaster.

While members of the family may not be willing participants in the events just described, they are willing participants in commercials and discussion programs, and they should have all of the advantages of any anticipated program, including a briefing of the program format, an understanding of what will be discussed—especially any sensitive topics, make-up, lighting and other production techniques. Although it may seem trivial and members of the family may be reluctant to ask for this information, they do compete with other TV and radio performers, and they should have the privilege of looking and sounding as well as they can. There is no excuse for a shiny pate on dad or unflattering shots of mother. In general, the use of children must be accompanied by consent forms from parents or guardians. Appearances on television, radio and film can be highly enjoyable and flattering experiences for the entire family, but some caution should be exercised in making a commitment.

Medical Personnel. Physicians are usually called upon in media to clarify matters concerning dangers to the environment, human and animal population, epidemic disease, preventative medicine, public health, crime, drugs, medical research, charity hospitals, insurance, socialized medicine and medical training. Some physicians and/or scientists head small teams of researchers and, therefore, serve as spokespersons for their accomplishments. In addition, physicians are exercising more influence outside the medical profession as members of a city council, school board and other civic groups.

When responding to media, physicians and scientists must be careful to do so in understandable terms, not only to the public in general but to the news reporters. Occasionally a physician's remarks when edited may result in a misleading statement for the public, and while it is incumbent upon the reporter to be accurate, he or she can only be accurate if the physician or scientist has been clear in the first place. Moreover, physicians and scientists would do well to give a public appearance of some warmth and understanding.

When using media as a teaching aid, complaints about physicians being "prima donnas" are rather common. Some physicians have a captive audience and they intend to lecture on media in the same way they would in the classroom, failing to take advantage of the audiovisual aids and expertise available to them from AV specialists. Audiovisual techniques are gradually being used by more physicians who have been taught by them and who wish to be experimental and innovative. Receptiveness to AV assistance would be a great help to physicians and medical instructors. As one TV specialist noted: "A physician will say, 'I've got to be back in an hour, and this is a one-hour lecture, so let's get on with it.'" To be sure the lecture can be recorded as is, but the better presentations are carefully preplanned with an audiovisual specialist.

Instructional design plays an important role in the development and production of self-instructional teaching packages and other complex audiovisual projects including motion pictures, videotapes, sound-slide presentations, exhibits and scientific brochures.

An early preliminary planning conference with the instructional designer will assure maximum efficiency and economy for your production. As the first step, concise definition of the objectives for your project will facilitate later decisions during development and production, and will provide the means for you to evaluate the effectiveness of your project. After the appropriate audiovisual medium is selected, the instructional designer can either develop a script based on information you provide, or guide you in writing your own script.

Once the final script is approved, the instructional designer will distribute and coordinate the production work to ensure maximum efficiency while maintaining continuity in the final project. Often the designer will direct shooting and recording sessions to assure that your objectives will be met. After final assembly, editing and refinement of the project is completed, the instructional designer can work with you to pre-test the program on a sample audience and then make any revisions that are indicated.

Finally, an evaluation of the program can be designed and conducted to assure that your objectives are valid and that they are met effectively.[5]

Developing areas in the health sciences suggest that administrative personnel, nurses and para-medical spokespersons will be utilizing media more extensively than they have in the past.

Large medical centers produce many programs for the public and for in-house use. These programs require performers of all types, who may or may not be medical personnel, to narrate and appear as presenters. Opportunities, therefore, do exist for an aspiring performer to gain experience and some money. Three specific examples include a call for actors to appear in a series of public service announcements on public health and the availability of community services; a request for a narrator to appear on camera and to provide the vocal continuity for a film on doctor-patient relationships; and a performer-producer for a radio series sponsored by a school of public health.

Politicians. Perhaps the best way for a politician to get a person's vote is to go door to door and visit with as many constituents as possible. In relatively small districts when the vote will be light anyway, this technique can be very effective and relatively inexpensive. For large areas it simply doesn't work. The politician cannot physically meet everyone and the politician needs the reinforcement of opinion that media can give. Politicians must tell their position on the issues and yet keep within the budgetary restrictions of the campaign. So, the campaign manager must decide what media purchases will do the job most effectively, what voters must be reached, who is likely to support the candidate, how these voters can be reached, what issues the voters consider most important, and what solutions they support. Various books in recent years, such as *The Making of the President,* illustrate the highly complex task of conducting a politician campaign.

The politician's physical appearance usually reflects a conservative mixture of the formal and the casual in multi-faceted roles ranging from business executive to laborer to member of the family. Smiling, confident, honest, credible, accessible, understanding—an indefatigable figure who may be caustically criticized by the opposition if he or she stumbles in the least way. During the period of the campaign a politician is seldom seen to tire, to be angry or unreceptive. Politicians are denied many human characteristics, and later when they have assumed public life, there seems to be some amazement on the part of the public that they had these qualities all along. Everything about the appearance of a politician is important. Managers make certain that make-up, clothing, diction and decorum will impress the public favorably. President John F. Kennedy maintained a suntan; but many politicians wear make-up almost constantly while campaigning so that they look good under intense lights as well as from a distance. Their clothes are immaculate, usually conservative and dark, with little or no jewelry or symbols of economic or social affiliation. If running regionally or locally, appropriate jargonese and dialect may be hinted at in the delivery of material, but often these things disappear if the candidate aspires to a national office, where clear regional affiliation might become a detriment. Most politicians take a steady course of noncommitment hoping to draw voters from all sectors of the public. Others make a broad commitment to, for example, a liberal or conservative philosophy, and base their statements accordingly. A heavy media entourage for popular candidates is bound to be a great strain on some, but most of them have a certain affinity for such attention.

Politicians stay away from adversaries and invest what media time they have to getting votes in areas where inroads can be made. Politicians pick places where they expect to have sympathetic crowds of admirers to make statements that might be carried on media. Politicians are usually in a hurry. They purposefully create the impression that there is great demand for their time, and often there is. They tend not to remain any longer than they have to, knowing that whenever they are around they are in the spotlight, and have a chance to make a mistake. A politician wants to make a winning case, to be pleasant, to gain votes and to leave, preferably without cross examination. Of course, politicians must reserve some time for cross examination, but they attempt to control this if possible—the press may be allowed a limited number of questions or the audience may be asked to submit questions in advance so that they can be screened for a prepared response. Control of media is the objective of the politician's campaign: Sell yourself and leave as a winner.

Some effective techniques for politicians during the '70s are to appear competent on the one hand while thoroughly familiar with the needs of the electorate on the other. The politician is frequently suitcase-carrying, tie-less, hat-less, in rolled up sleeves, concerned but optimistic and smiling, surrounded by admirers from all socio-economic levels, rooted in traditions of home, family, church and national loyalty. The politicians's environment is also important—hardworking staff, devoted family and friends, modest forms of transportation, certain speeches staged in a variety of environments from fields of corn to factory interiors to formal dinners.

A political campaign requires showmanship. Grooming for political life may begin earlier for politicians than in past decades, now that everyone has access to audio and videotape recorders. Politicians will tend to become better looking, attractive and trim, to have better speaking voices and oral language facility. They will be more conscious of cameras, recorders and press relationships. (Press secretaries representing politicians will have these characteristics, too.) In fact, young lawyers and aspirants for political office will do well to include media utilization as part of their education.

Religious Leaders. While religious services were relatively frequent and air time was gratis in the early days of radio, neither radio or television stations give much free time for services today, because of the great demand for air time that various denominations would seek under the FCC's Fairness Doctrine. About 600 radio stations in America specialize in religious programming, according to Dr. Ben Armstrong, executive secretary of the National Religious Broadcasters (NRB) association, thus making it possible in some markets for a listener to hear as many as 40 preachers each weekday. One television station runs 32 half-hour religious programs a week, paid for by the denominations. Religious programming is big business for the churches and synagogues and for both secular and religious stations.

For several years religious leaders have discussed the most effective ways of getting and holding an audience. The result has been an emphasis on personalities and effective communications on the part of the preachers themselves rather than on denominational services— Bishop Fulton J. Sheen, Billy Graham, Oral Roberts, Garner "Ted" Armstrong, the late Katharine Kuhlman, to name a few. In each of these speakers there is an evangelical intensity about "bringing the word of God" to the mass public, a kind of dynamic delivery which combines sincerity and a certain degree of showmanship. In every case the radio and/or televison minister has a sonorous voice and is rather good looking—some are handsome. The objectives are to bring God's word, sympathy and consolation to a special audience which, for one reason or another, finds solace in the presentation of the preacher and is willing to contribute monetary gifts in sufficient amounts to support the ministry. "Dr. James Engel, a marketing research specialist at the Billy Graham School of Communications at Wheaton College, states the matter flatly: 'We have conducted 61 studies for various broadcasters, and the conclusion is unmistakable: Christian media reach Christians, not the unsaved.' Similar research conducted by advertising agencies representing Christian broadcasters, seems to support this conclusion." Some programmers, facing these facts, are experimenting with a dual approach, presenting a traditional broadcast, aired on religiously oriented stations for their regular listeners and supporters, but also producing spots and five-minute programs more suitable for secular stations with a more diverse audience.[6]

Some religious leaders have become phenomenally successful. One is evangelist Rex Humbard, who conducts his World Outreach Ministry from the Cathedral of Tomorrow, Akron, Ohio.[7] Humbard claims that during 1977 his ministry will place "2,600,000,000 sermons in the minds of someone on earth." The Humbard group travels extensively, videotaping their appearances and his sermons in as many as five languages. The Cathedral of Tomorrow is a huge auditorium seating 5,000 people. For Humbard's sermon, "Fork in the Road," the 168-foot stage was draped in red with the tiered grand proscenium drape resembling that of the Radio City Music Hall. Suspended over the heads of the audience was a tremendous gold, lighted cross. On stage, the cast consisting of Humbard, his family, two associates, the Rex Humbard Family Singers (12 vocalists), a larger choir of over 30 voices and a 20-piece orchestra wore color-coordinated clothing in gold, blue and red. Humbard himself wore a red-brown suit with gold buttons, a medium gray vest, white shirt and figured gray and white tie which nicely concealed the tiny microphone clipped to it. The performers were all ages from teens to later life; Humbard admits to being 57. At both ends of the stage were one-story, white-columned porticos surrounding the dais for Humbard on the one side and a table with mail on the other. The entire one-hour production was "wholesome" in appearance and professional in every detail. An outline of the broadcast shows that the program is heavily promotional—"Let us hear from you." There was never any request for donations.

1. Humbard begins: "Bless the Lord, O my soul: And all that is within me. Bless His Holy Name." (Psalm 103, Verse 1) Theme music. Humbard introduces the cast and gives opening prayer.

2. Family Singers: "When I was in trouble Jesus looked at me."

3. Humbard promotes program: Services fed to Brazil and Yukon.

4. Soloist: "Liz," his daughter.

5. Humbard narrates brief videotapes of services in Canada and Japan, where thousands attend services.

6. Large choir sings "At the Cross."

7. Humbard introduces his associate evangelists who give testimonials and background: "I received the Lord at the age of six."

8. Perhaps hundreds in the audience come forth to be prayed for. A "Prayer Key" is promoted by showing the numerous mail requests for it. No charge.

9. Humbard promotes his album, copies of sermons and an extensive tour. His group averages one appearance every two days. Humbard invites everyone to attend his TV sermons. All materials and appearances are free.

10. Vocalist (his wife): "It is no secret what God can do."

11. Humbard reads and interprets the Gospel, speaking from a spiral-bound notebook for about 12 minutes.

12. Humbard promotes the program: "About 50 million watching today—a conservative estimate." Humbard asks audience: "How many are ready to meet the Lord?" About 30 came to the edge of the stage where he greeted some of them. Then, he included the television audience: "You beyond these walls . . . You by your television set." Humbard offers a prayer for the group. Humbard offers literature to everyone. Associate evangelist appeals to audience to write for literature, "Your New Life."

14: Evaluation

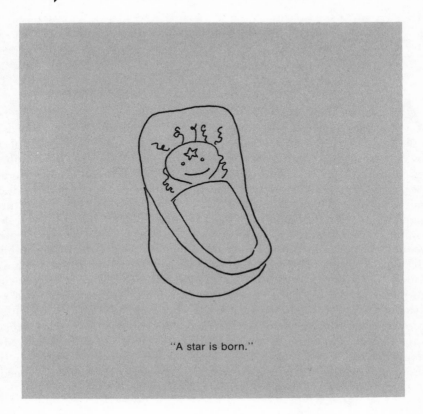

"A star is born."

Sources of Evaluation

Perspective

A PERFORMER'S WORK is evaluated critically by professional peers, critics, teachers and oneself. Virtually all evaluation is subjective opinion. The closest a performer can come to an empirical evaluation is by collecting data from ratings, box office receipts, perhaps the number of column inches in various publications, and awards and honors. Some performers measure media effectiveness in terms of increased product sales, votes received, attendance at services and crusades, and subsequent enrollments in TV classes. Occasionally an inconsistency between empirical data and subjective evaluation gives rise to the statement, "So the critics didn't like me. What do they know? The public likes me." Some of the most popular media performers of the day have failed to receive critical acclaim. Critical success does not necessarily predict popular appeal. The simplest and best understood form of evaluation is, of course, the salary and fringe benefits a performer receives. Multi-million dollar contracts for entertainers, newscasters, sports figures and media personalities suggest that some people are temendously effective in media utlization, and, therefore, the value of those performers to the media marketplace and the public is exceedingly high.

SOURCES OF EVALUATION

Generally, evaluation is of two types: quantitative and qualitative. A performer hopes to do well in both counts. The surest way for financial success is to have a large and loyal audience. A performer can acquire and control an audience to an extent. Many techniques are used to carry out a campaign to win public enthusiasm: (1) by producing quality work; (2) by appearing in a balanced exposure of media and live performances; (3) by avoiding overexposure; (4) by maintaining a positive media image through skillful promotion showing involvement in an exciting life; (5) by keeping an attractive personal posture when meeting the public and critics; (6) by giving one's talent unique and innovative exposure from time to time; (7) by complimenting your audience and associates; (8) by making your services available, and, in some cases, (9) by explaining to the public what you are doing and why.

Audience Feedback

An easy way of determing a performer's impact is through mail and telephone calls. Stations receiving lots of telephone calls for a performer sometimes count these calls and correlate them with the popularity of the performer.

Mail. Mail has the advantage of being easy to count and retain. It is a written statement that not only the station can respond to (and usually does) but so can the sponsors. While some performers may receive little mail, others get thousands of letters a week. In some cases an entire staff has to count mail and respond to letters. Some politicans and entertainers must sign their names thousands of times to provide enough souvenirs for the public. Receiving a response from a performer is sufficient motivation for a fan to write the letter. The opportunity to complain is also highly motivating and, indeed, these may be the only responses a performer will get, which can be depressing if taken out of perspective. Of course, every letter is not always favorable, but the level of criticism usually varies greatly. Even a letter of unfavorable comment may be considered as favorable because it shows viewer interest. A letter is equated roughly to a potential viewing audience of thousands. Some stations believe that one letter represents a potential viewing audience in the thousands, because so few viewers will take the time to write a performer. Now and then a top performer will receive mail inadequately addressed, but a diligent postal service delivers it. This is one of the benefits of being famous.

Ratings. The surest indicator of a performer's success is a high rating. A rating reveals the proportion of the audience that the performer's program receives compared with the competiton playing on the air at the same time. Each medium has its own audience; that is, TV programs are compared with other TV programs, and radio programs are compared with each other. Whatever share of the audience a program gets is equated to the probable number of persons viewing, each household having two or three viewers. Ratings indicate that some network anchor people are reading the news to 30 or 40 million viewers or listeners nationwide. The same rating locally may indicate a viewership in the thousands. Programs with small audiences such as those specializing in local public affairs may have a negative rating. Some stations consider that a "Minus 1" rating in a large market means that about 10,000 people are watching. The potential audience is said to be "delivered" to an advertiser at so many dollars spent per number of viewers or listeners; that is, cost per thousand (CPM). (M is 1000 in Roman numerals.) Gross figures are not sufficient for clients, however.

Advertisers want to know who is viewing or listening. Thus demographic breakdowns indicate the number of persons by age, sex, education, occupation or whatever else is tabulated. This breakdown tells sponsors whether the composition of the audience is appropriate for the products or services being sold. Granted the Osmond Brothers attract a certain audience. That particular audience in the opinion of the sponsor should consist of potential customers. Every performer has an image that sells to a certain audience, and advertising agencies try to match a client's product or service with the audience most likely to buy them because of watching performers they like on certain programs.

The best known TV rating system has been established by the A.C. Nielsen Company, a research firm based in Chicago. Nielsen has about 1,200 carefully placed recording devices called *audimeters* attached to various TV sets in homes throughout the nation. These home receivers constitute the base sample. Rating systems keep a record of viewers and programs either electronically or by means of a hand written diary. This is similar to casting a ballot for a program being watched; and because the rating company knows the demographics of the family involved, it can make projections concerning the composition of the audience. Keeping track of the listening and viewing habits of a nation with so few sample homes has come under a great deal of criticism at times, but ratings remain the speediest, simplest and so far the best indicators the industry has. A. C. Nielsen publishes its audimeter results "overnight" for New York City and Los Angeles. Separate reports of ratings are published for the 70 largest markets and Multi-Network Area (MNA), for national coverage (Nielsen Television Index (NTI)) and for local stations (called "sweeps"). Cursed as they are occasionally, rating systems dominate the broadcasting business. A high rating measured against competiton is the surest way of staying on the air, especially in prime evening hours. Three nationally recognized rating services for radio are the American Research Bureau (ARB), the Pulse Radio Survey and the Hooper Radio Survey. ARB serves both radio and TV principally by using the diary method.

Akin to ratings are box office receipts. Ticket sales for films, closed circuit TV presentations and live performances serve as measures of a performer's popularity. In cinema the top ten box office attractions are usually male stars with only one or two women having the same box office appeal.[1]

Another rating index used specially for performers is the TV-Q (Television Quotient). This devices scores a performer's familiarity to a TV audience and his or her appeal: Does the audience know the performer? Does it like the performer? A performer who scores high in each category is very employable. Likability is more important than familiarity, because the latter can be attained through promotion and time. Such profiles, determined by interviewing a sample group, are helpful in casting quiz shows and discussions having many celebrities.[2]

Product Sales. Another indicator that must be considered by a performer is product sales. Product sales includes the products advertised during spot announcements, products and services directly endorsed by performers, marketing exposure, and miscellaneous products and services using the performer's name or image. For example, the Bing Crosby family sells orange juice on behalf of Minute Maid. This product may be sold directly through a commercial appearing separately from program content in which they appear, through cutout pictures of the Crosbys in the supermarket shown with the product, or through various posters, folders or other items perhaps linking Florida, sunshine, oranges, health and the Crosbys. The marketability of a performer's media image is a measure of his value as a performer.

Professional Feedback

Professional feedback is the body of collected opinion and suggestions that a performer gets from those people he or she most respects. The course of a performer's career is anybody's guess. Happenstance plays a big part. When I spoke with Lindsay Wagner at a film conference in Windsor, Canada, she had successfully finished *The Paper Chase* and was looking for a new property, but hadn't found anything. No one would have supposed that she would become TV's bionic woman. Nevertheless, those who are in the business to make subtle comparisons, to refine judgments, to analyze public acceptance, to determine performer quality, to anticipate program trends—these people are very valuable to performers. Sooner or later this body of opinion will constitute the place the performer holds in media history. These are the people who chronicle the achievements of performers and assess them. Future historians and critics will depend upon the perspectives of these evaluators.

But for most performers history can wait, the evaluation of the present is of greater concern. A performer's appreciation of his or her career is often distorted, and so an agent, coach, producer or critic can be very helpful in indicating what is valuable and what should be changed to improve the presentation the next time. An agent's role may be that of a coach, thereby helping to groom a performer, but often the day to day discipline or training must remain with a coach because the agent simply hasn't sufficient time or knowledge to develop talent in addition to marketing it. The advice of a teacher is extremely important to a performer, as important as any other professional adviser such as in law or medicine, and the performer will do well to get the best he or she can afford. Some producers and directors will give assistance to performers; especially inexperienced ones. But they do this fleetingly in rehearsals and over coffee. Usually a performer can expect the producer or director of a program to comment either directly to the performer or to the agent. The proof of acceptance is when the performer is asked to work again, however. So while this fleeting feedback is useful, there is just too little of it and it comes too infrequently. The value of newspaper critics is that they give opinions often without having any personal relationship with the performer and these opinions are in a context of one who has seen an untold number of other performers in the same kind of work; so a clear, concise, honest outside opinion can be very revealing and stimulating to a performer. In fact, even a bad review can be an extremely helpful turning point in a performer's career if he or she uses the critic's suggestions wisely.

In order to make a judgment, the professional evaluators need to see and/or hear several presentations from the performer. After establishing a broad acquaintance, the evaluators are better able to help, if they feel the performer has ability. In practice, however, a performer appears often without a broad acquaintance by the critics. Some critics do not evaluate a new TV series until it has appeared two or three times so that they can offer a fairer judgment. One of the worst things that can happen to a performer is to be ignored.

Behavioral scientists have been slow to measure the probability of success in the arts, such as in commercials, programs and recordings. Even less has been done to scientifically pretest the probable success of a performer. Recent data research using galvanic responses of selected audiences has done so much to determine the probability of success in records and to analyze the weaknesses in a musical composition that a similar application is being applied not only to products but to viewing or listening to new talent. In his new Consumer Behavior Center in Dallas, Dr. Thomas Turicchi measures the success of a record by means of a galvanic skin response checked by electrodes attached to two fingers. The CBC sends record companies the responses of 56 carefully selected people—seven panels of eight persons each. They are broken down into three age groups: 12 to 17, 18 to 24, and 25 to 34. According to Dr. Turicchi, there are no geographical differences at the subconscious level, and so the data collected at this firm applies equally to other areas of the country.[3] High priced consultants are being called in "to news departments" to help determine audience preferences by means of similar surveys. Consequently, the news personality is emerging as even more important than the experienced journalist in his or her ability to retain a high audience rating.[4]

Journalistic Feedback

Journalists are very important to a performer, because every time a performer is mentioned in the press or on the air public attention is focused on the performer. The more attention the better. The three dominant ways a performer gets attention are through promotion, publicity and news coverage.

Unknown performers buy space and design ways of getting attention. This scheme is a promotional campaign paid for largely by the performer. A typical promotional campaign for a motion picture includes a press packet, screenings, parties and media appearances in each of the several cities selected for the tour. Advance press packets consist of biographies of all principal participants, feature items about the film, data and photographs. For *All the President's Men,* a stunning filmstrip and audio cassette describing scene construction was included. Occasionally buttons and other unusual items are sent to the press. After the performer arrives in town, a luncheon or cocktail party is held at a local hotel. These arrangements are often conducted by a local public relations firm in cooperation with the film company. The performer may appear in one place for the electronic press, burdened with tape recorders, and in another, where still photographers shoot pictures, for print media. The performer politely tells his or her story over and over, trying to make it seem fresh each time. After awhile it becomes routine with the same "amusing" items being retold to different groups. The performer is scheduled to appear on as many local TV and radio stations as possible with the higher rated ones having priority. NBC's Tom Snyder complained, for instance, that *Today* and *Meet the Press* got priority for guests over the *Tomorrow* program which he hosted. Many of the better known performers avoid personal appearance tours. They do appear at celebrity tournaments, roasts and certain benefits for which they are often paid at least a minimum sum and/or expenses. While these ventures are not strictly promotional, they serve that function.

There was a time when a celebrity would receive news coverage on local stations by merely getting on and off planes, in and out of cars and by making himself or herself available for interviews between flights at an airport. Few celebrities receive this kind of news coverage today unless they have enormous public interest value. To be newsworthy a celebrity may be involved in some event or mishap in the community, such as an accident or fight, then that, of course, is news. In a small community the participation in a charity ball or parade may receive news coverage; but more often this free media exposure is called "publicity." The difference between publicity and news is professional journalistic judgment. If the performer finds his or her activities in the news section of a paper or on a newscast, then a journalist has said they are newsworthy. If these activities appear in feature columns, then that is publicity. Popular gossip columnists, whether in print or electronic media, may wield considerable influence over public opinion which a performer or the performer's agent may actively seek. Performers crave favorable publicity because they can become widely known without paying for the attention. Information concerning marital problems, loss of valuables, sexual habits, media plans, relationships with the press and other performers, novel acts and travel have potential news or publicity value. A gag among some performers is the line, "Nobody knew me until I was sued."

Interviewing celebrities becomes a rather blasé task for some members of the media press corps. To illustrate:

Representatives from Columbia Pictures and a Houston public relations firm invited me to a press luncheon for Clint Eastwood, who was promoting his latest film *Play Misty for Me,* in which he was the leading actor. This was also his first attempt at directing. The interview was on Thursday, October 21, 1971, at the Warwick Hotel.

The Warwick is a posh old hotel. The interview was in the Don Quixote Room downstairs. Members of Houston radio stations and local press gathered about noon. Each man was given an ID to stick on his suit. Most of them were in their mid-20s. Two women were present. The film was to play simultaneously at four theaters. Everyone was supposed to have seen the film. According to promoters, Eastwood did not want to be interviewed by anyone who had not seen it. Few members of the media had seen it.

The bar was open. Everyone was very polite. Some former students now with the radio press corps carried tape recorders. At tables covered in white linen, fruit compotes were surrounded by dishes and silver. The press was obviously going to have a grand lunch. The only flaw in the surroundings was a two by two-foot paneled column stuck in front of the bar, thus eliminating any central focal point to the room.

About 12:45 Eastwood still had not shown up. The local promoter for one of the theater chains invited the two members of the major Houston newspapers and me to lunch with Eastwood in an adjacent room. The room was equal in size, but it looked larger because it contained only one table set up for about ten, the fruit compotes dotting the circumference of the table.

"We separate the TV people from the radio, so that they can get pictures. It just doesn't work when they are together." About one o'clock word came that Eastwood had just arrived from an earlier engagement in the city, and had gone to his room to freshen up. Placecards indicated that he was to be seated next to the movie columnists for the *Houston Post* and *Houston Chronicle.* I was thus removed one seat from the guest. We waited some more and then Eastwood arrived in the company of two PR persons.

He shook hands all around, saying, "All you Texans are tall."
He wore a dark suit and shirt, both in vogue, but nothing about his
attire would draw attention. We sat down. We were told to begin
eating. We discussed the weather: "It's nice here," he said. "Cold in
California."

"Houston has about five good days. This is one," a reporter
said.

A photographer from each newspaper snapped pictures
through the fruit compote. Questions flowed from the three of us
so that Eastwood hardly tasted his food.

"How did you happen to make *Play Misty for Me?*"

"My company owned the property. The girl who wrote the
story based it on a real experience, except that no murder really
occurred. I have been wanting to do the picture for some time. No
one else would do it, so my company decided to."

"This is the first time you've directed a picture. How did it
seem?"

"I was nervous the first day."

"Did you do the casting?"

"Yes. I cast some of the parts because of having seen some of
the actors work in previous films."

"Some of the small parts are very well done. The black maid
and the DJ, for instance."

The four moved to the main course: steak, potatoes mashed
into a frilly mold and another vegetable. The coffee flowed, but
Eastwood declined at first. The reporters reviewed his early days in
TV.

"I did 250 programs. The *Laramie* series and the pictures in
Europe. I wanted to see if I could do something else."

Eastwood's hair is fine and unruly. He had an even tan. His
cheeks were so rosy they looked flushed. He sat quietly, looking
down much of the time waiting for questions.

"Why did you have a nude scene in the film?"

"His relationship with her was all outdoors; all indoors with
the other girl."

"The concert seemed to bring the film nearly to a halt. I was
getting ready to go home. Then the film started up again."

"Well, it is a little bit different. If it works, then that's good. If
not, well—"

"In horror films, audiences become literal—"

"Yes. Some students wondered why the DJ didn't pick up the
flashlight before he entered the house. And, why didn't he have a
gun."

"Artistic license, I guess."

Eastwood has clear blue eyes. His very low pressure, unassuming response to everyone immediately maintains communication at a believable level.

"What are you going to do next?"

"I am acting in a film called *Joe Kidd*. We begin in November."

"Are you going to direct?"

"I don't know."

"Are you going to direct without acting?"

"My company owns a property right now in which I have a part. It's called *Breezy*."

Eastwood drank some black coffee and declined dessert. The TV people didn't show up. About two o'clock the PR people asked to conclude the meeting, so that he could go next door to answer the questions of the radio press.

One of the PR women entered to say, "Hello." "We met before a long time ago, but you won't remember me."

Eastwood hesitated—She was introduced—"Ah, yeah. Hi, Sue."

The PR group ushered him into the next room. One of the reporters said to me: "I hadn't seen his movie. But I guess I covered that pretty well. Well enough."

PERSPECTIVE

Every performer seeks perspective on what he or she is doing, and projects the probable degree of success. Because a performer's success is largely a mixture of circumstances as well as ability, chance is an important part of the performer's life. Whether a performer wants it or not insecurity is a way of life for beginning performers and even for established ones who, though wealthy, may find the public is no longer interested in them. A performer must be able to withstand the highs and lows that go with the work, postulating not that this variation is an indicator of ability but that it is an indicator of opportunity and ability. Although a performer can always feel discouraged, optimism and a faith in one's ability must prevail. It undoubtedly takes courage to be a performer.

Retaining Objectivity

When the performer has lost objectivity, his or her career is in deep trouble. If success has been too heady an experience, a decline is imminent, or if success has not been forthcoming, disaster of another kind may result. At times like these evaluation is especially necessary. Yesterday's press releases will not help a dead act. Only an objective revitalization has a chance of being successful. "On the TV show, we've died three or four times. If the first five minutes are an hour long and if I've asked a lot of questions, then I know we've died," Chicago TV personality Steve Edwards once said.[5] A performer must continually evaluate his or her efforts in order to strengthen any weaknesses.

Suggestions for Improvement

While specific suggestions for improvement can only be precisely addressed to an individual's presentation, certain general suggestions may be applicable to most performers who have hit a plateau in their careers: (1) a performer should take a vacation, completely forgetting his or her work; (2) a performer should try a different aspect of performance, such as singing instead of acting or outside reporting instead of anchoring; (3) a performer should try another medium or work "live" for a while; (4) a performer, in making public appearances, should talk about his or her career with the public to find out what it wants and likes; (5) a performer should watch other professionals doing similar things, and extract the variation he or she can incorporate in his or her own act; (6) a performer should change environments, perhaps countries, seeking new stimulation; (7) a performer should diversify his or her talents by going into other, but related, businesses; 8) a performer should volunteer to give benefits for other people in hospitals and schools, perhaps allowing these audiences to view pilot material; (9) a performer should return to school, to rigid practice sessions and strict discipline; (10) a performer should become part of a group of active people who are inspiring, exciting to be around and may provide good contacts.

Detrimental Criticism

A performer must remember that critics, agents, producers and all the others are, after all, only advisers. The performer must ultimately decide what is best and in which direction to go. Well meaning evaluators may be insufficiently schooled to evaluate a performer's work beyond their narrow preferences and experiences, so such opinion can be depressing and detrimental to the performer. A bad review can be very discouraging, for instance. A performer, therefore, should seek professional opinion—paid to help the performer solve his or her problem—rather than just opinion that's available. One's family, for instance, may make a judgment on a different set of standards than a professional evaluator. A professional looks toward aiding a performer in improving the quality of the presentation in anticipation of sharing some of the financial benefits or other recognition. Top professional people tend not to waste their time on performers who are not going to be successful. Generally speaking, the better the agent or producer the more in tune he or she is with what the public wants to see and hear—this is the individual or company a performer wants to retain to make professional judgments.

In short, place professional judgments in top priority, non-professional ones decidedly secondary and keep in mind that the performer must make the ultimate decision.

Protecting the Performer

Performers need a certain amount of nurturing. They should be placed at least for a while in an environment which will allow them to grow, to make mistakes without severe retribution, and to improve the quality of their performance. Some professional schools, high schools, colleges and universities do this. Local media, closed circuit and cable TV, nightclubs, dinner and community theaters, summer stock and off-off Broadway are places where performers can get experience. Very few performers become sensations overnight—the "overnight" on close scrutiny lasted 10 or 15 years. What Joseph Conrad wrote pertains to performers: an individual's vital, internal fire must be kindled and banked not smothered with criticism and adversity, so that the novice performer matures into the fine newsperson, politician, entertainer, teacher, advocate or other performer that media and the public need. This development doesn't just happen. It takes a willing individual, an understanding family, encouraging teachers, positive professional advice, lots of hard work and many years of experience in media.

Many performers, early in their careers, find that they can get constructive criticism by attending conferences and competitions such as those held annually at Northeast Louisiana University and those sponsored by Alpha Epsilon Rho, the national broadcasting fraternity. The basis for judging a radio announcer reading a commercial is, typically, on choice of material, communicative ability, copy interpretation and pronunciation. For a television announcer, judges consider communicative ability, eye contact, ability to take cues and pronunciation.

15: Careers

"It's tougher on top."

For those who wish to make a living from performing, some knowledge of the business aspects is essential.[1] Once sufficiently prepared, a performer tries to get a job. If fortunate, an audition is scheduled and a job materializes. Hardly on the first job, an aggressive performer is already looking for a better one and six months to a year later has found it. Having become somewhat established, the performer seeks an agent. The agent finds even more uses for the performer's talent, so that he or she has the main job plus free lance opportunities which increase the performer's recognition and income. The performer is invited to a larger market and probably joins a union, if membership has not been obtained earlier. The performer now enjoys regional celebrity status. The networks are watching the ratings and soon the performer's agent has gotten an invitation to do a movie or TV pilot or network contract. The performer gives it a try. Being successful overall, though experiencing ups and downs, the performer's career enables him or her to demand a tremendous salary and other benefits, more or less in direct proportion to the public's enthusiasm. In a few cases, superstars form their own companies packaging their own programs, and as the public's interest in the performer wanes, if it does, he or she may turn to producing or directing. If the public's adoration remains high, the performer may become a media legend.

KNOW WHAT YOU WANT

However a person may have procrastinated, the day of decision as to whether to be a performer will come. For most performers an opportunity will arise, and the performer must determine whether it is the right one. This rather profound, and certainly fundamental, decision in a person's life is at best a guess, based partly on education and partly on instinct, for no one can predict the outcome. Very few people, including performers, know what they want to do at an early age. Opportunity has a great deal to do with this decision. In my view, few performers are ready to take advantage of the opportunities they get. Each professional career in journalism or entertainment requires a different preparation, and so a performer must, as NBC anchorperson Jessica Savitch[2] told my class,

> Get in the right line. If you want to be in news, enter it with a real desire to report and present news. No news director wants to admit hiring just a pretty face, even though a news director may do this to get ratings. If you want to be an entertainer, know that you're good and that all you need is a chance to show what you can do. Few entertainers get hired who seem doubtful about their talents. Do not be dissuaded from becoming a performer because someone else says, "There are no jobs . . . The odds are too great . . . You'll never make it."

For that discouraged soul, there are no jobs and he or she would never make it. No one can decide except the performer, because no one else can say how much time, energy, study and work a person is willing to devote to performance or what opportunities will come along. If you know what you want, opportunity will come. Be ready to make use of it when it does.

Barbra Streisand is a case in point. Ms. Streisand was born in Brooklyn. Her father died when she was a baby. At age five she knew she wanted to be an actress, and as a teenager she worked in summer theater in upstate New York. In high school, she was an unhappy and unpopular student who never took part in activities. She rejected her mother's encouragement to take typing in case acting did not work out. She did work as a switchboard operator and usherette, however, and briefly studied acting. She finally won an amateur singing contest at a Greenwich Village nightclub, which led to other club dates. In 1961 she appeared in an off-Broadway show which closed after one performance, but she was so well received that club engagements followed. In 1962 producer David Merrick signed her for the Broadway musical, *I Can Get It for You Wholesale.* In 1964, she made her first hit single, "People," and the following year she won an Emmy for her first TV special, "My Name Is Barbra." She has become the top female box office attraction in films and has formed the First Artists production company.

TYPICAL OPPORTUNITIES

Typical entry points for performers are as part time or full time, weekend and odd-hour reporters for radio and TV news departments; disc jockeys, especially, in the smaller radio markets; community or public affairs directors having their own programs; vocalists who are regularly appearing at nightclubs and make records; sportscasters, weather people and farm reporters who can also do general news; presenters in closed circuit TV who appear as instructors, announcers or narrators for education, business and medicine; actors, who are type cast for commercials or are extras in films; models who appear in fashion shows and on commercials or are extras in films; representatives from various community organizations such as the Chamber of Commerce, philanthropic groups, churches, legal and medical professions, stock companies, banks, and automobile associations who provide a public service series. Cable TV systems and public radio stations probably offer inexperienced talent the greatest variety of on-the-air opportunities today, everything from announcing to gymnastic exercise programs.

Common advice, especially to women, is to qualify as a secretary or switchboard operator. This enables the performer to get station employment quickly, because a station needs many secretaries and turnover is high. Once employed, the performer would know when a better opportunity arises. Several independent and group-owned stations have the policy of promoting within the station, thus allowing those who are at the entry level to have preference when openings occur. This advice applies equally to men, but women should realize that they have only one-third to one-half of the roles men have in TV dramatic programs and comedies, and well over half of those depict the woman as a housewife, even in commercials and cartoons for children.[3] Although there is no universal way to get into media, two common patterns, referred to earlier, are "Get in any way you can" and "Get in the right line." The latter suggestion insists that you should at least get into the department you prefer.

Typical advertisements for radio and television performers are as follows:

"NEWS position open. Experience required—no license required."

"STAFF ANNOUNCER with production experience needed immediately by top rated adult contemporary station. Retirement, hospitalization and other generous benefits."

"ANNOUNCER with 3rd class and some experience needed for EVENING shift. Must be willing to relocate. Send tape and résumé. Medium market. Adult easy listening."

"ANNOUNCER needed for SPANISH language programming."

"SALES-ANNOUNCER needed with 2 years experience, 3rd class license. MOR format."

"TV COMBO opening in on-air weather, news gathering and writing, film shooting and editing. Medium market."

"FIRST PHONE needed with some NEWS background—must be able to do it all. Station in process of re-building from scratch."

PRODUCER/NEWSCASTER

*Education/back-
ground:* High school diploma, college degree preferred. Television experience in production of newscasts necessary, as is background of on-camera work as talent, reporter or news anchor—though experience as a regularly-scheduled anchorperson is not absolutely necessary.

Duties/skills: Person hired will be assigned to produce a half-hour daytime newscast and appear, either singly or in combination with another person, as talent on the program. Must have strong production background in news, with strength in newsgathering techniques, use of film and/or videotape, slides, pictures, etc., and, of particular importance, in newswriting for television. On-camera personality must be pleasing and authoritative, and person must be cosmetically attractive and possess ability to work well with others in on-air team.

WEATHERPERSON (Part Time)

*Education/back-
ground:* High school diploma, college degree preferred. Must have broadcast experience.

Duties/skills: Person hired must have working knowledge of weather, forecasting methods and terminology. Applicants will be required to demonstrate the on-camera presence and authority required of any television talent. Must be cosmetically attractive and able to converse ad lib with other personalities on the air.

Hours are weekend only, delivering weathercasts during early and late evening news programs.

SPORTS WRITER-REPORTER/BACKUP SPORTSCASTER

Education: High school diploma required, some college preferred.

Duties/skills: Person hired need not have prior experience as a television sports reporter. However, there must be a basic affinity for sports, including familiarity with terms, rules, players, teams, etc., in all phases of athletics: this is a highly-specialized field of reporting in which the presenter must be able to convey a sense of knowledge and expertise to the audience. Prior experience in related areas of journalism, particularly radio or television is preferred. Writing skills are required: television writing skills preferred. Person hired may, in addition to reporting duties, work as weekend sportscaster and as weeknight sportscaster when the Sports Director is absent. As much work will take place in the field, a knowledge of film/video tape operation and technique is most helpful.

TYPICAL PROCEDURE

"In order to get a job, I've got to have experience. In order to get experience I've got to have a job!" This frustrating dilemma is partly true and partly nonsense. With rare exceptions, a performer must have experience to get a paying job. Getting a job—any job—consists of someone having an opening and someone else being qualified to fill it. Talent agents, some schools and a few placement offices tend to know where the jobs are, and they match their clients or students with the openings. The task of matching performers and jobs is so large and varied that station personnel departments are constantly looking for new talent and replacements; they cannot depend solely on talent agents and schools having the right human resources when they need them. A performer, therefore, should provide identifying materials to talent agents, schools, placement offices and media personnel.

Letters of Inquiry

Many performers, about the time of graduation from college, blanket the top markets of the nation with letters of application. Some performers have sent as many as 200 letters. This is often a waste of time, because the performer may recieve only one or two potential job offers per 100 letters. More helpful is a letter addressed to a department head at a station in a city which the performer intends to visit. The letter, neatly typed and grammatically correct, should indicate that the performer would appreciate a visit, if possible, to see the station and department where the performer has always wanted to work and to ask the advice of the department head concerning a career in media. Usually the department head is very busy, but often grants a visit. Rarely is a performer turned away who has made an appointment in advance. This advice also applies to agents and casting directors at advertising agencies, in which case the performer may send a photograph along with a request for an appointment. If a response is not forthcoming, send follow-up inquiries later and try to make an appointment when you are in town, anyway. In New York information on agents, casting departments and directors may be found in the *Ross Reports* (sold by AFTRA), *Backstage, and Madison Avenue Handbook.* In smaller less well organized markets the Yellow Pages may be the only source.

Personal Interviews

One news director gets 35 letters of inquiry or application a month. He sees few applicants. To an extent, employment depends on reaching a level of acquaintance by letter or in person. The performer should try to see the employer in person—the personnel head, the news director—so that the performer can sell himself or herself in person. This may take a little doing, because a self-important secretarial staff may try to screen potential applicants. Do not be discouraged. Use relatives, friends, teachers and mutual acquaintances to get an appointment, if you need them. But get in! Most department heads—news directors, for instance—are very pleasant, a little flattered and greatly interested in new talent who present themselves in a serious manner. The performer does not ask for a job, because chances are the department head does not have one at the time, and thus the visit would end without any mutual acquaintance. Instead, the performer asks for whatever help the department head can provide—suggestions, contacts, job leads or anticipated opportunities. A typical response from a news director might be: "I do not have an opening right now, but I heard that Channel 5 is looking for someone." Or, "I suggest that you enroll in a school that will teach you media basics, and possibly get some experience in a smaller market. Then see me again. We may have something in six months or a year, because we intend to expand." Seldom does a job materialize at the moment of the interview, but very often ones does later, and the department head, if favorably impressed, will no doubt contact the performer assuming that he or she meets the necessary qualifications.

Do not expect the station to pay travel expenses. Be willing to go to the station at your own expense, if there is a chance for employment. Many network jobs have been obtained by aggressive people who were willing to invest in their own future. A department head is quick to notice an aggressive, yet attractive professional approach. Dress appropriately and moderately. Some stations purposefully conduct internship programs giving them an opportunity to look at talent before hiring. Sooner or later the performer is asked to fill out routine personnel application forms which are held for future reference. Note the current application form recommended by the NAB for station use.

Auditions

If there is an opening at present or in the near future, the performer will be asked to audition. An audition provides the station management with something concrete to look at and/or listen to and pass around to others at the station. An audition usually shows whether a person's appearance, movement and voice have sufficient impact on the management, few hiring decisions being made by one person. The performer should be less concerned about reading fluently (which can be improved in rehearsal) than with radiating a confident, warm and/or unique personality—that is, something marketable. Frequently the performer is asked to read copy without rehearsal or preparation. In fact, some news directors want to know whether a person is fluent at sight reading. This tells a lot about how the performer would sound in an

EMPLOYMENT APPLICATION

APPLICATION FOR EMPLOYMENT

NAME (LAST)	FIRST	M.I.	SOCIAL SECURITY NO.
STREET ADDRESS	CITY	STATE	ZIP CODE	TELEPHONE NO.

CHECK IF YOU ARE UNDER 18 ☐ OVER 65 ☐	POSITION DESIRED	SALARY DESIRED	DATE AVAILABLE

GRADE OF OPERATOR LICENSE FIRST CLASS ☐ SECOND CLASS ☐ THIRD CLASS W/ENDORSEMENT ☐	DATE ISSUED	BUSINESS MACHINES YOU CAN OPERATE	TYPING WPM	SHORTHAND WPM

LIST PHYSICAL DISABILITIES OR CHRONIC DISEASES WHICH MAY PRECLUDE YOU FROM CERTAIN JOBS

HOW DID YOU APPLY WITH US?

☐ NEWSPAPER ☐ EMPLOYEE ☐ AGENCY ☐ OTHER

IF ALIEN, LIST YOUR REGISTRATION NUMBER:

HAVE YOU EVER BEEN CONVICTED OF A FELONY? YES ☐ NO ☐
IF YES, EXPLAIN:

EMPLOYMENT HISTORY. LIST ALL EMPLOYMENT SINCE HIGH SCHOOL, LAST POSITION FIRST. INCLUDE MILITARY SERVICE

NAME OF EMPLOYER	FROM MO.	YR.	TO MO.	YR.	POSITION	SUPERVISOR	REASON FOR LEAVING
1.							
2.							
3.							
4.							
5.							
6.							
7.							

EDUCATION. CIRCLE HIGHEST GRADE COMPLETED—HIGH SCHOOL 9 10 11 12 – COLLEGE 1 2 3 4 – GRADUATE 1 2 3 4

NAME OF SCHOOL	LOCATION	COURSE OF STUDY	FROM MO.	YR.	TO MO.	YR.	GRADUATE
HIGH SCHOOL							☐ YES ☐ NO
BUSINESS OR TECHNICAL							DEGREE IN
COLLEGE							DEGREE IN
GRADUATE							DEGREE IN

I certify that the statements I have made are true, and I authorize the licensee to investigate the accuracy and completeness of the information provided.

SIGNATURE OF APPLICANT _____

BM608
Copyright 1976 NAB

DATE _____

adlib situation—what potential errors exist in voice, or judgment he or she might make, and whether there is a keen ability at word recognition. Generally, a professional department does not want to train a non-professional, for stations are not in the business of training people. They will acquaint an individual with the specific way they handle material and with their equipment, but they do not have time to train a

EMPLOYMENT APPLICATION (Reverse)

> **Applicants should not fill out this side of blank.
> It is for office use if applicant is employed.**

EMPLOYMENT RECORD

EMPLOYEE'S NAME		MARITAL STATUS	DATE OF STATUS
		SINGLE	
DATE HIRED	DATE OF BIRTH:	MARRIED	
		SEPARATED	
		DIVORCED	
		WIDOWED	

Make new entry on separate line for each change in rate and/or duties

JOB TITLE	DATES WORKED IN FROM TO	RATE OF PAY

IN CASE OF EMERGENCY CONTACT:

NAME	RELATIONSHIP	ADDRESS	PHONE NO.

Reason for Leaving: _____

Supervisor's Comments: _____

_____

_____

_____

_____

_____

Signed

DATE _____

novice. So, the audition is to show what the performer can do as a professional.

Radio news director Jay Williams, Dodge City, Kansas, recommends that applicants have: (1) an audition right away; (2) a consistent professional voice quality; and (3) a sense of humor. They must be (4) responsible, for professional radio is not a training ground; and (5) they must be able to read and project news on-the-air; (6) put feelings on the air through one's voice variations; and (7) most important, they must sound like they're having a good time.[4] An audition can be nerve wracking, but a performer should keep in mind that he or she probably would not get one if there wasn't some interest in his or her ability. Even a short audition takes staff time and equipment. Unlike theater or cinema, broadcast stations rarely hold open auditions. Management reviews auditions only of professional media performers. It is not uncommon for 40 or more professionals to audition for a new anchor position in a major market. Hundreds audition for parts in films and other media jobs. Typically, auditions are conducted selectively for those professionals who appear to be most qualified (they have established ratings in their markets) and have agents. The Casting Department at CBS, New York, auditions actors and actresses twice weekly for possible roles in soap operas and other programs. In this case the talent takes a résumé and photograph to the Casting Department where the performer is asked to present a contemporary scene which will enable the casting director to evaluate the talent for current dramatic formats.

Performers in commercials are usually cast through a casting department maintained by a local advertising agency or through an independent casting firm. Some photographers may serve as casting directors from time to time. A performer should be acquainted with casting agencies. If a performer gets a "call back" after an initial audition, he or she should try to perform the same way the second time, because apparently the performer's work was acceptable. Twenty or more auditions are not uncommon to get one spot. Regardless, preserve an air of confidence.

Résumés

Nearly every employer appreciates an in-hand reminder of the talent. A single photograph or "one sheet" showing a closeup of the person and giving minimum vita (name, telephone answering service, hair color, weight, age) is a common way of doing this. The pose should be appropriate to the job the performer is seeking, and the photograph should be made by a professional photographer who is in the business of making "head shots." The closeup should show what the performer actually looks like, including marks and lines of character in the face. Glossies are usually preferred over matte photographs, and all reproductions should be made from an 11 x 14-inch print. Some casting agencies may prefer a 2 x 2-inch color photograph.

A "composite" includes various photographs, principal credits and vita. A composite may not be sufficient for some actors and models, who then must provide a "book" of several photographs and additional information. Every performer's credentials should be assembled attractively, but they should not look as if the person has the experience of a veteran when, in fact, he or she has not. A little showmanship is desirable, but directness, good pictures and credits are what employers look for. After all, it would be a waste of everyone's time to get a job—because of a misleading composite—for which the performer was unqualified. If a performer shops around, most of this work can be done inexpensively. In addition, whenever the performer can be photographed on the job, follow-up postcards will serve as valuable reminders to agents.

A sample résumé:

JOHN JONES
Actor

Answering Service: Address:	Union Affiliations	Height: Weight: Eyes: Hair: Age Range:

EXPERIENCE

TELEVISION	Name of Program, Name of Series, Network or Station, Role, Date
RADIO	Name or Program and/or series, Network or Station, Role, Date
FILMS	Name of Film, Company, Role, Date
LEGITMATE THEATER	On and Off Broadway, Summer Stock, Dinner Theaters
INDUSTRIAL SHOWS	Name of Show, Company, Role, Date, Location
EDUCATIONAL PROGRAMS	Public Broadcasting, Closed Circuit Television, Audio-Visual Programs
TELEVISION COMMERCIALS	List upon request or list companies, not products
SPECIAL SKILLS	Athletic, musical, artistic, language and unusual abilities
EDUCATION	List universities, colleges, professional schools, certificates awarded, majors, dates

Audiotapes

An audiotape is not a substitute for a personal visit, but it is a help. Most radio stations do not fly in prospects for interviews unless they are established professionals, and so an audiotape may open the door for a novice if it is sent in advance of an interview or an effort to get one. An audiotape should be perfect—no mistakes, no apologies. It should consist of material pertinent to the job and the station format: news, weather, sports, DJ patter and/or an interview. A performer may include some work on the air, called an "air check," if he or she is already employed. Keep the tape short—from 5 to 15 minutes at most. Most program directors or news directors do not need to listen to a great deal to make a decision. They can ask for more if necessary. Occasionally a station will ask for specific items to be included in the tape; and so, a performer may have to write for details. A 7½ i.p.s., full-track audiotape is universally acceptable, but a high fidelity cartridge may also be all right. The audiotape should be clean, have leader and be neatly identified. Few station managers or program directors keep audiotapes of applicants; therefore, plan to send another tape if you apply again at a later date.

Videotapes

A 5-minute videotape can have the same format as an audiotape; frequently, however, the talent chooses only one. Videotapes should be made under professional conditions on high band, 2-inch color videotape at a professional recording studio—but narrow-gauge videotape may be sent to cable or closed circuit systems. Some schools have such recording studios and can do a respectable job. The performer is usually shot close up most of the time, with medium or long shots included as required. The performer presents five minutes of copy in a sampler format, with the most time devoted to the principal work for which the person is interviewing. Playback requirements should be investigated through the performer's letter of inquiry.

Videotapes are expensive—from $50 to $300 for a 5-minute master—and should be sent to stations selectively with return postage guaranteed. Needless to say everything about the tape should be perfect. Remember that the tape is designed to showcase the talent and not to exhibit the cleverness of the director, although imagination in selecting flattering shots and other directorial approaches should be encouraged. Management may screen dozens of videotapes in search of talent.

Credits

Employers always ask applicants, "What work have you done, and where have you done it?" The performer should have a list of all previous experience, especially on-air commerical jobs and films. These are "credits." A performer wants to be associated with top stations, film companies, networks and recording studios and/or well known people in the business. This association aids in establishing the reputation of the performer. The performer's record should also show that he or she has made progress to better stations, better markets, more responsibility, more money, more benefits. Some beginners, listing their credits on their employment forms, are surprised to learn that experience is more important to an employer than education, at least initially; but this should be expected. Paid experience indicates that a person is a professional performer progressing in a highly competitive business, that he or she is aggressive enough to get a job, and that some employer was willing to pay for his or her services. Each credit is listed with great care, especially by a novice who may not have many. As years go by the principal credits are listed until, of course, the performer is so well known that the networks, stations and film companies feel fortunate to get a contract with the performer no matter what the price.

PROFESSIONAL ASSISTANCE

As a performer becomes successful, he or she gathers quite a collection of other professionals to assist him or her. The first is likely to be one or more instructor(s) to develop one's talent; the next, an agent to get more work; the third, a business manager to invest the performer's money; the fourth, a lawyer to draw up contracts; the fifth, a companion or secretary to handle correspondence, personal maintenance, and in some cases protection; and the rest may be a pool of colleagues—writers, designers, artists—who produce the show when the performer becomes a star. A major TV program frequently requires the services of more than 150 people to support its star performer.

Schools

There are schools for everything. Schools are designed to keep performers within disciplinary guidelines—that is, they keep performers in practice, which is especially useful when the performer is not working constantly. Schools give a performer a chance to perfect his or her skills—voice, appearance, movement—and to bring these skills to the same degree of accomplishment as the competition provided by other performers. Schools enable a performer to become acquainted with other performers so that he or she can draw upon these other performers for ideas, inspiration and comparison. Schools often help performers find work, especially those entry-level jobs before the performer is experienced enough for an agent. Schools can be very expensive and time consuming; therefore, a performer wants to be certain the time and money promotes his or her career objectives.

Professional schools prepare a performer in a highly specialized way. Many entertainers—especially actors, dancers, and musicians—prefer professional schools. Colleges and universities may aid in the development of a performer's talent, but they usually do this within a broader context of a liberal arts curriculum. Journalists and some entertainers, recognizing that a broad understanding of all aspects of life is an advantage, follow this kind of education. A few schools offer short courses or workshops in performing for commercials, soap operas and announcing. These highly specialized classes may help to perfect a particular skill.

None of these schools should be confused with those few that claim short cuts to success. There are no short cuts at any price. A performer should examine the reputation of the school before entering it. Ask for a list of graduates or get the opinion of professional performers in the market. All schools do not have equal reputations for turning out people who are fully prepared. A school depends on its faculty and its graduates for reputation, and so should the performer. The performer should also get biographies of the faculty and should see the facilities.

A school contributes to the foundation of a performer's career, and so a proper choice is extremely important in the long run. Bad training can even retard a performer's progress. In general, a school should have a good physical plant, good facilities that are available to the students, a recognized faculty, a stimulating student body and an active community where there are professional media opportunities. Harold Niven's *Broadcast Programs in American Colleges and Universities* is an excellent reference. Obviously the top media markets of the nation attract thousands of hopefuls looking for opportunities, and so a beginner may wish to develop his or her skills in a smaller situation, remembering that someday he or she will have to compete in the large media markets, after becoming adequately prepared to do so. The sooner the performer believes he or she is ready to compete, the better.

Instructors

An instructor is not necessarily a performer, but instructors know what it takes to be a performer. They prefer searching for new talent. Some instructors may not have the appearance, voice or other characteristics to be a performer; instead, they may have the patience, concern, understanding, comparative knowledge, and intuitive sense for developing talent. A good instructor is very important to a performer. Besides discovering those with the greater potential, instructors encourage performers with the care of a gardener nurturing tender plants—giving discipline, love and attention when they need it, and finding opportunities for them. A performer's instructor may be the only source of human hope and inspiration a performer has through much of his or her career, knowing that regardless of success or failure the teacher is the one understanding person who knows the pitfalls a performer endures. Many fine teachers are found in high schools, colleges, universities and professional schools; a performer may meet others on the job. A performer is indeed fortunate to continue his or her education under the supervision of a highly respected news director, TV or film director, talent agent, producer or other mentor.

Talent Agents

After a performer is sufficiently well trained to be placed for continuous work, he or she is ready for a talent agent. Sometimes talent agencies take performers who show promise at an earlier stage; however, agents are essentially looking for persons whose abilities they can sell. A talent agent is a salesperson whose chief function is getting the performer jobs at the highest salary the market will bear, and for this service the talent agent gets a percentage of the payment negotiated for the talent, commonly 10 per cent of the gross. Thus, the more money the talent makes, the more the agent gets. The benefits of a talent agent to a performer are (1) an intimate knowledge of what is happening in the industry; (2) an optimum presentation of the performer's assets to buyers; (3) on-going contacts with talent buyers; (4) a detailed negotiation of the contract; (5) advice about career development, and, in some cases, the security of a friendly counselor. The principal drawbacks are that: (1) the agent may have to divide attention among many clients; (2) the agent may receive a commission from work the performer got himself or herself; (3) an agent may tend to favor the position of major buyers in negotiations; (4) the agent's advice may be bad, and the agent may benefit more from the association than the performer, in which case the performer should get a different agent.

Local talent agencies provide performers with job leads in their immediate vicinity. Agents in New York and Los Angeles provide talent for those markets and often for programs distributed nationally. Most celebrities in the business, whether in journalism or entertainment or sports, have agents. Generally, performers do not talk to anyone seeking their services; instead, they refer potential employers to their agents. The agent determines whether the performer should do the work and whether there is enough money and/or prestige in the job. The talent receives a secondary benefit in this arangement—any blame for being unwilling to meet a request is placed on the agent and not on the performer. An agent schedules the performer's commitments, making certain that proper decorum and amenities such as accommodations, receptions and billing are met in accordance with the contract.

The two largest talent agencies are the William Morris Agency, founded by William Morris in 1898, and International Creative Management, a subsidiary of Marvin Josephson Associates, formed in 1975 from the merger of various smaller agencies. The William Morris Agency is active in every type of media performance for national networks and large film companies. It receives 10 per cent commission from an individual performer or a talent package when it handles the performers for an entire program. There are four ways for a performer to come to the attention of a William Morris agent:

1. Be referred to a talent agent by a mutual acquaintance.
2. Be performing where an agent can see your work, such as in an off-Broadway play or "showcase."
3. Be an established performer.
4. If you are unknown, take an 8 x 10-inch photograph and your list of credits to the receptionist in the appropriate department (television, news, theater). Ask for an appointment with an agent and leave your materials. From time to time the talent agents review these materials and set up appointments with performers who look promising.

Meanwhile, there are a number of smaller agencies that may meet a performer's needs as well as or better than a large agency. Talent agents prefer three-year contracts, but performers may negotiate for shorter periods and with more than one agent, because many agents specialize in different media.

Managers

A performer may have need for a personal manager, business manager or lawyer. A personal manager may get from 5 to 50 percent to perform tasks similar to those of an agent. A personal manager has few clients, however, perhaps only one. In other words, a personal manager gives a performer "custom service." The combination of an agent(s) and personal manager may amount to 25 per cent of the performer's salary, but the combination should provide more than enough money for all of them, and this 25 per cent would go to government taxes anyway.

Business managers and lawyers (they may be the same) specialize in handling a performer's money. If a performer makes a lot of money, he or she should invest it wisely. There may come a time when the performer is out of work, with nothing much to live on for months or even years except the investments that were made when the performer was doing well. Many motion picture stars are wealthy today because of the money they invested with the help of managers in real estate, apartments and many other businesses. Business management has a certain risk of course, and the performer should select a completely reliable manager, who will make certain that the performer's investments are accounted for. Famous people are occasionally bilked out of great sums of money because of poor business judgment either by themselves or their business associates. So a reputable business manager is critical to a performer's financial security. Many performers receive only an allowance from their business managers. David Niven and John Wayne are two examples. Wayne was allowed only $100 a week for many years. This allowance covers expenses, but does not enable a performer to get carried away in what can be the heady experience of spending vast sums of money, especially by gambling or by living a life of luxury beyond the performer's means. While performers appear to make vast sums of money, frequently they spend equal amounts. For contracts involving much money or complex commitments over a long period of time, a performer or the talent agent is advised to pay for the services of a lawyer specializing in talent contracts.

Personal Staff

Performing can be a lonely life, especially for entertainers who are on the road as well as appearing in media; and many of them, particularly the women, take along a paid companion or secretary. The secretary may handle appointments, correspondence and the performer's personal upkeep; but she is usually much more, giving friendly advice and encouragement when needed. Occasionally a performer requires bodyguards—for example, entertainers who are immensely popular. Some stars are more fearful of being kidnapped than of being harmed (Sophia Loren, Audrey Hepburn). Contemporary Security Company, Los Angeles, and American Control, Inc., Washington, D.C., are two firms specializing in personal protection.[5] Other celebrities deny having bodyguards, but they do have experienced companions, chauffeurs and valets who protect them. The entourage of a top celebrity can be rather large and may even include animals. This can be a substantial overhead expense which a wise performer will keep at minimum.

The Production Company

A media superstar often forms a small production company for the express purpose of producing the star's programs. Captain Kangaroo (Bob Keeshan), for instance, has a company or unit of his own. This company consists of a team of media experts who collectively produce the vehicle in which the performer regularly appears. In fact, the resulting videotape series may then be owned not by the network but by the performer's company which syndicates the videotapes for years to come with a profit continually flowing to the performer as well as others. Some stars incorporate themselves because they can then package entire programs which serve as vehicles for their talent. This type of company may be a kind of repertory group working, sometimes exclusively, for one performer for years.

LEGAL AFFAIRS

Performers should be aware of the provisions in most contracts so that they can balance the desirability of these provisions along with the chance of getting a job. They must also be aware of certain laws pertaining to the limitations of program content and the conduct of a performer on-the-air.

Contracts

A performer may become involved in several kinds of contracts. Commonly, one is for performer services. But, in addition, other contracts may be written for scripts, musical compositions, performer endorsements for advertising or promotion, and for the development of audio or videotapes, films or other media entities which may be distributed for profit.

If a performer has an agent, the agent usually handles the contract, because it is in the agent's best interests for the talent to be well taken care of. Some performers, like newscasters who may not have agents, may want a lawyer to go over an individual contract with a TV or radio station. It is common for a newscaster to get more than $30,000 a year, and a contract for, say, five years with increments may amount to $250,000. The newscaster may wish to have his or her own lawyer read the contract. Some of the provisions of a contract include:

1. Basic salary and increments.
2. Amount of work to be done on and off the air.
3. Compensation for personal appearances.
4. Time off: vacations and holidays.
5. Fringe benefits: insurance, retirement, vehicle, office accommodations.
6. Release time to do other projects.
7. Billing and credits on the program(s).
8. Use of the performer's image or voice for endorsements or promotions.
9. Residuals, if any.
10. Expense account.
11. Staff assistance.
12. Period of the contract; provisions for early termination or renewal.

The NAB suggests the following outline for an employment contract:

EMPLOYMENT AGREEMENT ANNOUNCER/SALESMAN

This agreement made and entered into this _____ day of _____, 19__, by and between _____ (hereinafter referred to as the Station), Party of the First Part, and _____ (hereinafter referred to as the Employee), Party of the Second Part, WITNESSETH:

1. That Station shall employ the Employee for a term of _____ years from the date hereof as an announcer/salesman for duties consisting of but not limited to staff announcing, special program announcing, all duties associated therewith as assigned by the Station, selling, servicing, and collecting of advertising accounts as assigned by the Station.

2. That the work of the Employee shall be performed under the complete authority of the Station General Manager, or other person designated by the Station to exercise supervisory control. That Station shall have the sole right to exercise control over the method of presentation and the content of all program material produced in connection with the show or shows on which the Employee participates. That Station retains complete authority to allocate accounts and assign applicable work as may be necessary for the proper functioning of the business.

3. That Employee shall diligently and faithfully serve the Station in such capacity, shall devote his entire skill and energies to such service, and shall not perform on or permit his name to be used in connection with any other radio or television station or program, or to accept any other engagement, which will conflict with his performance for the Station, without prior approval and consent in writing by the Station. That Employee will not allow the use of or permit the use of his name, photograph, drawing, or other likeness of himself in any way with the giving of an endorsement, the advertising, or publicizing of any product which is competitive to a product advertised on the Station, and will not use his name, photograph, drawing, or other likeness of himself in connection with any other product without first securing approval and consent in writing by the Station. That Employee shall keep accurate accounts of all orders received by him, and of all other transactions undertaken by him in connection with said business. That Employee shall not communicate during the continuance of this agreement, or at any time subsequently, any information relating to the secrets of the Station relating to, but not limited to, the traveling, advertising, canvassing, and financial policies of the Station, nor any knowledge of the Station's trade secrets, methods, policies, or procedures which he then had or might from time to time acquire pertaining to other departments of the Station.

4. That Station may make use of the Employee's name, photograph, drawing and other likeness in connection with the advertising and giving of publicity to a Station program, or the advertising of the Station during the period beginning with the execution of this agreement and continuing up to ninety (90) days after the last broadcast rendered by the Employee under this agreement. That Station may make transcriptions of each broadcast on which the Employee performs and may make use of any announcing material supplied to the Employee. That the Station shall have the right to broadcast such transcriptions over any radio or television staion at any time without further compensation to the Employee. That any ideas, including but not limited to programs, themes, titles, characters, or titles which are developed by the Employee during the term of this contract and in connection with any duties performed by the Employee, shall be the property of the Station.

5. That Employee shall not accept or agree to accept from any person other than the Station any money, service or other valuable consideration for the inclusion of any matter as a part of the Station's program or in connection with the production or prepara- tion of any program or program matter intended for broadcasting. That Employee shall disclose to the Station General Manager the fact of such acceptance, agreement to accept, and other information of which he has knowledge concerning the offer of money, service or other valuable information for the inclusion of any matter as a part of the Station's program.

6. That Station shall compensate Employee a base salary of $_____ (_____) per month, in addition to a commission of _____ percent of all business sold by the Employee in each month in excess of a quota of $_____ (_____) a month. That quota shall consist of time charges only, provided further that the commission rate shall apply to time charges less agency commissions, discounts, rebates, adjustments, and all other deductions of any and every kind that are allowed by the Station in its sole judgment and discretion, either at the time of billing or subsequent thereto. That Station shall retain the authority to render an appropriate determination in the event of a dispute as to the credit for selling a particular account. That Station may, during the term of this agreement, make changes in the quota when deemed necessary to meet changing business conditions. That Employee's base salary shall be payable semi-monthly and commission earnings shall be paid monthly on the basis of the performance of programs sold. That upon program cancellation for any reason, Employee shall not be paid the commissions in connection with the cancelled program.

7. That either the Station or the Employee may terminate this agreement by giving to the other _____ months notice in writing.

That in the event of termination by the Employee during the term of this agreement, or in the event of termination of this agreement by the Station due to the Employee's breach of the terms of this agreement, the Employee shall receive commissions only on those programs sold by the Employee which have actually been performed up to the time of termination of employment. That in the event of the death of the salesman, or in the event of termination by the Employee due to an illness incapacitating him from attending to his duties for the Station or any competitor, The Employee or his estate will receive _____ percent of the commissions payable on programs sold by him and performed in the period of _____ weeks following the date of termination.

8. That in the event the services of the Employee are terminated for any reason, the Employee shall not accept employment involving either announcing activities or the sale of radio or television time within a radius of _____ miles from the Station's transmitter site for a period of _____ months following the date of termination.

9. This agreement shall remain in full force and effect until _____ and shall automatically renew itself from year to year thereafter unless written notice of termination or revision is given by either party to the other not less than thirty (30) days prior to the expiration of such annual period.

This agreement is signed and acknowledged by both parties in the presence of two witnesses this _____ day of _____, 19 ___.

_____
(Station Representative)

WITNESS:

_____
(Employee)

_____

_____

© National Association of Broadcasters

Salaries

A beginning performer takes whatever money he or she can get for services. Typically this means $10 to $15 for a one time appearance consuming about an hour of the performer's time on the job with no additional expenses. Most radio station commercials can be made in an hour or less. Reading weekend weather or sports on a local TV station may pay $25 to $35 per program. Emceeing an evening program on stage may bring $50 to $75. Reading a script about a half-hour in length for industry, medicine or education will probably pay the same amount, $50 to $75. A great deal depends upon how much money is available for the job and how highly the employer rates the performer's work. No performer should expect to live on the salary from his or her initial job; working a second job is common. The potential, once a performer is established, is substantial—and the top is virtually unlimited.

As a rule, guests on talk shows—including authors, scientists, doctors and others—appear free. Only on a few shows such as *The Tonight Show, Mike Douglas* and *Merv Griffin* will guests receive union minimum for appearing on an hour-and-a-half program; that is, $375.

In film, nonunion extras work for about $20 a day, plus a free lunch. The union extras make over $50 a day, plus fringe benefits and extra pay if they are asked to do anything out of the ordinary. "There are about 3,000 members of the Screen Extras Guild in the Los Angeles area, but only about a third of them work steadily. A few earn more than $10,000 a year, but not many. The annual income for most fulltime extras is closer to $5,000."[6] About 75,000 jobs are placed each year through Central Casting, a cooperative owned by the various film companies in the Los Angeles area.

Estimates of salaries for radio and telvision performers are difficult to make because of the variation in station profits, market size and requirements of the job. Of course, station management will attempt to get talent for the lowest possible figure, while the talent or its agent will try to get as much as the market will endure:

	Entry	*Established*	*Large Market-Network*
Annual Salary	$6,000–$13,000	$12,000–$50,000	$25,000–$90,000 +

TV news pays about as well as any performer category. The entry salary is from $100 to $250 a week. For example, Jane Pauley made $16,000 working for an Indianapolis TV news department in 1974, $55,000 as a Chicago anchor the following year, and over $200,000 as co-anchor of NBC's *Today*. One survey showed that 6.7 per cent of the women in news had an annual salary of $11,000 to $20,000; 46.6 per cent made $20,000 to $30,000; 9 per cent made $30,000 to $50,000 and 3 per cent made over $50,000.[7]

Radio news salaries are generally lower and peak much earlier. Disc jockeys earn $12,000 to $15,000 a year when established; a few make $50,000 or higher. A single radio commercial may pay only $15. A well known local person may get $75. In televison, a single commercial may pay as much as $10,000 for a day's work; $20,000 if it has national distribution; $50,000 if the performer is famous. Multimillion dollar contracts are not uncommon for top performers.

Occasionally a performer will appear on media gratis. He or she may have to sign a talent release form like the one prepared by Julian Clark Martin, of Vinson, Elkins, Searles, Connally & Smith, a Houston law firm, for the film, *The Second Door:*

University of Houston
HOUSTON, TEXAS 77004

Department of Communications
Journalism and Radio-Television
713/749-1745

January 20, 1977

Department of Communications
University of Houston
4800 Calhoun
Houston, Texas 77004

   RE: Film Entitled "The Second Door"

Dear Sir:

For good and valuable consideration, the receipt of which I hereby acknowledge as payment in full for my services as an actor in the above-described film and as payment in full for the permission herein granted.

I hereby consent to and authorize the use by the University of Houston, its assigns and representatives, of any and all film and photographs taken of me in connection with the film entitled "The Second Door," and of any reproductions of such film or photographs, for any purpose whatsoever, including without limitation, the sale, publication, display and exhibition of the film "The Second Door," without any compensation to me. I agree that the film and photographs and the negatives thereof shall constitute the sole property of the University of Houston and its assigns, with full right of disposition in any manner whatsoever.

As the University of Houston proposes to act on this consent immediately, I hereby declare it to be irrevocable, and I hereby release and discharge the University of Houston and its legal representatives, licensees and assigns from any and all claims whatsoever in connection with the use of my photograph in the film "The Second Door" and the reproductions thereof.

                                               _____
                                               Signature of Actor or Guardian

WITNESSED BY:

_____
Signature of Witness

Residuals

Sometimes a performer is very successful in a single role, and may or may not be successful in anything else. This performance may be in a media series or a commercial. The initial payment to the performer is followed by the continuous payment of a smaller amount every time the series or spot is shown. This is known as a "residual." A performer may receive payment for a number of years from a television series that originally ran only three or four years. Typical payouts, according to AFTRA and SAG contracts, are 75 per cent of the original compensation for the first and second replays; 50 per cent for the third, fourth and fifth replays; 10 per cent on the sixth; 5 per cent on the seventh and all additional replays.

Performer Rights

A performer's rights in regard to program content are the same as those guaranteed to the station licensee under the U. S. Constitution and the Communications Act of 1934, as amended in 1964. Performers will do well to maintain vigilance concerning those rights which enable them to do their work, such as sufficient freedom for members of the press in newscasts and fairness in airing controversial issues. By the late 1970s the trend in media was toward increased freedom on-the-air and greater access to information in program presentation. Performers should study their legal rights as mentioned in the documents below:

The First Amendment to the U. S. Constitution provides that "Congress shall make no law respecting an establishment of religion, or prohibiting the free exercise therof; or abridging the freedom of speech, or of the press; . . ." This provision is reflected in Section 326 of the Communications Act of 1934: "Nothing in this Act shall be understood or construed to give the Commission the power of censorship over the radio communications or signals transmitted by any radio station, and no regulations or condition shall be promulgated or fixed by the Commission which shall interfere with the right of free speech by means of radio communications." The term radio applies equally to television.

The Communications Act of 1934, as amended, includes:

Sec. 312 Assurance of reasonable access for political candidates.
Sec. 315 Assurance of equal time for political candidates.
Sec. 317 Assurance of fairness by means of record keeping.
Sec. 326 Assurance of programming without censorship.

The Federal Communications Commission's Fairness Doctrine.
U. S. Copyright Law as revised in 1976.

The Press. Whether a performer is called an anchorperson, newscaster, contributing reporter, commentator, moderator, panelist, analyst or presenter, his or her aspirations were summarized in a report by the Commission on Freedom of the Press:

1. A truthful, comprehensive, and intelligent account of the day's events in a context which gives them meaning.
2. A forum for the exchange of comment and criticism.
3. The projection of a representative picture of the constituent groups in the society.
4. The presentation and clarification of the goals and values of the society.
5. Full access to the day's intelligence.

Constitutional provisions in the First, Fifth, Sixth and Fourteenth Amendments regarding freedom of speech, press, due process and trial by jury are subject to constant reinterpretation.

Members of the press must also obtain appropriate credentials such as a press pass from local and/or state authorites so that they are permitted to move freely in carrying out assignments on-the-scene.

Political Candidates. Political candidates are extended utmost flexibility in the presentation of their views so long as they are not libelous, slanderous or obscene, and even these determinations must be made through the courts. Political candidates are further protected through legislation, namely Section 315 of the Communications Act. This law is frequently referred to as "equal time" for legally qualified candidates running for the same office, and in general, attempts to make certain that all political candidates have equal access to the airways in regard to length of programs, scheduling, rates and use. While the basic provisions may seem simple, the interpretations have become complex. Section 315 is commonly confused with the Fairness Doctrine which is not a law and does not offer equal time for controversial issues. Like the Fairness Doctrine, Section 315 should be studied in detail by those performers who must apply it often. Section 315 does not apply to bona fide newscasts, bona fide interviews, bona fide news documentaries, or on-the-scene coverage of a bona fide news event. These exceptions allow for the presentation of a candidate(s) who is incidental to the main thrust of the program without giving equal time to other candidates. Members of the legal department of the National Association of Broadcasters have prepared a guide *Legal Guide to FCC Broadcast Rules, Regulations and Policies,*[8] which should be studied by all candidates, along with the NAB's *Political Broadcast Catechism,* and pertinent laws and regulations.

Advocates. Editorialists, some commentators, opinion leaders and advocates are usually eager to present their views on media, and provided that representative spokespersons of other viewpoints are allowed to be heard, media are encouraged to air controversy. This is the spirit of the FCC's Fairness Doctrine issued in 1949. The Fairness Doctrine is itself controversial, extensive, complicated and open to interpretation. It encourages, but does not require, media to present controversial issues of public importance. If, however, a controversial issue is presented, it requires media to afford reasonable opportunity for the presentation of contrasting viewpoints and, if necessary, to seek representatives of contrasting viewpoints. Performers are thus obligated to advise management if program content is in any way controversial or unfair to any person or organization so that management can give full and fair opportunity to the other parties to respond. Such cases may inadvertently arise, for example, in a public affairs series. Specific procedures must accompany this opportunity when a controversial program involves a personal attack upon an individual or organization, when a licensee permits the use of facilities by a commentator or any person other than a political candidate to take a partisan position on the issues involved in a contest for political office or to attack one candidate or support another by direct or indirect identification, or when a licensee permits the use of facilities for the presentation of views regarding an issue of current importance. The performer must be aware that fairness extends to all matters of public concern wherein opinion is exercised, including civil rights, political issues and candidates, controversy within the media, health, education, national policy and the like. Because of its length the Fairness Doctrine should be consulted elsewhere, but the principal thrust of the FCC's Rules regarding personal attacks follows:

(a) When, during the presentation of views on a controversial issue of public importance, an attack is made upon the honesty, character, integrity or like personal qualities of an identified person or group, the licensee shall, within reasonable time and in no event later than *1* week after the attack, transmit to the person or group attacked (1) notification of the date, time and identification of the broadcast; (2) a script or tape (or an accurate summary if a script or tape is not available) of the attack; and (3) an offer of a reasonable opportunity to respond over the licensee's facilities.

(b) The provisions of paragraph (a) of this section shall not be applicable (i) to attacks on foreign groups or foreign public figures; (ii) to personal attacks which are made by legally qualified candidates, their authorized spokesmen, or those associated with them in the campaign, on other such candidates, their authorized spokesmen, or persons associated with the candidates in the campaign; and (iii) to *bona fide* newscasts, *bona fide* news interviews, and on-the-spot coverage of a *bona fide* news event (including commentary or analysis contained in the foregoing programs, but the provisions of paragraph (a) shall be applicable to editorials of the licensee). Sections (a) and (b) of the following F.C.C. Rules: 73.123 (AM); 73.300 (FM); 73.598 (Noncommercial Educational FM); and 73.679 (TV).

Performer Restrictions

Most laws concern themselves with restrictions and interpretations of specific points. The laws provide the general guideline, the cases the specific interpretation and the industry codes reiterate the legal sentiment. The principal restrictions for performers are defined in:

The U.S. Criminal Code,
§1304. Prohibition of lottery.
§1343. Prohibition of fraud.
§1464. Prohibition of obscene language.

The Communications Act of 1934, as amended,
Sec. 325 Prohibition of false distress signals.
Sec. 508 Prohibition of illegal compensation to performers ("payola").
Sec. 509 Prohibitions designed to insure fairness in contests.
Laws of Libel and Slander.
The American Bar Association,
Canon 35

What constitutes obscenity, fairness, libel and slander is being tested in specific court decisions, and performers are advised to consult them. Current industry debates include, for instance, performer endorsements: Should a performer endorse a product of which he or she has little or no practical knowledge? Those who say "yes" claim the public realizes the endorsement is part of an "act" or "dramatization." Those who say "no" claim endorsements, especially by celebrities, could mislead a potentially gullible public. Some network contracts prohibit performers from appearing in commercials while appearing in other capacities. A struggle of longstanding has been that of trials allowing media access and trials barring media. While recent legislation has tended to favor media access to government meetings and documents, various other areas such as media access to trials have not been completely resolved. The news person, therefore, can expect to have access to a day's intelligence, but from time to time such access will be in dispute because of its sensitive nature to the parties involved. Consequently in trials, usually for capital offenses, Canon 35 of the American Bar Association tends to prevail. Canon 35, which most broadcast journalists abhor, allows the presiding judge to restrict media coverage in reporting a court trial until legal findings are concluded.

Licensing

Section 318 of the Communications Act of 1934, as amended, requires that those who operate transmitting apparatus at broadcast stations shall be licensed. And so, in order to enhance their opportunities for employment, some performers—DJs, announcers and others—obtain licenses from the Federal Communications Commission. There are three classifications for a commercial license: a Radiotelephone Third Class Operator Permit with or without broadcast endorsement, Second Class, and First Class. Many performers, especially in radio, get the Third Class permit with broadcast endorsement by passing a relatively simple examination taken at the nearest office of the FCC. To obtain a permit the performer files appropriate forms (FCC Form 756 and FCC Form 756B) and a fee. If the applicant passes the examination and there are no doubts about his or her nationality, character or physical condition, a license is routinely issued. Assuming that the performer has not violated FCC Rules and Regulations, the permit is renewed upon application every five years. Normally the license is posted on the wall where the performer works. Except for a few standard broadcast stations using critical directional antenna arrays and television stations, licensees of AM and FM broadcast stations may employ third class operators for the routine station operation.

Some performers get the "First Phone" license so that they can meet requirements placed on engineers for reading meters and signing FCC forms, principally at radio stations wherein the studio and the transmitter share the same location. In this instance, the owner need hire only one person both to be on-the-air and to meet FCC requirements for transmitter operation. Although helpful, a First Class permit is not particularly useful to performers in the long run, because the larger stations do not expect this kind of service from performers. Materials for obtaining licenses can be obtained directly from the Federal Communications Commission.

Performer Ethics

In an effort to follow the spirit as well as the letter of the legal decisions, various industry organizations have developed ethical statements that reflect high standards for all aspects of media, including the contributions of performers. Performers should read certain sections of the National Association of Broadcasters Code of Ethics, Radio and Television Codes. In general, the Codes encourage high standards for

TEXAS ASSOCIATION OF BROADCASTERS'
"CODE OF ETHICS" FOR SPORTS ANNOUNCERS

Recognizing the responsibility to my listeners in describing the action, color and excitement in athletic contests, I shall abide by the following "Code of Ethics" for Sports Broadcasters.

"I shall remember that I am the guest of the participating schools and hosts of the game facility, and my appearance, demeanor and conduct will be such that I will be welcome to work there again. My performance will be, at all times, as professional as possible. I will refrain from the use of unfair, bias and prejudicial opinion, but not necessarily be impartial at all times. At no time will I belittle or attempt to discredit the Conference, the Schools or their Administrators, Faculty or any of their Employees. I will recognize the pressure under which the Coaches operate and will not pass judgement on their conduct or professionalism. I will not criticize the officials or time keepers. The players' performances should be given the benefit of the doubt. I will assume they are doing their best and performing as their coaches direct. I will remember that one player's ineptness is often the result of his opponent's expertise. I will affirm that I am a responsible, professional sports broadcaster and subscribe to this "Code of Ethics" to bring credit to my work, my broadcast station and sports broadcasters as a whole."

Radio Station_____ Date _____

Sports Announcer _____

all programming, especially those for children, by recognizing the powerful influence broadcasters (owners and performers) have on a community. Educational, religious, cultural, public affairs and news programs are pacesetters for high standards. Fairness, especially in news, commentary, and contests; humane treatment of individuals, even in dramas, and basic institutions such as marriage are upheld. Sex, violence, bias in any form (particularly racial or religious), derisive words, obscenity, profanity, smut, vulgarity, mental and physical cruelty, gambling, illegal and criminal acts, excessive use of alcohol, drugs, and misleading information, especially in advertising and news are discouraged. Although the performer will find the Codes of value, in the long run their execution requires sound adult judgment. A statement of ethics has been issued by various media groups such as the Radio Television News Directors Association. An example of a somewhat specific "Code of Ethics" was issued by the Texas Association of Broadcasters' for sports announcers, as illustrated.

Unions

Network operations, major film companies—those businesses which make a lot of money and whose programming has wide distribution—are usually unionized. Some exceptions may be found in states like Texas that have right-to-work laws. Houston, the nation's fifth largest city, is the largest non-union market in the nation. Most of the broadcast stations throughout the nation are non-union stations. Non-union performers get whatever compensation the market will bear; union performers get whatever the union contract agrees to or more. Generally, to enter a union a performer has to make enough money on the jobs covered by the union contracts. Everyone must join after the first performance, which is gratis. Some performers belong to more than one union. Actor's Equity Association (AEA) represents those who appear live on the legitimate stage, in stock companies and industrial shows, and the American Guild of Variety Artists (AGVA) covers nightclub performers. The American Federation of Television and Radio Artists (AFTRA) and the Screen Actors Guild (SAG) represent media performers. Contracts include all work whether live, film, tape, TV or radio.

AFTRA includes information specialists—news presenters, reporters, sportscasters; entertainers—performers, singers, dancers, specialists, animal acts; and commercial announcers. SAG, which was a theatrical motion picture performers' union, retains jurisdiction in that category, and represents performers in all TV shows and commercials made on film. AFTRA and SAG have established minimum wages, called "scale," with minimum rehearsal days and hours for a day and for a week. Wages are tied to the length of the show and the use—local, regional, network. There is one scale for principal performers, another for those speaking fewer than five lines—under five—and various other scales for extras, specialty acts, voice-over, dancers, singers' groups and choruses.

AFTRA and SAG contracts are complicated (about 50 pages long), in part, because they address themselves to various categories of performers, such as those in drama, comedy, variety, commercials or news. Essentially, contracts concern payment to and working conditions for performers.

A player (performer) is paid specified fees for each session. SAG has per day fees, but AFTRA works on a per program basis:

Sample per program figures for AFTRA:
Half Hour Program:

Principal performer	$260.00	9½ hours work, over last two days
Under 5 lines	125.75	5½ hours work, on the last day
Extras	70.75	

One Hour Program:

Principal performer	350.00	19 hours, over last three days
Under 5 lines	155.25	9 hours, over last two days
Extras	90.00	

Player compensation is determined by whether the player is on- or off-camera, whether appearing in a large or small market, whether the duration of service requires overtime, over night, weekends or holidays, or whether the program is distributed nationally or internationally, in which case residuals are paid. A player may be compensated for use of his or her own make-up, hair dressing, street or evening clothes, and travel time.

A player may expect certain working conditions such as adequate dressing rooms, first-class travel accommodations, rest periods, and protection from pay loss due to injury on the job. The SAG contract provides for protection of performers:

A. Where script or non-script stunts or script or non-script action sequences are required by producer, a qualified, professional stunt coordinator shall be engaged and be present on the set.

B. No actor shall be requested to perform a stunt or appear in an action sequence without prior consultation by the actor with the stunt coordinator, nor may any actor so perform without the approval of the stunt coordinator.

C. No actor shall be requested to work with animals without a qualified, professional animal handler or trainer present.

D. No actor shall be rigged with any type of explosive charge of any nature whatsoever without the use of a qualified special effects man.

E. In any or all cases described above, the actor's consent to perform shall, in each instance, be a requisite precondition.

The actor's consent shall be limited to the stunt described to the actor at the time consent was given, and no such consent shall constitute a defense to producer for any claim by the actor resulting from injury.

F. It shall be the policy of the parties to this agreement that players employed hereunder shall, to the extent possible, not be placed in hazardous or dangerous circumstances.

Union contracts include non-discrimination clauses that encourage the use of women and minorities:

A. Each signatory producer shall establish reasonable timetables and procedures to assure: a) equal employment opportunity for all minorities and women, and b) equitable "screen playing time" as well as fair representation of minorities and women which is truly reflective of the realities of society.

Producer agrees to file such plans with SAG within six months of the execution of this agreement. Producer agrees to report quarterly in writing to SAG the number of job engagements of actors and the number filled by each minority and women on a form to be mutually agreed upon in these negotiations.

It is agreed that joint meetings of the producer and the Guild and/or appropriate committees will be held when either party deems it necessary to review and discuss such reports and this program.

B. Women and minorities shall be utilized in non-descript stunts on a non-discriminatory basis.

C. When an actress requires a double for stunts, stuntwomen whose abilities lie within the field of the stunt work to be performed should be contacted before stuntmen are considered for the job.[9]

Penalties to producers and players are defined, if the conditions of the contract are not met.

The initiation fee for AFTRA is $300 for everyone, with $22 for the first six months dues. The initiation for SAG varies from $50 to $500 depending upon the region in which the performer joins. Dues are $25 for the first six months. In subsequent years dues are paid according to covered income. It is alleged that 80 per cent of the membership of these two unions makes less than $2,000 a year in the field.

Union contracts for musicians and writers describe similar benefits. The American Federation of Musicians (AFM) represents all musicians, and the Writers Guild of America (WGA) has jurisdiction over writer contracts in its two independent chapters WGA-East, and WGA-West.

GLOSSARY

Act: a performance. A display of a performer's ability.

Action: a verbal cue from the director to begin performing. Often extras are cued initially to create atmosphere, hence the cue, "Background action."

Actor/actress: a performer who appears in dramatic roles portraying someone other than himself or herself.

Actuality: the voices or sounds of an event at the scene.

Adlib: spoken remarks that are not written in the script.

AFTRA: a talent union called the American Federation of Television and Radio Artists. Referred to as "Af-tra."

AGVA: a union for variety artists called the American Guild of Variety Artists. Referred to as "Ag-va."

Air check: an excerpt from a broadcast illustrating how a performer sounds on the air.

Amplifier: an electronic device for increasing volume.

Announcer: various performers who present information, news, commercials, sports and weather. Narrowly defined, an announcer reads commercials, promotional spots and station continuity.

Apple box: an elevation, usually a box, used to raise actors to the correct height for a shot.

Aspect ratio: a reference to media screen dimensions—four horizontal units in width to three vertical units in height.

Audition: a selection and testing process wherein producers and directors determine which performers to hire.

Back timing: the process of predetermining where a performer should be near the end of a segment or program so that, with careful judgment, the program will come out on time.

B.G.: a term meaning background; i.e., maintaining music and/or sounds at a low enough volume so that the performer can be understood.

Bidirectional: a microphone pickup pattern resembling a figure eight that allows two (or more) performers to speak opposite each other while using the same microphone.

Blackout: a sketch, usually comedy. At its conclusion the scene goes to black; thus, a transition from one scene to another.

Bleep: an electronic interruption in a performer's verbal continuity, usually deleting a word or phrase considered in bad taste or legally injurious by program censors.

Blocking: the plotting of action by the director during rehearsals.

Book: a multi-purpose term referring (1) to the periodic listing of program ratings, (2) a script for a musical show, and (3) a performer's collection of credits and photographs. "To book" means to schedule a performer.

Break: to stop action, i.e., "to take a break." Also, to move talent and cameras to another set.

Breakaway: scenery or properties designed to break on cue.

Build: the gradual development of interest or tension in a segment to the point of climax.

Business: bits of characteristic action like smoking, knitting or shaking used by an actor or actress to portray a dramatic role.

Bust: to stop a performance, i.e., to cut or terminate the action.

Call: a warning to all performers for the beginning of a rehearsal or on-air session. Also, a notice of a need for performers; i.e., a casting call.

Cameo: a brief appearance in a drama.

C&W: a country and western music format for radio.

Canned: a prerecorded performance; i.e., one on tape or in a film "can."

Cattle call: a call for numerous extras.

Cardioid: a heart-shaped microphone pick-up pattern.

Cartridge: a small plastic box containing a tape loop that can be recued for immediate replay.

Cassette: a small reel-to-reel audio or videotape unit contained in a plastic box that is capable of playing an entire program.

Channel: a complete sound or signal path.

Charisma: the ability of a performer to consciously or unconsciously exude an enchantment or fascination which allows him or her to retain an audience.

Chroma key: a production technique which electronically inserts a performer into a television picture. Under these conditions the performer should not wear blue.

Character: a performer portraying a highly individualized or specialized role that typically does not resemble his or her own age or personality.

Cheating: an effort by a performer to create the illusion of talking directly to someone (as in an interview), while positioning the body for a maximum open relationship with the camera.

Circular response: the delivery of a message from a performer to the audience and the return of the audience's response to the performer.

Climax: the highest point of tension or interest in a performance or production.

Close: the conclusion of a program. Also, that relationship of a performer's body to a camera that allows the least expression, "a closed position."

Clothing: regular clothes worn on camera.

Cold: the reading of material without prior knowledge or rehearsal of it.

Communicant: the person who receives a message or stimulation from a performer.

Communication: the ability of one person to evoke a response and/or create an impression on another person.

Communicator: the performer who conveys the message.

Compatible color: colors that have good contrast in black and white.

Composite: a collection of photographs illustrating the versatility of a performer.

Concentration: undivided attention.

Condenser: a high fidelity microphone.

Conflict: dramatic opposition of the protagonist with one's self, another human being, society or fate.

Control room: a room adjacent to the studio. It contains audio and video consoles which are utilized by the director and engineers in program production.

Credits: a list of work experiences including all live and media performances. Also, a list of names and titles at the beginning and/or end of a program.

Critique: an evaluation of the strengths and weaknesses of a performance.

Cross: a movement from one place in the studio to another.

CU: a closeup shot; a detailed shot of part of a performer, usually the face.

Cue: a signal for a performer to begin the action.

Cut: a signal to stop the performance.

Cutaway: a camera shot diverted from the main action of the performers, but supplementing or reinforcing it.

Cyc: a reference to a cyclorama which is a huge curtain or plaster ("hard cyc") backdrop for a scene.

Diaphragm: a large muscle located between the lungs and the abdomen. It serves as a bellows in the breathing process. Also, a flexible element in a microphone producing electronic impulses.

Direct contact: eye-to-eye contact with a live audience and/or by means of looking directly into a camera lens.

Directional: the dominant pickup pattern of a microphone; i.e., uni-, bi-, omnidirectional or cardioid.

Double system: a method of film production in which the sound and picture are recorded separately, and synchronized later.

Director: the principal person responsible for the artistic development of a production.

Dress off: a direction to a performer to use a particular object or person as a reference mark or position for a shot.

Drive time: a reference to morning and evening periods when most people are going to and from work. Considered prime time for radio stations.

Dry run: a rehearsal which is not recorded or filmed.

Dub: a duplicate or reproduction of an original, hence, "to dub" a tape.

Dynamic: a microphone that works on the pressure principle.

Editall: a commercial name for a commonly used audiotape splicer.

ENG: an abbreviation for electronic news gathering, including instant direct relay from the scene and rapid videotape coverage.

Entrance: a performer's movement into view or recognition on microphone.

Exclusive contract: a legal agreement that binds a performer to one company or agent.

Exit: a performer's movement out of view or microphone pickup.

Extra: a performer without lines who contributes to the background, atmosphere or crowd scenes.

Fact sheet: an outline and/or list of titles or topics to be discussed on a program. A background sheet or biography of a guest. Sometimes called a "run down."

False move: premature action incorrectly begun by a performer.

F.C.C.: abbreviation for the Federal Communications Commission, a government agency controlling electronic media using airwaves, especially radio and television.

Featured player: a performer requiring special attention, although not a star.

Feed: a message sent from one performer to another, usually program segments as in a news "feed."

Feedback: a performer's response from listeners and viewers, critics and others associated with a production.

First phone: a first-class radio telephone operator's license issued by the Federal Communications Commission.

First team: the performers who will be doing the scene in front of cameras, not their stand-ins.

Freeze: to maintain an exact position.

Format: the overall structure of a program or series. A type of script listing major programming steps, including generally a scripted open and close.

From the top: an expression meaning start at the beginning.

Gain: an increase in the signal between the input and the output; to increase volume, as in "turn up the gain."

Gauge: the width of a tape or film. The common audiotape gauge is ¼-inch. Videotape gauges are ½-, ¾-, 1- and 2-inches. Film gauges are Super-8, 16, 35 and 70 millimeters.

Gogo: a sound absorbing screen used to isolate performers or instruments.

Gray-scale: the range of hues from black to white.

Guild: a term referring to unions for certain performers, writers and directors.

Hand signals: a silent method of sending instructions to performers while they are on the air.

Hand props: personal properties carried by a performer.

Hard news: a news story about an event having significant impact usually on many people. It often deals with disaster, economics and political events.

Head: an electro-magnetic device(s) within a tape recorder which enables the recorder to record, erase or playback a tape.

Head shot: a closeup of the face.

Heads up: a loud call on the set to warn people that overhead equipment is being moved.

Hold: to stop all movement in action or speech, usually for laughter or applause.

Hold it: to keep perfectly still; to maintain a position.

ID: identification of a performer by means of credentials or a station by announcing its call letters and location.

Idiot card: large cards with lines of dialogue or cues hand-held in easy view of the performer.

Image control: the selection of those attributes or cues which create a predetermined impression or stimulus within a viewer or listener.

Indirect contact: the focus of a performer's gaze at a multitude without addressing any person in particular.

Ingenue: an actress between 16 and 20.

Interference: an electronic disturbance such as static.

Jack: a female connector used to transfer current in sound devices. The counterpart of a plug.

Juvenile: an actor between 16 and 20.

Key light: the brightest major light source for a performer.

Key map: a locator map for news departments that send reporters to the scene.

Kicker: an amusing story at the end of newscast.

Kill: to cut, remove or get rid of action, lines or production elements.

Kinesics: a study of all body movement of communicative value.

Lag time: the moments before equipment is up to proper recording speed.

Lavaliere: a tiny microphone held around the neck by a lanyard or clip.

Leading man/woman: a performer having the major responsibility or role in a dramatic production.

Level: the volume of a voice as registered on a volume units meter or an audio console. "Give me a level" or "level check" is an engineer's request for the performer to keep talking until the audio equipment is adjusted properly.

Lines: the dialogue a performer must deliver.

Live: a performance in which the talent is working in the presence of an audience. Also, the direct transmission of a performance at time of origin.

Logo: a symbol, usually a visual design, for a station (call letters and/or news department) or a company advertising its services or products.

Looks: a direction in which the performer will be asked to "look" in order to match a previous shot, to prepare the audience for action, or to indicate the location of a person or object not in the shot.

LS: an abbreviation for long shot; that is, a full length view of a performer.

Marks: designations usually taped or painted on a studio floor indicating positions for performers.

Master: the original recording of a program, disc or film.

Media: an electronic conveyance utilized to disseminate entertainment and information to vast ("mass") audiences; specifically radio, disc and tape recording, television and film.

Message: a communication between a performer and other persons, animals, nature and certain objects.

Mixer: an electronic device, usually an audio console, used to combine sounds.

Modulation: an electrical strength of a signal as measured by a VU meter. "Over modulation" causes distortion in the audio quality.

Monitor: a television receiver without sound placed on a studio floor, news desk, or in a TV control room. Also, any of several audio receivers found in TV, radio or recording studios.

MOR: a term for a middle-of-the-road radio music format. Pronounced "more."

Morgue: a reference file of stories, photographs, films and tapes.

Motivation: the purpose or reason behind a performer's movement.

MS: an abbreviation for medium shot; i.e., a view of a performer from the waist up.

Nielsen: a term referring to a program rating (probably measured by the A. C. Nielsen Company) in which the performer appeared.

Omnidirectional: a circular microphone pickup pattern enabling all performers within its effective radius to share the microphone.

On: to be on the air.

One-liner: a role with one line of dialogue.

One sheet: a photograph with minimum vita, used for résumés or credits.

Open: the beginning of a program. Also, that relationship of the body of a performer to a camera that allows fullest expression, "an open position." A live or "open" microphone. "To open up" means to be freer in movement or interpretation.

Out-cue: those words constituting the final seconds of a segment, such as the final seconds of a song or news item. An out-cue is critically timed to match the upcoming segment.

Out takes: Rejected shots or scenes.

Overplay: to overemphasize dialogue or movement.

Oxide: a dull coating of iron particles carrying information on an audio-or videotape.

Pace: the overall rate or flow of continuity in a production.

Pad: a period of flexibility in the continuity that can be expanded or cut near the end of a segment so that it comes out on time.

Pager: a beeper device which is activated by a radio signal to call reporters.

Pancake: a water soluable make-up foundation.

Pan stick: a foundation in stick form used to cover difficult areas, such as beards.

Pantomime: the silent expression of an idea or emotion through body movement.

Patch: a temporary electronic connection between two pieces of equipment, usually connected by a "patch cord" through a rack mounted panel called a "patch panel."

Performer: anyone who appears on camera and/or microphone, especially those who are paid to do so ("media professionals") and those who do so because of their expertise in areas outside media ("community experts").

Narrowly defined, a person who appears in non-dramatic shows, actors and actresses appearing in dramatic ones.

Personality: the innate charm or essence of an individual. Also, a performer whose personal characteristics dominate whatever role he or she portrays is referred to as a "personality."

Phonation: the formation of a sound by means of the vocal mechanism, dominantly the lips, tongue, teeth and surrounding areas.

Photo double: someone who resembles the actor enough to be used in long shots, usually for stunts or dangerous action.

Pickup: the range within which a microphone can get a sound signal. A "pickup pattern" refers to the shape of the sensitive area surrounding a microphone. Also, to accelerate the pace of a program largely by means of responding more quickly to cues; to begin where action last stopped.

Pitch: the range of vocal sounds a performer can produce from deep tones with relaxed vocal folds through falsetto.

Playback: the replay of a performance on audio- or videotape.

Player: a performer; a common term used in union contracts.

Plug: a male connector which fits inside a "jack." Also, an unpaid remark or identification of a product or service, such as a performer's new book or latest film.

Post synchronization: a process in film production in which the sound is added after the picture has been recorded.

Potentiometers: dials or levers on an audio console that enable an operator to regulate volume. Also called "pots," "mixers," or "faders."

Presence: the optimum clarity of sounds. Also, the psychological status of being in the same room; i.e., present.

Presenters: any performer appearing live or in media. The term is commonly applied to news and information specialists.

Producer: the executive who arranges the business aspects of a production, including the contracting of a director and major performers.

Promo: a promotional announcement or reference.

Prompter: a human or electronic system of cueing talent.

Prop: an abbreviation for property. All objects necessary for the completion of a setting and for use by performers. Usually this includes furniture and smaller personal items; that is, "hand props."

Publicity: attention which media, especially news, gives to a performer without charge.

Quick study: a performer who can remember lines easily.

Range: the extent to which a performer can produce high to low pitch levels.

Ratings: an index of the relative number of persons tuned into a radio or television program.

Reel: a spool on which film or tape is wound. Reel-to-reel refers to a simultaneous transfer of film or tape from a supply reel to a take-up reel.

Resonance: the reenforcement of a vocally produced sound by means of a person's physical structure (bones, muscles, cartilage), acoustics and electronic devices.

Rewrite: a revision of a script to meet new standards or requirements.

Roll 'em: a film cue which means to start running cameras.

Rip 'n' read: a hasty presentation of news by means of tearing copy directly from a wire machine and reading it on the air.

Roll cue: a transitional statement that enables a performer to yield his or her presentation to another segment of the program.

RTNDA: an abbreviation for the Radio Television News Directors Association, a group devoted to upgrading standards for media news.

Run down: an outline of a segment or program. Sometimes called a "fact sheet."

SAG: a union called the Screen Actors Guild. Pronounced "sag."

Save the food: to fake the eating of food during a rehearsal until the actual take.

Scale: minimum union wages.

Scenario: a scene-by-scene outline of the principal action in a dramatic production.

Scene: a portion of a dramatic production, typically the moment of entrance to exit of a performer from a camera's field of view or microphone pickup.

Second unit: a film crew which shoots supplementary action not requiring major actors or the director.

Sequence: a segment of continuity from a longer work that tends to be a brief entity in itself.

Set: the scenery (walls, landscapes, panoramas) for a production. Also called the "setting."

Share: a give-and-take relationship between performers, as in an interview or dramatic scene.

Shot: a visual unit of a program or film during which an action occurs without interrupting the physical continuity by cutting or editing.

Sides: typed copies of a performer's part, including only his or her own speeches, stage directions and cues.

SIL: silent film.

Single system: a method of film production in which the sound and picture are simultaneously recorded on the same strip of film.

Slug: a one- or two-word identification for a new story.

SOF: sound on film.

Soft news: a news story having high human interest value, such as humor, novelty, gossip, sex and the like.

Source: the original event or person providing information for a news story. Also, a reference to equipment picking up audio-visual information; i.e., a microphone or camera.

Speed: the revolutions per second that are required for equipment to record sound and pictures. In cinema, sound speed is 24 frames per second; silent speed is 18 frames per second. Radio and recording studio standard speed is 15 inches per second.

Spot: a commercial or public service announcement. Also, a brilliant white light emphasizing the star performer. In dancing, "spot" refers to a fixed gaze a dancer maintains while making pirouettes.

Splice: to mend, usually to cut out a portion and rejoin the tape or film.

Stand by: a verbal or visual cue given just prior (usually 30 seconds) to a rehearsal or on-air program.

Stand-in: a substitute for the actual performer used to check lights and final preparations.

Straight: a role similar to a performer's natural characteristics and age.

Strike: to remove an item or setting.

Studio: a specially equipped room in which a performer rehearses or presents his or her act.

Summary: a prepared statement with which a moderator closes a program.

Talent: a collective term for all performers. Talent implies that the performer has exceptional ability.

Tag line: a performer's speech or final line at the close of a scene, act or production.

Talk: a radio or television format consisting of information, news, discussion and interviews. "All talk" implies that music is excluded.

Tally lights: tiny lights atop a television camera that indicate the camera is on the air.

Tape: any of several strips of plastic cut in various gauges and coated for different purposes such as recording sound and picture, filling blanks, mending and providing leader. "To tape" means to record.

Teaser: a short enticement at the beginning of a program; a preview. In news, it consists of headlines; in drama, it may be a dramatic highlight presented in or out of story context.

Throw away: to underplay a line or scene.

Time: a term with various meanings: "time" means the segment is over or time is up. "Running time" is the duration of any program or segment, usually measured in seconds. "Timing" refers to a performer's judgment in the delivery of material to receive maximum audience impact.

Toupee: a man's hairpiece.

Track: the portion of a film strip or tape that carries the sound impulse. Sophisticated sound recording requires sound elements to be recorded on different tracks; hence, monaural (one track) to multi-tracks.

Transplant: an operation which moves hair folicles from one part of the head to another (bald) area.

TV-Q: A measurement of audience response to a performer in terms of whether a performer is known and liked.

Unidirectional: a rather narrow microphone pickup pattern projecting in a single direction and designed for a single performer.

VO: abbreviation for voice over. A performer reads copy over silent tape or film.

Vocal quality: the audible characteristics of a voice including all of its nuances. A voice displaying a broad range of clear tones is considered to have high quality. A voice having excessive or unpleasing nasal, breathy, harsh or strident characteristics has low quality.

Voicer: a prepared presentation by an identified reporter.

Wind screen: a sponge rubber or latex sound-absorbing shield wrapped over a microphone to reduce wind noise and other extraneous sound when recording, particularly outdoors.

Wind up: a signal to end a segment, commonly the final 30 seconds. Also, called the "wrap up."

Wing it: to do the program without a rehearsal.

Wow: substandard audio caused from a recording being aired before it is up to speed.

Wrap: a signal to end a segment, commonly the final 30 seconds. Also called a "wind up."

Wraparound: an actuality around which a reporter adds a lead in and a final statement including his or her name and location.

NOTES

CHAPTER 1:

1. Barbara Delatiner, "Brinkley Focuses on His Image," *Newsday*, November 8, 1968.
2. Lloyd Shearer (ed.), "Intelligence Report," *Parade*, October 31, 1971, p. 18.

CHAPTER 2:

1. Tom Donnelly, "Impressions of male stars of television action series," The Los Angeles Times-Washington Post News Service, 1975. In *Houston Chronicle*, August 24, 1975, p. 9.
2. Kenneth Clark, *The Nude: A Study in Ideal Form*. Garden City, New York: Doubleday & Company, Inc., 1959.
3. Barbara Varro, "He's seen a lot of famous faces in the raw," *Chicago Sun-Times*, 1974. In *Houston Chronicle*, January 13, 1974, sec. 7, p. 3.
4. Clive Barnes describing Richard Burton's performance in *Equus* for the *New York Times, Houston Chronicle*, March 7, 1976, p. 29.

CHAPTER 3:

1. Alan Ebert, "Exercise Secrets of a Hollywood 'Body Doctor'," *Ladies Home Journal*, XCIV, No. 2 (February, 1977), p. 50.
2. Emily Wilkens, *Secrets from the Super Spas*. New York: Grosset & Dunlap, Inc., 1977.
3. Paul Taylor, University of Houston, September 27, 1972.
4. Robert C. Atkins, M.D., *Dr. Atkins' Diet Revolution: The High Calorie Way to Stay Thin Forever*. New York: David McKay Company, Inc., 1972, p. 113.
5. Stephanie Caruana, "Fatties Arise! You Have Nothing to Lose But Your Stored Fat Deposits!" *Playgirl*, October, 1973.
6. Marilyn Beck, "Fat Cats of Hollywood," *Zest, Houston Chronicle*, February 22, 1976, p. 7.
7. Judy Lunn, "The Underwear Movement," *Houston Post*, October 19, 1976, p. 3B.
8. Atkins, *op. cit.*, pp. 297–298. Adapted by Dr. Atkins from Metropolitan Life Insurance Co., New York. New weight standards for men and women. Statistical Bulletin 40.3, Nov.–Dec., 1959.
9. Shirley Pfister, "You'll like your face better in two weeks if you follow dermatologist's four steps," *Houston Chronicle*, July 27, 1975, sec. 7, p. 1.
10. Joan Crawford, *My Way of Life*. New York: Simon & Schuster, 1971, In "The Art of Looking Beautiful," *McCall's* Vol. XCVIII, No. 10 (July, 1971), pp. 55–56.
11. Mary Quant Cosmetics marketed a Mary Quant Colouring Box for men in 1976. It cost about $12.50.
12. Marce Zegar, "Hideaway Facelift," Marce Cosmetics, Ltd.

13. Barbara Varro, "He's seen a lot of famous faces in the raw," Chicago *Sun-Times*, 1974. In *Houston Chronicle*, January 13, 1974, sec. 7, p. 3.
14. Beverly Maurice, "Style—a la Princess Luciana," *Houston Chronicle*, March 17, 1976, sec. 7, p. 9.
15. Jason Thomas, "The 'Bald' Hairdo," Chicago *Sun-Times*, 1976. In *Houston Chronicle*, June 6, 1976, sec. 1, p. 7.
16. George Masters Press Book.
17. "Dentists assay attractive teeth in '76 candidates," *Houston Chronicle*, March 13, 1976, sec. 1, p. 12.
18. "Personality Mailbag," *Texas Magazine, Houston Chronicle*, October 17, 1971, p. 2.

CHAPTER 4:

1. Dennis L. Franz, "Who Would Ever Think To Ask Broadcasters about Broadcast Education," Colby, Kansas: Colby Community College, Summer, 1974, p. 14.
2. Leon Beck, "Minnelli Spurred on by Fanatical Crowd," *The Daily Cougar*, Houston, October 16, 1973.
3. Exercises suggested by actor's notebook from Theatre Under the Stars, Houston, Texas.
4. The International Phoenetic Alphabet is an accurate method of noting speech sounds and may be especially useful to those performers working with foreign words and phrases. For all practical purposes, however, it has never become widely used; instead, respellings of words that resemble actual pronunciation is common practice for media professionals. IPA is described in detail in Stuart Hyde's *Television and Radio Announcing*. Boston: Houghton Mifflin Company, Revised 1971. For details see pp. 55–78.
5. Walter Cronkite explained on the *CBS Evenings News* that English prefers "jun ta" but Spanish pronunciation is "hoon ta," March 24, 1976.
6. "Carter accent will soften, says linguist," *Houston Chronicle*, December 4, 1976, sec. 1, p. 14. "Atlas researchers study dialects of Southerners," *Houston Chronicle*, October 21, 1976, sec. 2, p. 6.
7. Charles H. Harpole, "Eric Report: Nonstandard Speech," *The Speech Teacher*, Vol. XXIV, No. 3 (September, 1975), pp. 226–231.
8. Kenneth F. Englade, "It's Rat Nass, But Prof Denies Texas Language," *Houston Chronicle*, March 4, 1976, Sec. 4, p. 5.
9. Paul Bravender, doctoral dissertation, Eastern Michigan University. Reported in *Houston Chronicle*, September 24, 1976, Sec. 4, p. 20.

CHAPTER 5:

1. M. Argyle, V. Salter, H. Nicholson, M. Williams, and P. Burgess, "The Communications of Inferior and Superior Attitudes by Verbal and Nonverbal Signals," *British Journal of Social and Clinical Psychology*, Vol. 9 (September, 1970), p. 230.
2. Dr. Cody Sweet, Nonverbal Communications, Inc., Mount Prospect, Illinois.
3. Ray L. Birdwhistell, *Introduction to Kinesics*. Louisville: University of Louisville Press, 1952, p. 3.
4. Leslie Irene Coger and Sharron Pelham, "Kinesics Applied to Interpreters Theatre," *The Speech Teacher*, Vol. XXIV, No. 2 (March, 1975), p. 99.
5. Sydney Pollack, University of Houston, September 29, 1975.

CHAPTER 6:

1. Joseph Conrad, *The Nigger of the Narcissus,* originally published, 1897. Doubleday, Page & Co., 1914. Copyright John Alexander Conrad, 1942.
2. William I. Kaufman (ed.), *How to Announce for Radio and Television.* New York: Hastings House Publishers, 1956, pp. 58–9.
3. Henry C. ("Hank") Ruark, "Exercise Your Execs on TV Before They Face Public," *Technical Photography,* December, 1976.
4. Prime Time School TV (PTST), a non-profit organization based in Chicago, urges teachers to use prime time TV programs to enhance learning. Kathryn Christensen, "Teachers using popular TV show as textbook," *Chicago Daily News,* 1977. In *Houston Chronicle,* January 8, 1977, Sec. 1, p. 9.

CHAPTER 7:

1. Ron Powers, "Superstar of the circus—Gunther Gebel-Williams," *Chicago Sun-Times,* 1976. In *Zest, Houston Chronicle,* July 4, 1976, p. 16.
2. "The 'peacock syndrome': the fitting of uniforms for fussy athletes," *Houston Chronicle,* Sec. 3, p. 4.
3. Laura Berman, "How Are Men and Women Different." *Detroit Free Press,* December 26, 1976, p. 1, Sec. D.
4. "The Taming of the Shrew," American Conservatory Theatre, PBS, November 11, 1976.

CHAPTER 8:

1. Jonathan Kandell, "Want plastic surgery? Go to see a Brazilian," *Houston Chronicle,* March 10, 1976, sec. 7, p. 10.
2. Kent Demaret, *The Many Faces of Marvin Zindler.* Houston: The Hunt Company, 1976, pp. 76–77.
3. Beverly Maurice, "Just putting your best face forward," *Houston Chronicle,* July 20, 1976, Sec. 7, p. 5.
4. ABC *Monday Night Special* with David Frost, May 3, 1976.
5. Molly Ward, "Nobody's Perfect," *Texas, Houston Chronicle,* February 2, 1975, p. 8.
6. Podine Schoenberger, "Dentist fashions better smiles for more sex appeal," *Houston Chronicle,* October 16, 1976, Sec. 1, p. 16.
7. Jack Barnes, "The View from the Top," *Texas, Houston Chronicle,* November 30, 1975, pp. 18–9.
8. Pat Reed, "Gone today, hair tomorrow," *Texas, Houston Chronicle,* December 5, 1976, pp. 7–12.
9. CBS, January 19, 1977.
10. Dick Cavett interview with Rudolf Nureyev, *Dick Cavett,* ABC-TV, July 24, 1974.
11. *Men Who Made the Movies:* Vincent Minnelli. KUHT, Houston, October 16, 1974.
12. Dwight Weist and Bob Barrons, *Basic TV Commercial Course Book.* New York: School of Television & Commercial Speech, revised September, 1975.
13. "Doctor says guests on talk shows have 'network nerves'," *Houston Chronicle,* January 22, 1977, sec. 5, p. 8.
14. Andree Beck, "Hard rock, planning key to Robert Hegyes success," *Zest, Houston Chronicle,* November 28, 1976, p. 5.
15. Patricia Shelton, "Living Inside the Pressure Cooker," *Zest, Houston Chronicle,* February 22, 1976, p. 6.

CHAPTER 9:

1. The author provided four students as stand-ins for the Vice Presidential Debate at the Alley Theater, Houston, Texas, on October 15, 1976.
2. Robert L. Hilliard, ed., *Radio Broadcasting: An Introduction to the Sound Medium.* Revised Edition, 1976. New York: Hastings House, Publishers.

CHAPTER 10:

1. Will Sinclair, *Audio Prompting,* 1971.
2. Angus Robertson, "Television Prompting," *Video & Audio Visual Review,* Vol. 2, No. 3 (March, 1976), p. 20.
3. *Houston Chronicle,* July 9–15, 1972, p. 6.

CHAPTER 11:

1. Based in part on suggestions from an actor's notebook developed by Theatre Under the Stars, Houston, Texas.
2. *The Tonight Show,* NBC-TV, January 31, 1977.

CHAPTER 12:

1. *News Media Keys,* published in New York and 35 markets by Jerry Leichter; *TV Publicity Outlets Nationwide,* Washington Depot, Connecticut, published by Harold Hansen; *National Radio Publicity Directory,* New York, published by Peter Glenn.
2. Leo Seligsohn, "Talk Shows," *Zest, Houston Chronicle,* April 18, 1976, p. 6.
3. Alvin Van Black, KPRC, Houston, February 2, 1977. See also, Alvin Van Black, "A Problem in Sensory Communication." Unpublished report, Department of Communications, University of Houston, Fall, 1973.
4. William I. Kaufman (ed.), *How to Announce for Radio and Television.* New York: Hastings House, Publishers, 1956, p. 31.
5. Vernon Scott, "Private Poll of a Game Show Host," United Press International. In *Houston Chronicle,* March 13, 1976, sec. 5, p. 5.
6. Charles Maher, "As an All-Round Play-by-Play Man TV's Curt Gowdy Had No Peers," Los Angeles Times-Washington Post News Service. In *Houston Chronicle,* April 16, 1972, sec. 2, p. 4.
7. *Tomorrow* with Tom Snyder, NBC-TV, May 28, 1976.
8. "Morning Mouth," *Texas Magazine, Houston Chronicle,* September 16, 1973, p. 6.
9. *Campus Workshop* #73, KHTV, Houston, February 15, 1975.
10. *Les Preludes,* film, 1960, and *"Les Chapeaux,"* WBAP-TV, Fort Worth, Texas, 1964. David Preston, choreographer; William Hawes, producer.
11. Dale Adamson, "Melissa Manchester walks a no-woman's land between first success and the future," *Zest, Houston Chronicle,* March 7, 1976, p. 26.
12. Michael Biel, "Broadcast Announcing Styles of the 1920's." Unpublished report presented to the Broadcast Education Association, March 16, 1974, p. 11.
13. *The Associated Press Radio-Television News Style Book.* New York: The Associated Press, p. 4.
14. Judith S. Gelfman, *Women in Television News.* New York: Columbia University Press, 1976, p. 13.
15. *Ibid.,* pp. 58–59.

16. The author was an extra in the film and a judge for the ballroom contest. He met the members of the cast and crew. Bud Yorkin was interviewed by Sharon Speer on *Campus Workshop* in March, 1972.
17. The author visited the *Lovin' Molly* set in Bastrop, Texas, on December 2, 1972 through the courtesy of producer Steve Friedman.
18. The author attended the rehearsal and evening performance of *Saturday Night Live* with Howard Cosell, at the Ed Sullivan Theatre, New York, on November 8, 1975 through the courtesy of Ron Muskowitz, CBS production supervisor.

CHAPTER 13:

1. Anita Klever, *Women in Television*. Philadelphia: Westminster, 1975, p. 31.
2. Kathryn Christensen, "Teachers using popular TV show as textbook," *Chicago Daily News*, 1977. In *Houston Chronicle*, January 8, 1977, sec. 1, p. 9.
3. Catherine Atwater Galbraith, "The Professor as TV Star," *American Film*, Vol. 2, No. 4 (February, 1977), p. 8.
4. Produced live from the Robert Carr Chapel, Texas Christian University, KTVT, Fort Worth-Dallas, December 13, 1960.
5. "Guide to Services. Medical Illustration and Audiovisual Education, Baylor College of Medicine." Houston: Baylor College of Medicine, 1976, p. 9. See also its companion: "Handbook for Effective Audiovisuals."
6. William C. Martin, "Religious Broadcasts Flourishing," *Houston Chronicle*, March 13, 1976, sec. 1, p. 14.
7. The $10.5 million cathedral complex houses the television studios, the staff of 50 that edits the Sunday tapes, administrative buildings and a restaurant. Humbard's two sons produce and direct the programs; his wife and daughter are singers on the show. Two-thirds of the cathedral's annual budget of $12 million goes for production and air time costs, according to his staff. Support comes largely from gifts of $5 and $10 a month from viewers. George Esper, "He was 'plain Bible talk,' guitar to minister to world," *Houston Chronicle*, October 10, 1976, sec. 1, p. 26.

CHAPTER 14:

1. The Quigley Publications' 45th annual poll of theater owners (1976) listed these top ten performers in order: Robert Redford, Jack Nicholson, Dustin Hoffman, Clint Eastwood, Mel Brooks, Burt Reynolds, Al Pacino, Tatum O'Neal, Woody Allen and Charles Bronson.
2. Bob Shanks, *The Cool Fire*. New York: W. W. Norton, Inc., 1976, p. 253–256.
3. Dick Saunders, "Picking Top 40 Hit Songs by Psychographics," *Zest, Houston Chronicle*, February 29, 1976, pp. 6–7.
4. David Chagall, "Only As Good As His Skin Tests," *TV Guide*, Vol. 25, No. 13 (March 26, 1977), pp. 5–10.
5. Millie Budd, "Stairway to the Stars," *The Texastar, Houston Post*, September 3, 1972, p. 6. *The Steve Edwards Show*, KHOU-TV, Houston.

CHAPTER 15:

1. In 1975 the total labor force for artists, entertainers and writers was estimated at 1,050,000. Of these, 7.4 per cent were unemployed with actors (35%) and dancers heading the list. Data on these occupations is very difficult to obtain. "Employment and Unemployment of Artists: 1970–1975," National Endowment for the Arts, April, 1976. Research Division Report #1.

2. Jessica Savitch, University of Houston, November 11, 1971. Ms. Savitch anchors the NBC *Nightly News* (Sundays).
3. For an extensive discussion of women on television see *Journal of Broadcasting*, Vol. 19, No. 3 (Summer, 1975), p. 291 (Seggar) and p. 301 (Verna).
4. Quoted in Dennis L. Franz, "Who Would Ever Think to Ask Broadcasters about Broadcast Education." Colby, Kansas: Colby Community College, Summer, 1974.
5. William Gilder, "Film stars' bodyguards must be 'diplomatic, never relax'," *Houston Chronicle,* October 10, 1976, p. 3, sec. 2.
6. William Overbend, "The wild, wild world of Hollywood extras," *Zest, Houston Chronicle,* April 18, 1976, p. 22.
7. Anita Klever, *Women in Television.* Philadelphia: The Westminster Press, 1975.
8. *NAB Legal Guide to FCC Rules, Regulations and Policies,* Washington, D.C.: National Association of Broadcasters, 1977.
9. *Screen Actor Newsletter,* May/June, 1977.

SELECTED RESOURCES

This list of resources for further study is suggested in addition to the trade publications such as *Advertising Age, Billboard, Broadcasting, Educational Broadcasting, Educational and Industrial Television, The Hollywood Reporter, Journal of Broadcasting, Radio and Television Age, Sponsor, TV Guide, Variety,* and the many fine biographies of performers in all media.

APPEARANCE

Buchman, Herman, "Film and Television Make-Up," a filmstrip. #210010. Hollywood, California: Olesen, 1535 Ivar Avenue. 90028.

Clark, Kenneth, *The Nude, a Study in Ideal Form.* Garden City, New York: Doubleday & Company, Inc., 1959.

Dicker, Ralph and Victor R. A. Syracuse, *Consultation with a Plastic Surgeon.* Chicago: Nelson-Hall, 1975.

Kehoe, Vincent J-R., *The Technique of Film and Television Make-Up for Color and Black & White.* New York: Hastings House, Second edition, 1969.

Lewis, John R., *Atlas of Aesthetic Plastic Surgery.* Waltham, Md.: Little, Brown & Co., 1973. Illustrated.

Linde, Shirley M. (ed.), *Cosmetic Surgery: What Can It Do for You?* New York: Pavilion Publishing Co., Revised edition.

Masters, George, and Norma Lee Browning, *The Masters Way to Beauty,* New York: E. P. Dutton, 1977.

Morini, Simona., *Body Sculpture: Plastic Surgery from Head to Toe.* New York: Delacorte Press, 1972.

Rees, Thomas D. and Donald Wood-Smith, *Cosmetic Facial Surgery.* Philadelphia, Pa.: W. B. Saunders Co., 1973.

Sanders, Keith P. and Michael Pritchett, "Some Influences of Appearance on Television Newscaster Appeal." *Journal of Broadcasting,* Vol. XV, No. 3 (Summer, 1971), pp. 293–301. Describes ideal newscaster.

VOICE

Associated Press, Regional Guides to Pronunciation. New York: Associated Press, revised.

Berry, Cicely, *Voice and the Actor.* New York: Macmillan, 1974.

Fisher, Hilda B., *Improving Voice and Articulation*. Boston, Mass.: Houghton Mifflin Co., 1975.

Hanley, Theodore D., and Wayne L. Thurman, *Developing Vocal Skills*. New York: Holt, Rinehart and Winston, 1962. Chapter on voice quality is especially helpful.

Hanneman, Gerhard J., and William J. McEwen, *Communication and Behavior*. Reading, Mass.: Addison-Wesley, 1975. Broad collection of materials from established writers in the field.

Linklater, Kristin and Douglas Florian, *Freeing the Natural Voice*. New York: Dramabooks, 1976.

Manser, Ruth B., and Leonard Finlan, *The Speaking Voice*. New York: Longmans, Green and Company, 1959.

Moncur, John P., and Harrison M. Karr, *Developing Your Speaking Voice*. Scranton, Pa.: Harper-Row, Second edition, 1972.

NBC Handbook of Pronunciation. Compiled by James F. Bender. New York: Thomas Y. Crowell Company, Third edition. Correct pronunciation for over 20,000 words and names.

Nist, John. *Handicapped English. The Language of the Socially Disadvantaged*. Springfield, Illinois: Charles C Thomas, Publisher, 1974.

Ogilvie, Mardel and N. S. Rees, *Communication Skill: Voice and Speech*. New York: McGraw-Hill Book Co., 1970.

Rossiter, Charles M., Jr., "Some Implications of Compressed Speech for Broadcasters," *Journal of Broadcasting*, Vol. XV, No. 3 (Summer, 1971), pp. 303–307. Suggests that newscaster delivery should be speeded up.

Schumacher, Walter, *Voice Therapy and Voice Improvement: A Simple and Practical Approach through Correct Muscle Usage*. Springfield, Ill.: C. C. Thomas, 1974.

Suderman, Lloyd F., *Artistic Singing: Its Tone Production and Basic Understandings*. Metuchen, N.J.: Scarecrow Press, 1970.

MOVEMENT

Birdwhistell, Ray L., *Kinesics and Context*. Philadelphia: University of Pennsylvania Press, 1970.

David, Martha, *Understanding Body Movement, An Annotated Bibliography*. New York: Arno Press, 1971.

Downing, George, *Massage and Meditation*. Westminster, Md.: Random House, 1974.

Hinde, R. A. (ed.), *Non-verbal Communication*. Cambridge: University Press, 1972.

Mehrabian, Albert, *Silent Messages*. Belmont, California: Wadsworth Publishing Company, Inc., 1971.

Sparger, Celia, *Anatomy and Ballet*. New York: Theatre Arts Books, Fifth edition, 1976.

Van Lysebeth, Andre, *Yoga Self-Taught*. Scranton, Pa.: Harper-Row, 1972.

STUDIOS: CINEMA PRODUCTION

Basic Production Techniques for Motion Pictures. Rochester, New York: Eastman Kodak Company, 1971. A brief overview on how to make films.

Brodbeck, Emil E., *Handbook of Basic Motion Picture Techniques.* Englewood Cliffs, N.J.: Prentice-Hall, 2nd edition, 1975.

McMurtry, Larry, "Here's HUD in Your Eye," in *In a Narrow Grave.* New York: Simon and Schuster, 1968, pp. 3–20. Describes life of film cast on location.

Mercer, John, *Introduction to Cinematography.* Champaign, Ill.: Stipes Publishing Co., Revised, 1974. Basic text in film making.

Roberts, Kenneth H., and Win Sharples, *A Primer for Film Making: A Complete Guide to 16 MM and 35 MM Film Production.* Indianapolis, Ind.: Bobbs-Merrill (Pegasus), 1971. Advanced instruction in film making.

Turell, Saul J., and Jeff Lieberman, "Performance," a film from *The Art of the Film* series. Chicago, Ill.: Perspective Films. 22-minute color film on acting in films.

Young, Freddie and Paul Petzold, *The Work of the Motion Picture Cameraman.* New York: Hastings House, 1972. The cameraman in a major feature film, procedures and equipment.

STUDIOS: RADIO & RECORDING

Burroughs, Lou, *Microphones: Design and Application.* Plainview, New York: Sagamore Publishing Co., Inc., 1977.

Gifford, F. *Tape A Radio News Handbook,* New York: Hastings House, 1977. Highly specialized, detailed, how-to-do it approach to tape for radio news.

Gross, Lynne S., *Self Instruction in Radio Production.* Los Alamitos, California: Hwong Publishing Company, 1976. Helpful for operating techniques, station procedures and laws.

Hilliard, Robert L. (ed.), *Radio Broadcasting: An Introduction to the Sound Medium.* New York: Hastings House, Revised edition, 1976. Includes a chapter on performing.

Nisbett, Alec, *The Technique of the Sound Studio: Radio, Record Production, Television and Film.* New York: Hastings House, Third edition, 1972.

Nisbett, Alec, *The Use of Microphones.* New York: Hastings House, 1974. A basic text.

Olson, Harry F., *Modern Sound Reproduction.* New York: Van Nostrand Reinhold Co., 1972. A complex book on various aspects of sound recording.

Oringel, Robert S., *Audio Control Handbook for Radio and Television Broadcasting.* New York: Hastings House, Fourth edition, 1972. How to operate radio and tape equipment.

Stokes, Geoffrey, *Star-Making Machinery: The Odyssey of an Album.* Indianapolis, Indiana: Bobbs-Merrill Co., 1976. An intimate look at the production of an album.

Woram, John M., *The Recording Studio Handbook*. Plainview, New York: Sagamore Publishing Company, 1976. Complex details of sound recording, largely for engineers, but musicians may find it useful.

STUDIOS: TELEVISION PRODUCTION

Englander, A. Arthur and Paul Petzold, *Filming for Television*. New York: Hastings House, 1976. Fascinating account of the contribution that film can make to television by the top BBC cameraman of *Civilisation, Alistair Cookes' America*, etc.

Millerson, Gerald, *The Technique of Television Production*. New York: Hastings House, 9th edition, 1972. Comprehensive basic text.

Paulson, C. Robert, *ENG/Field Production Handbook*. New York: Broadcast Management/Engineering, 1976. Guide to using mini video equipment.

Quick, John and Herbert Wolff. *Small-Studio Video Tape and Production*. Reading, Mass.: Addison-Wesley Publishing Company, Second edition, 1976. Aimed at industrial and educational users, including performers.

Zettl, Herbert. *Television Production Handbook*. Belmont, California: Wadsworth, 1976, third edition. An excellent text, a standard in the production field.

MEDIA PROFESSIONALS: GENERAL

Dusenbury, Delwin B., *Television Performance*. Cincinnati: International Thespian Society, 1969.

Hilliard, Robert L., *Writing for Television and Radio*. New York: Hastings House, third edition, 1976.

Newcomb, Horace, *TV: The Most Popular Art*. New York: Anchor Books, 1974. Discusses popular network formats.

Poteet, G. Howard, *Published Radio, Television, and Film Scripts: A Bibliography*. Troy, N.Y.: Whiston Publishing Co., 1975. A list of available sources for radio, television and film scripts.

ANNOUNCING

Chester, Giraud, Garnet R. Garrison and Edgar E. Willis, *Television and Radio*. Englewood Cliffs, New Jersey: Prentice-Hall, Inc., fourth edition, 1971. Includes a chapter on announcing.

Fisher, Hal, *The Man Behind the Mike*. Blue Ridge Summit, Pa.: TAB Books, 1967. Good advice and many exercises for announcers.

Hyde, Stuart W., *Television and Radio Announcing*. Boston: Houghton-Mifflin, 1971. Includes a discussion of the International Phonetic Alphabet and many exercises.

Lewis, Bruce, *The Technique of Television Announcing*. New York: Hastings House, 1966. A manual for those who work on camera.

Weist, Dwight and Bob Barrons, *Basic TV Commercial Course Book*. New York:

School of Television & Commercial Speech, revised September, 1975. Text for a popular professional school.

ENTERTAINERS

Chester, Giraud, Garnet Garrison and Edgar Willis, *Television and Radio.* Englewood Cliffs, N.J.: Prentice-Hall, Inc., Fourth edition, 1971. Chapter on acting.

Kingson, Walter K., and Rome Cowgill, *Television Acting and Directing: A Handbook.* New York: Holt, Rinehart, & Winston, 1965.

Klein, Maxine, *Time, Space, and Designs for Actors.* Boston, Mass.: Houghton Mifflin Co., 1975. Chapters 13 and 15 are especially useful to TV actors.

Lawrence, Sharon, *So You Want to Be a Rock & Roll Star.* New York: Dell, 1976. A behind-the-scenes look at what it takes to become an R&R star.

Passman, Arnold, *The Deejays.* New York: Macmillan, 1971. A history of music on radio.

Quinn, Sally. *We're Going to Make You a Star.* New York: Simon and Schuster, 1975. Describes the difficulties in becoming a network TV performer.

NEWS & INFORMATION

The Associated Press Radio-Television News Style Book. New York: The Associated Press, 50 Rockefeller Plaza, revised.

Bliss, Jr., Edward, and John M. Patterson, *Writing News for Broadcast.* New York: Columbia University Press, 1971. A well written analysis of all aspects of broadcast news.

Brady, John, *The Craft of Interviewing.* Cincinnati, Ohio: Writers Digest, 1976. A detailed approach to interviewing.

Cavett, Dick, and Christopher Porterfield, *Cavett.* New York: Harcourt Brace Jovanovich, 1974. Cavett's life and comments on talk shows.

Conversations with Eric Sevareid. Washington, D.C.: Public Affairs Press, 1976.

Dary, David, *Television News Handbook.* Blue Ridge Summit, Pa.: TAB Books, 1971. *Radio News Handbook,* revised. Companion books well written.

Diamond, Edwin, *The Tin Kazoo—Television, Politics and the News.* Cambridge, Massachusetts: The MIT Press, 1975. Discusses news formats and the audience.

Fang, Irving E. *Television News: Writing, Filming, Editing, Broadcasting.* New York: Hastings House, Revised edition, 1972.

Gelfman, Judith S., *Women in Television News.* New York: Columbia University Press, 1976. Several women in news describe their progress and responsibilities.

Green, Maury, *Television News: Anatomy and Process.* Belmont, California: Wadsworth Publishing Co., 1969.

Hall, Mark W., *Broadcast Journalism: An Introduction to News Writing.* New York: Hastings House, Revised edition, 1978. All types of news stories.

I Can Hear It Now. Columbia Records. Narrated by Edward R. Murrow, Walter Cronkite 1919 to 1949, and the Sixties.

Marzolf, Marion, *Up From the Footnote: A History of Women Journalists*. New York: Hastings House, 1977. Includes the emergence and increasing stature of women in the broadcast media.

Miles, Donald W., *Broadcast News Handbook*. Indianapolis, Indiana: Howard W. Sams & Co., 1975. A fine text oriented to radio news.

O'Connor, John J., " 'Today'—why it seems like only yesterday," *Zest, Houston Chronicle*, January 16, 1977. New York Times News Service.

"Radio News: a primer for the smaller operation." Washington, D.C.: National Association of Broadcasters, 1974.

Siller, Robert C., *Guide to Professional Radio and TV Newscasting*. Blue Ridge Summit, Pa.: TAB Books, 1972. A guide to various aspects of broadcast journalism by experienced newsman.

Small, William, *To Kill a Messenger: Television News and the Real World*. 1970. A newsman looks at the problems in TV news.

SPORTSCASTING

Barber, Red, *The Broadcasters*. New York: The Dial Press, 1970.

Coleman, Ken, *So You Want to be a Sportscaster*. New York: Hawthorn Books, 1973. Useful hints on several aspects of sportscasting.

Johnson, William O., Jr., *Super Spectator and Electronic Lilliputians*. Boston, Mass.: Little-Brown, 1971. Revised articles from *Sports Illustrated*.

Klages, Karl W., *Sportscasting*. Lafayette, Ind.: Sportscasters, 1963.

COMMUNITY EXPERTS

Armstrong, Ben, and LaVay Sheldon (eds.), *Directory of Religious Broadcasting: 1976*. Morristown, N.J.: National Religious Broadcasters, 1976. A listing of stations and producers in religious broadcasting.

Benson, Dennis, *Electronic Evangelism*. Nashville, Tenn.: Abingdon Press, 1973. A guide for churchmen using mass media.

Biegel, Len, and Aileen Lubin, *Mediability: A Guide for Nonprofits*. Washington, D.C.: Taft Products, Inc. A handbook for laymen in the uses of media for public service.

Brown, James W., Richard B. Lewis and Fred H. Harcleroad, *AV Instruction: Technology, Media and Methods*. Although more for a AV producer, the performer may find it useful.

Ellens, J. Harold, *Models of Religious Broadcasting*. Grand Rapids, Michigan: Eerdmans, 1974. Four models for religious broadcasting including Graham, Roberts, Sheen.

Gilbert, Robert E., *Television and Presidential Politics*. Quincy, Massachusetts: Christopher Publishing House, 1972.

Jones, G. William, *Landing Rightside Up in TV and Film*. Nashville, Tenn.: Abingdon Press, 1973. Tells how best to use TV and film to communicate to youthful audiences.

Lewels, Francisco J., Jr., *The Uses of the Media by the Chicano Movement: A Study in Minority Access.* New York: Praeger Special Studies, 1974. A good introductory discussion.

Mickelson, Sig., *The Electric Mirror: Politics in an Age of Television.* New York: Dodd, Mead, 1972. Experiences of network news broadcaster.

Minow, Newton, John Bartlow and Lee M. Mitchell, *Presidential Television.* New York: Basic Books, 1973. Campaign and non-campaign uses of TV in politics.

Murray, James, *To Find an Image: Black Films from Uncle Tom to Superfly.* Indianapolis: Bobbs-Merrill, 1973. Includes interviews with major black film personalities.

Political Broadcast Catechism. Washington, D.C.: National Association of Broadcasters, Eighth edition, 1976. Laws and regulations pertaining to politicians on the air.

Shapiro, Andrew O., *Media Access: Your Right to Express Your Views on Radio and Television.* Boston: Little, Brown, 1976. A how-to-do-it approach for community advocates.

Teachers in Television and Other Media. Washington, D.C.: National Education Association, 1973. Short booklet on teacher rights in regard to programs.

Zelmar, A. C. Lynn, *Community Media Handbook.* Metuchen, N.J.: Scarecrow Press, 1973. Useful to groups trying to get a message disseminated.

EVALUATION

A. C. Nielsen Company, 2101 Howard Street, Chicago, Illinois 60645.

American Research Bureau, 4320 Ammendale Road, Beltsville, Maryland 20705.

Kuhn, William, *Why We Watch Them: Interpreting TV Shows.* New York: Benziger, Inc., 1970. An analysis of the appeal of major network program formats.

Schramm, Wilbur, *Men, Messages, and Media: A Look at Human Communication.* New York: Harper & Row, 1973. Discusses process of communication and political impact of communication.

Whitaker, Susan, and Rod Whitaker, "Relative Effectiveness of Male & Female Newscasters," *Journal of Broadcasting,* Vol. 20, No. 2 (Spring, 1976), pp. 177–183. Finds no significant difference in believability, acceptance, effectiveness or preference.

CAREERS

Academy Players Directory. Academy of Motion Picture Arts and Sciences. Los Angeles. Lists more than 8,500 performers with pictures and agents.

The American Film Institute Guide to College Courses in Film and Television. Washington, D.C.: Acropolis Books, 1975. Lists film course offerings, including performance, at U.S. schools.

Ashe, Jim, *Broadcast Announcer: 3rd Class FCC Study Guide.* Blue Ridge Summit, Pennsylvania: TAB Books, 1974.

Chase, Chris, *How to Be a Movie Star or a Terrible Beauty is Born.* New York: Harper & Row, 1974. How an actress survives when she is not working.

Ewing, Sam, *You're on the Air!* Blue Ridge Summit, Pa.: TAB Books, 1972. A career guide for high school students entering small or medium stations.

Federal Communications Commission. FE Bulletin No. 4. Washington, D.C.: Federal Communications Commission, 20554, or any field office. General information on operator licenses and permits.

Harwood, Kenneth, "Earnings & Education of Men & Women in Selected Media Occupations," *Journal of Broadcasting,* Vol. 20, No. 2 (Spring, 1976), pp. 233–237. Says performers often enter as announcers then go into management in mid-career.

Jackson, Gregory, *Getting into Broadcast Journalism: A Guide to Careers in Radio-TV.* New York: Hawthorn Books, 1974. Aimed at young people looking for broadcasting careers.

Joels, Merrill E., *How to Get into Show Business.* New York: Hastings House, 1970. Discusses relationship of business and talent.

Kahn, Frank J., (ed.), *Documents of American Broadcasting.* New York: Appleton-Century-Crofts, 1968. Useful to news and information specialists.

Klever, Anita, *Women in Television.* Philadelphia: Westminster, 1975. A broad perspective on careers women have in television including performance.

Marzolf, Marion, *Up From the Footnote: A History of Women Journalists.* New York: Hastings House, 1977. Good background on women's media careers.

Niven, Harold, *Broadcast Programs in American Colleges and Universities.* Washington, D.C.: National Association of Broadcasters, 1771 N Street, N.W., Fourteenth Report, 1975. Lists institutions, faculties and facilities offering instruction in broadcasting.

Shanks, Bob, *The Cool Fire.* New York: W. W. Norton & Company, Inc., 1976. Management looks at talent.

Swearer, Harvey F., *Commercial FCC License Handbook.* Blue Ridge Summit, Pennsylvania: TAB Books, 1972. Prepares performer for FCC's first, second and third phone licenses.

Taubman, Joseph, *Performing Arts Management and Law.* New York: Law-Arts Publishers, Inc., 1972. A complex, detailed look at contracts and legal matters, in two volumes.

Walker, Alexander, *Stardom.* New York: Stein and Day Publishers, 1970.

TALENT AGENTS

Creative Management Associates, Inc., 8899 Beverly Blvd., Los Angeles 90048.
William Morris Agency, 1350 Avenue of the Americas, New York 10019.

UNIONS

Actors' Equity Association (AEA) (AFL-CIO), 165 West 46th St., New York 10036.

American Federation of Musicians (AFM) (AFL-CIO), 641 Lexington Ave., New York 10022.

American Federation of Television and Radio Artists (AFTRA) (AFL-CIO), 1350 Avenue of the Americas, New York 10019.

American Guild of Musical Artists (AGMA) (AFL-CIO), 1500 Broadway, New York 10036.

American Guild of Variety Artists (AGVA) (AFL-CIO), 1540 Broadway, New York 10036.

Screen Actors Guild (SAG) (AFL-CIO), 7750 Sunset Blvd., Hollywood 90046.

Screen Extras Guild (SEG) (AFL-CIO), 3629 Cahuenga Blvd. W., Los Angeles 90068.

Writers Guild of America East, Inc. (WGAE), 22 West 48 St., New York 10036.

Writers Guild of America West, Inc. (WGAW), 8955 Beverly Blvd., Los Angeles 90048.

INDEX